At the Court of Versailles

Gilette Ziegler

AT THE COURT OF
VERSAILLES

Eye-Witness Reports from the Reign of Louis XIV

TRANSLATED BY
SIMON WATSON TAYLOR

A Dutton  *Paperback*

ILLUSTRATED

New York
E. P. DUTTON & CO., INC.
1968

CONTENTS

ILLUSTRATIONS

INTRODUCTION

For more than fifty years, Versailles was the centre of the history and intrigues of the French Court. It was here that Louis XIV consolidated his power, signed his treaties, entertained his mistresses and established the religion of etiquette.

We know the principal facts of this famous reign, and the great days of Versailles, but the daily life of the Court is less familiar to us since the historians of the epoch were not always particularly interested in this aspect. Nevertheless, the throng of courtiers, foreign guests and palace servants included reporters, some of them respectful, some servile, some malicious. . . . Their accounts are not necessarily accurate, but they succeed in recreating the atmosphere that reigned in this curious establishment which housed the royal weekends and, in 1862, became the actual seat of government. Gilette Ziegler has called upon a few of these witnesses to relive for us the day-to-day events that form the thread from which the glittering tapestry of the *Grand Siècle* was woven.

A FEW DATES

1661
Death of Cardinal Mazarin:
the real reign of Louis XIV
begins.
— Marriage of the Duc
d'Orléans, the King's brother,
to Henrietta Anne of England
(Henriette d'Angleterre).
— Commencement of the
King's love affair with Louise
de la Vallière.
— Disgrace of Superintendent
Fouquet.
— Birth of the Dauphin.

At Versailles:

Work starts on the remodelling
of the courtyard and façade of
the château of Louis XIII.

1662-3
Trial of Fouquet.

The King's first journeys to
Versailles, where work is pro-
gressing on the construction of
the buildings of the forecourt,
the Orangerie, the avenues....

1664

First great fête at Versailles.

1665
Death of Philip IV of Spain,
father-in-law of Louis XIV,
who later claims the Spanish
Netherlands for his wife.

Pavilions are constructed for
the King's favourites.

1666
Death of the Queen Mother,
Ann of Austria.

1667
The War of Devolution, against
Spain. The campaign in
Flanders turns into a gay
military promenade.
— La Vallière becomes
Duchesse de Vaujours. Mme de
Montespan comes into favour.

Enlargement of the central
avenue. Construction of the
Grand Canal.

1668
Campaign of Franche Comté
and Treaty of Aix la Chapelle.

First projects for the Château
Neuf. Great festivities to
celebrate peace.
—Mlle de Scudéry and
La Fontaine's 'promenades' at
Versailles.

1669

Construction of the three main
buildings: the Château Neuf.

1670
Secret treaty of Dover with
England, negotiated by Madame,
the King's sister-in-law.
— Death of Madame.

First pavilion constructed on
the site of the hamlet of
Trianon.

1671
Monsieur takes as his second
wife Charlotte Elizabeth of
Bavaria, known as the Princess
Palatine.
— The King prepares for war
against Holland.
—Disgrace of the Comte de
Lauzun.

Project for the creation of the
town of Versailles. The Grand
Canal completed. Building of
the Chapel.

1672
Beginning of the third
Dutch War.

Inauguration of the Chapel.

1673
Second campaign of Franche
Comté, against Spain, the allies
of Holland.
— Legitimization of the King's
bastards.

Six rooms of the royal apartments are completed.

1674
Campaigns of Alsace and
Franche Comté.
— Victory of Senef.
— The Rohan plot.
—Invasion of Alsace by the
enemy.

The Château Neuf is finished.
Beginning of lengthy visits to
Versailles: Mlle de La Vallière
leaves the Court. 'The widow
Scarron' becomes Mme de
Maintenon.

1675
Turenne re-establishes the
situation in Alsace.
—Death of Turenne.

Mme de Montespan leaves the
Court, then returns.

1676
Execution of the Marquise de
Brinvilliers.

1677

Louis XIV decides to transfer
his residence to Versailles,
where work continues on the
construction of apartments for
the Court.

1678
Capture of Ghent.
—Peace treaty of Nijmegen.

Mansard presents his plan for
the new residence.
Commencement of the southern
wing, of the Pièce d'Eau des
Suisses, and of the Bassin de
Neptune. ...

1679
Beginning of the 'affaire des
poisons'.
— Mlle de Fontanges appears to
have replaced Mme de
Montespan.

The Cour de Marbre acquires
its ornamentation.
—Commencement of work
project at Marly.

1680
Development of the 'affaire des poisons'.

The Dauphin marries Marie Christine of Bavaria. (Mme de Maintenon appointed Mistress of the Wardrobe to the future Dauphine.)
—Mlle de Fontanges becomes a duchess. A special medal is struck in honour of Versailles.

1681
Death of Mlle de Fontanges.

Completion of the 'Grands Appartements' of the King and Queen.

1682

Birth of the Duc de Bourgogne. Versailles becomes the seat of government. The southern wing completed.

1683
Death of Colbert.

Death of Queen Marie Thérèse. Secret marriage between the King and Mme de Maintenon?

1684
Beginning of the dragonnades against the Protestants.

Completion of the Galerie des Glaces. Commencement of the northern wing. Project for bringing water from the Eure to Versailles.

1685
Revocation of the Edict of Nantes.
— Death of Charles II of England and accession of James II.
1686
Death of the Great Condé.

The Doge of Ghent makes an act of submission before the King in the presence of the entire Court.

The ambassadors of Siam at the Court. Opening of the Maison Saint-Cyr.
—The King operated on for a fistula.
—Water is pumped from the Seine to Versailles.

1687

Construction of the Grand
Trianon.

1688
*War of the League of Augsburg.
— Ravaging of the Rhenish
Palatinate.*

1689
*Flight of James II of England
and his establishment at Saint-
Germain.*

Esther *performed at Versailles.
—Fénelon becomes tutor to the
Duc de Bourgogne.*

1690
*Victory of Fleurus.
—Death of the Dauphine.*

*All construction work finally
completed.*

1691
*Siege of Mons.
—Exploits of Jean Bart.*

*Saint-Simon arrives at the Court.
—Jean Bart received at
Versailles.
—Mme de Montespan leaves the
Court.
—Death of Louvois.*

1692
*Siege of Namur.
—Victory of Steinkirk.*

*Marriage of the Duc de Chartres
(the future Regent) to Mlle de
Blois; and of the Duc du Maine,
natural son of Louis XIV, to
Mlle de Condé.*

1693
Victory of Nerwinden.

1694 (or 1695)
*The 'open letter' from Fénelon
to the King,* Lettre à Louis
XIV.

*Saint-Simon begins to make
notes for his proposed
'Mémoires'.*

1695
*Fénelon named Archbishop of
Cambrai.*

1696
Treaty of Turin with Savoy.

Marie Adélaïde of Savoy, betrothed to the Duc de Bourgogne, arrives at Versailles.

1697
Publication of Fénelon's 'Explication des Maximes des Saints'.
— *Peace of Ryswick.*
— *The Prince de Conti elected King of Poland.*

The Quietist affair excites the Court of Versailles.
—*The Duc de Bourgogne's marriage celebrated at Versailles.*

1698
Treaty of The Hague (between France, Holland and England).
— *Bossuet publishes his 'Relations sur le Quiétisme', a bitter attack upon Fénelon.*
—*Disgrace of Racine.*

1699
Condemnation of Fénelon's book.

Final construction work on the Royal Chapel.

1700
Death of the King of Spain, Charles II.

The Duc d'Anjou proclaimed King of Spain at Versailles.

1701
Beginning of the war of the Spanish Succession.
— *Death of Monsieur, brother of the King.*
— *Death of James II of England.*

1702
Beginning of the revolt of the Camisards.

1703
Vauban named a Marshal of France.

1704
*Defeat of Blenheim and
invasion of France.*

*Birth of the Duc de Bretagne,
son of the Duc de Bourgogne.*

1705

*Death of the infant Duc de
Bretagne. Birth of his brother,
bearing the same title.*

1706
*Defeat of Ramillies.
— Vauban publishes his
'Projet d'une Dîme Royale'.*

1707
Death of Vauban.

1708
Defeat of Oudenarde.

*Intrigues against the Duc de
Bourgogne.*

1709
*Terrible year of famine.
—Battle of Malplaquet.
—Destruction of Port Royal.*

1710

*Birth of the future Louis XV.
Marriage of the Duc de Berry.
Completion of the Royal
Chapel.*

1711
*Death of the Grand Dauphin,
at Meudon.*

1712
Victory of Denain.

*Death of the Duchesse de
Bourgogne (February 12), of
her husband (February 18),
of their eldest son (March 8).*

1713
Treaty of Utrecht.

1714
Treaties of Rastadt and Baden.   *Death of the Duc de Berry.*
—Royal testament, instituting a
Council of Regency during the
minority of his successor.

1715   *The Persian ambassador*
received at Versailles.
—Death of Louis XIV (Sep-
tember 1). Louis XV leaves
Versailles for Vincennes.

THE FAMILY OF LOUIS XIV

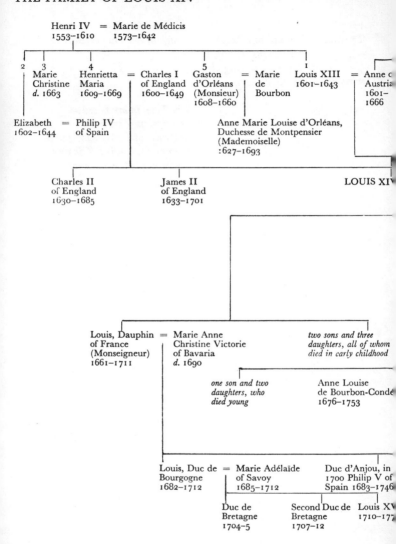

Henri IV = Marie de Médicis
1553–1610   1573–1642

2	3	4		5		1	
Marie	Henrietta	= Charles I	Gaston	= Marie	Louis XIII	= Anne of
Christine	Maria	of England	d'Orléans	de	1601–1643	Austria
d. 1663	1609–1669	1600–1649	(Monsieur)	Bourbon		1601–
			1608–1660			1666

Elizabeth = Philip IV
1602–1644   of Spain

Anne Marie Louise d'Orléans,
Duchesse de Montpensier
(Mademoiselle)
1627–1693

Charles II   James II   LOUIS XIV
of England   of England
1630–1685   1633–1701

Louis, Dauphin = Marie Anne   two sons and three
of France   Christine Victorie   daughters, all of whom
(Monseigneur)   of Bavaria   died in early childhood
1661–1711   d. 1690

one son and two   Anne Louise
daughters, who   de Bourbon-Condé
died young   1676–1753

Louis, Duc de = Marie Adélaïde   Duc d'Anjou, in
Bourgogne   of Savoy   1700 Philip V of
1682–1712   1685–1712   Spain 1683–1746

Duc de   Second Duc de   Louis XV
Bretagne   Bretagne   1710–1774
1704–5   1707–12

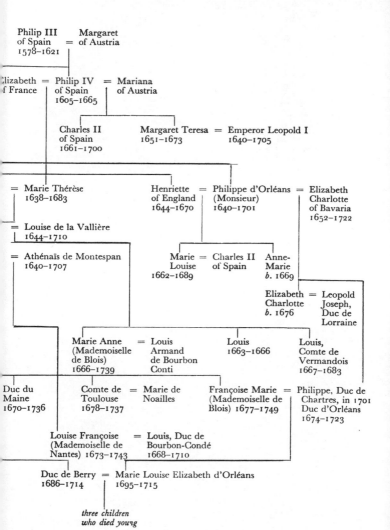

Philip III
of Spain = Margaret
1578-1621   of Austria

Elizabeth = Philip IV = Mariana
of France   of Spain   of Austria
            1605-1665

Charles II   Margaret Teresa = Emperor Leopold I
of Spain   1651-1673   1640-1705
1661-1700

= Marie Thérèse   Henriette = Philippe d'Orléans = Elizabeth
  1638-1683   of England (Monsieur)   Charlotte
                                 1644-1670   1640-1701   of Bavaria
= Louise de la Vallière   1652-1722
  1644-1710
                                 Marie = Charles II   Anne-
= Athénaïs de Montespan   Louise   of Spain   Marie
  1640-1707   1662-1689   b. 1669

                                          Elizabeth = Leopold
                                          Charlotte   Joseph,
                                          b. 1676   Duc de
                                                       Lorraine

                 Marie Anne = Louis   Louis   Louis,
                 (Mademoiselle Armand   1663-1666   Comte de
                 de Blois)   de Bourbon   Vermandois
                 1666-1739   Conti   1667-1683

Duc du   Comte de = Marie de   Françoise Marie = Philippe, Duc de
Maine   Toulouse   Noailles   (Mademoiselle de   Chartres, in 1701
1670-1736   1678-1737   Blois) 1677-1749   Duc d'Orléans
                                                              1674-1723

                 Louise Françoise = Louis, Duc de
                 (Mademoiselle de   Bourbon-Condé
                 Nantes) 1673-1743 1668-1710

        Duc de Berry = Marie Louise Elizabeth d'Orléans
        1686-1714   1695-1715

                  three children
                  who died young

THE ILLEGITIMATE CHILDREN OF
LOUIS XIV

The King's issue by Mlle de La Vallière:

In 1663 a son, Charles—died at age of two.
— 1665 a son, Philippe—died at eleven months.
— 1666 a daughter, Marie Anne, legitimized and married to Prince Louis Armand de Conti.
— 1667 a son, Louis, Comte de Vermandois, legitimized—died at age of sixteen.

By Mme de Montespan:

In 1669 a daughter, Louise—died at age of three.
— 1670 a son, Louis August, legitimized with the title of Duc du Maine.
— 1672 a son, Louis César, legitimized with the title of Comte de Vexin—died at age of eleven.
— 1673 a daughter, Louise Françoise, legitimized, called Mlle de Nantes, married to Louis de Bourbon-Condé.
— 1674 a daughter, Louise Marie, legitimized, called Mlle de Tours—died at age of seven.
— 1677 a daughter, Françoise Marie, legitimized, called Mlle de Blois, married to the Duc de Chartres, future Regent.
— 1678 a son, Louis Alexandre, legitimized with the title of Comte de Toulouse.

By Mlle de Fontanges:

In 1679 (December) a son, who died in January 1680.

(The above list includes only the children of the known favourites)

CHAPTER I

THE DECOR AND THE CAST

We had scarcely reached the top of the hill from which we suddenly saw displayed below the magnificent palace whither we were bound, than La Belle Etrangère burst forth in admiring tones: 'What do I see,' she asked, 'crowning magnificently the rising ground ahead of us which commands so delightful a stretch of country? Is that what you name the little house of the greatest King on earth?'

'Yes,' I answered, 'that is Versailles, Madame.'

MADELEINE DE SCUDÉRY: *La Promenade à Versailles*

🕮

What was Versailles? Until 1661, it was, according to André Félibien, Sieur des Avaux et de Javercy, architect and historiographer of the King's Buildings, a simple hunting-lodge:

This château, which Louis XIII had had built for himself, then comprised a simple structure consisting of two wings and four pavilions.

Louis XIV had been there occasionally while still a child. The Gazette *of April 8, 1651, reported:*

The King has been pleased to divert himself by the pleasures of the chase in the vicinity of the Château of Versailles. The Maréchal de Villeroi, His Majesty's tutor, who was in attendance upon him, requested the Président de Maisons, Superintendent of Finances, captain of this château and that of Saint-Germain to arrange a banquet. The King graciously honoured this repast with his presence and was extremely satisfied with the arrangements, for although His Majesty had not permitted his own retainers to serve at the function it seems that the meal was efficiently supervised by officials who gave magnificent service to His Majesty and his whole Court, pre-

siding at tables where food was served to guests without delay
as soon as they presented themselves.

*Ten years later, the King decided to have a more sumptuous
palace built at Versailles, although the site, if one is to believe
Louis de Rouvroy, Duc de Saint-Simon, was far from enchanting:*

Versailles, the saddest and most barren of places, with no
view, no wood, no water and no earth, for it is all shifting
sand and marsh, and the air, consequently, is bad . . .

*Work began in the autumn of 1661. Its scope was modest to
start with.*

*The roofs were repaired; two new main buildings were
erected to house kitchens, on the right, and stables, on the left,
with living rooms on the first floors; two pavilions at the
entrance were set aside for the King's Musketeers; to the south,
an orangery was in process of construction. The King made
frequent visits to check on the progress of the works. On
February 17, 1663, M. Petit, steward and general factotum
of Minister Jean Baptiste Colbert, wrote to him:*

My Lord, immediately the King arrived yesterday at Versailles, he enquired what new work had been done since the
previous occasion His Majesty had been there and whether
the works were making progress. We told him that the frost
was preventing us from working on the completion of the
plastering of the interior of the main buildings and pavilion of
the kitchens and stables (buildings of the forecourt) but that
all these surfaces were lathed and could be finished in three
weeks of good weather and that His Majesty should receive
satisfaction from our diligence then; that it was not possible to
work on the Orangerie or on the two small pavilions at the
head of the demi-lune in entering the forecourt until the frost
was over, that the plumbing and roofing of the main buildings
and pavilions of the said forecourt was completed and that, in
a short time, His Majesty would see much interior carpentry
completed.

Our labourers, to the number of eighty, are working as I described to you in my letter. I am assured that a fresh team is due to arrive on Monday and these I shall put immediately to work. 350 labourers are working mightily at shifting the earth for the Orangerie and the demi-lune from the end of the *grand parterre* and are also working on the garden of the Vieux Château.

In 1664, the royal dwelling began to take shape. Sebastiano Locatelli, a Bolognese priest visiting France, described it in these terms:

Versailles is a fine château begun by Louis XIII and completed by the reigning king. There is plentiful game in the vicinity. An aviary constructed of copper wire contains, I think, an example of every bird known to man. Indeed, I was shown more than forty species which I had never yet seen or even heard of. As regards the buildings, hunting facilities, comfort and pleasure, Versailles excels all the King's other châteaux, even Fontainebleau.

Three great roadways leading from the Cours la Reine in Paris to Versailles have already been started and will gradually be improved. They will be twenty-one miles in a straight line, planted with four lines of trees and divided into three pathways: the central pathway, to be paved for the use of carriages, will be four perches wide; the two flanking pathways, each a perch wide, will be raised, so forming a sort of levee. All this will cost the King a great sum of money, for this region is very hilly, and these hills must be levelled out over a distance of seven miles; it is true that they are not very high, and contain no stones. If these roadways are ever completed they will surely be unparalleled throughout the world.

All this did, indeed, cost a great sum of money, and Colbert, who accumulated the functions of Comptroller General of Finances and Superintendent of Buildings, wrote to the King on September 28, 1665:

Your Majesty has just returned from Versailles. I beg him to permit me to report to him a few words of thought which I have vouchsafed to him before and which he will, if it please him, pardon as deriving from my zeal in his service. This mansion is concerned far more with the pleasures and diversions of Your Majesty than with his glory, and since he has made it clear to the world how much more highly he regards the latter than the former, there being no doubt that this indeed represents the feeling of his heart, so that one may safely speak freely to Your Majesty upon this matter without running the risk of displeasing him, I would think myself to be betraying the allegiance I owe him if I did not tell him that, while it is entirely right that after the great and constant application he is pleased to give to affairs of State, with the admiration of the entire world, he should grant some time to his pleasures and diversions, nevertheless great care must be taken that these do not become detrimental to his glory.

However, if Your Majesty desires to discover where in Versailles are the more than 500,000 écus spent there in two years, he will have great difficulty in finding them. Will he also deign to reflect that the Accounts of the Royal Buildings will always record the evidence that, during the time he has lavished such vast sums on this mansion, he has neglected the Louvre, which is assuredly the most superb palace in the world and the one worthiest of Your Majesty's greatness . . . And God forbid that those many occasions which may impel him to go to war, and thus deprive him of the financial means to complete this superb building, should give him lasting occasion for regret at having lost the time and opportunity.

Your Majesty knows that, apart from glorious actions of war, nothing celebrates so advantageously the greatness and genius of princes than buildings, and all posterity measures them by the yardstick of these superb edifices which they have erected during their life. O what pity were the greatest and most virtuous of kings, of that real virtue which makes the greatest princes, to be measured by the scale of Versailles! As for myself, I confess to Your Majesty that, notwithstanding his reluctance to increase the cash payments, had I been able to foresee that this outlay of money would have become so high, I would have preferred to make over to him cash warrants so that I might be spared knowledge of the expenditure.

During the following years, the King multiplied his short stays at Versailles, even in winter. A Counsellor of the Parlement, Olivier Lefèvre d'Ormesson, noted in his Journal, in March 1667:

Having decided to spend the three days before Ash Wednesday at Versailles, the King desired that all who came there between Saturday and Tuesday should wear masks. He had great tables prepared for the regalement of his guests and announced that all masked parties would be welcomed most courteously. The whole Court lavished great expense on the magnificent preparations, and I can say as a beholder that nothing more beautiful may ever have been seen, yet it was a very lonely occasion; only three or four carriages of masked people came from Paris. The King was much put out, seeing that no one was there to witness his splendour. There were very few masked parties at Paris, for most people had little joy in their hearts.

In 1668, the construction was set in hand of the three new blocks surrounding the original building which would eventually form the Château Neuf. This activity was greeted with great despair by Colbert, according to Charles Perrault, author of the famous Contes, who was Controller of Buildings:

When the old château was completed, M. Colbert scarcely had time to rejoice at seeing a royal mansion whose construction was finished and which he would only have to visit two or three times a year, from then on, to supervise necessary repairs, before the King resolved to add several new buildings in which to house his Council of State more commodiously in the event of a stay lasting several days. Work commenced on several buildings which failed to please him when they were half finished and were promptly torn down again; then work started on the three main buildings which surround the Petit Château and face on the gardens. When these buildings, designed by M. Le Vau, were completed, they were beautiful and magnificent to look at but it was now seen that the old palace lacked any correct proportion or architectural relationship to the new edifice. It was suggested to the King that this small château should be razed and replaced by buildings more in harmony and scale with those which had just been built. But the King was adamant. In vain it was pointed out to him that large sections of the house were in a state verging on ruin: he ordered any necessary restoration to be undertaken and, suspecting that some attempt might be made to botch the repair so that he might be persuaded to order its demolition, he stated with some emotion that they might tear down the whole building but that he would have it rebuilt exactly as it was without a single change.

Félibien des Avaux *adds:*

Since His Majesty has such piety for the memory of his late father as to forbid the demolition of anything he had built, all the buildings that have been added do not prevent us from seeing the old palace as it was formerly, except that the court-yard has been paved with marble, and enriched with fountains and statues, while aviaries have been set up in its corners and the façades ornamented with gilded balconies, and in fact the whole of the inside and outside has been embellished so as to blend more harmoniously with the great buildings which now surround it. . . . The blocks which the King has had joined to the old building are together called the Château Neuf or Grand Château. They face on the garden and on the courtyards which separate them from the little château, to which they are joined nevertheless by great stairways communicaing with the upper apartments.

The works produced a number of accidents. Workmen were frequently injured, and their families punished if they dared protest. Lefèvre d'Ormesson *notes, during the month of July 1668:*

Two notable incidents have just occurred. First, a woman who had lost her son when he fell from a scaffolding while working at Versailles, and who had nevertheless been taxed by the local court of justice, overwhelmed with grief, presented a blank petition to draw attention to herself and, indeed, the officials present asked her laughingly what claim she was making; at which she started hurling abuse at the King, calling him whoremonger, knave of a king, tyrant and a thousand other stupidities and extravagances, so that the King was astonished and demanded if she was in fact referring to him. To which she replied 'yes' and continued her tirade. She was seized and condemned on the spot to be whipped; being taken to the Petites Maisons, the whipping was administered to her by the mayor of Saint-Germain with extreme rigour, yet this woman uttered not a single sound, suffering this torment like a martyr and for the love of God. Many have condemned this severe punishment, saying that the woman should have been treated as mad and confined in the Petites Maisons, and thus the general outbreak of anger and indignation provoked by this punishment would have been avoided.

In a second incident, a sixty-year-old man who, overcome by rage, had uttered similarly outrageous sentiments, was accused of having said that the King was a tyrant and that there were still Ravaillacs and courageous and virtuous people. This man was judged by the Provost Marshal, together with the Maîtres des Requêtes of the district of Juilley and others who were at Saint-Germain, and was condemned to have his tongue cut off and to be sent to the galleys. Some members of the court had favoured a death sentence . . . It is said that the cutting off of the tongue is an entirely new penalty for even blasphemers are only condemned to have the tongue pierced.

In 1671, the King decided to encourage the creation of a town around the Château, where work was still in progress, and where the Court's sojourns were becoming increasingly frequent, despite the fact that the courtiers did not always succeed in finding a room or even a corner for themselves. In addition, at each visit their apartment—or garret—was changed according to the royal whim. Saint-Simon has recounted the manner in which the Marquis de Dangeau, the King's favourite and the confidant of his amours, succeeded in obtaining accommodation:

Seated at play one day with the King and Madame de Montespan, during a period when the work on the great extensions to Versailles was just beginning, Dangeau importuned the King for accommodation for himself, and the King, who was already overwhelmed with similar pleas, began to joke with him about his talent for improvising verses (although, if the truth be told, the results were rarely good) and suddenly challenged him to compose verses around some extremely uncouth rhymes which he gave him, promising him a lodging if he could accomplish this feat on the spot. Dangeau accepted the challenge and after a few moments filled all the rhymes and so won his lodging.

Mansart now presented his plan for the extensions to Versailles: two new wings, work on which continued from 1678 to 1689. Visitors to the Château complained incessantly at the lack of comfort and the bad air. Marie de Rabutin-Chantal, Marquise de Sévigné, writes, on October 12, 1678:

The King wishes to go to Versailles on Saturday, but God, it seems, wills otherwise, because of the impossibility of getting the buildings in a fit state to receive him, and because of the great mortality afflicting the workmen, of whom every night wagons full of the dead are carried out as though from the Hôtel-Dieu. These melancholy processions are kept secret as far as possible, in order not to alarm other workmen.

And the Italian fortune-teller Primi Visconti, an expert at divining the future from people's handwriting, who for ten years lived in Paris and at the Court, made the following remark about Versailles:

The air is foul there. In addition, the putrid waters infest this air so vilely that during the month of August everyone fell ill, the Dauphin, the Dauphine, the courtiers, everyone there, I think, except the King and I myself. Yet the King insists on living there.

In 1682, the King even transferred the seat of government there. By this time, work had been started on the scheme for drawing water from the Seine by means of hydraulic apparatus at Marly and sending it to Versailles by an underground

aqueduct.[1] *The place remained surrounded by building debris
and scaffolding. On August 27, 1684, the Marquis de Dangeau
writes:*

During this last week, the sum of 250,000 livres has been
spent on Versailles. Every day 22,000 men and 6,000 horses
were working there.

*In 1686, Versailles finally had a water supply, but a more
ambitious project was under way, designed to bring water from
the Eure. However, according to the Abbé de Choisy, courtier
and diplomat, in his Mémoires:*

The King having learned, sometime at the beginning of
1686, that the majority of the princes of Europe, jealous of
his glory and fearful of his power, were leaguing together
against him and busy concluding hostile agreements, and that
the Emperor was even considering making peace with the
Turks in order to turn his armies around to face the Rhine,
he himself decided to put himself in a state of preparedness to
resist the combined strength of so many conspiring nations,
and therefore resolved to effect economies in his treasury by
cutting down on unnecessary expenses. The previous year, he
had spent fifteen millions on building works, but he allocated
only four millions for the current year, ordering that while
those aqueducts for bringing water from the River Eure to
Versailles which had already been started should be kept in
good repair, the rest of the great undertaking was to be postponed to a more convenient time when his need for money
would be less great. This resolution was admirable, but he had
not the strength to keep it. The desire to see a river at Versailles was stronger and the works continued.

*These works were nevertheless interrupted, two years later,
at the outbreak of the war of the League of Augsburg, and, at
the end of 1689, the royal palace was considered completed.
According to Saint-Simon, it was far from being a model of
comfort:*

[1] Previously, it arrived in small quantities, pumped by windmill power from
the Étang de Clagny near the Bièvre.

His apartment [that of the King] and that of the Queen
suffer from the most dreadful inconveniences, with back-views
over the privies and other dark and malodorous offices. The
astonishing magnificence of the gardens is equalled only by the
bad taste with which they are designed, and it is disheartening
that they are so little used. To reach the coolness of the
gardens' shade one is forced to cross a vast, scorching plain at
the end of which there is no alternative, at any point, but to
climb upwards or downwards, and the gardens end with a
very small hill. The flint surfacing burns one's feet, but without it one would constantly be plunged into soft sand or black
mire. The violence done to Nature everywhere is repellant
and disgusting. The innumerable water-courses pumped or
otherwise guided in from all directions makes the water itself
green, thick and muddy; it provokes an unhealthy and per-
ceptible humidity, and gives off a vile odour. . . . From the
vantage point of the gardens, one may enjoy the beauty of the
whole design, but the palace itself looks as though it had suffered a conflagration in which the top storeys and the roofs
had been destroyed. . . . One could go on listing indefinitely
the defects of this enormous and enormously costly palace
and its even more costly outhouses.

Who, then, lived in this 'enormously costly' palace?
First of all, the King, his wife Marie Thérèse, the Queen
Mother, Anne of Austria (until 1666), and the heir to the
throne, the Dauphin.
In the second rank were the Sons and Daughters of France,
their children and grandchildren, and—at the same level, in
*the scales of etiquette—*Monsieur, *the Duc d'Orléans, his wife,*
who died in 1670 and was soon replaced by the second
Madame, *Charlotte Elizabeth of Bavaria, the Princess Palatine;*
and Mlle de Montpensier, grand-daughter of Henri IV and
first cousin of the King.
The next category comprised the Princes of Royal Blood
(going back, in the male line of descent, to Hugh Capet).
These were the princes of Condé, progeny of the House of
Bourbon; the Great Condé; his son who inherited the father's
appellation of Monsieur le Prince; *his grandson Louis de Bour-*
bon, called Monsieur le Duc; *his brother Armand, Prince de*

Conti, father of two sons: Louis Armand and François Louis, who both carried the title of prince, the latter being the darling of the Court at the same time as being the object of the King's most intense dislike. Etiquette placed all cardinals and certain bishops in the same rank as these princes.

The final group was composed of the Dukes and Peers, *in previous times holders of the kingdom's principal fiefs (the King had the right to create new dukedoms and peerages), and the foreign princes: Dukes of Lorraine, Savoy, Nevers (House of Mantua), Longueville (rulers of Neuchâtel) and Rohan (descendants of the House of Brittany).*

The royal favourites were in a privileged position which was soon fixed as being between that of the Princes of Royal Blood and that of the Dukes and Peers—a position occupied also by Louis XIV's bastards before being declared 'true princes of royal blood' at the end of his reign.

One grade lower were the supreme officers of the armed forces: marshals, admirals and so on; and the great officers of state: ministers, secretaries of state, chancellors, comptrollers-general of finance, all of these being accommodated at Versailles.

And then came the countless holders of great traditional royal offices: Grand Almoner, Grand Chamberlain, Master of the House, Master of the Robes and Gentlemen of the King's Chamber, Grand Master of Ceremonies, Provost Marshal, Master of the Royal Hunt, Master Falconer, Master of the Wolf-hunt, Master Harbinger, Master Pantler, etc. . . .

There were four office-holders for most of these posts, since duties were 'quartered', with each occupant serving for three months in one year. As Primi Visconti *noted:*

The expenses of the Royal Household are particularly high as a result of the system of quartering which quadruples the number of servants and retainers, who amount to more than seven thousand heads, not counting the soldiers of the Royal Household, consisting of four thousand foot-soldiers of the Gardes Françaises, the Swiss regiment, a company of halberdiers, one of archers, one of sentries, and about three or four thousand cavalrymen; Royal Bodyguards, Life-Guardsmen and Light Horse, their officers being held in great esteem.

One may add to this list, finally, the foreign visitors, the ordinary courtiers[1] on the look-out for an official appointment or a favour, the King's scribes and historiographers, the architects, painters and musicians, the staff of the various Households (Household of the King, of the Queen, of Monsieur, of Madame . . .) each with their own servants—a total of probably more than fifteen thousand people all living at the palace in the effulgence of the royal presence.

Jean de La Bruyère, who was tutor to the Great Condè's grandson, has given us a view of the Court in the context of a celebrated passage:

It is a country in which the joys are visible but false, and the sorrows are hidden but real. Who would believe that the enthusiasm for entertainments, the applause at the brilliant plays of Molière and at the Harlequinades, the feasts, hunting parties, ballets and tournaments conceal so much disquiet, so many cares and conflicting interests, so many hopes and fears, such lively passions and such serious matters?

Primi Visconti said more simply:

I wish you could see the Court. It is an absolute confusion of men and women. Well-known personalities of all kinds are welcomed here. Since the nation is somewhat frivolous by nature, the result is a great mixture of different types, a continuous buzz of activity, which prompted the Duke of Palestrina to remark to me the other evening: '*Ceci est un vrai b ...*'[2]

On the other hand, Cardinal Maldacchini, when he visited France for the first time, seeing all these gentlemen and ladies mingled together, exclaimed: '*Oh! quelle cocagne! Oh! quelle cocagne!*'[3]

Now let us allow the witnesses to speak for themselves.

---

[1] All noblemen. But only the titles of princes of the blood, dukes and peers, foreign princes were official. The other titles: marquis, comte, chevalier, and so on were attached to estates, belonged to these, and might be sold with the estates to any member of the nobility.
[2] 'This is a real b[rothel].'
[3] 'Oh! what fun! what fun!'

CHAPTER II

LA VALLIÈRE:
THE SPRINGTIME OF
VERSAILLES

This tender and mutual love, however irregular, accompanied
by all the delicate consideration which it is capable of inspiring
in two impassioned lovers, provided the original reason for the
expeditions to Versailles and thereafter for all the amusements
and gay parties elaborated there to flatter the passion of a king
in love.

EZECHIEL SPANHEIM : *Relation de la Cour de France*

PRINCIPAL PERSONALITIES MENTIONED IN CHAPTER II

KING LOUIS XIV, son of Louis XIII and Anne of Austria.
Twenty-five at the time, and very handsome. 'He wears
his dark blond hair fairly long, he has a high forehead, the
colour of his eyes is blue rather than black, the pose is
aquiline, the outline of the face round . . .' (Locatelli).

QUEEN MARIE THÉRÈSE OF SPAIN, daughter of the King of
Spain Philip IV. Small and fat, the same age as the King and
passionately in love with him. But, according to Mlle de
Montpensier, 'she always had the idea in her head that people
despised her and this made her jealous of everyone.'

The QUEEN MOTHER, ANNE OF AUSTRIA. 'She had been one
of the greatest beauties of her century.' (Mme de Motteville).

JEAN BAPTISTE POQUELIN, who acted under the name of
Molière.

JEAN BAPTISTE LULLY, later to become superintendent of
the King' Music.

LA VALLIÈRE, LOUISE DE LA BAUME LE BLANC, favourite
of Louis XIV whom, according to Bussy-Rabutin, 'she loves

so strongly that it is clear to see that she would have loved him just as much had he been a simple squire and she a great queen.'

JEAN FRANÇOIS, MARQUIS DE LA VALLIÈRE, brother of the favourite, who derived considerable advantage from his sister's privileged position.

LOUIS JOSEPH, DUC DE GUISE, descendant of the great Henri de Guise.

NICOLAS FOUQUET, VICOMTE DE MELUN ET DE VAUX, Superintendent of Finances, disgraced and imprisoned by Louis XIV in 1661.

MME DUPLESSIS-BELLIÈRE, friend and confidante of Fouquet.

Monsieur PHILIPPE D'ORLÉANS, brother of Louis XIV. 'No woman was able to accomplish the miracle of inflaming the heart of this prince,' said Mme de la Fayette, putting it delicately.

Madame HENRIETTE D'ANGLETERRE, wife of Monsieur. Beautiful and flirtatious, she possessed, again according to Mme de la Fayette, 'black eyes burning with such a flame that men were unable to look at them for long without feeling their heat.'

ARMAND DE GRAMMONT, COMTE DE GUICHE, son of the Maréchal de Grammont. 'Beautiful as an angel and full of love,' claimed Bussy-Rabutin.

FRANÇOIS RENÉ DU BEC-CRESPIN, MARQUIS DE VARDES, courtier of Louis XIV, imprisoned and exiled, who regained the King's favours twenty years later.

OLYMPE MANCINI, COMTESSE DE SOISSONS: niece of Mazarin, married to the Comte de Soissons, Colonel-general of the Suisses.

MME DE NAVAILLES: SUZANNE DE BEAUDÉAN DE NEUIL-LANT, married to the Duc de Navailles, a lady-in-waiting to Queen Marie Thérèse and supervisor of her maids of honour.

PHILIPPE DE LORRAINE-ARMAGNAC, known as the CHEVA-
LIER DE LORRAINE, 'looking like the painting of an angel,'
according to the Abbé de Choisy, and a very intimate friend
of Monsieur. Brother of Monsieur le Grand (the Comte
d'Armagnac).

FRANÇOIS DE NEUFVILLE, MARQUIS, later DUC DE VIL-
LEROI, brought up with Louis XIV, a captain in the Guards,
later an army commander with an unbroken record of defeat
in the field, and eventually a marshal of France.

JEAN BAPTISTE COLBERT, Comptroller of Finance. In reality,
directed the entire administration, justice, the interior, commerce, industry, the Navy, building works . . . and concerned himself also with facilitating the King's love affairs.

DUC DE MAZARIN: ARMAND CHARLES DE LA PORTE,
MARQUIS DE LA MEILLERAYE. Having married a niece of
Mazarin's and become Duc de Mazarin through an entail in
his favour, he had inherited a fortune of 28,000,000 livres
from the cardinal. A puritan, he personally smashed with a
hammer all those statues bequeathed to him by the cardinal
which he considered insufficiently clad. He was the laughing-stock of the Court.

*In the month of October 1663, the Court made its first long
stay at Versailles. For the diversion of his guests, the King had
summoned Jean Baptiste Poquelin. The registers of Charles*
Varlet de La Grange, *Molière's pupil and favourite actor, contain the following entry:*

On Thursday, the eleventh day of October, the company
left for Versailles, on the orders of the King. We performed
*Le Prince Jaloux ou Don Garcie, Sertorius, L'École des Maris,
Les Fâcheux, L'Impromptu de Versailles* (so-called because of
the newness of the piece and the place where it was played),
Le Dépit Amoureux, and once again *Le Prince Jaloux*. For the
whole performance, received from M. Bontemps, the King's
chief valet de chambre, 3,300 livres from the privy purse.

*But these performances took place unostentatiously in a little
theatre hastily set up in the vestibule of the Château. The*
Gazette de France *recorded that:*

On October 22nd, Their Majesties, after visiting Versailles to enjoy the pleasures of the chase and all the other diversions which so charming a place may offer, returned here [to Paris] accompanied by Monseigneur le Dauphin and the whole Court.

A few months later, on May 7, 1664, Versailles' history as a centre of elegant entertainment truly began, with the Plaisirs de l'île Enchantée, *a series of performances lasting seven days, for which Lully had written a new score. The gazette-writer* Carpentier de Marigny *thus described the first day of the* divertissements *which were staged in front of the* Château, *with the* Tapis Vert *for background:*

In the four avenues radiating from the *rond*, great porticos had been set up, decorated inside and outside with His Majesty's armorial bearings and symbols. The dais jutted out from the entrance into the *rond* and, behind it, stretching into the *allée*, tiers of benches had been set up in the form of an amphitheatre, to seat 200 people.

As soon as the Queens had arrived, a great fanfare of trumpets and kettledrums announced the fact that the Paladins were ready to enter the lists.

The knights commenced the *course de bague*.[1] The contest was disputed for a long time between the Duc de Guise and the Marquis de La Vallière, who finally won, and although no prize had been proposed for this contest, the Queen Mother, who cannot refrain from lavishing gifts at the least opportunity, rewarded the skill of the Marquis de La Vallière by presenting him with a diamond-encrusted sword and scabbard . . .

At nightfall the arena was lit by countless flambeaux and, the knights having retired, there appeared the Orpheus of our days—I am referring of course to Lully—at the head of a great company of performers who, after approaching the Queens in short steps in time to their instruments, divided into two columns passing on each side of the high dais and proceeding alongside the palisades bordering the *rond*. At the same time,

---

[1] The game consisted in riding at full gallop past a stake, lance in hand, and unhooking and carrying off one or more of the rings hanging from it.

there emerged from the avenue on the right-hand side the Four Seasons: Spring on a great Spanish horse, Summer on an elephant, Autumn on a camel and Winter on a bear. The Seasons were accompanied by twelve gardeners, twelve reapers, twelve wine-harvesters and twelve old men. They indicated the difference between their Seasons by flowers, wheatsheafs, fruits and mirrors, and carried on their heads great bowls in which were heaped the ingredients of the collation which was to follow . . .

The Controllers of the King's Household, costumed to represent Abundance, Joy, Cleanliness and Good Cheer, supervised the setting up between the high dais and the other side of the *rond* of a great crescent-shaped table decorated with festoons and embellished with a great display of flowers, and soon as this had been covered by the Appetizers, Meats and Delicacies, the barrier was drawn aside in the centre to allow Their Majesties to pass, together with the ladies who were invited to the collation. . . This superb banquet lasted until the early hours of the morning.

On the following day, May 8th, Molière's Princess de'Élide was performed on a stage set up in the centre of the Allée Royale; while on May 11th Les Fâcheux was performed in the little improvised theatre in the vestibule, followed by Tartuffe ou l'Imposteur on the following day. The members of the audience appear to have remained discreetly silent as regards their reaction to this last play. But an anonymous Account of the Plaisirs de l'île Enchantée (which appeared in 1665) remarked that:

This evening, His Majesty commanded the performance of a play entitled *Tartuffe* which the Sieur de Molière had written against hypocrites, but although it was found extremely diverting the King perceived in the play such comparisons between those in whom a true devotion gains God's blessing and those whose vainglorious boasting of good deeds is yet accompanied by the performance of evil deeds, that his extreme delicacy in questions of religion was not able to endure this juxtaposition of vice and virtue, wherein one might be taken for the other. Consequently, although he did not question the good intentions of the author, he forbade any performance of this play before the public and even denied himself the pleasure of seeing it again, for fear that his own appreciation might be abused by others less capable of making a judicious assessment of the story.

But the Tartuffe *affair does not seem to have provoked much excitement among the courtiers, who remained charmed with the variety of pleasures offered them. And the true queen of these festivities, the woman who provided the inspiration for this gay atmosphere at Versailles of youthfulness and love, was Louise de la Baume Le Blanc de La Vallière, maid-of-honour to the Duchesse d'Orléans, and since three years the King's mistress.*

Was La Vallière really the tender-hearted, fragile beauty immortalized by Alexandre Dumas in Le Vicomte de Bragelonne? *Witnesses disagreed as to her beauty, but all paid tribute to her gentleness and unselfishness. The Abbé de Choisy, courtier and diplomat who has left us some fascinating* Mémoires, *was one of those who knew her best:*

It is a pleasure to speak about her. I spent my childhood by her side. My father was chancellor to the late Monsieur and her mother was the wife of Madame's chief maître d'hotel.[1] We must have played blind man's buff and musical chairs together a hundred times or more, but once she had tasted the joys of the King's love she no longer wished to see her old friends nor even hear their names mentioned, so completely had she surrendered to this all-embracing passion.

Mademoiselle de La Vallière was not one of those exquisite beauties whom one admires without loving. She was extraordinarily lovable and La Fontaine's verse: 'Her charm was more beautiful even than her beauty' might well have been written for her. She had a lovely complexion, blonde hair, an agreeable smile, blue eyes and so tender and yet so modest a gaze that it won the beholder's heart and esteem equally. For the rest, not very witty, though she polished her mind every day by assiduous reading. No ambition, no points of view, more apt to dream about the object of her love than to please

[1] 'Madame': the Duchesse d'Orléans, wife of Louis XIII's brother.

him, completely enclosed in herself and her passion, the sole passion of her life, setting honour above everything and risking death on several occasions rather than allow anyone to suspect her fragility; gentle, generous and shy, she was always conscious of her failings and strove ceaselessly to overcome them.

Lefèvre d'Ormesson, *on the other hand, was struck by the royal favourite's singular lack of beauty, and said so quite frankly:*

I was at the King's Mass, which was attended by the Queen, Monsieur le Dauphin, Monsieur, and Mlle de La Vallière, whom the Queen has taken into her retinue in deference to the King's wishes, in which she is exceedingly wise. This young lady did not seem to me to be at all beautiful; her eyes are remarkably lovely, as is her complexion, but she is skinny, hollow-cheeked, her mouth and teeth are ugly, the tip of her nose is bulbous and her face is far too long. I must admit that I was surprised to find her so unattractive.

The Lieutenant-captain of the King's Musketeers, Charles de Baatz, Seigneur d'Artagnan, also mentioned La Vallière in the Mèmoires *which were written for him by Captain Gatien* Sandras de Courtilz:

People made fun of her limp and, above all, of her thinness. She certainly was thin and this affliction, if one may call it thus, resulted from her life at the Court, for she was nothing less than fat when she first arrived. Since the King honoured her with his favours, she had two children by him which might well have passed for love-children since each was more beautiful than the other. But this made her so thin that she became positively emaciated.

But according to the Bolognese priest Sebastiano Locatelli, *the young woman had other talents:*

Perhaps, reader, you may be curious to know why so great and noble a King has found it possible to demean himself so far as to love a maid-of-honour of his brother's wife? Moreover, her beauty is nothing out of the ordinary, her figure is far from elegant, she limps slightly, but it is true that she has very beautiful eyes, though they are not black.

The reason is that the King is now able to enjoy at leisure the pleasures which peacetime affords. He loves hunting and he knows, having observed her several times, that not even the professional hunters themselves can excel her in swordsmanship, pistol shooting and horse riding. I once saw her at the Tuileries, which are the King's pleasure gardens in Paris, mount and ride a Barbary horse bareback, stand upright on its back while it was in full gallop and reseat herself again, repeating this manoeuvre several times, aided only by a silk cord passed through the horse's mouth in lieu of bridle. Her skill was so extraordinary that one might almost suspect her of being in league with the devil, for no one, however accomplished a horseman he might be, had ever seen such a spectacle. Her teacher was a Moor, one of the King's grooms, and I have on several occasions seen this Moor perform the feat which I have described.

La Vallière had, in fact, attracted others in addition to the King. Soon after her entry into the Court she had been noticed by Superintendent Fouquet, who had sent her his regular procuress, Mme Duplessis-Bellière, with a proposition, but the rebuff she received resulted in a furious letter to her protector:

I still quiver with rage every time I think of the haughtiness with which that little demoiselle de La Vallière treated me. To secure her good will I had complimented her on her beauty, which is in fact very slight. Then, having revealed to her that you would always see that she lacked for nothing and that you had set aside 20,000 pistoles for her, she flared up at me, saying that 200,000 livres could not make her take even one false step, and she repeated this statement to me in so contemptuous a tone that, though I had omitted no effort to mollify her before taking my leave of her, I fear strongly that she may mention the matter to the King, in which case we must take appropriate precautions. Do you not think it might be advisable to forestall her by stating that she had asked you for money and that you had refused her? That would make all her complaints suspect.

How did this royal love affair start?—As a result of a fairly comical amorous entanglement. When his brother married Henrietta Anne, daughter of King Charles I of England, thenceforward to be known as Henriette d'Angleterre, the King had immediately decided that this young woman, whom he had known as a child, was now extremely seductive, and he made no effort to conceal his admiration.

Mme de La Fayette, *author of* La Princesse de Clèves, *who also wrote a* Histoire de Madame, *related that the intimacy between the King and his sister-in-law had begun to create a scandal in the Court in 1661 and that the Queen Mother had become most upset. Meanwhile:*

The King and Madame, without ever confiding in each other concerning their mutual feelings, continued to live in a manner which made it clear to everyone that there was more between them than mere friendship . . .

Rumour grew so strong, and the Queen Mother and Monsieur reproached the King and Madame so vigorously that they began to come to their senses and probably for the first time made some practical reflections on the situation. In any case, they resolved to avoid provoking any further gossip and, for some obscure reason, agreed that the King should start a love affair with some young lady at the Court . . .

Among those ladies considered capable of becoming suitable partners to the King, three young ladies at the Court were most often mentioned: Mlle de Pons, Mlle de Chêmerault and Mlle de La Vallière. Mme de La Fayette *continues:*

With Madame's connivance, he [the King] began to make love to all three ladies indiscriminately, rather than choose one of them in particular. However, he soon made up his mind: his heart declared itself for Mlle de La Vallière, and although he continued to flirt with the other two and even remained quite assiduous in his attentions towards Mlle de Chêmerault, it was to La Vallière that he devoted his care and his affection.

But Bussy-Rabutin, *cousin of Mme de Sévigné and author of the* Histoire amoureuse des Gaules, *offered a simpler version of the facts:*

It is certain that she [La Vallière] loved the King by her own inclination, more than a year before he ever met her, for she often told a certain lady, one of her closest friends, that she wished he were not of so exalted a rank. It is common knowledge that the teasing she endured as a result reached the ears of the King, so that he became curious to meet her, and since it is natural for a generous heart to love those who love him, the King loved her from that moment onwards. It is not that he was impressed by her physical appearance, but he was truly fond of her. Telling the Comte de Guiche that he wanted to arrange a marriage between her and a certain marquis who was a friend of the count, the latter remarked to the King that his friend liked beautiful women. 'Well, by God,' said the King, 'it is true that she is not beautiful, but I will be generous enough to him to make him desire her.'

Three days later, the King, while visiting Madame, who was ill, in her apartment, stopped first in the anteroom and held a long conversation with La Vallière. The King was so charmed by her liveliness of mind that, from that moment onwards, his fondness became love. He remained only a moment with Madame, but he returned the following day and every succeeding day for a month, which led everyone to think that he was in love with Madame.

The Queen began to become jealous of La Vallière, despite the King's precautions and the discretion of his mistress. François Langlois de Motteville, attached to the King's suite, wrote:

On my return from a short journey to Normandy which I made at that time [1662], I found that the Queen was in childbed prior to the birth of Anne Elizabeth of France. One evening, when I had the honour to be in her company, standing in the alcove by her bed, she motioned to me with her eyes, directing my attention to Mlle de La Vallière who was just then passing through the bedroom on her way to take supper with the Comtesse de Soissons, and said to me in Spanish: '*Esta doncella con las arracadas de Diamantes, es esta que el Rey quiere.*'[1]

---

[1] 'That young woman with the diamond ear-rings is the one the **King loves**.'

I was taken aback by this remark, for I knew that the Court was most concerned at the time to keep this secret from her; I said something to the Queen in reply which was vague enough to avoid either agreement or disagreement and, so as to give her a little courage in facing events, I tried to convince her that all husbands, without ceasing to love their wives, were usually unfaithful in this way.

But someone else had become upset by the King's passion for La Vallière, and this person was the Duchesse d'Orléans, Madame; having had a brief flirtation with her brother-in-law, Louis XIV, she was enraged to see him paying so little attention to her now.

Charles Auguste Marquis de La Fare, *commander of the Dauphin's Company of Life-Guards, has related how Madame thought of revenging herself:*

When Madame realized that she was not really the object of the King's frequent visits but was serving as a pretext for him to see La Vallière, she harboured great resentment against both of them and, with revenge in mind, discussed the matter with the Comte de Guiche, eldest son of the Maréchal de Grammont, a well-built young man whose lively spirit and courage were matched by his boldness. At the same time, the Comtesse de Soissons, seeing that the King had surrendered to La Vallière's charms, started a love affair with the Marquis de Vardes who, though no longer in his first youth, still retained his youthful qualities of amiability and wittiness, an ingratiating manner and even a youthful figure. It is thought by some that he started his liaison with the countess on the orders of the King and that the King was his confidant. What is certain is that this inveterate courtier did what he did through ambition rather than love, and that he was just as put out as were the countess and Madame when he saw that La Vallière's hold on the King was complete.

These four people, that is to say Madame and the Comte de Guiche (whose infatuation for her had made him completely irresponsible), the Comtesse de Soissons and Vardes, began to plot together to eliminate La Vallière so that they might remain in control of the Court. They decided that if, by some means, the young Queen could be provided with positive proof of the King's commerce with La Vallière she would become so angry and would so provoke the Queen Mother's anger against him that the King would have no choice but to give up his mistress. They then wrote a letter to her, purporting to come from her father the King of Spain, warning her of the King's unfaithfulness. This letter was composed by Vardes and translated into Spanish by the Comte de Guiche, who prided himself on his linguistic accomplishments. He did at least know Spanish, that is certain.

The letter was delivered in due course, without anyone suspecting it true origin at the time. The young Queen, who loved her husband passionately, all the more so because he in turn had genuinely loved her during the first year of their marriage, was overwhelmed with grief. The Queen Mother took her side, but though the King was extremely vexed and anxious, he refused to abandon his mistress. His ill humour was visited upon those who had been bold enough to attack him in so hurtful a manner. Yet he was so far from suspecting the true source of the letter that he summoned Vardes, for whom he had a high regard and felt great affection, and sought his opinion as to which member of the Court might have dared offer him such injury.

Vardes, shrewdly and spitefully, diverted suspicion towards Mme de Navailles, one of the Queen's ladies-in-waiting. Her austere principles had recently caused displeasure to the King, since she had ordered railings set up barring access to the avenues leading to the quarters occupied by the Queen's maids-of-honour, so preventing him from continuing to visit Mlle de La Mothe-Argencourt, to whom he had been mildly attracted, egged on by the Comtesse de Soissons whose constant objective was La Vallière's downfall. Mme de Navailles and her husband were promptly expelled from the Court, without explanation . . .

Meanwhile, Vardes remained closer to the King than any other man at Court and the one whose advice the King sought most constantly. But unfortunately for him, the expulsion of the Comte de Guiche from the Court because of his relations with Madame resulted in that princess conceiving some infatuation for Vardes, as a result of which she tried to make him give up the Comtesse de Soissons. The countess not only succeeded in keeping her lover, but was so pleased with herself as a result that, at a ballet performance one day, she related her account of the matter to those around her, an account which enraged Madame when it reached her ears.

The quarrel between Madame and the countess became increasingly bitter, and Vardes, to please his mistress, committed an imprudence which was unpardonable in a man of his years and experience. What happened was that, finding the Chevalier de Lorraine, Monsieur's favourite, together with Mlle de Fiennes, daughter of Madame, he said to him in mocking tones: 'Come, Monsieur, a prince of your constitution playing around with soubrettes! Are you then exhausted by your mistresses?' This jest, which the Chevalier de Lorraine repeated to his friend the Marquis de Villeroi and which was quite probably overheard by others in any case, soon reached the ears of Madame. She complained to the King, and Vardes was sent to the Bastille. At first it was thought that he would only be detained there for a few days, but his enemies at Court succeeded in further embittering Madame by revealing to her the secret of the letter purporting to come from the King of Spain. The King's anger was all the greater because he saw himself betrayed by the two who were closest and dearest to him, the Comtesse de Soissons and Vardes. Vardes was consigned to a dungeon in the citadel of Montpellier, while the countess was exiled to the province of Champagne of which her husband was governor.

La Vallière now had all the intriguers ranged against her. And the King's love had borne its fruit. By the end of 1663, everyone was remarking on the poor woman's pale, sickly appearance. In the month of December, Lefèvre d'Ormesson noted in his Journal *a curious story involving a Court physician by the name of Boucher:*

On Tuesday, December 18th, the Marquise de Villeroi was in labour and so prayed Boucher not to make other appointments or at least to leave news as to where he could be found. It is said that Boucher, arriving at Mme de Villeroi's apartments on Wednesday morning after being sought for all night.

explained that he was at home the previous evening when a carriage drew up and he was invited into it. Once inside, he had been blindfolded and the carriage had driven off at full speed. After a short time, it halted outside a house, where he was guided up the stairs, his eyes still blindfolded, and into a room where the blindfold was removed. He found himself in a bedroom, where he saw a lady lying in bed, masked, and surrounded by ten or twelve persons who were not masked; the bed itself and the room's hangings were draped with sheets. Having delivered this lady, he was blindfolded once again, re-escorted to the carriage and driven home after having been paid most handsomely.

Boucher is supposed to have told this to Mme de Villeroi, having arrived just in time to deliver her successfully of a son. And it is claimed that the masked lady whom he had delivered of a child was none other than Mlle de La Vallière.

The date and the facts are perfectly correct. Colbert *was made responsible for looking after the child—a boy—and noted in his* Mémoires:

Regarding the feeding and care of the baby, I decided to entrust it to Beauchamps and his wife who had been in service in my family and now lived in the Rue aux Ours. Observing the secrecy which the King had commanded in the affair, I told them that one of my brothers had had this child by a young lady of quality and that to save his honour I was obliged to assume responsibility for the new-born infant and so desired them to feed and care for it, which they very gladly agreed to do.

But La Vallière's opponents at the Court also included the puritan faction which was shocked, or pretended to be shocked, by the royal liaison. In December 1664, Lefèvre d'Ormesson *writes:*

I wish also to record a true story involving the Duc de Mazarin. On Sunday, a week ago, he made up his mind to warn the King of the scandal that his conduct with Mlle de La Vallière was causing throughout his kingdom, so, after taking communion, he went to the Louvre to attend the King's levee. Having told the King that he desired to speak to him in privacy, His Majesty invited him into his closet where M. de Mazarin, after making all sorts of excuses for the liberty he was taking, told him that his conscience had troubled him for some time, that he had just taken communion, and that he could no longer refrain from informing His Majesty of the scandal he was causing at the Court through his relations with Mlle de La Vallière.

The King let him say his piece, demanded: 'Have you quite finished? I have known for a long time that there was something wrong with you there,' touching his hand to his forehead as he said this, then retired. Everyone condemns M. de Mazarin's zeal, for he has neither the authority nor the character to deliver this type of admonition.

CHAPTER III

THE KING ENJOYS HIMSELF

La Vallière, so 'tis said,
Is losing favour fast.
The King goes to her bed
With boredom unsurpassed.
Now Montespan takes o'er;
Things—as we've seen before—
From hand to hand get passed.
                    (Song, 1667)

❦

PRINCIPAL PERSONALITIES MENTIONED IN CHAPTER III

CHARLOTTE DE GRAMMONT, PRINCESSE DE MONACO, daughter of the Maréchal de Grammont and sister of the Comte de Guiche. Married to Louis Grimaldi, grandson of Honoré II of Monaco and son of Hercule, Marquis de Baux.

PÉGUILLAIN: ANTOINE NOMPAR DE CAUMONT, MARQUIS DE PUYGUILHEM (sometimes written Péguillain), later Duc de Lauzun. This 'straw-haired little man', ('*ce petit homme blondasse*') so called by Saint-Simon, forms the subject of Chapter V.

CATHERINE DE LA BAUME, daughter of Alexandre de Neufville-Villeroi.

MME DE MONTESPAN: FRANÇOISE ATHÉNAÏS DE MORTEMART, married to the Marquis de Montespan, and the King's favourite.

CLAUDE MARIE DU GAST D'ARTIGNY, COMTESSE DE ROURE, friend of Mlle de La Vallière.

MME DE MONTAUSIER: JULIE D'ANGENNES, daughter of

Mme de Rambouillet, married to the Duc de Montausier and one of the Queen's ladies-in-waiting.

LOUIS DE PARDAILLAN DE GONDRIN, MARQUIS DE MONTE-SPAN. He did not resign himself to the rôle of cuckold. A judicial separation between him and his wife was ordered, on July 7, 1674, the decree citing the Marquis's dissipation of his fortune and the cruel treatment he had inflicted upon his wife.

The ARCHBISHOP OF SENS, uncle of the Marquis de Monte-span, who supported his nephew's cause. The Abbé Boileau noted that this archbishop ordered a woman of the town of Sens who, like the Marquise, was openly living in concubinage, to perform public penance, and had the ancient canons against violations of the laws of religion posted throughout his diocese.

HENRI DE MASSUÉ, MARQUIS DE RUVIGNY, French Ambassador to England.

FRANÇOIS DE NEUFVILLE, MARQUIS (later DUC) DE VILLEROI, a favourite of Louis XIV and later a Marshal of France (already mentioned in Chapter II).

Louis XIV was not a faithful lover. Already by the end of 1664 it was being whispered that the Princesse de Monaco, daughter of the Maréchal de Grammont, would very probably supplant La Vallière. The Marquis de La Fare is the source of our information about this royal flirtation:

Although Mlle de La Vallière remained the queen sultana, the King nevertheless desired to possess the Princesse de Monaco, daughter of the Maréchal de Grammont; up till then her favours had been awarded to Péguillain,[1] her cousin, famous later under the name of the Comte de Lauzun, who had known her from childhood, having lived as a boy at the Hôtel de Grammont where the marshal treated him like one of his own children.

He was still very much in love with her, and on good terms with the King, but he spoke to the King on the subject of

[1] Puyguilhem.

Mme de Monaco with such arrogance and pride that he was imprisoned in the Bastille. However, what might well have ruined him, in fact made his fortune: the King cared little about Mme de Monaco, but conceived such a high opinion of Péguillain from that moment onwards that he did him great favours, as we shall see.

And Lefévre d'Ormesson *notes in his* Journal, *during the month of July 1665:*

Today [Tuesday July 28th] M. de Péguillain was sent to the Bastille for having spoken to the King with extraordinary insolence. It seems that he was annoyed because Mme de Monaco, the object of his passion, was accepting the King's blandishments, and having told this lady that he possessed letters of hers which would cause her downfall she thought it best to speak to the King about it to prevent him carrying out his threat. The King summoned Péguillain, and after a fairly long meeting about which no one has any details, the King finally told him that he would be obliged to send him to Guiana. Péguillain replied that he refused to go there, that he would never again serve him, but that he would not serve his enemies either, for reasons of honour, for he loved his country, and so he continued in the same extravagant style. To which the King remained unmoved, saying simply that he was being foolish. Then he had him arrested. Everyone agrees that Péguillain must be completely out of his senses.

Anonymous messages were very much in vogue in this Court. In a letter to Marie Louise de Gonzaga, Queen of Poland, dated August 25, 1665, the Prince de Condé *relates:*

The Marquis de Villeroi has recently developed symptoms of extreme infatuation for Mme de Monaco, daughter of the Maréchal de Grammont, and although she has received his advances coldly and has even sent several messages to him through friends of hers, advising him to abandon any thoughts he might have in her direction, he continues to pester her with his amorous advances . . .

In fact he and Mme de La Baume resolved together to write

to Mlle de la Vallière an unsigned letter in disguised hand-writing, warning her of the King's love for Mme de Monaco, hoping that Mlle de La Vallière would be in a strong enough position to oblige the King to break with Mme de Monaco. They composed and sent this anonymous letter but it failed to have the desired effect. Mlle de La Vallière is perfectly sure of the King's affection for her and quite incapable of jealousy. She simply showed the letter to the King, without comment or question; he was shrewd enough to guess that it could only have been written by M. de Villeroi, since he was the only love-sick courtier around capable of such folly, Puyguilhem being in the Bastille and so not in a position to write letters. There was no one else upon whom suspicion might fall so, knowing the friendship which existed between M. de Villeroi and Mme de La Baume, he felt sure that she would be able to throw some light on the matter: he spoke to her about it, and she confessed. The Marquis de Villeroi was also obliged to admit his guilt to the King who was gracious enough to pardon him. Can any more fantastic a situation be imagined?

The Prince de Condé *is also our informant as regards the amusements which Versailles offered during this summer of 1665. On September 18th, he writes:*

The King returned yesterday from Versailles where he had remained four days. On the first day, he took a hart and a buck, accompanied by all the ladies who rode wearing embroidered jerkins and hats. They followed the hunt most efficiently, especially Mlle de La Vallière, riding with one of Madame's daughters; they kept well on the heels of the hounds and no man could have gone faster than they.

The following day, there was a new play written by an actor called Molière. This man has an extraordinary wit and follows the ancients, in all his plays, in making sport of the vices of his century. In this last comedy of his, he attacks physicians . . .

Puyguilhem, meanwhile, spent only six months in the Bastille before being readmitted to the King's good graces. But he had sworn to revenge himself, and he began by preventing

a particular rendezvous between the lovers. The Abbé de
Choisy *explains how he managed this:*

Mme de Monaco found it necessary to confide in one of
her lady's-maids that the King was to come and visit her two
hours after midnight, for the lady's-maid slept in her anteroom and without her co-operation the King could not con-
veniently have access to her apartment. She naturally supposed
that the young woman would serve her faithfully.

This lady's-maid more or less kept the secret, as she had
promised to, except that she told M. de Lauzun of the rendezvous and that it had been arranged that, at two o'clock, the
King would walk down the corridor of Mme de Monaco's
apartment, and would find the key which this girl would have
taken care to leave beforehand in the door of the anteroom
where she slept.

M. de Lauzun paid handsomely for this piece of information
and only demanded of the girl that the key should already be
in the door by one in the morning. So, when everyone seemed
to have retired for the night, M. de Lauzun himself passed
down the corridor, double-locked the door, took the key and
withdrew.

The girl and Mme de Monaco were both aroused by the
noise of the lock-springs, and were still discussing their predicament when the King arrived at two o'clock as he had promised.
But how could he get in? No explanation was possible at that
hour and through a closed door. The King went away again
and it was not until a long time afterwards, when M. de Lauzun
was arrested, that he learned by whom and how this door was
locked.

*Puyguilhem, however, was by no means satisfied with this
petty vengeance. During the following month of May, he
inflicted a brutal punishment on the Princesse de Monaco by
crushing one of her hands under the wooden heel of his shoe.
The Prince de Monaco and his friends made vociferous protests; Guiche, in exile in Holland, was advised of the disgraceful
treatment to which his sister had been subjected. But the King
refused to allow Puyguilhem to be punished, declaring himself
convinced that only clumsiness was involved. The King des-*

cribed the official version of the story in a letter to the Comte
d'Estrades, his envoy at The Hague, dated May 18, 1666; it
was hardly convincing:

You must know, then, that last Monday, being at Versailles,
we were gaming, in the salon, for a piece of jewellery worth
12,000 pistoles, and the ladies were all seated prettily on the
floor, to be more comfortable. I was standing up and watching
the play closely, to see who was winning. At one moment I
stepped back two paces to get a better view, so that those who
had been standing between me and the wall were obliged to
withdraw to each side, including Puyguilhem who, moving
away somewhat hastily in order to make room for me, most
unfortunately stepped by chance on Mme de Monaco's hand
which was, as I have explained, resting on the floor to
support her, but covered by her skirt so that it could
not even be seen, an unhappy circumstance which led to the
following scene. First, this princess spent some time examining
her fingers and showing them to the ladies surrounding her,
complaining that she had been hurt, then suddenly she raised
her voice and accused Puyguilhem of stepping on her hand.
Now she started weeping, got to her feet, hurled to the ground
in a fit of rage a book she had been holding, and dashed into
another room, where she burst into tears in the presence of
several people who were quite unable to console her or to
make her consider that it had been pure mischance and that
there could have been no possible intention to injure her, and
even less to offend her deliberately. Puyguilhem, for his part,
made every conceivable show of regret and despair for what
had happened and offered not only to make any amends
demanded of him, despite the fact that it had been pure clumsiness, but even to throw himself out of the window that very
instant if that could content the princess and persuade her that
he had been very far from having any intention of vexing her.

Around this time, rumours began to circulate about a love-
affair between the King and Mme de Montespan, the Queen's
lady-in-waiting, who had, it was said, vowed to seduce him.
But according to Primi Visconti:

This beautiful lady with her penchant for banter and mockery, did not at first attract the King. One day, when he was at table with Monsieur, his brother, he even joked about her; noticing how assiduously she was attempting to please him, he is supposed to have said: 'She tries hard, but I want nothing of it.'

La Vallière was pregnant for the third time when her eldest son died in July, 1666, at the age of two and a half (her second child, born in 1665, died when eleven months old). She gave birth to a daughter in October, and Queen Marie Thérèse also gave birth to a daughter, on January 2, 1667, but according to Lefèvre d'Ormesson, the King did not seem particularly concerned by the latter event:

A fortnight after the Queen's delivery, at the Court performance of ballet together with farcical pieces by Molière and the Italian troupe, the King was to be seen sitting side by side with Mlle de La Vallière.

While the Prince de Condé *noted:*

In the midst of all these entertainments, the ladies were engaged in a thousand intrigues. What really embitters them, at the bottom of their hearts, is that they are extremely jealous of Mlle de La Vallière and there are very few among them who do not envy her acutely.

In the spring, the King prepared to support by force of arms the rights of Queen Marie Thérèse to the succession to the Spanish possessions, resulting from the death of his father-in-law, Philip IV of Spain. But before leaving for the campaign in Flanders, he announced a piece of news which threw the Court into a turmoil: Mlle de La Vallière was created Duchesse de Vaujours and her daughter, Marie Anne, was recognized and legitimized!

The Marquis de Saint-Maurice, *ambassador to France of the Duke of Savoy, wrote to his master on May 17, 1667:*

The King has acknowledged the daughter he has had by

Mlle de La Vallière, has named her Marie Anne de Bourbon, has purchased an estate in Poitou adjoining that of La Vallière, and has elevated it to a duchy and peerage under the name of the duchy of La Vallière. He has presented it to the mother and her daughter and after their deaths the duchy will become extinct. Vaujours cost 800,000 livres. The King, in declaring his daughter Marie Anne legitimate and in creating La Vallière duchess, has simultaneously declared to the Queen that he would never touch her [La Vallière] again in his life and it is said that he is firm in these resolutions and faithful in his assurances.

At the same time, Louis XIV announced that only the ladies of the Queen's Household, with the Queen herself, would accompany him to Flanders. Madame and her maids-of-honour would not make the voyage. La Vallière realized that a new star was rising on the horizon: Athénaïs de Mortemart, Marquise de Montespan, a beautiful calculating young woman who had determined to become the royal favourite and was manoeuvring skilfully to achieve this objective, as La Fare explains:

While the King was thinking about Mme de Monaco, Mme de Montespan had begun to think about him and was shrewd enough to do two things at the same time: first, she gave the Queen an extraordinary impression of her virtuousness by taking communion in her company every week; secondly, she insinuated herself so successfully into the good graces of La Vallière that she was constantly to be seen by her side. By these means, she contrived to be permanently in the King's immediate entourage and she did all that she could to please him, in which she succeeded very well, being plentifully endowed with wit and charm, in contrast to La Vallière who was sadly defective in these qualities.

The King had requested the Queen to leave for Amiens, where he was to join her later. Suddenly La Vallière, despite the royal orders, decided to leave as well: she was determined to see Louis and speak to him. Mlle de Montpensier, cousin of the King (known since the Fronde under the name of La Grande Mademoiselle), relates in her Mémoires:

Leaving Compiègne, we went to La Fère. While the Queen was playing cards that evening, I noticed that all around her were talking in low voices and behaving strangely. I went to my room to unravel these mysteries, and learned that Mme de La Vallière was due to arrive on the following day. It was this that was occupying the Queen's thoughts, for she was most vexed by this news.

The following day I was dressed early in the morning. I went to the Queen's quarters because she had said that she would be leaving as soon as she was up and dressed. I was most surprised to find Mme la Duchesse [de Vaujours], the Marquise de La Vallière [sister-in-law of the favourite] and Mme du Roure sitting on trunks in her anteroom. They greeted me, saying that they were so tired they could hardly remain upright, not having had any sleep that night. I asked them if they had seen the Queen. They said no. I entered her closet and found her in tears. She told me that she had just vomited and was too weak to move. And Mme de Montausier shrugged her shoulders and repeated to me several times: 'You see the Queen's condition.' Mme de Montespan was making even more vigorous exclamations, to make it clear to everyone how much she pitied the Queen and how well-founded her grief was.

The Queen set out for church, to take Mass in one of the tribunes. The Duchesse de La Vallière went downstairs and the Queen had the door locked in case she should try to come up again. But despite all these precautions, La Vallière came up to her just as we were about to climb into our carriages. The Queen did not say a word to her. And at dinner she ordered that no food was to be offered her. The conversation in our carriage that morning was entirely centred on her. Mme de Montespan said that she admired her boldness in daring to confront the Queen; she said: 'It is certain that the King did not authorize her to come, and when she left she must have been quite aware of the displeasure she would surely cause him and the harsh reception she would certainly receive from the Queen ... God protect me from being the King's mistress!

If I had that misfortune, I would certainly never have the effrontery to face the Queen.'

The following day, the Queen, who had slept overnight at Guise, had forbidden her officers to permit anyone to leave before her, but:

When Mme de La Vallière was on top of a promontory from which she could see the army, she sent her carriage jogging across the fields as fast as it would go. The Queen saw this and was overcome by rage. Everyone had begged Mme de La Vallière not to go ahead, warning her that the Queen would be bound to report to the King the way she had behaved. When the King arrived and came up to the Queen's carriage, she pressed him most urgently to enter; he was reluctant, saying that he was covered with mud. When the King had dismounted and the Queen had stepped to the ground, he spent a short moment with her, then went straight to Mme de La Vallière who did not put in an appearance again that evening.

The journey continued, but after the capture of Douai and Tournai, the King rejoined the ladies at Compiègne:

While he was stopping there, he visited Mme de Montespan every day in her room, which was just above that of the King. One evening, at dinner, I heard the Queen complain to the King that he had not come to bed until four in the morning, and when she asked him the reason he replied that he had had to work exceedingly late. While saying these words, he turned his head aside so that no one might see him laugh. Fearing to do likewise, I dared not lift my eyes from my lap.

On August 27th, Lille capitulated to the French. At the beginning of September, the victorious Louis XIV returned to Saint-Germain, and the ambassador of the Duke of Savoy, Saint-Maurice, noted for his master:

The King spoke for a while to Mme de Montespan and, the following day, as they took their places in the carriage, he was sitting in the back with the Queen, and had this lady seated on the portière by his side and conversed with her throughout the journey; and the cream of the jest is that apparently the Queen still has no suspicion whatsoever of this affair and that the King continues to encourage her jealousy of La Vallière.

A refrain about the two favourites had already reached the Court from Paris, and was being sung discreetly:

> One is lame and has a stick,
> The other's tough and red and thick.
> While nothing's thinner than the first,
> The second's fat enough to burst.

On October 2nd, La Vallière was delivered of a fourth child, which, like the preceding ones, was taken in charge by Colbert. Louis XIV was preparing the invasion of the Spanish Franche Comté. The campaign was launched on February 2, 1668, and was over in three weeks. Peace was signed at Aix la Chapelle on May 2nd, and was celebrated at Versailles by a series of magnificent fêtes which took place in July: the first performance of Georges Dandin ou le Mari Confondu, *a ballet by Lully entitled* Le Triomphe de Bacchus, *a great ball and, to finish up with, a remarkable fireworks display, described for us by* Félibien des Avaux, *the King's historiographer:*

By a prodigious transformation, the château appeared truly to be the palace of the Sun. All the intersections of the avenues were suddenly illuminated by antique statues of all hues. In an instant, all the balustrades were bordered with flaming urns which decorated and lit up at the same time the vast reaches of this superb park. Suddenly one heard an almost heroic harmony: the explosion of a thousand fireworks, followed immediately by a thousand plumes of fire soaring up from the fountains, the woods and the shrubberies, and shooting from the gaping jaws of the lizards, frogs and other animals which surrounded the basins . . .

The Marquis de Saint-Maurice *considered these fêtes somewhat extravagant:*

Never have such beautiful water and firework displays been seen. They have cost the King more than 500,000 livres.[1] Everyone says that he would have done better to give this money to the demobilized soldiers. The ladies and gentlemen of quality have also made excessive expenditures in their private capacity; some have spent as much as 15,000 livres on French point-lace: one merchant has sold 80,000 livres worth. I have had to spend nearly 4,000 livres on adorning myself, my wife, my daughter and her children, and in my opinion I have never spent money so uselessly; I console myself with the thought that when one is among madmen one must be mad oneself.

From this year, 1668, Mlle de La Vallière and Mme de Montespan were to find themselves living in close proximity for six years. Mme de Caylus, *cousin and protégée of Mme de Maintenon, from whom more will be heard later on in this narrative, confirms this fact in her* Souvenirs:

So the King fell in love with Mme de Montespan while Mme de La Vallière was his *maîtresse déclarée*, and Mme de Montespan came to live with her in the capacity of *maîtresse peu délicate*, sharing the same table and sometimes the same house. At first the latter was in favour of this arrangement, either because in this way neither the public nor her husband would guess the true situation, or because she simply did not care, or perhaps because her pride relished the pleasure of seeing her rival constantly humiliated, while her confidence in the King's affections led her to fear nothing from the other's charms. Whatever may have been the reason, they certainly lived together.

But one day, being annoyed with the King for some other reason (which often happened to her), she complained about this communal existence with a bitterness which she did not really feel, saying that she found the King lacking in delicacy in tolerating the situation. To mollify her, he replied most gently and tenderly and ended by assuring her that this establishment had developed imperceptibly. 'Imperceptibly for

[1] 100,000 livres, according to the accounts of the Royal Buildings.

you, perhaps,' answered Mme de Montespan, 'but very perceptibly indeed for me.'

If we are to believe the evidence of the Abbé de Choisy, the King was rather amused by the whole situation:

When he returned from hunting, he went to Mme de La Vallière's apartment to remove his boots, powder himself and change his clothes; then, after scarcely saying good-day to her, he would pass into Mme de Montespan's apartment and stay there the whole evening.

But a troublemaker had arrived in the shape of M. de Montespan, who, having perceived his misfortune somewhat tardily, had come to protest. But according to Mme de Caylus:

He was generally considered a dishonest man and a fool. If, at the beginning, he had resolved to remove his wife from the Court, the King, however infatuated he might have been, would have been incapable of asserting his authority against that of a husband, but M. de Montespan, far from being concerned with his marital rights, arrived with the sole idea of profiting from the situation, and his subsequent actions were motivated entirely by spite resulting from the fact that he failed to get his own way.

The deceived husband's foolish behaviour aroused more amusement than sympathy in the Court, as Mlle de Montpensier makes clear:

He came to me one evening and repeated a harangue which he claims to have delivered to the King, during which he quoted countless passages from the Scriptures and made many arguments to oblige him to return his wife to him and to fear the judgment of God. I told him: 'You are mad. No one will ever believe you actually delivered this speech; it is made up for the benefit of the Archbishop of Sens, your uncle, who is ill-disposed towards Mme de Montespan.' I was at Saint-Germain the following day and said to Mme de Montespan: 'Come and take a walk with me. I have seen your husband,

and he is madder than ever. I scolded him thoroughly and told him that if he did not hold his tongue he deserved to be locked up.' She said in reply: 'He is a laughing-stock in the Court. I am ashamed that not only my parrot but my husband too serve to amuse the riff-raff.'

Anne Marguerite Petit, *wife of the Capitaine Dunoyer, staying at Toulouse, where M. de Montespan had retired, wrote at a later date to a friend at the Court:*

Although M. de Montespan is not reticent in talking about his wife's conduct, he does not like to be made fun of on this subject and, despite his natural courtesy and good breeding, he has not dealt gently with those ladies who have tried to be humorous about the matter. Not long ago he was playing at lansquenet; his card, a king of hearts, was the first to be taken and since he was cursing his luck, a présidente who was of the company, wishing to show her wit, said to him: 'Ah! Monsieur, it is not the king of hearts which has caused you the greatest grief.' M. de Montespan, irritated both by the loss of his card and by this présidente's ill-conceived jest, retorted: 'If my wife is worth a Louis, then you are worth thirty sols' (*'Si ma feme est à un Louis, vous êtes à trente sols'*).

Some time after this exchange, he made up a masked party with a few of his friends and went with them to a ball at which this présidente was presiding as queen. Here, he slashed her with a whip in full view of everyone, then left the ball without being recognized. Everyone realized that it was he who had struck the blow, but because it could not be proved and because the lady had provoked this assault, no more was said about it.

In the spring of 1669, the Court was alarmed by rumours of a plot against the King, the details of which remain obscure. But a man named Marsilly was arrested, and Lefèvre d'Ormesson *recounts the affair in his* Journal:

On Saturday, June 22nd [1669], a man was broken on the wheel, whose history is worth relating. He was named Le

Roux, Sieur de Marsilly, a native of Nîmes. He was a Huguenot. Claiming that he had been unjustly dealt with in some matter of finance, he swore to revenge himself on the King. First he went to England, where the Duke of York warned M. de Ruvigny of Marsilly's presence, and they arranged that M. de Ruvigny should hide behind a curtain, where he heard this man boast to the duke of all the vile actions he proposed to undertake against the King.

After M. de Ruvigny's report was received, it was decided to capture the man, and M. de Turenne selected a certain Mazel, captain of cavalry, with four others, to follow him everywhere and capture him. Mazel, accompanied by his four horsemen, tracked him through Holland and thence into Switzerland, where they attacked him in a village, seized him and took him back to France.

He was put in the Bastille, where he said that if they treated him well he would reveal some most important matters. Then, when his trial was under way, he resolved to die by his own hand. Having got possession of a small knife, he cut off his genitals entirely, meaning to die slowly from loss of blood, and so that he should not be discovered and saved he had gathered all the blood in a basin and hidden it. He had eaten nothing since Saturday, June 15th, and finally, to bring death more quickly still, he had cut all the flesh from his little finger and broken the bone. On Thursday, June 20th, thinking himself so near to death that he had foiled the executioner, he revealed what he had done, showed the knife and the parts he had cut off his body, and also the preparations he had made to hang himself if his other means had failed. As a result of this knowledge, his trial was promptly concluded on the following day and on the Saturday he was sentenced by the Lieutenant Criminel together with the Châtelet by royal commission, and condemned to be broken on the wheel, which sentence was executed at midday and his corpse dragged through the streets.

When he had been brought before the judges, he had played dead, keeping his eyes closed and giving no sign of consciousness, but once on the scaffold he burst into paroxysms of obscene rage against the King. General horror is felt at the schemes and behaviour of this miserable creature, and astonishment at the force of will which allowed him to mutilate himself, for there is no example known of so extraordinary an action.

A grocer has also just been confined to the Bastille, after being denounced for plotting some treachery against the person of the King.

THE DEATH OF MADAME. POISON?

It is advantageous that the period of mourning for Madame
has resulted in the discontinuation of the sale here of Venetian
point-lace.

(Letter from Colbert to the French Ambassador to Venice, 1670)

※

PRINCIPAL PERSONALITIES MENTIONED IN CHAPTER IV

PHILIPPE CHEVALIER DE LORRAINE (already mentioned in
Chapter II).

LORD EDWARD MONTAGU, English Ambassador to France.

HENRI DE LA TOUR D'AUVERGNE, VICOMTE DE TURENNE,
second son of the Duc de Bouillon and the most illustrious
military commander of his time.

MARGUERITE DE ROHAN-CHABOT, MARQUISE DE COA-
QUIN, married to Malo de Coaquin, and a lady-in-waiting to
the Duchesse d'Orléans.

GABRIEL DE ROCHECHOUART, DUC DE MORTEMART, father
of Mme de Montespan.

The ABBÉ DE LA RIVIÈRE, BISHOP OF LANGRES, formerly
an agent in the service of Mazarin, and uncle of the Chevalier
de Lorraine.

MICHEL LE TELLIER, Secretary of State; in 1666 he handed
over this office to his son Louvois, while keeping the title of
Minister.

1. *Versailles* (between 1664 and 1668), by Patel

2. *Louis XIV*, by Le Brun

JEAN BAPTISTE COLBERT, Comptroller of Finance (already mentioned in Chapter II).

The COMTE DE VAILLAC, captain of the Duc d'Orléans's bodyguard. His wife is the duchess's Mistress of the Wardrobe.

The COMTE D'AYEN, son of the Duc de Noailles and captain of the King's Bodyguard.

POLASTRON DE LA ILHIÈRE, lieutenant in the King's Bodyguard.

RUZÉ, MARQUIS D'EFFIAT, Equerry to Monsieur. Together with the Comte de Beuvron, the Chevalier de Lorraine, the Comte de Marsan and the Marquis de Villeroi, constitutes the small band of very intimate friends of Philippe d'Orléans: 'In this Prince's circles,' said Primi Visconti, 'they spoke of young men in the same way that a group of love-sick men would ordinarily speak of young girls.'

MARIE-FRANÇOISE DE MONTMORIN, COMTESSE DE GAMACHES, one of Madame's ladies-in-waiting.

JOACHIM SEIGLIÈRE DE BOISFRANC, Monsieur's treasurer.

ELISABETH ANGÉLIQUE DE MONTMORENCY, DUCHESSE DE MECKLEMBOURG.

FEUILLET, dean of the church of Saint-Cloud.

ANTOINE VALLOT, the King's chief physician.

JACQUES BÉNIGNE BOSSUET, at this time Bishop of Condom.

BERNARDIN GIGAULT, MARQUIS DE BELLEFONDS, diplomat and soldier, a Marshal of France since 1668.

ALBERT DE GRILLET, COMTE DE BRISSAC, commander of the King's Bodyguard.

The Court was in the throes of many other intrigues as well, in particular the veiled hostilities between the Duchesse d'Orléans, Madame, and her husband's favourite, the Chevalier de Lorraine. The Abbé de Choisy, *in his* Vie de Daniel de Cosnac, *notes that:*

The Chevalier de Lorraine, looking like the painting of an angel, placed himself entirely at Monsieur's disposal and soon became his favourite, dispensing favours and giving orders in so lordly and authoritative a manner that he might have been taken for the master of the house. Madame spoke with horror of this disgraceful situation, about which she complained first of all to Mme de Saint-Chaumont, a close friend of the Bishop of Valence.

And this Bishop of Valence, Daniel de Cosnac, *himself recounts how he had put Madame on her guard against the Chevalier de Lorraine, and how at first Madame hoped to succeed in tearing Monsieur away from this very singular friendship:*

Madame answered me that if it was simply a question of proffering him good advice, she had some to give, assuring me that the Chevalier de Lorraine was madly in love with Mme de Monaco, and that since Mme de Monaco was her dearest, most faithful friend, she would encourage her to respond to M. le Chevalier's love. I replied to her: 'I do not know either Mme de Monaco or M. le Chevalier sufficiently well to be able to advise Your Royal Highness how successful such an approach may prove.' She replied: 'You may take my word for it.'

It took only a few days after this conversation for Madame to begin to revise her opinion. I have already mentioned that Monsieur had demanded of the Chevalier de Lorraine that all his feelings of loyalty should be directed towards himself rather than towards Madame. The Chevalier no doubt realized that such single-minded devotion was essential if he was to retain Monsieur's regard, and chose the good fortune which he expected his relationship with Monsieur to bring, in preference to the real or feigned love he felt for Mme de Monaco. He let it be known on several occasions that he belonged entirely to Monsieur and was absolutely opposed to Madame. Indeed, the Chevalier made open show of his hostility towards, and almost contempt for, Madame. Madame realized, rather late in the day, that she had been ill-advised to place any hopes in Mme de Monaco, who failed to fulfil the rôle allotted to her by Madame, having, in any case, no influence over the Chevalier.

Meanwhile, Louis XIV was preparing his war against Holland and seeking England's support. For this, he had need of Madame. He had spoken of his plans to Turenne, who now became the victim of a curious adventure, described by La Fare:

The King had told the great man in confidence of his plans to humble the Dutch and make war on them. They then judged that in order for this plan to succeed it would be necessary to involve Charles II, King of England, taking advantage of his affection for his sister, Henriette d'Angleterre. Lord Montagu, the English ambassador, who was one of Madame's circle of friends and wanted to turn this friendship to good use, persuaded the King that she was the best possible person to negotiate such an alliance. The King then entirely changed his attitude towards Madame, and whereas he had very often neglected her previously, she now suddenly became the most powerful figure at Court.

There developed a very close relationship between herself and M. de Turenne who, as I have said, was a party to these secret plans. He visited Madame every day and so came to know the Marquise de Coaquin, sister of M. de Soubise, a young lady who, although not particularly beautiful, was most piquant in appearance, and was Madame's favourite at that time. Neither the age of this great warrior[1] nor his wisdom saved him from falling in love with her and his infatuation was such that he even went so far as to tell her the State secret.

Monsieur was extremely vexed to see his wife—with whom he was already displeased—suddenly acquire such importance in the eyes of the King, and although he guessed she must be involved in some affair of consequence he was quite unable to find out what it was. But the Chevalier de Lorraine, his favourite, soon rescued him from his embarrassment. This young man was the most handsome, likeable and witty person in the entire Court. He promptly laid siege to Mme de Coaquin

[1] Turenne was fifty-nine years old at the time.

and it must be admitted that her resistance did not last long. She revealed to him Madame's involvement in the King's plans, and the State secret which M. de Turenne had confided to her.

Monsieur was infuriated with his wife and complained to the King about the disgraceful way in which he had been treated, informing him that he knew all the facts they had tried to hide from him. It did not take long to discover from what source his information had come, and M. de Turenne was overcome with embarrassment and humiliation when the King reproached him for allowing himself to become infatuated with Mme de Coaquin. He remained very ashamed of this incident all his life. M. le Chevalier de Lorraine told me that, long afterwards, when they were on perfectly good terms again, and he had wanted to discuss this adventure with M. de Turenne, the latter had replied, quite amusingly I think: 'We can speak of it whenever you like, so long as the candles are extinguished beforehand.'

But suddenly the Chevalier de Lorraine became the object of the King's wrath and was arrested on January 30, 1670. Saint-Maurice hastened to describe the affair to his master, the Duke of Savoy:

Here, Monseigneur, is the unvarnished truth, written by Mme de Montespan to M. le Duc de Mortemart, her father, and related to me by her intimate and well-loved friend Mme de Tambonneau. But I beseech Your Royal Highness that no one may know that I have divulged all these names to him.

The Abbé de Rivière, Bishop of Langres, possessed two abbeys within the appanage of Monsieur. Since the Abbé was old and in feeble health, Monsieur had long been awaiting his death so that he might present them to the Chevalier de Lorraine. He mentioned this to the King at Chambord, but the King answered him that since the Chevalier was not a priest his conscience would not permit him to give his assent, and that furthermore the Chevalier's dissolute existence made it inappropriate that he should possess benefices. Monsieur having begged him urgently to give his agreement, His Majesty repeated that he could not, but that out of consideration of the fact that Monsieur was so attached to the Chevalier, and despite the fact that he himself had very little esteem for him, he would award him a pension of 40,000 livres when the said abbeys became vacant.

After Monsieur had reported all this to the Chevalier de Lorraine, they both indulged in many mocking jests at the expense of the King's conscience because of all the ladies with whom His Majesty was involved, and these jests were reported to him. The King also accuses the Chevalier de Lorraine of the infamous crime of sodomy with the Comte de Guiche and even with men who have been burned at the stake in Grève for that crime.

The Bishop of Langres died on Thursday morning and Monsieur promptly told the King that he had given the abbeys to the Chevalier de Lorraine, but the King replied that he refused his assent. Monsieur retorted that it was an accomplished fact. His Majesty repeated that he would prevent him. And so they both became very heated, and those in attendance realized that they were disputing some matter but did not know what it was. After leaving chapel, the King left Saint-Germain for Versailles. Monsieur retired to his own quarters, utterly crushed, shut himself up in a closet with the Chevalier de Lorraine, told him what had happened, and said that since the King was treating him in this fashion he intended to leave the Court immediately. The Chevalier begged him not to do so, since such an action would harm both their interests. Monsieur summoned M. le Tellier and spoke to him in heartbroken tones, complaining about the King's conduct, then flew into a rage and swore that certain people had instigated the King to behave thus badly towards him. M. Le Tellier attempted to calm him and, when he went on in the same tone, asked him if he wished him to write to the King, setting out all that he had just said. Monsieur answered that he did wish him to do so, and the minister then went and wrote a letter to the King, which the King received and read without any comment or reaction. M. Colbert had also arrived at Saint-Germain meanwhile, so Monsieur summoned him too and spoke to him as angrily as he had spoken to M. Le Tellier.

At nightfall, the King arrived at Versailles and went straight to Mlle de La Vallière's apartment. Mme la Duchesse d'Orléans sent him a gentleman to tell him that she was unable to leave the Château Neuf, and begging him to be good enough to visit here there for a matter which was of the greatest importance to her. His Majesty went there immediately. Madame begged him to consent that the Chevalier de Lorraine should have his abbeys. He replied that he could not consent. She asked him to do so as a personal favour to her. He persisted in his refusal, remarking to her that she seemed to have forgotten very quickly the slights she had received at their hands. She declared that she put the satisfaction of Monsieur above her own interests, that the Chevalier de Lorraine was a young man and would mend his ways, begged the King to pardon him and, seeing that he was not going to give in, threw herself at the King's feet with tears in her eyes, confessing that what would be hardest of all for her would be to have to part from his person, but that she was obliged to follow Monsieur, who had resolved to quit the Court.

The King withdrew, saying that since his brother was parting company with him on these grounds, he was determined to punish those responsible for fomenting trouble between them. He first gave orders that the guard of Monseigneur le Dauphin, who lodges in the Château Neuf, should be strengthened, and then that all the avenues should be patrolled.

The Comte de Vaillac, the captain of Monsieur's Body-guards, noticed these preparations and advised his master, who replied that he knew the reason, and showed signs of regret. M. Le Tellier entered Monsieur's room and told him that the necessity of his service to the King obliged him to secure the person of the Chevalier de Lorraine, but that he would be sorry to be forced to have the Chevalier arrested in Monsieur's apartment and in his presence. Monsieur replied to him that, since the King was using him in this fashion, he would leave immediately for Villers-Cotterêts. The Minister put it to him that he should not travel so far, but should go rather to Saint-Cloud, which was within easy reach of the Court, although it was not yet known when he might be able to return there. Monsieur told him in no uncertain terms that he wished to live at least 300 leagues away from the King, that he intended to go away and that he would never come into the presence of the King again except with the Chevalier de Lorraine at his side. Then, turning to the Chevalier, he assured him of his continuing friendship and told him to follow M. Le Tellier. They left together. The Chevalier asked him what he had to do, and said that he was ready to obey the King's orders. M. Le Tellier answered him that, for his part, he had no orders to give him.

When they were in the Cour of the Vieux Château, the Comte d'Ayen together with the Chevalier de La Ilhière, arrested him. They demanded his sword, then escorted him away. He asked the Comte d'Ayen where he was taking him, and was told: 'To my room . . .'

So the Chevalier slept at Saint-Germain that night, and was not taken to the Bastille. He was asked how many servants he wanted, and that he might choose those he desired; he chose two of his gentlemen and two men-servants. He left on Friday, in a carriage, accompanied by a lieutenant of the Bodyguards with a strong escort. He is to go to Pierre-Encise; others say his destination is the citadel of Montpellier, or perhaps Collioure on the frontiers of Catalonia.

Monsieur, furious, went off to sulk at Villers-Cotterêts, then returned and submitted to the King's inclinations, for, adds Saint-Maurice:

It seems certain that orders have been sent for the Chevalier de Lorraine to be set free, provided he first pays an extended visit to Rome or Malta. The King will give him a pension of 10,000 écus, and the abbeys which were the cause of his misfortunes will be given to the Abbé d'Harcourt, his brother. So the whole affair is finally resolved according to the King's desires.

The secret Treaty of London was signed, and Madame returned to Paris in triumph. A few days later she was dead. Mme de La Fayette, her confidante, wrote this account of her death:

On June 25, 1670, a week after her return from England, Monsieur and she went to Saint-Cloud. On her first day back, she complained about a pain in her side and a stomach-ache, things to which she was subject. Despite this, since it was very warm she desired to bathe in the river. M. Gueslin, her chief physician, made every effort to dissuade her but, despite his advice, she bathed on the Friday, but on the Saturday she felt so ill that she did not bathe.

I arrived at Saint-Cloud on the Saturday at ten in the evening. I found her in the gardens. She told me that I would find that she was looking poorly and that, indeed, she was not feeling well. She had taken supper as usual and walked in the moonlight until midnight. On the following day, June 29th, she arose early and went downstairs to visit Monsieur, who was bathing; she stayed with him for quite a long time then, leaving his room, she came straight into mine and did me the honour of telling me that she had spent a good night.

Shortly afterwards I went up to her apartment. She told me that she was in a peevish mood, but the ill-humour of which she spoke would have constituted radiant happiness in other women, so incapable was she of bitterness or anger. As she spoke to me, she was informed that Mass was about to be celebrated. She went to attend it, then, coming back into her room, leaned against me and said to me in the kindly tone which was so typical of her, that her bad humour would quickly vanish if she could have the chance of conversing with me, for she was so tired of all the people around her that she could not stand them any longer.

She then went to watch the progress of a portrait which an excellent British artist was painting of Mademoiselle, and she began speaking to Mme d'Epernon and myself about her journey to England and about the King, her brother. This conversation pleased her and revived her spirits. Dinner was served, and she ate normally. Then, after dinner, she lay down on some cushions, which she often did when in an informal atmosphere. She had me sit down beside her, so that her head was half in my lap.

The same English artist was painting Monsieur; the conversation ranged over a number of subjects while she continued to sleep. During her sleep, her expression changed so completely that, after looking at her closely, I was surprised and thought that her gentle spirit must show its radiance through her face, because she looked so attractive when awake but so unattractive when asleep. Yet I was wrong to make this reflection, since in truth I had seen her asleep on several previous occasions and had never noticed her to look less amiable than when awake.

When she awoke, she got to her feet, but looked so unwell that Monsieur was surprised and pointed it out to us. She then went to the drawing-room, where she walked for some time with Boisfranc, Monsieur's treasurer, and during her conversation with him she complained several times of the pain in her side.

Monsieur started going downstairs to get ready to leave, having decided to go to Paris, but he came across Mme de Mecklembourg on the stairway and went up again with her. Madame left Boisfranc and came up to Mme de Mecklembourg. As she was speaking to her, Mme de Gamaches brought her and myself a glass of chicory water which she had asked for some time ago. Mme de Gourdon, her Mistress of the Wardrobe, presented it to her. She drank it, then, while with one hand she replaced the glass in the saucer, with the other she clasped her side and exclaimed in tones which betrayed great suffering: 'Ah! What a pain in my side! Ah! What pain! I cannot bear it any longer!' She went red as she spoke these words, then, to our astonishment, grew pale and livid. She continued to cry out and told us to help her away, that she could no longer stand up. We took her under the arms. She could hardly walk and was bent almost double. We undressed her as quickly as possible. I supported her while others unlaced her. She continued to moan and I noticed that she had tears in her eyes. I was astonished and moved to pity, for I knew her to be the most long-suffering person in the world. I said to her, while kissing her arm which was around my shoulder as I supported her, that she must be suffering terribly. She replied that the pain was unendurable. We placed her in bed and as soon as she was lying down she cried out more loudly than ever and tossed from one side to the other, like a person in the last throes of suffering. Meanwhile, someone had gone to fetch her chief physician, M. Esprit. He arrived, said that it was colic and ordered the usual remedies for such cases. But her pains continued to torture her. Madame said that her sickness was greater than they supposed, that she was going to die, that someone should go and fetch her a confessor . . .

Monsieur was standing by her bed. She embraced him and said to him with a gentleness which would melt the hardest heart: 'Alas, Monsieur, you have not loved me for a long time. That is unjust, for I have never failed you.' Monsieur appeared to be very moved, but he made no reply . . .

Suddenly, she demanded that the potion of which she had taken a draught should be examined, insisted that maybe some-one had mistaken one bottle for another, that she had been poisoned, she knew she must have been poisoned, and called for an antidote.

I was standing in the bedside alcove, near Monsieur, and although it would never have occurred to me to suspect him of such a crime, nevertheless a normal feeling of awareness of human depravity made me study him attentively. He gave no sign of being either moved or embarrassed by Madame's opinion. He fell in with Madame's desires in ordering that oil and antidotes should be brought, so that this unfortunate suggestion might be proved to her to be unwarranted. Mme Desbordes, her first Lady of the Chamber, who was absolutely devoted to her, assured her that she had prepared the potion herself and had also drunk from it, but Madame continued to insist on wanting oil and antidotes. Both were administered to her.

Mlle de Montpensier was on the point of going out with the Queen when she heard the news; according to her, this is how Monsieur acted in these circumstances:

The Comte d'Ayen said to me: 'Madame is dying! The King has commanded me to find M. Vallot and to bring him to Saint-Cloud with all possible speed.' When I was inside the carriage, the Queen said to me: 'Madame is failing fast, and the worst of it is that she believes she has been poisoned.' I exclaimed in horror, saying: 'Oh, how terrible! That is a dreadful report!' And, without thinking what I was saying (for I had no reason to suppose there was any truth in the rumour) I asked her what the poison had been. She told me, in reply, that Madame had been in the drawing-room at Saint-Cloud in good health, and had asked for a draught of chicory water to be prepared for her. Her apothecary gave her the potion and as soon as she had drunk it she began to cry out that she felt a fire in her stomach, and had continued crying out, so that emissaries had been sent to inform the King and to find M. Vallot. The Queen expressed her great grief and mentioned very briefly the vexations which Monsieur had caused Madame, and remembered that when Madame had left for England she had wept bitterly, so it seemed that she must have foreseen her unhappy end. A gentleman whom the Queen had sent to bring back a report arrived. He said that Madame had charged him to tell her that she was dying, and that if Her Majesty wished to see her alive she begged her very humbly to visit her soon, for if she lingered she would find her dead.

We had been walking alongside the canal. Now we climbed into our carriage and went to find the King, who was at supper at that time, because he was taking the waters. The Maréchal de Bellefonds advised the Queen not to go to Madame, and she seemed undecided. I begged her to permit me to go in her stead, but she raised objections. However, at that moment the King appeared and said to her: 'If you wish to come, here is my carriage.' The Comtesse de Soissons joined us. In mid-route, we crossed paths with M. Vallot, who was returning from the scene; he told the King that it was only a colic, and that her ailment would be neither prolonged nor dangerous. On arrival at Saint-Cloud, we found that hardly anyone was showing any concern, and Monsieur seemed most astonished to see us.

We found her lying on a cot which had been prepared for her in the bed alcove. She was quite dishevelled; she had not been able to relax sufficiently for it to be possible to prepare her hair for the night, her chemise was unfastened at the neck and wrists, her face was pale, her nose pinched, and she looked like someone already dead. She told us: 'You see the state I am in.' We began to cry. Mme de Montespan and Mme de La Vallière appeared. Madame was making terrible efforts to vomit, while Monsieur was saying to her: 'Madame, try hard to vomit, so that you will not be choked by this bile.' She was clearly upset to see how calm everyone around her remained, despite the fact that her sufferings should have been enough to arouse everyone's pity. She spoke in a very low voice to the King for a few moments. I approached her and took her hand, she squeezed mine and said to me: 'You are losing a good friend who was beginning to love you very much and to get to know you as well.' I could not reply for weeping. She asked for an emetic. The doctors said that that would be of no use to her, that these sorts of colic lasted sometimes nine or ten hours, but never longer than twenty-four. The King tried to reason with them, but they did not know what to say to him in reply. He told them: 'It is unheard of to let a woman die without giving her any help at all.' They looked at each other and said nothing. People were chatting and laughing, coming and going, as though Madame had not been lying there on the point of death . . .

Monsieur came up to me, and I told him: 'No one seems to realize that Madame is on the point of death and that she is in need of communion with God.' He replied that I was right. He remarked that his own confessor was a Capuchin friar who was fit only to accompany him in his carriage so that the public should be persuaded of his piety, but that a different man would have to be found to speak with her about death: 'Who could we find whose name would look good in the *Gazette* as having assisted Madame?' I answered him that the most desirable qualities in a confessor for such an occasion should be goodness and skill in exposition. He said to me: 'Ah! I know the man: the Abbé Bossuet, who has been named to the see of Condom. Madame used to entertain him occasionally; so let him perform the task.'

According to the Abbé Le Dieu, Bossuet's secretary, it was Madame who asked for the Bishop of Condom:

It was from Saint-Cloud, in the middle of the night, that she sent to Paris on three successive occasions to find him, and fearing that she would never see him again, because she was in increasing pain, she entrusted to Monsieur a valuable ring with a large emerald stone (worth 100 louis), to give to him as a mark of her esteem and gratitude. But he arrived soon enough to receive this favour from the princess herself and to help her to die in grace.

Mme de La Fayette also mentions the gift of this ring and adds:

As M. de Condom continued to speak to her of God, she suddenly felt a desire to sleep, which was in fact a symptom of her physical weakening; she asked him if she might take a few minutes' rest. He said that she might and that meanwhile he would pray to God for her.

M. Feuillet remained at the head of her bed and almost in the same moment Madame told him to bring M. de Condom back, for she felt sure that she was about to die. M. de Condom approached and gave her the crucifix; she took it and kissed it fervently. M. de Condom continued to speak to her and she replied to him with as much lucidity as if she had not been ill, while still holding the crucifix pressed to her mouth. Only death made her release it. Her strength left her, she let the crucifix drop and lost her power of speech at the same moment that life left her. Her agony lasted only a moment and after two or three little convulsive movements of the mouth, she expired at two in the morning, nine hours after she first started to feel ill.

Hugues de Lionne, *Secretary of State for Foreign Affairs, wrote immediately (on July 1st) to Colbert de Croissy, French Ambassador to England, to inform him of the departure of the Maréchal de Bellefonds who had been entrusted with the task of conveying to King Charles II the condolences of Louis XIV as well as giving him a detailed account of the autopsy performed on the body of Madame. He adds:*

Since, when great princes die suddenly, the public invariably suspects that the deaths may have been hastened, and since, in this particular instance, as a result of Madame's violent illness, many people in attendance brought all sorts of remedies of their own, nostrums, powdered viper and other dubious means of counteracting poison in the body, the King and Monsieur desired that her body should be opened in the presence of our most famous doctors, and that the English Ambassador should be present and should bring with him any experts he might wish. The ambassador brought an English physician and one of the King of England's surgeons, and the dissection commenced in the presence of these gentlemen and of more than a hundred other persons who were in the room. As each part was examined, stomach, liver, heart, lungs, spleen, intestines, etc., an exact description was recorded of the state in which it had been found. In this manner, a very comprehensive report was compiled, which was signed by all the doctors and surgeons, and notably by the two English doctors, without any difference of opinion being recorded by any of them.

Everyone was still haunted by the suspicion: was Madame poisoned? The English Ambassador to France, Lord Montagu, wrote to Lord Arlington on July 15th that he had seen Madame on her death-bed:

I then took the liberty of asking her if she thought she had been poisoned. Her confessor, who was present and overheard my question, admonished her: 'Madame, accuse no one and offer your death to God as a sacrifice.' This prevented her answering me, and although I repeated the same question several times, her only response was to shrug her shoulders. I asked her to let me have the casket in which she kept all her letters, so that I might send them to His Majesty and she authorized me to demand them of Mme de Bordes, but that lady was in such a state of fainting and weeping from grief at seeing her mistress so gravely ill that Monsieur took the opportunity to seize the casket before she had recovered.

D'Artagnan, *in his* Mèmoires:

The King found it quite impossible to believe that anyone could have been so wicked as to make an attempt on the princess's life in this way. Nevertheless, from the moment she had begun to feel ill she had insisted repeatedly that she had been poisoned. Such words demanded investigation, and so the King ordered that her body should be opened up in the presence of his principal doctors.

Either the doctors had been bribed or Madame really had died simply of a colic, as had been claimed; in any case, all these doctors certified that after examining the royal remains from one end of the body to the other they had discovered no signs whatsoever of poisoning.

And Saint-Maurice, *on July 2nd, reported to the Duke of Savoy:*

As a result of the rumours sweeping Europe that the late Madame was poisoned, I feel obliged to inform Your Royal Highness what happened when her body was opened up. The English Ambassador was present together with all the English who were here and physicians and surgeons from his country, and there was a great throng of people who happened to be at Saint-Cloud at the time, for the doors were open here to all sorts and qualities of people.

The stomach of the princess had swollen in the most extra-ordinary way since her death. The very first incision of the bistoury into her body released such a vile stench that all those taking part in the dissection were obliged to withdraw, and could only approach the corpse once more after furnishing themselves with masks against this evil odour. No formal traces of poison were found; the one slightly suspicious element was the discovery in her stomach of a hole with blackened lips, but the physicians and surgeons agreed that it was the result of a carelessly directed incision made by a bistoury. The body was found to contain a great quantity of bile, and the liver was quite putrid.

The Duc de Saint-Simon *did not know this epoch, but he possessed sources of information, and as far as he was concerned there was no doubt whatsoever that Madame had been poisoned. Here is his account:*

Madame was at Saint-Cloud, and for some time had taken refreshment at about seven in the evening, consisting of a glass of chicory water. One of her valets was entrusted with preparing it. He used to place it in a cupboard in one of Madame's anterooms, with its glass, etc. This chicory water was in a pottery or porcelain jug, and was always accompanied by a jug of plain water, in case Madame should find the chicory water too bitter and wished to dilute it. This anteroom was a public passage for anyone wishing to visit Madame, and there was never anyone on duty in it. . . .

The Marquis d'Effiat had already spied out these facts. On June 29, 1670, passing through this anteroom, he found the moment he had been waiting for: there was no one in the room, and he had already noticed that he was not being followed by anyone else on their way to visit Madame. He turned aside, went to the cupboard, opened it, emptied the contents of his phial into the chicory water, then, hearing someone coming, seized hold of the other jug containing plain water, and as he was replacing it the valet whose duty it was to prepare this chicory water shouted, came running up to him and asked him brusquely what he was doing at the cupboard. D'Effiat, without showing the least embarrassment, begged his pardon, saying that he was dying of thirst and that, knowing the cupboard contained water—showing him the jug of plain water—he had not been able to resist the temptation to take a drink. The manservant continued to grumble, but the marquis simply excused himself once more in a conciliatory fashion, then entered Madame's room and started greeting and chatting to the other courtiers present, still perfectly cool and collected. What happened an hour later belongs to another story, and has in any case created a sufficient stir already throughout Europe.

Madame died on Monday, June 30th, at three in the morning, and the King was overwhelmed with grief. It seems that during that day he received hints as to the true circumstances: apparently the valet had not kept silent, and it was also suspected that Purnon, Madame's first maître d'hôtel, may have been in the conspiracy, because of the intimate relationship he maintained, in the servants' quarters, with d'Effiat. After going to bed, the King got up during the night and summoned Brissac who was commander of his Bodyguards and absolutely loyal; on his arrival, he ordered him to choose six reliable, discreet members of the Bodyguards, to go and pick up the steward and to bring him to his study by way of the back stairs. This was carried out before dawn. As soon as the man was produced to the King, he asked Brissac and his chief valet to withdraw. Then, assuming a countenance and a tone of voice calculated to strike terror into any heart, after examining him from head to foot, the King said: 'My friend, if you confess everything, and if you answer truthfully the questions

I am going to ask you, whatever you may yourself have done I pardon you and the matter will be forgotten as far as you are concerned. But take care not to conceal the least fact from me, for if you do you will never leave this room alive. Was Madame not poisoned?'

'Yes, Sire,' he replied.

'Who poisoned her?' asked the King, 'and how was it done?'

He replied that it was the Chevalier de Lorraine who had sent the poison to Beuvron and d'Effiat, and then described the events I have just set down. Then the King, repeating his assurances of forgiveness coupled with threats of death, demanded: 'And my brother, was he in the know?'

'No, Sire, none of the three of us was stupid enough to tell him; he is incapable of keeping a secret, and we should all have been lost.'

At this reply, the King exclaimed 'ha!' in the voice of a man suddenly relieved of a burden of suspicion, and said: 'That is all I wanted to know; swear that it is the truth.' Then he recalled Brissac, and ordered him to take this man somewhere away from the Court and then let him go free immediately. It was this very man who related the whole story, many years later, to M. Joly de Fleury, procureur général of the Parlement, who told me in his turn.

However, the Chevalier de Lorraine was not to remain in disgrace for long. On February 12, 1672, Mme de Sévigné wrote to her daughter:

The King asked Monsieur, who had just returned from Paris: 'Well, brother, what are they talking about in Paris?' Monsieur replied: 'Sire, they are talking a great deal about the unfortunate Marquis.'[1] 'And what are they saying?' 'They are saying that it was because he wanted to speak on behalf of another unfortunate.' 'And which unfortunate is that?' asked the King. 'The Chevalier de Lorraine,' replied Monsieur. 'Why,' said the King, 'do you still think about this Chevalier de Lorraine? Do you really care so much? Would you show true affection towards anyone who would restore him to you?' 'In truth,' replied Monsieur, 'it would be one of the greatest

[1] The Marquis de Villeroi, who had been expelled from the Court.

pleasures of my whole life.' 'Well,' said the King, 'I shall make you this present. The courier left two days ago. When he returns, I shall dispatch orders. The Chevalier shall return to your side as my gift, and I ask only that you remain grateful to me for this all your life. Indeed, I will be even more generous, because I appoint him a maréchal de camp in my Army.'

At these words, Monsieur threw himself at the King's feet, embraced his knees for a long time and kissed his hand with unbounded joy. The King lifted him to his feet, saying: 'Brother, that is not how brothers should embrace each other.' And he embraced him fraternally.

The return of, and the favour shown to, a man who was the object of such grave suspicions scandalized a great number of people. In a letter written in cipher to Lord Arlington, Lord Montagu *argued that the King of England should intervene:*

I write to you at the present time only to inform Your Lordship about a happening which I think, however, you already know about: that is, that the Chevalier de Lorraine has not only been allowed to return to the Court but has been appointed to serve in the Army with the rank of maréchal de camp. If Madame was indeed poisoned, as most of the world believes, certainly the whole of France regards him as her poisoner and is justifiably astonished that the King of France should have so little consideration for the King our master as to permit him to return to the Court, in view of the insolent manner in which he constantly behaved towards the Princess during her lifetime. My duty compels me to tell you this, so that you may acquaint the King with this news; and if the King thinks fit, he should speak to the French Ambassador in the strongest possible terms, for I can assure you that he would be doing himself an injustice if he were to endure this matter.

CHAPTER V

WHAT TO DO ABOUT LAUZUN?

Strato is born under two stars: unlucky and lucky in the same degree; his life is a novel; no, it lacks probability; he has had no adventures; he has had beautiful dreams; what am I saying, one does not dream in the way that he has lived.

LA BRUYÈRE

PRINCIPAL PERSONALITIES MENTIONED IN CHAPTER V

ANTOINE NOMPAR DE GAUMONT, MARQUIS DE PUYGUILHEM, later DUC DE LAUZUN (already mentioned in Chapter III).

LOUIS D'OGER, CHEVALIER then MARQUIS DE CAVOYE, Grand Marèchal des Logis of the King's Household.

FRANÇOIS MICHEL LE TELLIER SIEUR DE CHAVILLE, MARQUIS DE LOUVOIS, Secretary of State for War.

LOUIS AUGUSTE DE BOURBON, DUC DU MAINE, natural son of Louis XIV and Mme de Montespan.

HORTENSE MANCINI, DUCHESSE DE MAZARIN, niece of Mazarin.

MARIE DE ROHAN-MONTBAZON, DUCHESSE DE CHEVREUSE, married first to the Duc de Luynes, then to Claude de Lorraine, Duc de Chevreuse, involved in all the plots against Richelieu and Mazarin. Now seventy years old.

PHILIPPE, MARQUIS DE COULANGES, ambassadorial attaché, correspondent of Mme de Sévigné. His wife, Marie-Angélique du Gué-Bagnols, was to become later a great friend of Mme de Maintenon.

CHARLES DE SAINT-MAURE, MARQUIS, then DUC DE MONTAUSIER, tutor to the Dauphin. Married to Julie d'Angennes, daughter of Mme de Rambouillet.

CÉSAR PHOEBUS, MARÉCHAL D'ALBERT, descendant of the sovereigns of Navarre.

LOUIS GUILHEM DE CASTELNAU, COMTE DE CLERMONT-LODÈVE and MARQUIS DE CESSAC, Master of the King's Wardrobe.

JEAN-FRANÇOIS VATEL, maître d'hôtel of Superintendent Fouquet, then of the Prince de Condé at Chantilly.

DIANE CHARLOTTE DE CAUMONT, COMTESSE DE NOGENT, lady-in-waiting to Mlle de Montpensier.

The COMTESSE DE FIESQUE, known as 'La Reine Gilette', celebrated for her warlike exploits during the Fronde, and for her intrigues: 'She took no trouble,' said Bussy-Rabutin, 'to obtain lovers; when a man chose to make approaches to her she neither put on a show of severity to get rid of him nor a show of gentleness to retain him . . .'

GASTON, DUC DE ROQUELAURE had been Lieutenant-General of the Armies of the King during the Fronde. Reputed to be the ugliest man in France, but both witty and clever.

HENRI LOUIS D'ALOIGNY, MARQUIS DE ROCHEFORT, fought under Turenne and became a marshal of France in 1675.

GEORGE VILLIERS, DUKE OF BUCKINGHAM, son of the famous minister, favourite of the King of England, and loved by Anne of Austria. Laden with honours by King Charles II, soldier and poet, in love with the King's sister Henrietta before she became Duchesse d'Orléans.

LOUIS DE MORNAY, MARQUIS DE VILLARCEAUX, uncle of a certain Demoiselle de Grancey, aged fifteen whom he tried to thrust into the arms of Louis XIV.

CHARLOTTE DE BAUTRU, MARQUISE DE RANNES, friend of Mlle de Montpensier, wife of a Lieutenant-General of the

King. 'A very dry woman,' commented Primi Visconti, 'covered in make-up and wholly lacking in personality.'

At the moment of Madame's death, an astonishing affair was on the point of breaking out, but the Court mourning held the news back for six months: it involved a projected marriage between Mlle de Montpensier, daughter of Gaston d'Orléans, cousin of the King—and none other than Puyguilhem, Comte de Lauzun, known for his contentious behaviour towards the Princesse de Monaco. This younger brother—who had become a count because his elder brother had renounced his father's inheritance, the estates being heavily in debt—had remained, despite his bad character, the favourite of Louis XIV, who tolerated conduct in him which he would not have countenanced from anyone else. Loménie de Brienne, Secretary of State for Foreign Affairs, reports an anecdote illustrating this fact:

Puyguilhem and Cavoye were standing behind the King, three paces away from His Majesty, and adopting a haughty attitude to each other. There was only M. de Noailles, captain of the Bodyguards and myself between the King and them. We were on the great stairway of the Louvre. Suddenly Cavoye's wig flew to the ground. The King turned round and I, who was two steps lower than he was, held up my cloak to prevent His Majesty seeing something which was grossly disrespectful to his presence. I said to him: 'Ah! Sire, there are some things which Your Majesty should not see.' He expressed his gratitude to me, saying: 'You are quite right.' But he spoke a few words to the combatants, finishing with: 'Thank Brienne for having prevented me from seeing who you are. Withdraw, and do not return again.' And turning towards me, the King said: 'I thank you. You have spared me the pain of being angry and punishing a person I love.'

The King had even promised Lauzun the post of Grand Master of the Artillery, but the latter talked too much. Louvois, Minister of War, intervened to prevent the appointment. Lauzun refused to admit defeat, and Saint-Simon, told about the whole affair later on, set it down as follows:

He went in search of Mme de Montespan to tell her of his anxiety [regarding the opposition to his assuming this post], and begged her to use her influence on his behalf. She promised him miracles and kept him happy in this way for several days. Then he became tired of all the double-dealing he suspected was going on around him, and since he still could not guess from what quarter the opposition was coming he decided on a course of action which would be incredible if it were not attested by everyone who was at Court at the time. He coaxed into his bed Mme de Montespan's favourite chambermaid, for he was prepared to make use of any means to protect his interests and secure information, and used the girl to help him carry out the most dangerous and foolhardy scheme it is possible to imagine.

Despite all his love-affairs, the King never failed to share the Queen's bed eventually, although sometimes at a very late hour. To be more at his ease, therefore, he often joined his mistresses in bed after dinner. Puyguilhem had himself hidden by the chambermaid under the bed in which the King was due to lie with Mme de Montespan, and, by listening to their conversation, learned that it was Louvois who was blocking his appointment, heard the King express his anger that the secret had been given away, and his resolution to punish him by not giving him the Artillery post, which would also save continual quarrels between Puyguilhem and Louvois and the necessity for him to have to adjudicate these quarrels. He heard all the remarks about him made by the King and his mistress, and especially those by Mme de Montespan who, after promising to use all her influence on his behalf was now busy denigrating him to the King. A cough, the least movement, any chance event might have revealed the presence of this reckless creature, and then what would have become of him? It is one of those stories which make one laugh out loud and yet appal one at the same time.

He was luckier than wise and was not discovered. The King and his mistress finally got out of bed. The King dressed again and went to his own quarters, while Mme de Montespan began to get herself ready for a performance of a ballet which she was to attend, and at which the King and Queen and the whole Court would be present. The chambermaid pulled Puyguilhem from beneath the bed, and he was apparently still so immaculate that he did not even need to return to his apartment to tidy up, for he went straight up to the door of Mme de Montespan's dressing-room, and leaned against the door-post.

When she emerged to go to the ballet performance, he held out his hand to her and asked her in honeyed and respectful tones if he might flatter himself that she had deigned to mention his cause to the King. She assured him that she had not failed to do so, and proceeded to invent for his benefit a list of services which she claimed she had just performed on his behalf. During this recitation, he occasionally interrupted her credulously with some question, to lead her even further into mendacity, then, approaching his mouth to her ear he informed her that she was a liar, a rogue, a jade, and a dog's whore, and repeated to her word for word the entire conversation between the King and herself. Mme de Montespan was so flabbergasted she could not utter a word and hardly had the strength to make her way to where the ballet was to take place, she was trembling so much in all her limbs. When she reached her seat, she fainted in front of the whole Court. The King went to her in alarm and had some trouble in reviving her.

That evening, she told the King what had happened, and was quite convinced that it must have been the devil himself who had informed Puyguilhem so promptly and so precisely of all that they had said about him while in bed. The King was furious about all the insults to which Mme de Montespan had been subjected, and exceedingly puzzled as to how Puyguilhem could have been so exactly and promptly informed. Puyguilhem, for his part, was enraged at having lost the Artillery command, so that for the next few days an atmosphere of constraint between the King and himself became evident. Having the privilege of the *grande entrée* Puyguilhem soon saw a chance of catching the King alone and took it. He mentioned the Artillery to him and impudently called upon him to keep his promise. The King had replied that he was no longer bound by it since the post had been offered Puyguilhem only under pledge of secrecy and that the latter had failed to maintain that secrecy. Thereupon, Puyguilhem walked away a few steps, turned his back on the King, drew his sword and broke the blade in two with his foot, crying out in fury that he would never in his life serve a prince who broke his word so scurvily. The King, who was beside himself with rage, made perhaps the finest gesture of his whole life: he turned away immediately, opened the window, threw his cane out of it, remarked that he would have been sorry to have struck a man of quality, and walked off.

At the time, an epigram concerning Lauzun, the King and Mme de Montespan, which was circulating in Paris, was attributed to Lauzun himself:

> Your Majesty's new game
> Was unkind and unfair;
> I'm laughing all the same—
> For her no more I care.
> My mistress you may claim.
> God, she's a bore today—
> But may you find her gay;
> I'll wash my hands and say
> She's ugly, old and grey.

During December 1670, two intrigues created excitement at Court. First, the 'affaire des boucheries' which set Mme de Montespan and Colbert at loggerheads. The Marquis de Saint-Maurice *explains the matter:*

The butchers' shops of Paris produce a considerable revenue which had not been exactly calculated hitherto; it had been thought that this revenue belonged to the city, but it was discovered that the butchers' shops were the property of the King. Having been informed about this, Mme de Montespan asked the King to award her this bounty, which he granted her, each being under the impression that it might bring in 50,000 écus a year at the most.

Being acquainted with these plans, the butchers first offered 100,000, then 150,000, although some warned her that these were exaggerated estimates and that she would be lucky to receive a revenue of 50,000 écus. M. Colbert got to know about these negotiations and informed the King, pointing out to him that none of his predecessors had ever made a gift of this importance. His Majesty, who is thrifty by nature, began to change his mind about the proposed gift of revenue, despite his love for the proposed beneficiary. When Mme de Montespan realized what was going on she exploded in a violent rage against the minister. He, for his part, to get rid of his enemy, tried to supplant her in the King's favours with the Duchesse de Mazarin, and the Comtesse de Soissons and the Duchesse de La Vallière joined with him in this scheme, which was set in motion and masterminded by old Mme de Chevreuse. And that is how things stand at present.

Then, a few days later, came an astounding piece of news: Mlle de Montpensier had sent an emissary to the King, asking his permission to marry Lauzun whom she had loved for nearly a year, and His Majesty, encouraged by Mme de Montespan, who had made up her quarrel with Lauzun, did not say no. The astonishing news spread immediately. Mme de Sévigné wrote to M. de Coulanges on December 15, 1670:

I am going to tell you something utterly astounding, surprising, marvellous, miraculous, triumphant, astounding, unheard of, singular, extraordinary, incredible, unforeseen, vast, tiny, rare, common, glaring, secret until today, brilliant and enviable; in short, something unexampled in past ages except for one single instance which is not really comparable; something we find impossible to believe in Paris (so how could anyone at Lyons believe it?), something which makes everyone exclaim aloud in amazement, something which causes the greatest joy to Mme de Rohan and Mme de Hauterive; something, in short, which is to happen on Sunday next, when those who are present will doubt the evidence of their eyes; something which, though it is to be done on Sunday, may well remain unfinished on Monday . . .

But Mme de Sévignè wrote to the same Coulanges, on December 31st, after paying a visit to Mlle de Montpensier:

Mademoiselle was writing; she told me to come in, finishes her letter and then, since she was in bed, beckoned me to sit by her in the bedside alcove; she told me to whom she had been writing and why, and also of the splendid presents she had made the night before and the title she had conferred on him; that there was no suitable match for her in any of the courts of Europe, and yet, she said, she was determined to get married. She related to me, word for word, a conversation she had had with the King, appeared overcome with joy at the prospect of being able to make a man happy, and mentioned, with great tenderness, the merit and gratitude of M. de Lauzun. To all of this I replied: 'Upon my word, Mademoiselle, you seem very happy, but why did you not promptly conclude this affair last Monday? Do you not realize that so great a delay is giving time and opportunity to the whole kingdom to talk, and that it is absolutely tempting God, and the King, to protract so extraordinary an affair at this great length?' She agreed that I was perfectly right, but was clearly so sure of success that what I said made little or no impression on her at the time.

Mme de Sévigné was right to fear that the King might change his mind, for this is exactly what happened. But Lauzun was still confident of carrying off this master stroke of marry-ing a princess of royal blood boasting an income of some 600,000 or 700,000 livres a year. And, according to La Fare:

He despatched this affair so smartly and so energetically that everyone was taken by surprise when the Duc de Montausier and the Maréchal d'Albret went to the King one day to ask for the hand of Mademoiselle on his behalf, saying that they came not only as relatives and friends of M. de Lauzun, but as deputies, so to speak, of the nobility of France who, they claimed, would deem it an act of great honour and great grace if the King would permit a simple gentleman of quality to marry a princess of this rank; they then supported their plea with several examples of similar matches throughout history.

The King, who had already been persuaded by Mme de Montespan to grant his favourite all he desired, received his envoys favourably and agreed that Mademoiselle should do as she pleased. The princess, drunk with love, and Lauzun, drunk with vanity, both thought their affairs were now settled, and the latter was foolish enough to postpone the wedding for a few days, so as to have time to arrange all the ceremonial and ostentatious display which his vanity demanded, as though he were marrying someone of his own social level. During this short period of time, the entire Royal Household, the Ministers and the Court joined in opposing this marriage. The Queen Mother, who never involved herself in controversy, spoke very strongly to the King. Monsieur was even more outspoken, and M. le Prince de Condé told the King, quite respectfully, that he would attend the wedding mass of the *cadet* Lauzun and, on leaving, would put a bullet through the man's head with his pistol.

Attacking on another flank, the Archbishop of Paris used various pretexts for procrastinating in the matter of issuing banns for the marriage, persuaded to this course of action by Le Tellier and Louvois who were both declared enemies of this little upstart. But what finally brought about the collapse of the affair was the intervention of Mme Scarron, a highly intelligent woman who had been entrusted by Mme de Montespan with the care of the children she had had by the King, and who was then her principal confidante. Mme Scarron pointed out to Mme de Montespan the storm she would draw upon herself in supporting Lauzun in this affair, and that the royal family and the King himself would eventually reproach her for the course she was urging him to take. She was so persuasive, that Mme de Montespan, who had initiated the whole affair, broke it, and at the end of three or four days Lauzun and Mademoiselle received orders to proceed no further in their marriage plans. This thunderbolt dashed all Lauzun's hopes to the ground and, at the same time, exposed Mademoiselle to public scorn, for although this marriage had seemed an extraordinary idea when first announced, it seemed merely ridiculous now that it had been broken off . . .

Returning from Languedoc, a few days after the wedding had been called off, I came across M. de Lauzun at Saint-Germain, in the apartment of a relative of mine with whom he was on excellent terms, and after asking me if I had not felt sympathy for him in his misfortunes he began to talk of Mme de Montespan in tones of such indignation and loathing that he seemed almost to have lost all self-control. Indeed, when I returned to Paris to visit a lady with whom I was madly in love, who happened to be also a friend of M. de Lauzun, I felt impelled to say to her: 'Your friend Lauzun is a lost man, he will not last more than another six months at Court.'

Mlle de Montpensier was in the depths of despair, as Mme de Caylus relates:

Mademoiselle, of weak constitution and subject to violent movements which were physically exhausting to her, did not hide her grief. After the rupture of her marriage, she retired to her bed and received visitors like a bereaved widow, and I heard someone tell Mme de Maintenon that she was crying in her despair: 'He would have been there! He would have been there!'—that is to say: 'in my bed', since she was pointing to the empty space beside her.

As for Lauzun, his luck held out for a little longer still. The King thought no doubt that he owed him some compensation, for, on January 9, 1671, a letter from Saint-Maurice to the Duke of Savoy informs us that:

M. de Lauzun has been officially declared favourite, the King having given him *carte blanche* to enter his study and his bedroom, as though he were the First Gentleman of the Chamber, a privilege accorded to no one else, not even to those furnished with *billets d'affaires*. But the Court is mistaken in thinking that the King has made him a present of 100,000 louis d'or; M. de Lauzun is interested in neither money nor honours after losing the fortune which seemed so close within his grasp. He has declared that his only desire is to acquire sufficient money to pay his debts, and to serve the King for the rest of his days in any capacity which may please His Majesty.

Duringthe spring of the same year, La Vallière, overwhelmed by the humiliations to which she had been subjected, decided to leave the Court. The Princess Palatine (Charlotte Elizabeth of Bavaria, second wife of Monsieur, Duc d'Orléans) wrote at a later date:

The King's behaviour towards her [La Vallière] was so harsh and sarcastic as to be insulting. One day, while passing through La Vallière's apartment on the way to that of Mme de Montespan, the King, egged on by Mme de Montespan who was accompanying him, picked up La Vallière's little dog, a pretty spaniel named *Malice,* and threw it at the duchess, saying: 'Here, Madame, is some company for you: it should prove sufficient,' a remark which was all the more insulting insofar as he was not even remaining in her apartment but simply passing through on his way to that of his more recent mistress.

And Saint-Maurice *informed the Duke of Savoy, on March 20, 1671, that:*

The King no longer goes to bed with Mlle de La Vallière, so everyone believes; her rival will not tolerate it. Besides being consumptive, the poor lady has been receiving treatment for two months for a wen on her neck, under the right-hand side of her jaw, which obliges her to go around swathed in bandages. Nevertheless, she often walks out with the King and her pride is vastly flattered thereby . . .

Lauzun was assigned the task of bringing Mlle de La Vallière back to Versailles, after she had suddenly decided to retire to a convent. According to Mlle de Montpensier:

The Court left for Versailles on the first day of Lent. There had been a ball at the Tuileries, at which neither Mme de Montespan nor Mme de La Vallière had appeared; the reason for their absence became known on the day we were due to leave: La Vallière was so displeased with her rival's success that she had decided to immolate herself in the convent of the Filles de Sainte-Marie at Chaillot. The King despatched M. de Lauzun and M. Colbert to the convent, and M. Colbert eventually brought her back with him.

The King and Mme de Montespan both continued to weep bitterly in the carriage; so did I, but for a very different reason. When Mme de La Vallière arrived, the tears dried up quickly. Everybody had approved of her previous resolution and therefore agreed in thinking her stupid to have returned.

During this same month, a scandal rocked the Court: the Marquis de Cessac, the King's Master of the Wardrobe, was caught cheating at cards! Mme de Sévigné reports:

An event has just taken place which is the talk of all Paris: the King has ordered M. de Cessac to resign his post and to quit Paris immediately. Do you know why? For having cheated at play and so winning 500,000 écus with marked cards. The man who made these cards was interrogated by the King himself: he denied the fact at first; but, upon the King promising him a pardon, he confessed that he had followed this trade for a long time. It seems that the affair will not stop here, for he furnished several houses with these marked cards. It was some time before the King could bring himself to disgrace a man of Cessac's quality, but, seeing that everyone who had played with him for the last two months had been ruined, he decided that he could not in conscience do less than bring this roguery to light.

The other newsworthy event occurring that same April was the Vatel affair, described by a witness, Jean Herault de Gourville, who had been charged with organizing the reception for the King given by the Prince de Condé at Chantilly:

I had sent members of my staff into the various neighbouring villages with supplies of provisions for men and horses, so that as the guests arrived at Chantilly they could immediately be issued with vouchers indicating the village where they were to be lodged. A number of tents had been set up on the lawn at Chantilly, containing dining tables, for serving those guests who customarily dined in the King's company, and more tents were set up in other parts of the grounds for feeding the other guests as soon as the tables filled up. Each tent was staffed with servants to serve the food and drink, most of them Swiss, who had been specially hired for the occasion. Vatel, M. le Prince's supervisor, a most experienced and efficient man, was in general charge of all the catering arrangements. On the following day, which was a day of abstinence, Vatel arose at daybreak, and found to his vexation that the supplies of fresh fish he had ordered had not yet arrived; he went to his room, locked the door behind him, placed the hilt of his sword against the wall and promptly ran himself through.

After the door had been broken down and the body discovered, someone came and woke me up in the boathouse, where I was sleeping on a bed of straw, to give me the news. My first instruction was that the body should be transported by cart to the parish church half a league away for burial. At that point the fresh fish began arriving. M. le Duc arose as soon as he learned of Vatel's death, and took charge of things so efficiently that people hardly noticed that Vatel was no longer there to give orders.

Lauzun remained in favour with the King throughout the voyage the latter made to his armies, and during the whole of 1671. But on November 25th came a dramatic turn of events. In Mlle de Montpensier's words:

While I was at table, Wednesday evening, someone came up to Mme de Nogent, who was dining with me, and whispered something to her; she left the table, followed by the other ladies. I passed the time in chatting to some of my retainers in the dining-room, then the Comtesse de Fiesque came up to me and started saying: 'M. de Lauzun ...' I thought she was telling me that he was here, and had been let into my dressing-room by way of the wardrobe closet. I went straight there, saying aloud: 'What manners! He is supposed to be at Saint-Germain, and now suddenly he is here!' The Comtesse de Fiesque repeated to me: 'No, what I just said to you was that he has been arrested!' I was so overwhelmed by this announcement that I remained speechless for a long while and was hardly in a fit state even to notice that Mme de Nogent had fainted away. Finally, I asked who had brought this news. Rollinde told me that one hour after arriving at Saint-Germain, M. de Rochefort had gone to M. de Lauzun's room and arrested him there and taken him directly to that of the captains of the Royal Bodyguards. This confirmation that the news was indeed true left me in a state of complete and indescribable desolation.[1]

The Marquis de Saint-Maurice *told his version of the story to the Duke of Savoy:*

I will commence this letter by relating all that I know about the disgrace of the Comte de Lauzun, since I have no doubt that Your Royal Highness will be impatient to learn the details, which I have obtained from a reliable source.

On Wednesday, he left Paris together with the Duc de Roquelaure, and arrived at Saint-Germain about seven in the evening. As was his usual custom, he went straight to his room and shut himself up there for several hours; he used to seclude himself in this fashion every day, sitting alone, dreaming, often in the dark. The Marquis de Rochefort, captain of the locally-based Bodyguards, who was his colleague and friend, had orders from the King to take him prisoner.... He knocked so loudly and insistently at the door of the Comte de Lauzun's room that the latter was obliged to open it, whereupon he arrested him with the usual formal courtesies. The Comte de Lauzun exclaimed: 'Who? *Me?*' and retreated in disbelief. When he was asked to hand over his sword, he threw it on the ground; then, when he was ordered to unlock the door to his closet so that his personal papers might be sequestrated, he refused to hand over the key, saying that none of his papers were relevant to his service to the King and that he would rather see the door broken down than hand them over voluntarily.

The general opinion at the Court is that he realized his position had become insecure, and was consequently thinking of leaving the Kingdom. With this aim in view, it seems that he had been accumulating funds by selling silver plate and pieces of jewellery, and that he had been engaged in a massive correspondence with people in different foreign countries, in particular with the Duke of Buckingham; it seems, further-more, that these letters had been intercepted and shown to the King, who considered the plans and schemes outlined in them

[1] But according to Lefèvre d'Ormesson in his *Journal*, Lauzun was arrested by d'Artagnan and escorted by him and a hundred musketeers to Pignerol.

3. *Philippe d'Orléans*
(Monsieur)

Henriette d'Angleterre
(Madame)

4. *Mlle de La Vallière,* by Nocret

Mme de Montespan and the Duc du Maine, by Mignard

to be disloyal, and decided that it was necessary to take pre-
cautionary measures against their author. However, those
courtiers most addicted to speculation claim that his disgrace
results from being involved in the Villarceaux intrigue, having
attempted to advance Mlle de Grancey's cause with the King;
they say that it was he who incited Villarceaux and attempted
thereby to create a rift between the King and Mme de Montespan, with whom he was on extremely bad terms, as he was
with M. de Louvois . . .

On the other hand, Mademoiselle hinted to one of her
intimate friends that Lauzun was probably arrested for having
called Mme de Montespan a 'fat tripe-seller'. If that is true, he
must be not only insolent but crazy to say such a thing, since,
quite apart from the respect owed to a lady whom the King
loves, the lady in question, though well moulded, is certainly
not fat.

*But Mlle de Montpensier continued to think about her
beloved Lauzun, and Giovanni Battista Primi Visconti, the
graphologist and fortune-teller who had arrived in France in
1673 and was well established at the Court, relates the following story in this connection:*

One evening, I was so tired that I retired to my bed earlier
than usual, but shortly after I had lain down a servant came
to tell me that the Comtesse de Fiesque and the Marquise de
Rannes wished to see me. I got up. They were sitting in a
carriage with another lady who was listening to them. I got
in, and we drove to the house of Mme de Rannes, where we
found a mass of carriages and people. After I had entered the
house, a tall, veiled lady approached me, and although she tried
to disguise her voice I knew her immediately to be Mlle de
Montpensier. But I feigned ignorance, and followed her into
her closet. Mademoiselle was of fitful humour, and seemed
unable to keep still, now sitting on a footstool, now on a sofa,
then finally, after an hour's conversation, leaning back against
a Chinese table, which broke under her weight, so that the
princess fell down on top of it and I, who had tried to save her
from falling, slipped and landed on top of her on the ground.
All the ladies in the room rushed up, and God knows what

thoughts ran through their minds as they saw me lying there on top of her. In the end, everybody burst into laughter, except for Mme de Rannes, who saw that 200 pistoles-worth of china was lying scattered under the collapsed table. Amid this confusion, Mme de Nogent, the Comte de Lauzun's sister, appeared upon the scene, and the conversation started up again. I was proffered a letter for analysis, and deduced from it a description of Lauzun, an outline of his fortunes and misfortunes, and the fact that he would be imprisoned but would be set free in six or seven years' time. Mademoiselle and Mme de Nogent were both convinced that I must have been informed about the course of events. . . . Mademoiselle asked me to state whether or not she was married, to which I replied in equivocal terms. Then, what goings on! Now she burst into tears, now she laughed or sighed, depending upon my answers to her questions, all of which had to do with Lauzun. Mademoiselle was indefatigable, but eventually her ladies-in-waiting persuaded her that dawn was about to break, and that she should retire: it was then that she revealed her identity to me, instructing the ladies of her suite to bring me to her residence in the future and asking me to visit her as often as possible.

CHAPTER VI

A REPUBLICAN PLOT

On September 11, 1674, as a result of a letter written to the King by the Sieur de Cauzé, a gentleman studying at the home of van den Enden, the Chevalier de Rohan was arrested and taken to the Bastille.

NICOLAS DE LA REYNIE, First Lieutenant of Police

PRINCIPAL PERSONALITIES MENTIONED IN CHAPTER VI

FRANÇOISE D'AUBIGNE, widow of the poet Scarron, later Marquise de Maintenon, favourite and morganatic wife of Louis XIV.

LOUIS, CHEVALIER DE ROHAN, PRINCE DE GUÉMÉNEÉ. Formerly the Master of the Royal Hunt (Grand Veneur), but obliged to resign from his post.

HORTENSE MANCINI, DUCHESSE DE MAZARIN, who left her husband for the Chevalier de Rohan: 'If the ugliness of the husband and the attractiveness of the lover provide any excuse for a woman, then she might well be excused,' commented La Fare. (Already mentioned in Chapter V.)

MME DE LIONNE, née Paule Payen, wife of the Secretary of State, Hugues de Lionne, 'beautiful and unbelievably dissolute,' according to Mme de Sévigné.

GILLES DU HAMEL, SIEUR DE LA TRÉAUMONT, gentleman of Normandy, leader of a group of malcontents.

GUILLAUME DUCHÊNE, CHEVALIER DE PRÉAULT—nephew of La Tréaumont.

ANNE SARREAU, known as the MARQUISE DE VILARS, accomplice of La Tréaumont.

PRINCE WILLIAM OF ORANGE, Stadtholder of Holland, later King of England.

The COUNT OF MONTEREY, Governor-General of Flanders, under the orders of William of Orange.

FRANS AFFINIUS VAN DEN ENDEN, Dutchman, scholar and conspirator, living in France since 1671.

The COMTE DE BRISSAC, commander of the Royal Body-guards (already mentioned in Chapter IV).

LOUIS BOURDALOUE, Jesuit and Preacher in Ordinary to Louis XIV.

RENÉE MAURICE D'O DE VILLIERS, mistress of the Chevalier de Rohan.

MME DE SOUBISE: ANNE DE ROHAN-CHABOT, married to her cousin the Prince de Soubise, and one of the Queen's Ladies of the Palace. ('Her beauty accomplished all the rest,' said Saint-Simon.) The King's mistress.

MME DE THIANGE: GABRIELLE DE ROCHECHOUART-MORTEMART, sister of Mme de Montespan.

The French armed forces had occupied—and evacuated—Holland, and conquered the Franche Comté. At the age of thirty-five, Louis XIV was a glorious but far from popular king. His subjects reproached him for going to war, and his courtiers reproached him for not being sufficiently aggressive. Louis Henri Loménie de Brienne *reports some insulting remarks about the King made by the Comte de Guiche after being wounded in the arm and shoulder at the battle of Texel:*

This braggart, he said to some courtier, makes us break our arms and legs every day, but he has not exposed himself to a single musket shot. The King heard him, but pretended to have heard nothing.

And La Fare *mentions, in his* Mémoires, *that the precautions taken by Louis XIV on the occasions of the crossing of the Rhine and the siege of Maastricht were held up to ridicule:*

They [the precautions] did not redound to the credit of a nation which, however rashly, took a pride not only in braving danger but in seeking it out. I know that bravado is not inherent in the character of a king, but nevertheless, if he wishes to lead others in great exploits, he must not appear too obviously reluctant to face the consequences, especially if he affects the reputation of being a warrior and a hero.

Mme de Montespan was now supreme at the Court. Her three children were legitimized by a royal decree of December 20, 1673, as had previously the son and daughter born to La Vallière. And in November 1675, all the Queen's maids-of-honour were dismissed, to everyone's surprise. Mme de Sévigné *had this to say about the latter event, in a letter to Mme de Grignan:*

All the Queen's young ladies were dismissed yesterday, for reasons which remain obscure, although it seems probable that one of them was considered to be a dangerous element, so all were sent away to avoid public gossip.

She added, on December 1st:

There is no doubt whatsoever that *Quanto* [Mme de Montespan] found that the quarters of the maids-of-honour bred a hydra-headed monster, and that the only solution was to chop off all the heads. For, otherwise, what does not happen today may yet happen tomorrow.[1]

---

[1] According to Voltaire (*Le Siècle de Louis XIV*) the reorganization of the royal establishment resulted from the unfortunate liaison between one of the maids-of-honour and the King. This incident was celebrated by the Sonnet of the Abortion, which included these verses:

  Little creature which love created through a crime,
  And which honour has destroyed by a crime in its turn. . . .

The dangers attaching to the status of being a young woman in a Court notorious for its frivolous and lecherous character were resolved by replacing the twelve maids-of-honour who so embellished the Queen's suite with twelve 'ladies of the palace'.

Primi Visconti *explains this incident in the same fashion:*

The Court was abuzz with rumours that the King was making free with Mlle de Théobon, Mlle de La Mothe, and others
among the Queen's maids-of-honour. He is even supposed to
have had designs on the Chanoinesse de Ludre. Mme de Montespan was shocked, claiming that these young ladies were bringing the Court into ill repute; in any case, she enlisted the aid of
the Duchesse de Richelieu, the Queen's lady-in-waiting, who
was entirely devoted to her, to arouse the Queen's scruples.
The Queen, who was a true saint, asked the King to dismiss
these young ladies, and he did so.

*Together with the favourite's three children, now acknow-
ledged, their governess had made a discreet entry into the
Court: this was the widow Scarron, shortly to be known as
Mme de Maintenon, but at that juncture no one was interested
in her presence. At this same time Louis XIV, in a spirit of fair-
mindedness, no doubt, expressed to La Vallière his desire to see
their daughter, Mlle de Blois, now eight years old, make her
first official social appearance. The début took place on
January 12, 1674, with Mme de* Sévigné *as a witness:*

Mlle de Blois is quite ravishing, and the King and the whole
Court are enchanted with her. While the ball was in full swing
she went up to Mme de Richelieu and said: 'Madame, could
you please tell me, perhaps, if the King is pleased with me?'
Then she passed by Mme de Montespan and said to her:
'Madame, are you not greeting your friends today?' In fact,
her childish wit and charm captivated the hearts of everybody
present.

*This sop to Louise de La Vallière's maternal pride was not
sufficient to keep her attached to the Court, and she decided to
retire to a convent, as she had planned to do three years
previously.*
*On April 19th, the King's first favourite heard Mass and
then went to the house of the Grand Carmelites in the Faubourg Saint-Jacques, after first making her farewells at the
Court and cutting off her blonde tresses with her own hands.*

Everyone admired her air of serenity. But Bussy-Rabutin *was ungentlemanly enough to write:*

The conversion of Mlle de La Vallière provides convincing proof to me that God draws people to him by the most diverse ways. He would have had some difficulty, if one may be permitted to put it so bluntly, to pluck this penitent from the hands of her lover, yet jealousy achieved just that miracle. The more I think about her loud self-condemnations of her past life, the more it seems to me that she was motivated by revenge rather than humility and hoped by this attitude to condemn her rival's behaviour.

Louis XIV had other things to occupy his mind. He was still at war against Holland and Spain. In France itself, Guienne, Languedoc, Dauphiné and Provence were seething with discontent over excessive taxation. Seditious posters had appeared on the walls in Normandy, and a plot against the security of the State had been discovered.

On September 11, 1674, at about midday, the Chevalier de Rohan was arrested at Versailles, as he emerged from the chapel where he had been hearing Mass.

Who was Rohan? A grand seigneur, *son of Mme de Guéménée, who had been the devoted friend of Cardinal Mazarin. The King's playmate when they were both children, Louis de Rohan had now been his Master of the Hunt for four years. He had the reputation of being something of a daredevil, an inveterate gambler and a Don Juan, and was the lover of the actress Du Parc (for whose favours he contended with Racine), of the Duchesse de Mazarin, of Mme de Thiange, possibly of Mme de Montespan. . . . La Fare tells us:*

No man of the epoch could compare with him in elegance, good looks and finely shaped limbs. It may seem petty and base to praise the shape of a man's legs, but one should not scorn the gifts of nature, however trifling they may be, when they are present in a state of perfection.

For the rest, he was a mass of contradictions. When he wanted, he could be gay and witty, but as often as not he was dull and moody. Excitable and easily provoked, a so-called witticism was always on the tip of his tongue. At times, he was capable of pursuing lofty ideals and honourable and courageous courses of action, but at other times he was equally capable of feeble judgement and ill conduct, as he showed in a squabble he had with the Chevalier de Lorraine, who came better out of it than he did; the Chevalier de Rohan claimed originally that one day, while on horseback, he had struck the Chevalier de Lorraine with his cane, but he was later forced to retract the whole story, after inventing increasingly mendacious versions of the incident.

This same Chevalier de Rohan had, on an earlier occasion, had a dispute with the King himself, while the latter was still young and under the tutelage of the cardinal. The exchange, which helped to create his reputation for recklessness, was briefly as follows:

A group, which included the King, was playing for high stakes at the house of the cardinal. The Chevalier de Rohan lost steadily and found himself at the end heavily in debt to the King. It had been agreed beforehand that all payments of money would be in louis d'or, but after counting out 700 or 800 in this coinage to the King, he proceeded to count out about 200 Spanish pistoles. The King refused to accept these, saying that he wanted louis pieces. So the Chevalier de Rohan promptly took back the 200 Spanish pistoles and threw them out of the window, remarking: 'Since Your Majesty does not want them, they are good for nothing.'

The King was vexed at this and complained to the cardinal about the Chevalier de Rohan's insolence. The cardinal, speaking as his tutor, replied: 'Sire, in this matter the Chevalier de Rohan has behaved like the King, and the King has behaved like the Chevalier de Rohan.' This light-hearted statement saved the Chevalier de Rohan from public reproach, and allowed the King to swallow his injured pride and even to form a favourable view of the chevalier which he might have put to some profit had he had the experience and the inclination.

Daniel de Cosnac *reported that Rohan had openly proclaimed himself to be devoted to Madame (Henriette d'Angleterre, Duchesse d'Orléans):*

Vanity persuaded him that Madame would be grateful to him if he contrived to insult the Chevalier de Lorraine. He probably had no other designs on the princess's affections than that which would have resulted from the Chevalier de Lorraine's hostility; in any case, he sought a quarrel with the latter, and afterwards boasted of having struck him. The Chevalier de Lorraine denied this flatly, and the King ordered the Duc de Noailles to reconcile the two parties. The Chevalier de Rohan then not only disavowed the deed of which he had boasted but even signed a disclaimer; yet, the very same day, he wrote to ten of his friends that in order to avoid the rigours of the law against duelling, he had thought best to deny an encounter which had nevertheless taken place exactly as previously described. These messages came to the notice of the Chevalier de Lorraine and Monsieur, and the quarrel broke out anew.

From this period onwards, Rohan was never free of money troubles. The King disapproved of his too frequent escapades; he had sold his post of Master of the Hunt; and then, after a new altercation with the Chevalier de Lorraine, he was confined in the Bastille for a month. On his release, he took part in the Dutch campaign as an ordinary volunteer, but although he was wounded the War Minister, Louvois, refused to grant him any compensation. At a later date, Louis Urbain Lefèvre de Caumartin *told Voltaire:*

The Minister's arrogance and harshness so angered M. de Rohan that, after this interview, he came straight to my apartment in a state of extreme nervous tension, threw himself on to a day-couch and swore: 'Either this —— of a Louvois dies, or I do!'

From then onwards, the embittered young courtier was ready for any crazy enterprise. Primi Visconti, *the Italian fortune-teller, knew Rohan well and relates:*

The first time I met Rohan was at a reception given by the Comtesse de Soissons. As usual, her place was filled with members of the nobility. Mme de Lionne rather fancied the chevalier, and begged the Comtesse de Soissons to obtain my opinion about him. The countess came up to me, clutched me by my hair and drew my head close to hers to obtain this confidential information. I told her that Rohan seemed to me to be an unregenerate malcontent, and that prison and scaffold were painted on his face. Mme de Lionne cried out that I was mad; then, proclaiming herself a physiognomist, she asserted that Rohan was the most delightful man in the world and that she was proud to admit that she loved him. It must be said that she had allowed herself to behave rather freely in public with the young men of the Court, squandering her money as a lover would do on his mistresses . . .

After being told of my prediction, Rohan refused to speak to me for two months. But during the beginning of September, when his disposition towards me appeared to have become more favourable, I assured him that these predictions were a mere amusement for me; at the same time, I advised him to beware of an imminent act of treachery by a woman or by a whole group of people. The countess was playing cards with a group of guests at that moment. Rohan boasted to me in reply that he feared no woman; there was one, he said, who was bitterly hostile towards him, but he claimed that when he had chanced to meet her at the Opéra a few days earlier, a few feigned tears on his part had served to melt her heart completely. There was not a woman alive, he added, capable of resisting him when he chose to exercise his charms.

But it was not a woman who was to bring about Rohan's downfall. He no longer had any post at the Court, and had become an embittered man, swamped with debts, at the end of his resources, when he happened to meet a man he had known in the army—a man similar to himself, according to La Fare, *but more intelligent and more willing to risk his life.*

This man was Gilles du Hamel, Sieur de La Tréaumont, a gentleman of Rouens, who had abandoned his military career to become the guiding spirit, in his own province, of a small group of malcontents which included in its ranks his nephew, the Chevalier de Préault, and his neighbour, Anne Sarreau, known as the Marquise de Vilars.

This group had conceived the project of helping Holland in its war against France by facilitating a landing by the Dutch in Normandy. The province was crushed by taxation and ripe for rebellion; nearly all the armed forces were engaged outside the kingdom, the coast was badly guarded, and the moment seemed propitious.

It seems, in fact, that the conspirators soon enlarged their scheme; according to the witnesses whose reports follow, they had intended to organize the kidnapping of the Dauphin, the overthrow of the King and the proclamation of a Republic! In any case, their manifesto, which was included among the evidence offered in the Rohan trial and has survived together with the entire dossier, was a thoroughgoing project for the establishment of a republican government:

The aim is to found a popular State which shall be invincible, flourishing and eternally developing, through the unity and energy of all the people, towards general prosperity and liberty.

On the first day, the citizens shall be summoned to assemble, without arms, in their own parishes, to participate in discussion about their liberty and their submission, which is to say that they shall recognize no masters other than the free nobility and people.

All public offices, jurisdictions, judgments, etc., shall be suspended until the people and the nobility have elected leaders to govern them according to laws established by themselves and subject to change or modification according to their desires.

Under these circumstances it will be necessary to provide armed support for our sacred cause, and for this purpose the twelve nobles who are provisionally at the head of their regional group of armed volunteers shall assemble their men in each parish after midday to choose among themselves a commander, a lieutenant and a colour-bearer. Voting will be secret. The one gaining most votes among the armed group will become commander; the second, lieutenant; and the third, colour-bearer. These commanders and lieutenants, six hundred in all, shall constitute the military Council which, on a predetermined day, shall elect in each parish twelve of the wisest and most prosperous citizens to form a civilian Council composed of three hundred members.

This Council will concern itself, following the instructions formulated by the community, with:

Matters of finance, annual census of the district, provisions, urban improvement, fortifications and public works.

Indigent widows and orphans, who ought not to be treated with scorn. Needy families, public health, and precautions to be taken against the plague and other contagious diseases.

Art, industry and commerce.

Occupations useful to the Republic.

Litigation and the rights of citizens.

People guilty of theft, homicide and, above all, of actions constituting an attack upon liberty.

Marriage questions and the augmentation of the population.

Adulterers who prey upon women, and all those whose conduct is injurious to public morals.

The instruction of children in the fine arts and, above all, in a knowledge of the idea of liberty.

Alliances and treaties with other cities, peoples and nations.

To sum up, everything of importance today, including the periods of military service which citizens will be required to undergo, although the conditions for such service will be set out by the military Council . . .

No one shall be considered a citizen until he has reached the age of twenty-one or served three years as a soldier. Any man aged twenty-one who has not completed three years' military service shall be required to fulfil this duty before being granted citizen's rights.

All the nobles, ecclesiastics and inhabitants of small towns and villages shall be deemed to be citizens of the city of which their town or village is an adjunct.

No distinction shall be made between Catholics and Protestants, so long as both factions show themselves to be good citizens, defend the cause of freedom, and refrain from intruding questions of religion into State affairs.

The plot was hatched during the spring of 1674; by the end of that year more than sixty people had been arrested as conspirators. The anonymous author of a letter now in the manuscript collection of the Bibliothèque Sainte-Geneviève (and published by the then Conservateur in 1758) claimed to have inside information about these treasonable activities:

I have spoken to individuals who have had access to the most secret documents produced in evidence at the trial; and in addition, I entertained yesterday in my room for three hours a gentleman who is a friend of mine and had been asked by the Marquis de Bray, brother of Mme de Vilars, to attend to the disposition of his body if he were to be executed, and it is from this gentleman that I learned details about the plot, since our conversation dealt entirely with this sad affair ...

Still according to this same anonymous witness, La Tréaumont had made contact, during April, with the Count of Monterey, Prince William of Orange's military commander in the Netherlands, and had assured him that:

... Normandy was ripe for rebellion, and that the Dutch had only to provide a fleet carrying six thousand men, weapons to arm twenty thousand, siege engines and 2,000,000 livres. Furthermore, he was in touch with a great nobleman who would join the rebel cause on payment of 30,000 écus. And in this same letter he, La Tréaumont, demanded 20,000 écus for himself, asserting that his name was so well-known in that province that it would encourage the inhabitants to support this project which he begged the Count of Monterey to undertake.

The Count of Monterey had an agent in France, a seventy-year-old scholar named Affinius van den Enden, who is mentioned by Paul Pellisson, the King's historiographer, in a letter dated September 21, 1674:

He is Flemish by origin, but has lived for many years in Paris, or rather in Picpus, and his name is van den Enden. He is a school teacher by profession, and takes in pupils as boarders to teach them Latin. You may have noticed his house; the door has a grille and carries a plate with his name on it. I believe it is this house which is generally known as the *Hôtel des Muses*. Here is how the plot was discovered: among the young schoolboys was a thirty-four-year-old man, a Frenchman who had spent a long time in Flanders and had been severely wounded in the war. He had recently decided to have this man teach him Latin (it seems that he was considered an excellent teacher) with a view to entering the Church.

This thirty-four-year-old 'schoolboy', Cauzé de Nazelles, relates in his Mémoires *how he succeeded in foiling the Rohan—La Tréaumont plot. He had been lodging in van den Enden's house for some months and had come to acquire a very high opinion of him when:*

Some time in July I first noticed that La Tréaumont visited him frequently. I had known this man while he was an officer in the army and knew that he had an exceedingly bad reputation. He used to enter by a secret door at the end of the garden, unlocking it with a key he had in his possession, and took the most careful precautions to avoid being seen. Later on, he brought the Chevalier de Rohan with him, through that same door and using the same discretion. The sight of the Chevalier de Rohan surprised me. It seemed incredible to me that a man of his rank should have any dealings with La Tréaumont, who was regarded by the troops as being entirely without honour and was furthermore known as a dangerous character capable of committing any crime.

Thanks to van den Enden's daughter, Marianne, Cauzé was able to spy on the conspirators for some time, and one day overheard a conversation between van den Enden and La Tréaumont which left him in no further doubt since it concerned a project of kidnapping the Dauphin while he was in Normandy, and even of capturing the King at Versailles! Cauzé *continues:*

The 550 Guards' uniforms would soon be ready, and the friendly elements who were to wear them were standing by in readiness. These sympathizers were all courageous and experienced men. The horses had been positioned so that they could be assembled in one unit in the space of a few hours. Arms would be distributed at the appropriate moment. The only important question that remained was to know the day when Monseigneur le Dauphin was due to leave his wolf-hunting expedition in the woods of Normandy.

The Prince usually hunted alone except for a single piqueur, following the first relay, so ten conspirators dressed as Guards would be sufficient to capture him and take him to the coast, where a vessel was already positioned to bring him out to the Dutch fleet which would be in the vicinity. The other 'Guards' would divide into two groups: ten of them would be a sufficient force to capture Honfleur, where La Tréaumont would be waiting to let them through the gates, and the rest of the force would proceed immediately to Versailles where the chief prize awaited them . . .

But even now, Cauzé hesitated to denounce the plot:

I had no scruples as far as La Tréaumont was concerned: he was a notorious scoundrel who was bound to come to a bad end. But I was utterly dismayed at the involvement of the Chevalier de Rohan, one of the most distinguished figures in the whole of France, whose name and family I respected, and whom I knew to be in desperate financial straits. I had equally great esteem for van den Enden, and was horrified at the thought that this man of rare parts and extraordinary ability, so highly regarded by all scholars and so estimable in every way, would be utterly ruined by an accusation in this matter. I was full of regret for the unhappy situation in which this family found itself . . .

I finally made up my mind that same evening to go and give an account of events to the Marquis de Louvois, Secretary of State for War, who was then in Paris. I requested an audience with him to inform him of a most urgent matter of the utmost concern to the King. I was introduced immediately into his presence, and he listened to me most attentively, without interrupting me. When I had completed my account, he told me that everything I had just related to him was of the greatest importance, but that he was surprised that I had delayed so long in informing him, since what I had seen in the beginning had been sufficient to oblige me to warn him immediately . . .

The author of the anonymous letter now in the collection of the Bibliothèque Sainte-Geneviève, relates the outcome of the affair:

As soon as the King was informed of this treason, he gave orders to the Comte d'Ayen, captain of his Bodyguards, to instruct the Sieur de Brissac, their commander, to arrest the Chevalier de Rohan as he emerged from Mass. This was done, and the Chevalier was taken to the room of the Sieur de Brissac, where he asked for food. This was brought to him after the commander had obtained the King's permission.

After dinner, he was taken by carriage to the Bastille. I saw him leave there, the day of his execution, half-dead already, his lips blue, his face pale and distorted like that of a corpse, leaning on the arms of Père Talon and Père Bourdaloue, and hardly able to stand upright although apparently making every effort to control himself.

Sandras de Courtilz, in a book about Rohan called Le Prince Infortuné, *provides further details of events:*

An officer of the Royal Bodyguards had the King's order to require the Chevalier de Rohan to surrender his sword as he came out from hearing Mass. There had been some discussion previously as to whether or not he should be arrested, since the known facts did not provide sufficient evidence against him to convict him of felony. M. Colbert, who had married his eldest daughter to the Duc de Chevreuse who was related on his grandmother's side to the house of Rohan, had been of the opinion that it would be unwise to proceed too hastily against the prince, who might yet be shown to be innocent. But the battle of Senef took place a few days after the question of the Chevalier's arrest had been discussed, and the baggage of the captured Marquis d'Affentar was found to contain a pouch inside which was a memorandum concerning the money that had been sent to the Chevalier de Rohan and to La Tréaumont as the price of their treachery. This discovery resolved all doubts, and orders were given immediately for their apprehension.

And Sandras de Courtilz *describes La Tréaumont's arrest:*

Brissac was accompanied by a small party of Bodyguards when he confronted La Tréaumont. La Tréaumont would not have been surprised to see Brissac enter his room alone, but seeing him at the head of a force of armed men his guilty conscience allowed him to guess immediately the reason for his arrest. The traitor begged Brissac to grant him one favour in the name of their ancient friendship, namely that he be allowed to enter his closet to pack some personal linen and other articles which he wished to take with him. Brissac permitted him to retire, but La Tréaumont's real intention was not to pack a bag but to get his hands on two pistols he had in the closet. Reappearing with these, he fired one at Brissac but missed him and the shot hit a guardsman who was behind Brissac; since La Tréaumont still had a pistol left to fire, Brissac, who was a brave man and an old soldier who was used to being shot at, called out to him: 'Fire! Fire!' The guards accompanying him thought he was addressing them, and seeing that La Tréaumont had missed their commander with his first shot and fearing that his second shot might be more accurate, they opened fire on the unhappy man, wounding him mortally, so that he died half an hour later.

Among the documents of the criminal trial of the Chevalier de Rohan (in the department of manuscripts of the Bibliothèque Nationale) is a sheet of paper on which La Tréaumont penned his last words, in reply to a question asked him by Brissac:

I have nothing to tell you and have never admitted to you that I am a criminal, but neither fear, which has never overtaken me, nor your threats will ever drag anything . . . out of me.

It seems from another source, that La Tréaumont survived for several hours. Paul Pellisson *writes, on September 14th:*

The guard wounded by La Tréaumont has died and he is in scarcely better condition according to what the King said yesterday evening. Two manifestos were discovered among his belongings, one in French to arouse the people of Normandy against the King, and another one, in Latin, which was, so I am informed, a kind of project for the reformation of the State.

Meanwhile Cauzé de Nazelles, *acting under Louvois' orders, was spying on the movements of Mme van den Enden, whose husband had vanished. In his words:*

I followed her, and pointed her out to the commander of the small brigade posted at the gates of the city, and we continued to follow her, with some of his men, as far as the Quai des Augustins, where the commander hailed a hackney carriage and beckoned me to get in with him, while three of his guards followed in a second carriage. She stopped at Le Bourget, at an inn which she entered just as we drove up. Van den Enden and she were in a room on the top storey of the house. They were in the process of laying out the tattered clothing and long false beard in which he was about to disguise himself. When we burst in, they were greatly taken back, and I myself was in great distress at the circumstances in which I now confronted them. Seeing me surrounded by Royal Body-guards, he thought at first that they had arrested me as his accomplice and made every effort to convince the officer that he had never confided a word of his plans to me and that I was entirely uninvolved, that, on the contrary, I had always spoken of the King to him in terms of the greatest respect and loyalty. In so defending me he was making an open confession of his crime and, from this moment onwards, he realized that his doom was sealed.

During October, a number of other confederates were arrested: Rohan's mistress, Renée Maurice d'O de Villiers, who remained faithful to the memory of her lover until the end of her life; a young chevalier enamoured of the Marquise de Vilars; and various other malcontents suspected of having knowledge of the plot. . . . Too many arrests, in the opinion of the Lieutenant of Police Nicolas de La Reynée, writing to Colbert on October 16th:

The Bastille affair seems to be developing into a more extensive criminal prosecution than I would think desirable. We are learning, and no doubt will continue to learn, fresh facts every day, and if the authorities determine to follow every potential clue I fear that the proceedings may become hopelessly protracted.

In addition, I am not persuaded of the wisdom of bringing so many people to trial at the same time and of so filling the prisons; and I fear that the justice which all expect to be meted out to the truly guilty, and the terror which these sentences should inspire, may be lessened in effect by a general feeling of horror at this multitude of defendants and criminals, so that their very numbers will make them appear less criminal in the eyes of the public.

Rohan was meanwhile under interrogation by Claude Bazin de Bezons, a cunning and ruthless magistrate about whom Primi Visconti *relates:*

It is said that he was so vicious that, when he fell down in a fit of apoplexy, which happened often to him, for he was small and fat, one had only to say to him: 'Monsieur, the accused has confessed' for him to recover immediately.

Comte Armand de Monchy, *Bishop of Verdun, wrote to Bussy-Rabutin on November 26th:*

The Chevalier de Rohan is to be sentenced today. He has been on the *sellette*,[1] wearing a new costume and seeming entirely composed. He does not believe he will die. I think he deserves pity in that, according to rumour, he will be put to the question, and in my view torture is worse than death. It is said that he admitted the plot for the Normandy uprising during interrogation, then denied it when on the *sellette*. His intention, most probably, was to obtain money from the enemy and then make absolutely no attempt to keep his side of the bargain. But, in my view, such conduct still merits death.

[1] A small wooden seat on which those accused of capital crimes were obliged to sit before sentence was pronounced.

A few days before the death of the Chevalier de Rohan, his mistress, Renée Maurice d'O de Villiers, arrested, then released, wrote him a last letter:

If I did not know you to be strong in character and courageous in the face of death, I would take great pains to prepare you gradually and to teach you how little hope you should repose in life. But since you have never feared anything, I do not believe that you will feel fear at losing a life which you have so often held in contempt and the loss of which you should regard as a blessing rather than a misfortune, since your death will deliver you from a horde of miseries, will save you from new crimes, and will afford you a path to salvation by offering your death as a sacrifice to God for the expiation of your faults. For you are truly a victim, whom La Tréaumont has immolated to his ambition, and whose name, friendship and weakness he has most cruelly abused. Start then, Monsieur, to have recourse to God, employ all the little time which remains to you to work for your salvation; reflect in horror on all the pernicious errors which La Tréaumont put into your head and with which he had poisoned your mind and your heart. My one desire is to inspire you, in this, with the feelings which overwhelm my soul, for despite the feebleness of my sex, I wanted with all my heart to seem criminal to your judges, so that I might be quit of a life which has become odious to me. I can assure you that I would never ask either God or the King to prolong my life one moment longer than necessary, but, alas, neither my imprisonment nor my enemies were able to blacken my innocence. Therefore, Monsieur, I find myself reduced to dragging my chains so long as it may please God, and the one thing that prevents me from complaining about my fate is that it permits me the liberty to pray to God on your behalf for the rest of my days.

Of this you may be certain, as you may be equally certain that no one was ever more truly your friend and your humble servant than Renée Maurice d'O.

Van den Enden was put to the question, but Rohan was spared torture. On either November 27th or 28th (witnesses disagree on the date), Rohan, the Chevalier de Préault and the

Marquise de Vilars were beheaded, and van den Enden was hanged in the rue Saint-Antoine, near the Bastille. Bayle, *author of the* Dictionnaire Historique et Critique, *wrote on December 15th to his friend Minutoli:*

It is said that though Père Bourdaloue had spent five or six days trying to reconcile the Chevalier de Rohan to the idea of death, when the moment came for the chevalier to leave on his short journey to the scaffold he found his penitent in a state of despair and absolutely unresolved to die. The Reverend Father invoked all his rhetorical resources and propounded every conceivable argument in favour of resignation without making the slightest impression. So he went up to some of the captains of the Guards who were stationed at the gates of the Bastille and in the surrounding streets and begged them to come to his aid, saying that he had exhausted his theological resources and his powers of persuasion. So a captain of the Guards named Magalotti went with him and addressed the chevalier in an extremely brusque fashion, exhorting him to die in the most picturesque terms, saying: '*Par la Tête Dieu*, Monsieur le Chevalier, *you* afraid of death? A fine thing for a man of your profession to be scared of dying! Why, *Mort Dieu*, Monsieur, just imagine you are in the forward trench with a hundred cannon-balls whistling past your ears and singeing your wig! Pretend you have just given the order to attack!' This was better received than all the Jesuit's moralizing, and the criminal found himself capable of contemplating the prospect of death without terror as a result of this very Christian exhortation.

Rohan's death created discontent among the courtiers. La Fare *considered it regrettable that no one had had the courage to ask the King to grant a reprieve to the ill-fated prince:*

Rohan had enjoyed the favours of Mme de Thiange, the sister of Mme de Montespan, and some people claim that he had been in love with Mme de Montespan herself. Although she had not reciprocated his passion, she was greatly affected by his death but did not have the courage to intercede on his behalf. Yet I heard it said that the King was half inclined to grant a reprieve of his own accord. Le Tellier and Louvois both emphasized to him that, under the existing circumstances, it was necessary to make an example, and that this occasion provided him with an opportunity to make a great example at the least cost to himself, since the Chevalier de Rohan was of noble and ancient lineage yet without followers or friends, on bad terms with his mother and his entire family, none of whom dared invoke the King's mercy.

The public disapproved exceedingly of this fact and bitterly reproached his mother, as well as his relative, Mme de Soubise, who was at that time on very good terms with the King, it seems, although their liaison was unavowed. Mme de Montespan, the King's *maîtresse déclarée* since many years, was reproached equally for failing to act, but this is not the first instance in which she has shown herself to possess a hard heart and to have little sense of pity or gratitude.

The epilogue to the whole affair is provided by Jean Rou, an Avocat of the Parliament, who had been imprisoned in the Bastille 'for having advanced facts contrary to the dominant religion,' who relates, in his Mémoires, *how he came to know the Chevalier d'Aigremont during the course of his captivity:*

Aigremont was a gentleman from the Normandy border regions who had found himself involved unwittingly in the Rohan affair because of Mme de Vilars, with whom he had recently fallen in love.

This chevalier had become exceedingly depressed at being involved in this complicated intrigue, and soon after obtaining his *liberté de cour* [permitting him to move freely within the Bastille] he had made a point of seeking my company rather than that of the other *bastillards*, all of whom he despised.

He told me one extraordinary story concerning the last tragic chapter in the history of this lady [de Vilars]. Since all the accomplices in this affair were in separate custody, he was unable to obtain any reliable information concerning the execution of the four condemned persons, Rohan, the Vilars woman, Préau, and the Fleming, van den Enden. But, acting out of a sense of disquiet or foreboding, he had piled pieces of furniture on top of each other under a small window set high up in the outside wall of his cell, facing the rue Saint-Antoine, where some scaffolds had been set up near a gallows. When he had climbed to the top of his improvised structure and was able to see what was going on in the crowded street, the first sight to meet his eye was the head of his beautiful mistress in the process of falling from her shoulders as the executioner chopped it off. His shock was so great that he fell off his scaffolding, almost as dead as the woman who had been the darling of his heart. He revived after a few moments of unconciousness. Several times thereafter he repeated to me and to others the description of this dismal spectacle, and even a year and more after the event his recollection of it would plunge him once again into the fit of mental derangement which had so affected him at the time of the tragic event . . .

He was finally released from the Bastille, on condition that he served the King at his own expense during the forthcoming campaign. He died while standing a few paces away from his commanding officer, the Marquis de Renel, and most people considered that the unfortunate man was shot in the back on orders from above, so that his punishment would be sure even though the processes of justice had been unable to condemn him.

CHAPTER VII

THE TRIUMPH OF
LA MONTESPAN

Mme de Montespan, not only beautiful but endowed at that
time with a sharpness of wit which is said to be the prerogative of
the Rochechouarts, was arrogant, capricious, and the prey to
a temper which did not spare even the King. The Queen herself
experienced some of her arrogance and was often heard to say:
'This whore will be the death of me.'

DUCLOS: *Mémoires Secrets pour Servir à l'Histoire de Louis
XIV et de Louis XV*

PRINCIPAL PERSONALITIES MENTIONED IN CHAPTER VII

MME D'ELBEUF, niece of Turenne and mother of the man
who Mme de Sévigné referred to as 'le petit Elbeuf.'

COMTE DE SAINT-HILAIRE, lieutenant-General of Artillery
in Turenne's Army.

COMTE HAMILTON, Maréchal de Camp in the same Army.

COMTE DE LORGE DE DURFORT, nephew of Turenne, who
was to become a Marshal of France in 1676.

COMTE DE ROYE, another of Turenne's nephews.

MME DE SOUBISE, briefly the King's mistress (already mentioned in Chapter VI).

The DUCHESSE DE LA FERTÉ née DE LA MOTHEHOUDAN-
COURT, enamoured of the King.

MARIE ISABELLE DE LUDRE, CHANOINESSE DE POUSSAY,
a lady-in-waiting to the Queen, then to Madame (second
wife of the Duc d'Orléans).

PHILIPPE, CHEVALIER DE VENDÔME, brother of the Duc de Vendôme and Grand Prieur of France.

ISAAC DE BENSERADE, Court Poet to Louis XIV.

MARIANNE FRANÇOISE PAJOT, daughter of Mlle de Montpensier's apothecary.

LOUIS DE MEDAILLAN DE LESPARRE, MARQUIS DE MONTATAIRE.

It was one year, now, since La Vallière had left the Court. The Imperial troops had gained a foothold in Alsace, and it had needed Turenne's campaign of January 1675 to repel the invaders. For the first time since the beginning of the reign of Louis XIV, fortune in war had turned its back on the standards emblazoned with the fleurs de lys. The King was now thirty-seven years old and his health was unsatisfactory.

Some observations about the King's state of health appear in the Journal de la Santé du Roi *(edited successively by* Vallot, d'Aquin and Fagon) *for this year 1675:*

The beginning of this year and the end of last year after the solstice were foggy, there was little rain or hail, and a wind nearly always blew between midday and sunset, consequently a very great measure of humidity intruded itself into people's bodies and entered the brain, thus furnishing matter for obstinate colds and inflammation of the lungs, as we noted at the end of the season. And because these frequent changes of atmosphere did not permit His Majesty to take exercise out of doors, the King found himself to be rather heavy in spirit, and on January 7th he was attacked by a violent dizzy spell which left him with a kind of ague and a weakness in the thighs for the rest of that day, although these symptoms disappeared after he had enjoyed a good night's sleep. The ailment provided the occasion to represent to His Majesty his need for a purge.

Mme de Montespan's power was now at its height, although no one at the Court liked her particularly. The Princess Palatine, *Monsieur's second wife, made no attempt to conceal her dislike:*

La Montespan was whiter-complexioned than La Vallière; she had a beautiful mouth and fine teeth, but her expression was always insolent. One had only to look at her to see that she was scheming something. She had beautiful blonde hair, and lovely hands and arms, which La Vallière did not have, but at least La Vallière was clean in her person, whereas La Montespan was filthy . . .

Once Mme de Montespan was watching a military parade, and when the German soldiers marched past they began shouting '*Königs Hure, Hure!*' That evening, the King asked her how she had enjoyed the parade, and she replied: 'Very much indeed; only I find the Germans would perhaps be better advised not to call everything by its right name, since I had someone explain to me what they were shouting out.'

According to Mme de Caylus, this lovely woman was cold-hearted:

One day Mme de Montespan's carriage ran over a poor man while crossing the Pont Saint-Germain, and the other ladies who were with her, Mme de Montausier, Mme de Richelieu, Mme de Maintenon and some others, were all horror-struck, as would be natural on such an occasion. Only Mme de Montespan remained unmoved and even reproached the other ladies for showing alarm, saying: 'If your reactions were really the consequence of your kind-heartedness and compassionate nature, you would feel the same degree of regret at learning of a similar incident which had occurred far away from you.'

On April 11th, Maundy Thursday, a rumour started sweeping Versailles: Mme de Montespan had been refused absolution by a priest in the town!

Languet de Gergy, a protégé of Bossuet, who later became chaplain to the Duchesse de Bourgogne, explains in his Mémoires what actually happened:

Being at Versailles for the celebration of some solemn occasion, one of the women in Mme de Montespan's suite went to confess herself in the parish, and approached one of the officiating priests, a M. Lécuyer. The chambermaid, who was pious, was gratified with the quality of the instruction she had received from her confessor, and said so to Mme de Montespan on her return. The latter, hoping that this confessor would prove well-disposed towards her, resolved to have the same priest confess her, but was greatly astonished when she heard the holy man say to her: 'Can it be that same Mme de Montespan whose behaviour shocks the whole of France? Come, come, Madame, cease your scandalous conduct first, then come and throw yourself at the feet of the ministers of Jesus Christ!' These crushing words, uttered with uncompromising scorn for sinfulness, completely confounded her false piety, and she stormed out in a rage, and went straight to the King to complain and to demand revenge for the insult she had suffered. She was so ill-instructed in matters of religion that she claimed that a confessor was bound to receive any penitent and give absolution and had no power to refuse to do so. The King, better instructed than she, did not agree with her reasoning, and since she continued to argue he called for the Bishop of Meaux (it was M. Bossuet at that time). This prelate gave his decision without hesitation, stating that the confessor not only might refuse absolution, but was bound to do so in certain cases. He even went so far as to say that the situation in which the lady found herself was such that no confessor would feel able to grant her absolution.

What happened next is related by Mlle de Montpensier:

While we were at Versailles during Lent, at Easter-time, Mme de Montespan left the Court. We were all most surprised by this withdrawal. When I got back to Paris I went to visit her in the house the other side of the Vaugirard gates, where her children lived. Mme de Maintenon was with her. She was receiving no one. Everyone was aware that she had returned to Paris, though people were discreet enough not to mention the fact in public. However, it was known that M. Bossuet, at that time tutor to Monseigneur, went there every day, disguised under a capacious grey cloak.

And Mme de Scudéry *(the wife of Georges Scudéry) wrote, on April 16th, to Bussy-Rabutin:*

It is said that the King and Mme de Montespan have parted, despite their great mutual love, simply on a religious principle. It is said, too, that she will return to the Court, but will not be lodged at the Château and will never see the King except in the Queen's presence. I doubt whether such an arrangement could last for long, for a great danger would exist that love would regain the upper hand.

Which is exactly what happened, according to Mme Caylus:

The break between them occurred during a period when a jubilee was being celebrated.[1] The King possessed a religious sense which never abandoned him even during the periods of his most extreme misconduct with women, while indulging the one weakness in his character. He was otherwise absolutely sober and steadfast in his conduct, and heard Mass every day of his life, except on two occasions only while he was leading the army in battle.

Well, when the day of this Jubilee I have mentioned arrived, these two lovers, troubled by their consciences, decided—or thought they had decided—to part. Mme de Montespan came to Paris, visited churches, fasted, prayed and wept for her sins. The King, too, resigned himself to this separation in a truly Christian spirit. When the Jubilee, however inappropriate it may have been, was over, the question was raised as to whether Mme de Montespan could properly return to the Court. The opinion of her relatives and friends, even the most virtuous, was that she should return: her birth and rank demanded her presence there, and she could live there in no less Christian a fashion than elsewhere. The Bishop of Meaux agreed, not realizing apparently that flight is the sole solution in such cases. One difficulty remained: how could Mme de Montespan appear before the King unprepared? It should be arranged for them to see each other privately before meeting in public, to avoid the embarrassment which a surprise encounter might have caused.

[1] The writer's recollection appears confused: the Jubilee was celebrated in 1676, and all other witnesses agree that the favourite's provisional dismissal occurred in April 1675.

Following this line of reasoning, it was thought best that the King should visit Mme de Montespan in her own house, but it was agreed that in order to avoid the slightest breath of suspicion he should be accompanied by some of the most respectable and high-minded ladies of the Court, who would be present during the interview, so that the King and Mme de Montespan should not be left alone.

The King visited Mme de Montespan, as arranged, but during their conversation he gradually drew her into a window recess. They talked together in low voices for a long time, wept, and behaved in exactly the way that reunited lovers behave. Finally, the King bowed deeply to these venerable ladies, while Mme de Montespan made a low curtsey to them, and they then passed into an adjoining room. . . . The result of this reunion was Mme la Duchesse d'Orléans—on whose face and in whose spirit it is impossible not to perceive traces of this struggle between love and the Jubilee; the Comte de Toulouse came later.

Apropos of the Duchesse d'Orléans—she assumed the title on marrying the son of Monsieur, Duc d'Orléans and future Regent of France—the Princess Palatine had some doubts about the circumstances of her birth, and writes:

I once knew a German gentleman, dead now for a long time, who swore to me that Mme la Duchesse was the daughter not of the King but of the Maréchal de Noailles. He marked the exact day and hour when he saw the marshal enter La Montespan's house, and Mme la Duchesse was born exactly nine months later. This German was named Bettendorf. He was a brigadier in the Guards. He was mounting guard before La Montespan's door when the marshal, who was captain of the company, arrived and went in.

On June 4th, Mlle de La Vallière made her profession in the Order of Carmelites in the rue Saint-Jacques; Mme de Scudéry comments:

And then I was present when Mlle de La Vallière took the veil. She performed the action with great piety. I think she

never looked more beautiful or more content. She should be
happy if only because she no longer has to lace up Mme de
Montespan's stays. If the truth be told, she was a real martyr.

And Mme de Sévigné:

This beautiful and courageous person performed this action,
just as she performed all her actions in life, in a noble and
charming manner. Everyone present was astonished at her
beauty; but even more astonished that M. de Condom's sermon
was by no means as divine as had been anticipated.

*Mme de Montespan was back at the Court, and the Château
of Clagny was being constructed for her near Versailles. On
June 28th, Mme de* Sévigné *wrote to her daughter:*

Your judgment is excellent regarding the *Quantonova*: if
she is astute enough not to return to her old ways, she will
secure so much power and glory that the peak of her achievements will rise above the clouds. . . .

And on July 3rd:

You cannot imagine the extent of her triumph, surrounded
by her workmen, who number twelve hundred. The palace of
Apollidonus and the gardens of Armida combined may give
some faint indication of the splendour of this place. The wife
of her steadfast friend [i.e. the Queen] visits her, as does the
rest of the royal family in turn. She is elevated above all the
duchesses, that is a fact.

Primi Visconti *records that during July:*

The King visited Clagny for the first time and lunched in
private with Mme de Montespan, not having seen her alone
since Easter.

While there, he received the news of Turenne's death. The
pious ones immediately attributed this misfortune to the re-
newal by the King of his sinful behaviour. That evening, while
the courtiers were crowded round the table where the King

was accustomed to dine, he appeared and immediately said in a tone of great gravity: 'We have lost the father of our country.' All those present became pale and remained silent.

Turenne was killed at Salzbach on July 27th, and the whole country went into mourning. Mme de Sévigné *wrote to her daughter on August 28:*

Mme d'Elbeuf is staying for a few days with the Cardinal de Bouillon, and asked me yesterday to dine with them so that we might speak of their affliction. Mme de La Fayette was also present. We all said what was in our hearts and wept a great deal. She had a beautifully painted portrait of the great hero, which she showed to the gentlemen of his suite who all arrived at eleven o'clock. These poor people were heart-broken and already clad in mourning dress. Three gentlemen who saw the portrait were so affected that they seemed about to swoon, and sobbed out aloud. . . . When one of the gentle-men was sufficiently composed, we asked him our sad questions and he told us the details of the Marshal's death.

That evening, he wished to confess, and gave out the orders for the evening before entering the confessional. He intended to take Holy Communion the following day, a Sunday. With the aim of engaging the enemy, he mounted his horse at two o'clock that Saturday, after taking a meal. He was accompanied by a great number of his officers, but made them all wait thirty paces away from the high ground from which he wished to survey the scene. He told the young Elbeuf: 'Nephew, remain where you are, you are circling me so often you will have me recognized by the enemy.' M. d'Hamilton was close to the spot he was making for, and called out to him: 'Monsieur, come this way, you are liable to be fired upon in the direction you are going.' 'Monsieur,' he replied, 'I will certainly withdraw, since I do not in the least wish to be killed today.' While turning his horse he noticed Saint-Hilaire, who doffed his hat and said to him: 'Please cast a glance at the battery I have just set up over there.' Our heroic leader began to back his horse up, and while still in motion was struck by the shot which had just severed Saint-Hilaire's arm with its hand still holding the hat, and now pierced his own body after

breaking his arm. Saint-Hilaire was still looking at him. He
did not fall off immediately but was carried off by his horse
towards the spot where he had left the young Elbeuf, slumped
over the horse's pommel; suddenly the horse pulled up sharp
and he fell into the arms of his followers. He opened his eyes
wide twice, opened his mouth, then expired. Part of his heart
had been torn away. M. d'Hamilton ordered that the confusion
of shouting and lamenting should cease, and also took away the
young Elbeuf, who had prostrated himself on the body,
clutching at it and quite hysterical with grief. A cloak was
thrown over the corpse, and it was carried to a nearby thicket,
where those present stood silently around it, awaiting a carriage to transport it to the Marshal's own tent. There, M. de
Lorge, M. de Roye and many others gazed grief-stricken at the
remains, but realized that they must put aside their grief and
think of the weighty matters of war which confronted them.
A military service was conducted in the camp, and the atmosphere of grief and despair was indescribable. . . . Another scene
of mourning followed when the body was transported away
from the army: everywhere the cortège passed there were
demonstrations of grief, culminating in the arrival of the coffin
at Langres, where those escorting the body, more than two
hundred strong, preceded it, in mourning dress, followed by
the local populace. All the clergy wore ceremonial garb and
conducted a solemn service in the town, covering the expenses,
which amounted to 5,000 francs, by raising a collection, which
was soon done, and enabled them also to conduct the procession to the next town and pay the expenses of all those taking
part.

*People were beginning to talk about Mme de Montespan's
protégée, the widow Scarron, who had been granted the estate
of Maintenon by the King, and thenceforward assumed the
name of her new property. She had cared devotedly for the
children of the love affair, and during the summer she used to
take the crippled little Duc du Maine to take the waters at
Barrège. Mme de Sévigné, writing on August 7, 1675, had this
to say about the relationship between the favourite and the
governess:*

5. *Nicolas Fouquet,*
by Bourdon

*Jean Baptiste
Colbert*

6.
Louis, Duc de Saint-Simon,
by Vanloo

Jean Molière
by Mignard

This beautiful friendship between Mme de Montespan and her *amie*, who are on voyage at present, has in fact been a positive aversion for the last two years, an unshakeable bitterness and antipathy. You may well ask the reason: here it is. *L'amie* is so proud that she has rebelled against the other's orders. She takes no pleasure in obeying the mother but would be only too delighted to please the father. She travels for his sake, not at all for love of her. *L'amie* is blamed for being too friendly with this vainglorious creature, but no one thinks it will last long. . . . This news has been a supreme secret for the past six months but is now spreading gradually.

The King was no longer concealing his friendship for the governess, and another letter from Mme de Sévigné *to her daughter informs us that* l'amie *is 'even more triumphant than the other' (i.e. Mme de Montespan):*

She has won over everyone; all of her neighbour's chambermaids are entirely loyal to her, and one will hold out her cosmetic jar, kneeling in front of her, while a second brings her gloves and a third soothes her to sleep. She acknowledges nobody's presence and I think that, in her heart, she must be laughing at all this subservience.

Meanwhile, Mme de Montespan found herself contending with rivals who do not appear to have given her much cause for alarm, according to Mme de Caylus:

It is true that the King was not the most faithful lover in the world and conducted several other love affairs during his liaison with Mme de Montespan, but she seemed quite unconcerned and mentioned them only when of ill-humour or else to amuse herself. I am not sure that she was so indifferent to the intervention of Mme de Soubise, although she gave no signs of caring. Mme de Montespan discovered this intrigue through Mme de Soubise's habit of wearing a certain pair of emerald pendant earrings each time that M. de Soubise had just left for Paris. Noticing this, she kept a close watch on the King's movements and found that the earrings were indeed a signal for a rendezvous. Mme de Soubise's husband was made of different stuff than that of Mme de Montespan's, so these precautions were necessary.

This husband had eleven children by his wife, and Primi Visconti *remarked that:*

Her continual pregnancies disrupted the King's amorous inclinations, since she was no longer beautiful while pregnant. Otherwise, she was beautiful, with a fine figure, but she had red hair.

This particular love affair of the King's did not last long. Mme de Sévigné, *on September 2, 1676, noted that:*

... The vision of Mme de Soubise passed by quicker than a flash of lightning. Reconciliation is complete. The other day, at the gaming table, *Quanto* was leaning her head affectionately on the shoulder of her *ami*. This affection was doubtless meant to convey to everyone that she was more securely entrenched than ever.

But on September 30th she wrote:

It is generally believed that *l'ami* is no longer in love, and that *Quanto* hesitates between the consequences which would follow a return to favour and the danger of no longer asserting her interests and so provoking a search elsewhere. Apart from that, she resists the idea of the relationship becoming one of friendship: so much beauty combined with so much pride could hardly bear to accept the second place. Jealousy is rife, but jealousy has never prevented events taking their course. There is no doubt that the good woman [Mme de Soubise] has been favoured at least with glances and gestures and, although everything you say about her is perfectly true, the fact remains that she is A RIVAL and that is already a great deal. Most people think that she has more sense than to raise the standard of such perfidy, with so little likelihood of enjoying it for long.

If one is to believe Saint-Simon, Mme de Soubise was to retain the King's friendship long after their brief affair was over:

Her charms had made it possible for her to gain a close insight into the King's secret thoughts, and she was able to make use most advantageously of this knowledge as a result of the close relationship which still existed between them. Her ambition led her to give herself to the King to the degree that his devotion to the other would permit him, and she was content to enjoy his favour when his devotion resolved him to repudiate her, knowing well how to put the King at his ease and even to make use of his devotion to the other to improve her own position, under the pretext of keeping her husband ignorant of past events, despite the fact that his ignorance was entirely feigned.

But many other women were pestering the unfortunate King; according to Primi Visconti:

The one who really annoyed the King was the Duchesse de la Ferté, who followed him everywhere and wooed him in public as I might flirt with a young girl. To make matters worse, the Duc de la Ferté arrived at a Court ball one day, masked, with a pair of horns set with diamonds attached to his forehead. The King ignored these antics. But, one day at Versailles, when he was about to go on an outing, he asked that the Princesse de Soubise should be invited to join him in the Queen's carriage, in which he was sitting. La Ferté, who was present, was so overcome with rage against Mme de Soubise that she exclaimed aloud: 'She is too old by now to lay any claim to him.' La Soubise turned to the King and said: 'Your Majesty witnessed the manner in which I was insulted?' The King replied: 'I will remedy that.' Later, he made it clear to the Maréchal de la Mothe that his daughter, Mme de La Ferté, bored him and that she was excluded from the Court.

At the beginning of 1676, a new favourite put in an appearance. The Princess Palatine *described her thus:*

Mme de Ludre, who had been the King's mistress, was an extremely beautiful woman. She was the maid-of-honour of my predecessor and, after her death, of the Queen. When the Chamber of Maids-of-Honour was disbanded, Monsieur retained the two young ladies who had gone from his suite to that of the King, that is to say Mlle de Ludre and Mlle de Dampierre. Mlle de Ludre had the title of Madame because she was a canoness in Lorraine.

The King had paid no attention to this belle while she was with the Queen, but he became enamoured of her as soon as she joined my retinue. Her reign lasted two years. La Montespan warned the King that Ludre had skin blemishes all over her body, resulting from a poison which Mme de Cantecroix had tried to make her take when she was still only twelve or thirteen years old, at a time when the old Duc de Lorraine was so infatuated with this child that he wanted to marry her. Apparently the poison exploded and splashed over her, marking her skin from head to foot. As a result, the marriage was prevented. The appearance of her face was saved by careful medical attention, but from time to time she still has attacks of sickness from the effects of the poison on her skin.

And Primi Visconti:

I saw her often, and was even her confidant at the time she was being courted by the Chevalier de Vendôme, although she refused to entertain his proposals unless they involved marriage. The chevalier decided that her claims were set too high, despite the fact that the old Duc de Lorraine had had ambitions to marry her. . . .

Acting on no other grounds but the general opinion that she was the object of the King's affections, all the princesses and duchesses used to rise to their feet when she approached, even in the presence of the Queen, and sat down again only when Mme de Ludre made the appropriate gesture, in exactly the same way as used to happen with Mme de Montespan. It was this mark of distinction offered to Mme de Ludre which allowed the Queen to discover the King's latest infidelity, since no one had thought of mentioning the matter to her . . .

The Queen had become inured to these infidelities, but Mme

de Montespan's rage knew no bounds. At the Tuileries, I have seen Mme de Ludre and Mme de Thianges look daggers at each other. Mme de Montespan did her utmost to discredit her rival, but in the end Mme de Ludre compounded her own destruction: her only adviser was a poet named Benserade and her confidante was a certain Marianne, married to a certain Montataire. They were a curious pair of worthless associates. This woman Marianne, desiring to advance her husband's cause, persuaded Mme de Ludre to use him as an intermediary between herself and the King. His Majesty was so astonished to find himself confronted by Montataire that he immediately broke off relations with Mme de Ludre and sent word to her that she should withdraw to a convent, offering her 200,000 livres which she was reluctant to accept.

Bussy-Rabutin *also mentions this refusal:*

If Mme de Ludre's refusal of the present offered her helps to bring her lover back to her, then I shall consider her to be remarkably artful. Otherwise, I shall say with old Senneterre that an honourable nature does not put a shirt on a man's back. Or: those who lack bread have no business appointing generals.

And Mme de Sévigné *celebrated La Montespan's final victory in a letter dated June 11, 1677:*

Ah, my child, what a triumph at Versailles! what reinforced pride! what a solid establishment; what a second Duchesse de Valentinois! What pleasure, even, resulting from the whole history of misunderstanding and absence! what a recovery of possession! I spent a whole hour in her apartment: she was lying in bed, fully dressed and made-up, taking her rest before the *medianoche* [midnight supper]. I presented her your compliments, and she answered most kindly, praising you highly. Upstairs, her sister, arrogating to herself all the pride of Nikë, cast mocking reflections upon the unhappy Io [Mme de Ludre] and laughed at the idea that she could have been so bold as to complain about her. Just picture to yourself everything that selfish pride can suggest in its moment of triumph, and you will not be far from the mark.

It is said that the young woman will soon resume her former place among the ladies that attend upon Madame. She was seen yesterday, taking a solitary walk with La Moreuil, in the garden of the Maréchal du Plessis . . .

THE BRINVILLIERS SCANDAL

The atrociousness of the crimes and the quality of the accused person demand absolutely positive proof.

NIVELLE, advocate of the Marquise de Brinvilliers

PRINCIPAL PERSONALITIES MENTIONED IN CHAPTER VIII

NICOLAS DE LA REYNIE, First Lieutenant of Police at Paris.

NICOLAS DESMARETS, nephew of Colbert. Later Comptroller-General of Finance.

MARIE MAGDELEINE D'AUBRAY, MARQUISE DE BRINVILLIERS, daughter of a Counsellor of State, accused of having poisoned her father and her brothers.

GODIN, called Sainte-Croix, alchemist, lover of Mme de Brinvilliers.

BRIANCOURT, secretary of Mme de Brinvilliers, and her accuser.

GUILLAUME DE LAMOIGNON, Premier Président of the Parlement of Paris.

PIERRE LOUIS DE REICH, SEIGNEUR DE PÉNAUTIER, Receveur Général du Clergé and Trésorier de la Bourse of the States of Languedoc.

MME DE LIONNE, wife of Secretary of State Hugues de Lionne (already mentioned in Chapter VI).

PALLUAU and MAUDAT, commissioners of the King, who interrogated Mme de Brinvilliers.

The Court occasionally allowed itself to be moved by the miserable conditions which were the lot of the common people throughout the kingdom. A typical incident is described by Mme de Sévigné:

Here is a little story of something that happened three days ago: a poor passementerie maker of the Faubourg Saint-Marceau was taxed ten écus for mastership dues; he did not have the money, and was pressed relentlessly for payment. When he asked for time to pay, he was refused, and they came and seized his humble possessions—bedstead and porringer. Seeing himself destitute, he went mad with rage and despair and cut the throats of three of his children who were in the room; his wife rescued the fourth child and escaped. The wretched man is in the Châtelet, and will be hanged in a few days. He says that his one regret is not to have killed his wife and the child she saved. I swear to you, daughter, that this is as true as if you had seen the whole thing with your own eyes . . .

But the official version, that of Nicolas de La Reynie, First Lieutenant of Police of Paris, writing to Colbert, differed somewhat:

Monsieur Desmarets has written to me by your order, Monsieur, that you have been informed of rumours concerning a miserable ribbon-maker of the Faubourg Saint-Marcel who is supposed to have killed or wounded four of his children, and concerning a menacing gathering of sellers of eau-de-vie. Regarding these matters, I have the honour to inform you that various ill-disposed individuals have attempted to insinuate that a demand made to this poor artisan for payment of tax made him so desperate that in his madness he wanted to kill his wife and children; it is also asserted that a great crowd of people were present at the scene of the crime.

However, Monsieur, in accordance with your instructions, no taxes of any kind have been levied on any artisan of Paris. I have even taken the step, following your orders, of making it clear to this community of ribbon-makers, which is both numerous and impoverished, that they were free to continue

following their customary way of life. So it is very certain
that no such tax demand was made, and that the dreadful event
resulted solely from a fit of madness which seized the unfortunate man and which has been very evident since his arrest.
There is no more truth, either, in the story that his house was
thronged with people at the time; all that happened is that a
crowd gathered after the incident, as is usual in cases where
something extraordinary is known to have occurred. The
district superintendent makes regular reports to me on the
daily events in his area, and if any such event had occurred,
you can be sure that I would not have failed to give you a full
account.

The people, who habitually seize upon these kind of un-
usual tragedies, have set up their version in doggerel on the
Pont Neuf and have distributed a song-sheet. I have ordered
all those that are found to be torn down or confiscated,
although these broadsheets speak only of the tragedy that a
father should be so cruel as to kill his own children.

*But soon the Court was to be enthralled by a more serious
matter: Marie Magdeleine d'Aubray, daughter of a Counsellor
of State, married to the Marquise de Brinvilliers, was accused
of having poisoned her father and her two brothers so as to
inherit the family fortune.*

*The affair began in 1672, with the death of Godin, known
as Sainte-Croix, a former captain, an alchemist, and Mme de
Brinvilliers' lover. Among his effects was found a small case
filled with phials of poison, together with a note asking that
the case should be handed over to his mistress, who had meanwhile fled to England.*

*In March 1676, she was arrested at Liège and brought to
Paris. Sensational revelations were generally anticipated, since
Sainte-Croix was suspected of having placed his phials of
poison at the disposal of some highly-placed individuals.*

*On April 29th, the Marquise de Brinvilliers appeared, by
virtue of her privilege of nobility, before the highest jurisdiction of the kingdom: Grande Chambre and Tournelle sitting
together. Père Pirot, Jesuit and Docteur en Sorbonne, who
had been appointed to assist the accused during the final stage
of her trial, relates how he came to receive this commission:*

On Tuesday, July 14, 1676, the P.P. [Premier Président Lamoignon] sent Père de Chevigny to me to require my attendance at his house. . . . We were shown into his library, and shortly afterwards he joined us there. He did me the honour of telling me that the task he had in mind for me represented the greatest possible mark I could have of his confidence in me, that the commission with which he wished to charge me was extremely painful, that he was fully aware of its difficulty and regretted having to ask me to undertake it.

What we ask of you, he continued, is to have the charity to help prepare Mme de Brinvilliers for death, since it seems almost certain that we shall be bound to condemn her to the supreme penalty. We may say this without prejudice because although we have not yet seen her on the *sellette*, she will appear on its tomorrow, and apparently the death sentence is sure to be pronounced. By that time, it will be too late to take the necessary measures to provide her with the help of which we believe her to be in need in order to die in a Christian manner. It is for this reason that we thought best to speak to you today.

Her mentality dismays us. We worked yesterday on her case until eight in the evening: she was confronted in the chamber with Briancourt for thirteen hours on end, and today for a further five hours, and she has withstood these confrontations in the most self-assured manner possible. She showed great respect for the judges, but complete contempt for the witness with whom she had been confronted, accusing him of being a valet, a chronic drunkard who had been dismissed as a result of his dissolute behaviour, asserting that it was intolerable that his evidence against her should be heard at all, mocking him for the tears that he was now shedding at the memory of her brothers' deaths, while he accused her of having admitted to him that she had poisoned them, and telling him that he was a villain to weep in front of all these gentlemen and that such hypocrisy sprang from a base and ignoble character. She said all this without passion, and during the whole five hours that we observed her today, her calm expression never varied.

There you see, Monsieur, he continued, the bold or rather callous soul which we have to place in your hands. We pray that God's grace may touch her, but we are also concerned, for the sake of the public, that her crimes should die with her, and that she should make a full confession which will prevent any possible continuation of these crimes. Otherwise we shall not be able to ensure that her poisons do not continue to do her service after her death. We are not asking you to express your personal feelings on this matter, we wish simply to represent to you what is the public interest.

Why was the public interest invoked? Why was it so important that La Brinvillier's crimes should die with her? Because some fairly exalted individuals were in danger of being compromised in the affair, notably Pierre Louis de Reich, Seigneur de Pénautier, Trésorier de la Bourse of the States of Languedoc and Receveur Général du Clergé. A letter from him had been found in Sainte-Croix's case. And after the death of his alchemist friend he had visited Mme de Brinvilliers and handed over a large sum of money to her. In this connection, Primi Visconti *reported:*

Rumour has it that Mme d'Aubray's [Brinvilliers's] misdeeds and secrets have been so thoroughly brought to light that Pénautier cannot escape involvement. He is the son-in-law of Counsellor Le Boults, who had already extricated him from a criminal charge of the same nature once before; this Counsellor had so much influence at the Parlement that the King is supposed to have remarked: 'If I was involved in a lawsuit with Le Boults, I would lose the case.' This Pénautier was suspected of having poisoned M. de Saint-Laurent, so as to obtain the post of Receveur Général of Languedoc. Mme de Lionne lived in a house where Pénautier had once lodged; one day, while completing her toilet in front of her mirror, worms started dropping on her from the ceiling. A search discovered the head of a corpse. Some claimed that it was the head of the lackey who had proffered Saint-Laurent the drink containing the poison and whom Pénautier had effectively silenced by killing him, pretending that the man had left for Italy. But Pénautier had removed suspicion from himself by convincing the authorities that it was only an anatomical figure.

The cause of Pénautier's arrest was the discovery of a note signed by him in Sainte-Croix's poison-case. But he was a man with money and friends. When the trial was about to begin, the Counsellor Le Boults paid 10,000 écus to Mme d'Aubray on his behalf, although she was no longer counting on him, considering him to be a bankrupt debtor. The widow of Saint-Laurent, who had been making a great fuss with petitions, suddenly shut her mouth. And, in fact, at the end of one year Pénautier was out of prison again.

The King is supposed to have stated that a man with four millions to his name would never be found guilty by the Parlement. Louvois hated Pénautier because he was an ally of Colbert's, and Pénautier had acquired a bad reputation through trying to buy Court offices for Sainte-Croix. You should know that Pénautier's outward appearance of being an honourable gentleman, aided by all the loans and gifts of money he has made, are sufficient to have the entire French clergy flock to his support, for he is their Receveur Général.

It transpired that Mme de Brinvilliers had indeed been a close friend of Pénautier's. On April 29th, she wrote him a letter from prison which was intercepted:

I learn through my friend that you intend to help me in this matter in which I am involved. Believe me, your intervention would make me eternally grateful to you, coming on top of all your kindnesses of the past. This is why, Monsieur, if you have this intention, I beg you to act without delay and to discuss with the individuals who will come to see you how best you may go about arranging matters. I feel it would be prudent that you should not show yourself too much in public, but your friends must be kept informed of your whereabouts, for the Counsellor has questioned me at length about your activities.

Pénautier was finally arrested on June 15th. And Mme de Sévigné wrote to her daughter on July 10, 1676:

Pénautier has been confronted with La Brinvilliers. It was a most melancholy interview, since they were accustomed to meet in more agreeable circumstances! She has so often threatened that, if she dies, she will make many others die with her, that there is little doubt she will say enough to seal his fate, or at least to have him put to the question, which is a dreadful thing. This man has a vast number of influential friends, to whom he did favours while holding his two posts. Nobody doubts that money is flying in all directions, but if he is convicted not even money can save him.

Père Pirot *persuaded his charge to confess her crimes, and described the penitent's change of heart:*

Monsieur, she said to me, let me be left in peace until to-morrow. I will reveal my criminal activities to M. Palluau. I will confess to him that I did poison my father, that I did have my brothers poisoned, and that I intended to poison my sister. I cannot tell you the ingredients of the poisons which I used and which were used on my orders: all I know is that toads were used in one recipe, and that others consisted entirely of rarefied arsenic.

The confessor then raised the question of the guilt of Pénautier, whom the Marquise had accused:

Monsieur, she said, I have no knowledge at all that he had commerce with Sainte-Croix about poisons, and I could not accuse him of such involvement without betraying my conscience. But since a note from him was found in the poison-case, and since I have seen him countless times in Sainte-Croix's presence, I thought it possible that their friendship had extended to a trafficking in poison. With this doubt in my mind, I took the risk of writing to him as though I already knew him to be guilty in this respect, since this could do me no harm in my present position. I reckoned to myself thus: if they were indeed allies in the trafficking of poisons, Pénautier would think that I knew of his involvement, writing to him in those terms, and that that would persuade him to act on my behalf in his own interests, for fear that I should betray his guilt and, on the other hand, if he was innocent, my letter was of no consequence to him and could not harm him. —I would risk nothing but the indignation of someone who was far from declaring his support for me or offering me any aid, even had I never written him a word.

Père Pirot *adds:*

I did not witness her interrogation, and do not know what was the substance of her declaration, but when she was returned to my charge she assured me that she had told all she knew, and that she had affirmed to the commissioners Palluau and Maudat that had I seen her earlier she would have confessed everything that much earlier. After her interrogation she was put to the question. I did not see her from half-past seven in the morning until two in the afternoon, when she reappeared, deeply affected by what she had undergone, her face, which was usually so pale, burning red, her eyes glowing, her mouth set in a grimace, her heart beating feebly.

And here are the last moments of the Marquise de Brin-villiers. On July 16th, her confessor accompanied her on to the scaffold and made her repeat a final prayer for the redemption of her soul:

'My soul emerged from you, Lord, may it enter into you again. You are its origin and its principle. If it please you, Lord God, remain its centre and its end.'

It seemed to me that she had only just repeated after me the last of these words when I heard a dull thud which made me cease speaking. This was the death stroke administered by the executioner. He severed her head so skilfully that I did not even see the blade descend, although my gaze was directed at the head which he had just cut off. I still do not know what kind of an instrument it was that he used, having never seen it either sheathed or unsheathed. The noise of the stroke was like that of a butcher's cleaver chopping meat on a block. I never noticed that the executioner had felt her neck to judge the best point at which to strike. He said nothing to Mme de B., who was kneeling there with her neck stretched out. He severed it so neatly that it remained for an instant on the trunk before falling. Indeed, I feared for a moment that the executioner had misaimed and would have to strike a second time.

But my fear was immediately dispelled when the head fell on to the floor of the scaffold, rolling slightly backwards and leftwards, while the trunk fell forward on top of a plank which had been placed in front of her, crosswise. I observed all this without horror, and was quite unaffected by the sight of the head lying there at one side, with very little blood issuing from it, and the body lying nearby, also with very little blood issuing from it.

A great number of courtiers witnessed the execution, including Mme de Sévigné:

At last it is all over. La Brinvilliers is in the air; after her execution her poor little body was thrown on to a great pile of faggots and burnt, and her ashes were dispersed by the wind, so that whenever we breathe we shall inhale some particles of her, and by the communication of the minute spirits we shall be infected with the desire of poisoning, to our great surprise. . . . At six o'clock, she had been carried in a cart, naked under her shift, and with a rope round her neck, to Notre Dame, to perform the *amende honorable*, after which she was put again into the same cart, where I saw her lying back against a heap of straw, in her shift, and with a nun's cornet on her head, with a holy man on one side of her and the executioner on the other. Indeed, the sight made me shudder. Those who saw the execution say she mounted the scaffold with great courage. I was on the Pont Notre-Dame with the Baronne d'Escars. Never have so many people been seen in Paris, and never has the city been so excited by a single event or followed events with such single-minded attention.

CHAPTER IX

A DAY AT VERSAILLES

Those who imagine that these are merely matters of ceremony
are gravely mistaken. The peoples over whom we reign, being
unable to apprehend the basic reality of things, usually derive
their opinions from what they can see with their eyes.

LOUIS XIV

PRINCIPAL PERSONALITIES MENTIONED IN CHAPTER IX

LOUIS DE LORRAINE, COMTE D'ARMAGNAC, Grand Écuyer
of France, known as 'Monsieur le Grand'.

JACQUES LOUIS DE BERINGHEN, COMTE DE CHÂTEAU-
NEUF.

PHILIPPE DE COURCILLON, MARQUIS DE DANGEAU (see
the Table of Sources).

MME D'ELBEUF, niece of Turenne (already mentioned in
Chapter VII).

*How did the Court at Versailles live? From 1672 onwards,
the Court was usually centred at Versailles, but not continuously, since the King still made stays at Saint-Germain and
Fontainebleau, making the voyage in a massive moving operation, with armies of carriages and carts transferring from one
palace to the other everything considered necessary for the
royal comfort and pleasures, including furniture, theatre
scenery and props, and even tapestries taken down from the
walls. At the beginning of the reign, the gazetteer Loret
described such a journey:*

> To give last week a novel start
> A suite of coaches did depart
> With all the luggage of the King
> Who next day too went travelling,
> And from that desert all did go,
> From vast and lovely Fontainebleau.

Primi Visconti, *who lived at the Court from 1673 onwards, recorded with amazement the sight of the King and his suite setting out on such a journey:*

It is a fine spectacle to see Louis XIV setting out, surrounded by his Royal Guard, carriages, horses, courtiers, valets and a great throng of people, all in a state of complete confusion, running and shouting around him. It is exactly like the queen bee leaving her hive accompanied by her swarm.

Visconti *goes on to describe the daily routine involved in the King's life at Versailles:*

All his daily actions are strictly regulated. He always arises at eight o'clock, and remains with his Council from ten o'clock until midday, when he and the Queen attend Mass, accompanied by members of the royal family. At one o'clock, after hearing Mass, he visits his favourites until two o'clock, at which hour he dines, always with the Queen and always in public. The rest of the afternoon he spends hunting or taking the air, and very often he holds another Council. From nightfall until ten o'clock he converses with the ladies, or plays cards, or attends a play or a ball. At eleven o'clock, after supper, he returns once more to the apartments of his favourites. He always sleeps with the Queen. Thus he divides the hours of his day and his night between his public affairs, his pleasures, his devotions and his duties.

To hope to obtain a favour from the King, it was necessary to station oneself somewhere where he was due to pass by—preferably as he was leaving the Cabinet du Conseil. The method of obtaining an audience with Louis XIV during that

period has been described by François Grandet, Counsellor at
the Présidial¹ of Angers, who later became mayor of that city.
According to his account, he had gone to Paris, in February
1676, to intercede in favour of the priests of the Angers
seminary, threatened with expulsion by their Jansenist bishop.
Having won the support of the Archbishop of Paris, it was
arranged that he should be presented to the King by the Grand
Écuyer of France, the Comte d'Armagnac:

A moment before His Majesty was due to leave the Cabinet
du Conseil, M. le Grand went in and approached the captain
of the Guards unit then on duty, asking his permission to
present me, which he immediately agreed to. Moreover, he
left his post, where he was awaiting the King, and approached
me to ask if I was the person of whom M. d'Armagnac had
spoken to him. When I replied in the affirmative he informed
me that I was not well placed, because as soon as the King left
the Cabinet to go to Mass, the throng of courtiers following
him would prevent me getting near enough to speak to him.
He said that I should take up a position at the threshold of the
door which connects the King's Apartment with the Salle des
Gardes, and that since the Salle des Gardes was both broad
and long, those accompanying would disperse somewhat and
I would be free to speak with the King at leisure . . .

The moment that the King reached the doorway where I
was standing, M. d'Armagnac assisted me by approaching the
King and telling him that I was the person His Majesty had
ordered him to present to him. I bowed, holding my petition
in one hand, and explained to His Majesty the substance of
the matter, while the King, slackening his pace, gave me all
his attention. Seeing that I was still holding my petition in my
hand instead of presenting it to him, His Majesty said to me:
'Give me your petition, and be assured that these gentlemen
will receive full justice.'

Now without my petition, I went downstairs and towards
the Chapel, where I related my good fortune to M. de
Châteauneuf, who had come up to me to ask what the King

---

¹ A tribunal composed of at least nine counsellors or judges, which tried
minor civil actions, and sometimes crimes of brigandage. The Présidiaux
were instituted by Henri II in 1551.

had said to me. When I told him that I had handed over my petition to the King at his command, he said: 'Your audience was completely wasted: when the King changes his clothes this afternoon, before going hunting, the petition will remain in the pocket of the first coat, and it will be as good as lost.'

Mass was celebrated in the Chapel. La Bruyère *has described the scene, with the King kneeling down on a velvet cushion, in the Royal Tribune facing the altar:*

The great ones of the nation assemble each day, at a certain hour, in a temple which they call a church. At the far end of this temple is an altar consecrated to their God, at which a priest celebrates sacred and redoubtable mysteries named saints. The great ones form a vast circle at the foot of this altar and remain standing, their backs turned to the priest and the holy mysteries, and their faces lifted towards their king, who is to be seen on his knees in a tribune; and it seems that their minds and their hearts are concentrated on him alone. This procedure would seem to indicate a sort of subordination, for the people appear to adore the prince and the prince to adore God.

Then came the main meal, an important affair if we are to judge by the number of employees of the Service de la Bouche (the royal table) which totalled 498. The King had a robust appetite, and according to the Princess Palatine:

I have often seen the King eat four plates of soup of different kinds, a whole pheasant, a partridge, a large plate of salad, two thick slices of ham, a dish of mutton in a garlic-flavoured sauce, a plateful of pastries and then fruit and hard-boiled eggs. Both the King and Monsieur are exceedingly fond of hard-boiled eggs.

And, in a later observation, she speaks of the royal table manners:

The Duc de Bourgogne [the Dauphine's son] and his two brothers had been taught the polite innovation of using a fork while eating. But when they were invited to the King's table at supper, he would have none of it and forbade them to use such a tool. He would never have had occasion to reproach me in that matter, for I have never in my life used anything to eat with but my knife and my fingers.

Saint-Simon has described the ceremonial surrounding the service of dinner:

The dinner was always *à petit couvert*, that is to say by himself in his room, at a square table . . . The meal was fairly substantial, for in the morning he ordered either a *petit couvert* or a *très petit couvert* to be prepared, though even the latter comprised a number of dishes, and three separate courses, not counting fruit. When the table had been set, the principal courtiers entered the room, followed by others who had permission to attend. Then the First Gentleman of the Chamber went to inform the King that the meal was ready to be served, and served the meal himself, if the Grand Chamberlain was not there . . .

I have often seen Monsieur, either just arrived from Saint-Cloud to see the King, or else coming from the *conseil des dépêches*, enter the room alone, hand the King his napkin and remain standing. A little later, the King, noticing that he was not going away again, would ask him if he would not like to be seated, whereupon Monsieur would bow and the King would order a chair to be brought. A *tabouret*[1] was then placed behind him. A few moments later the King would say to him: 'Brother, be seated.' Monsieur would bow again, and remain seated until the King had finished his meal, continuing to present the napkin to him.

It should be noted that Molière never ate with the King (any more than did anyone else); the story about Louis XIV welcoming the playwright to his table was invented by Mme Campan, the teacher of Louis XV's daughters. Saint-Simon states categorically:

Except when with the Army, the King never ate in company

[1] A kind of folding stool provided for those privileged to sit in the presence of the King.

with any other man, wherever he may have been, not even with the Princes of the Blood, although when one of the princes married, the King sometimes arranged a wedding banquet and then might join him at table.

After his meal, the King often decided to go on an outing, usually in his carriage and far from the Château, since, according to the Princess Palatine:

Although Versailles possesses the loveliest promenades in the world, no one except myself ever walks in them. The King is always telling me: 'You are the only one who enjoys the beauties of Versailles.'

The occasional moves to Saint-Germain or Fontainebleau involved certain discomforts en route, if we are to believe Saint-Simon, *writing at a later date:*

During these journeys, there was always a vast store of provisions of various kinds, including meats, pastries and fruits. The expedition would not have covered a quarter of a league before the King would be asking the ladies in his carriage whether they did not care to eat something . . . Then they were all obliged to say how hungry they were, put on an air of jollity, and set to with good appetite and willingness, otherwise the King became displeased and would show his resentment openly. . . . As for the needs of nature, they could never be mentioned, and in any case, any such needs would have proved most embarrassing to the ladies in the party, with the carriage preceded and followed by detachments of the Household cavalry and the Royal Guards, and equerries riding by the doors, raising a dust that covered everyone in the carriage. The King liked fresh air and insisted on having all the windows lowered; he would have been extremely displeased had any lady had the temerity to draw one of the curtains to keep out the sun, the wind or the cold. There was no alternative but to pretend not to notice that, nor any other kind of discomfort . . . To feel sick was an unforgivable crime.

In fact, the courtiers were subject to an iron discipline. Ezechiel Spanheim *notes that at Versailles:*

Everything is more stiff, more reserved, more constrained and also less free than is typical of the nation's general character. Even the entertainments and fêtes which the King often arranges for the principal ladies of the Court seem to lack spontaneity and appear stiff and formal, with a sense of constraint reigning over the pleasures.

But happily, everyone was able to relax at the gaming tables, playing frantically for high stakes in an atmosphere which was not only tolerated, but approved of, by the King. In a letter to her daughter dated October 9th, 1675, Mme de Sévigné comments:

They play for enormous sums at Versailles. In Paris *hoca*[1] is forbidden, under pain of death, and yet the King and his Court play it: for 5,000 pistoles to change hands in a single morning is nothing.

The Princess Palatine *adds confirmation:*

The players behave like madmen, one screaming aloud, another striking the table so hard with his fist that the whole room echoes with the sound, a third uttering blasphemous oaths so terrible as to make one's hair stand on end; they all appear to be completely out of their minds.

And the young Marquis de Feuquières *writes to his father:*

Mme de Montespan's gaming has reached such excessive proportions that losses of 100,000 écus are common. On Christmas Day, she ended up losing 700,000 écus, despite the fact that during the day's play she had wagered 150,000 pistoles on three cards and won; it is perfectly easy to win or lose fifty or sixty times in a quarter of an hour, playing that game lansquenet.[2]

[1] An Italian game, introduced into France during the era of Mazarin: the players placed stakes on a board divided into thirty numbered squares; if the number they had wagered on came up they won twenty-eight times the amount of the stake.

[2] The écu was worth 3 livres, the pistole 10 livres, the livre approximately 2 francs-or.

Certain courtiers, such as the Marquis de Dangeau, lived from their gambling. Saint-Maurice asserted that Dangeau's entire existence was bound up with the fortunes of the gaming table. And Mme de Sévigné calculated that he was able to credit to his account book sums such as 200,000 francs won in ten days, and 100,000 écus won during a single month. Primi Visconti *comments wrily on the gambling mania:*

The Queen's favourite game is *hombre*, but she is so simple-minded that she loses continuously, and the Queen's losses provide the poor Princesse d'Elbeuf with her sole means of support. This gaming, if it continues at the present intensity, will be the Court's finest source of revenue. It is a general fault in France, especially among the ladies. The art of conversation is a finished thing; nowadays people are simply concerned with making some money one way or another. The money they win is not hoarded, it is needed to cover the vast cost of feeding and dressing themselves.

It was, indeed, absolutely necessary to have a constant flow of money coming one's way, in order to maintain a ruinously extravagant way of life. Courtiers often wheedled favours for their friends in return for substantial cash payments. In the view of Mme de Motteville:

The King's establishment is like a vast market, where there is no choice but to go and bargain, both to maintain one's own existence and to protect the interests of those to whom we are attached by duty or friendship.

But gambling often gave way to ballets and various divertissements *given in the gardens, to which the general public were admitted, for, in the words of* Louis XIV, *in his* Mémoires:

The people enjoy pageantry and display. In this way we retain their loyalty and devotion, sometimes more effectively, perhaps, than by just rewards and benefits.

But on most occasions, the King spent the hour between

*seven and eight o'clock playing billiards in the Salon de Diane,
with refreshments being served in the Salon de Vénus. These
rooms were known collectively as 'l'appartement'. The
Princess Palatine confessed to being bored to distraction in
that atmosphere:*

The *appartement* is an absolutely intolerable experience. We
all troop into the billiard room and lie on our stomachs or
squat, no one uttering a word, until the King has finished his
game. Then we all get up and go to the music room where
someone is singing an aria from some old opera which we have
heard a hundred times already. After that, we go to the ball,
which lasts from eight to ten o'clock. Those who, like me, do
not dance have to sit there for hours without budging for an
instant, and can neither see nor hear anything except an
interminable minuet. At a quarter to ten, we all follow one
another in a quadrille, like children reciting the catechism, and
then the ball is finally over.

*Three times a week, plays were performed, but many mem-
bers of the public of that era would have agreed with the
Duchesse d'Osnabrück (aunt of the Princess Palatine), who, on
a visit to Versailles, declared:*

I found so many people to occupy my time and thoughts
that I took very little notice of the plays. There was terrible
overcrowding in the audience, and the heat was unbelievable;
I came to the conclusion that the pleasures of the Court of
France are mingled with many inconveniences. We refreshed
ourselves by drinking lemonade.

*Despite all this, the discomfort, the boredom, the courtiers
seem to have been passionately attached to the way of life,
and were inconsolable when away from Versailles. Mme de
Sévigné gives an account, in one of her letters, of the return
of the Marquis de Vardes, exiled twenty years previously to
Montpellier,[1] whom the King had graciously pardoned:*

He arrived on Saturday morning, looking quite extra-

[1] See Chapter II.

ordinary, and wearing an ancient *justaucorps à brevet*[1] in the style of those worn in 1663. On entering the King's chamber he went down on one knee . . . The King told him that he had not recalled him so long as his heart was wounded, but that he now recalled him with a whole heart, and that he was glad to see him again. M. de Vardes replied most eloquently and emotionally, and the gift of tears which God has given him was well in evidence on this occasion. After this first interview, the King caused M. le Dauphin to be called, and presented him to him as a young courtier. M. de Vardes recognized him and bowed to him. The King said to him laughingly: 'Vardes, what a stupid thing to do, you know quite well that you do not bow to anyone when in my presence.' M. de Vardes replied in the same tone: 'Sire, I no longer know anything, I have forgotten everything, Your Majesty will have to pardon me even thirty stupidities.' 'That I will,' said the King, 'you have twenty-nine left.' Later, when the King made fun of his coat, M. de Vardes said: 'Sire, when a man is so wretched as to be banished from your presence, he is not only unfortunate, he becomes ridiculous as well.'

---

[1] A blue great coat, embroidered with gold and silver, which the King authorized certain courtiers to wear by issuing them with a royal warrant. According to Mlle de Montpensier, these costumes were renewed every two years.

CHAPTER X

LA VOISIN:
THE 'AFFAIRE DES POISONS'

Paris one year went crazy over
A dame who practised as a soothsayer.
Every occurrence was referred to her:
Whether you lost a hanky or a lover,
Or had a husband who refused to die,
A jealous wife or a vexatious mother,
Or any other suchlike bother,
Straight to the Pythoness you'd hie . . .*
                                    LA FONTAINE

*Translation by Sir Edward Marsh, La Fontaine: *Fables*, 7, 'The Two
Soothsayers', Everyman's Library, London.

※

PRINCIPAL PERSONALITIES MENTIONED IN CHAPTER X

JEAN RACINE and NICOLAS BOILEAU-DESPRÉAUX, poets
and war correspondents.

CATHERINE DESHAYES, 'La Voisin', midwife and poisoner.

ADAM COEURET, known as Le Sage and ABBÉ GUIBOURG,
accomplices of La Voisin.

LA VIGOUREUX and MARIE BOSSE, poisoners.

MARIE ANGÉLIQUE DE SCORAILLE, DUCHESSE DE FON-
TANGES, one of Madame's maids-of-honour, and the King's
mistress.

MLLE DES ADRETS, another of Madame's maids-of-honour.

PÈRE DE LA CHAISE, Jesuit and the King's confessor.

RUBANSTEL, MARQUIS DE MONDÉTOUR, Lieutenant-Colonel of the Royal Guards.

Accused of being clients of La Voisin:

MARIE CHARLOTTE DE ROQUELAURE, DUCHESSE DE FOIX.

ANNE LOUISE DE CREVANT D'HUMIÈRES, COMTESSE DE VASSÉ.

FRANÇOIS LOUIS DE MONTMORENCY, DUC DE LUXEMBOURG, Marshal of France.

MARIE ANNE MANCINI, DUCHESSE DE BOUILLON, niece of Mazarin.

MARIE LOUISE D'ALBERT, PRINCESSE DE TINGRY, sister-in-law of the Duc de Luxembourg.

BENIGNE DE MEAUX DE FOUILLY, MARQUISE D'ALLUYE.

JACQUELINE DE GRIMOARD DE BEAUVOIR, DUCHESSE DE POLIGNAC, daughter of the Comtesse du Roure.

CLAUDE HUGUES DE LEZEY, MARQUIS DE LUSIGNAN, brigadier of cavalry.

LOUIS JOSEPH, DUC DE VENDÔME, great-grandson of Henri IV and Gabrielle d'Estrées.

ANTOINE DU PAS, MARQUIS DE FEUQUIÈRES.

The King was still waging war against Holland, Spain and the Holy Roman Empire. After some reverses, victories were being won once again. In 1677, Racine and Boileau were appointed royal historiographers and charged with preparing accounts of the battles, for, according to Primi Visconti:

Racine was in fashion, and so was Despréaux, his inseparable companion. They were known as 'the philosophers'. I knew them both: Racine is a pedant, but Despréaux is a man of judgement who has composed several extremely witty satires. He once confided in me that he concerned himself with history because he was obliged to, rather than because it inspired him.

For her part, Mme de Sévigné was indignant to see such a mission confided to two bourgeois:

Four days ago, the King said to them: 'I am sorry that you did not come on the last campaign;[1] you would have seen war, and it would have been a short trip for you.' Racine replied: 'Sire, we are two bourgeois who possess only town clothes; we ordered some country clothes, but the places you attacked were captured so quickly that the clothes were not ready in time.' This was pleasantly received. Ah! I know a man of quality [Bussy-Rabutin] to whom I would have confided the writing of my history, had I been his master, rather than to those two bourgeois. That would have been worthy of posterity!

During the spring of 1678, the King achieved victories at Ghent and Ypres. Racine was following the campaign and took notes:

The King, approaching Valenciennes, received the news that Ghent was invested and that the town and the château held only 500 infantry soldiers and 1,500 horses.—Zeal of the peasants in this frontier area.—Savagery of the peasants at Cateau-Cambrésis. At one league from Valenciennes, the King showed me seven towns, all visible in a single sweep of the eye, which are now in his possession, and added: 'You will also see Tournai, a town which is well worth my venturing something in order to keep it.'—On our arrival at Valenciennes, the King was so weary that he did not have the energy to go upstairs to his room.

Ghent, March 4th. The King, arriving at eleven in the morning, found Ghent invested by the Maréchal d'Humières. He dined, and then supervised the allocation of quarters and made a tour of inspection of the siege positions . . . In the evening, work was started on the trenchworks. M. de Maran ordered the excavation of the approach trench which was subsequently used in the attack on the right wing which has been named the Navarre attack. On the following day, the trench was opened on the left wing by the Regiment of

[1] The Maréchal de Créqui's campaign in Alsace (October 1677).

Guards. . . . The Spaniards in a miserable state, surrendering because starving. The governor, old and bearded, would say only this to the King: 'I desire to surrender to Your Majesty, and that is all that I have to say to him.'

While all this was going on at the front, the greatest scandal of the entire reign was brewing and was about to burst into the open.

On September 21, 1677, an anonymous note found in a confessional box of the church of the Jesuits in the rue Saint-Antoine revealed that a plot was on foot to assassinate the King. Some of the confessors acknowledged that most of their penitents had accused themselves of having poisoned somebody. La Reynie, *First Lieutenant of Police of Paris, had this comment about the use of poison:*

Human life is practically up for sale. This poison is almost the sole remedy used in family embarrassments. Impiety, sacrilege and all kinds of abominations are widespread throughout Paris, the countryside and the provinces.

On December 5th, Louis de Vanens, alchemist and purveyor of philters, was arrested, together with his female accomplice, La Finette. Their interrogation revealed the names of others: La Vigoureux, wife of a tailor, was seized the following year, as was Marie Bosse, fortune-teller by cards. Finally, on March 12, 1679, it was the turn of Catherine Deshayes, wife of Antoine Voisin or Monvoisin, midwife, and her chief accomplice, Le Sage.

The revelations of the accused soon involved many members of the haute bourgeoisie *and personalities at the Court. On April 7th, the King named a special commission to investigate these matters. This was the Chambre Royale de l'Arsenal, also called the Chambre Ardente, because, according to the* Mercure Galant *of that month:*

In other times, criminals of high birth were judged in a room whose walls were covered in black mourning drapery and which was lit only by torches.

The Affaire des Poisons *was about to commence. On April 19th,* Contarini, *the ambassador of the Doge of Venice, wrote a confidential letter to his master:*

Most Serene Prince: with the habit of poisoning becoming established in a nation, and with several members of the nobility and the common people standing accused of complicity in so odious a crime, it seems that the Parlement's judgements have not been pronounced with the severity required by so delicate a matter. In consequence, the King has delegated some members of his Council of State and several officers of justice,[1] to conduct the enquiry, and has established a tribunal, which he has named the Chambre Ardente, to judge the accused. The prison of Vincennes and the Bastille are filled to overflowing with these people. They are mostly women of the nobility and the bourgeoisie. The Premier Président of the Parlement has represented to the King the blow which the Parlement had received, seeing itself deprived of its accustomed rights of jurisdiction, and has boasted of its immaculate justice, hoping to persuade him to spare the Parlement this stigma and this affront. But the King held firm and refused to yield to these remonstrances. One day soon we shall be in possession of the melancholy facts which this tribunal will reveal.

According to Primi Visconti:

The Chambre Ardente set up at the Arsenal caused a great stir at the time, for, besides the poisonings, it investigated all sorts of superstitions and vices; it seemed like a State inquisition of conscience. All France trembled, especially at the sight of even Princesses and Marshals in flight, or in prison, on mere suspicion.

Colbert was strongly opposed to this tribunal. Apart from the fact that it was costing the King's exchequer a great deal of money, he was alarmed at the scandalous picture of the nation that its revelations were establishing. Louvois, on the

---

[1] Eight Counsellors of State, and six Maîtres des Requêtes—among whom was the Lieutenant of Police of Paris, Nicolas de la Reynie.

contrary, supported it; it was his own creation, and he had himself suggested it to the King. . . .

. . . Associated with Le Sage was a certain Voisin who, under pretext of divination and magic, had turned his house into an abode of evil and a dispensary for drugs and perfumes which were suspected of being poisons. It is certain that she had brought about many abortions, and she collected all kinds of herbs. Most of the ladies of Paris seem to have visited her; she had drawn up a list of their names together with their requirements. It was given out at the time that the Duchesse de Foix had asked the means of increasing the size of her breasts and that Mme de Vassé wanted to develop larger hips and become taller; many of them wanted the secret of making men fall in love with them, and some of them wanted to displace Mme de Montespan. However, La Voisin boasted that it was through her arts that Mme de Montespan and Louvois remained in favour.[1]

During this time, other intrigues were building up at the Court. The governess of Mme de Montespan's children, that Mme de Maintenon who had achieved a position of such influence in the King's unofficial family, wrote on March 17, 1679, to her confessor, the Abbé Gobelin:

You know how great is my need that you should pray to God for me. I ask you, too, to pray and to have prayers said for the King, who is hovering on the brink of a precipice.

The precipice is an eighteen-year-old girl of extraordinary beauty, newly arrived at the Court, who had already conquered the King's heart.

Who was she? Ezechiel Spanheim, tutor to the son of the Elector Palatine, and envoy extraordinary at Versailles, tells us:

It was Mlle de Fontanges, daughter of the Comte de Roussille, a distinguished gentleman of Auvergne, who came to the

[1] Primi Visconti himself was nearly compromised; he recounts elsewhere that the Lieutenant of Police La Reynie had heard it said that 'as a man of science I had been much sought after and that I was in a position to know and reveal many things, but the commissioners laughed in his face and the King sent word that he stood guarantee for me.'

Court in the year 1679 to take up a post as one of Madame's maids-of-honour, and with the conscious determination, abetted by her own family, to make the King her lover.

Her youth, her beauty, such as had not been seen at Versailles for a very long time, and a figure, bearing and appearance capable of surprising and charming a Court so concerned with gallantry and romance soon produced the effect she had intended, despite the fact that her mind was dull and her opinions terribly provincial. The Duc de La Rochefoucauld, one of the courtiers on the most intimate terms with the King, performed the rôle of go-between in this affair of the King's heart, and experienced no difficulty in persuading the lady to agree to his proposals.

To this account, Primi Visconti *adds:*

The King was tired of Mme de Montespan. She had gained so much influence over him that she practically dominated him. She had borne two more children and she had grown extremely stout: indeed, while she was descending from her carriage one day, I had a glimpse of one of her legs, and I swear it was almost as broad as my whole body . . .

Marsillac [La Rochefoucauld] was involved in the intrigue, and had no difficulty in playing his part, since Mlle de Fontanges wanted nothing better. He [the King] then travelled to Paris, at night, escorted only by a few Bodyguards, and went to the Palais Royal. Mlle des Adrets opened the door of the apartment of Madame's maids-of-honour, and this was the first occasion on which the King possessed Mlle de Fontanges.

Despite the darkness, the King's return was observed by early risers. When he was staying at Saint-Germain, he used to make similar journeys by night, by way of the park, to the Château Neuf [of Versailles]. Once, when he noticed that someone had seen him passing, he had the man followed and arrested by his Guards: it was Villeroi. This mishap cost Villeroi a temporary banishment from the Court.

Mlle de Fontanges was soon given the apartment adjoining the King's study. This room had a chandelier which was kept lit at all times, but a room had been prepared for her at some distance from the closet, above the King's bedroom, and the

7·
*Elizabeth Charlotte of
Bavaria (the Princess
Palatine)*

Mme de Sévigné,
by Mignard

8. *Jean Racine*

Nicolas Boileau,
by Rigaud

King went up to her, or else she herself would descend a little staircase which led down from the study to the royal bedroom. But in public the King pretended that he did not know her.

On March 22, 1679, Bussy-Rabutin wrote to his friend Erard du Châtelet, Marquis de Trichâteau, governor of Semur:

Mme de Montespan left Saint-Germain for Paris, in a great hurry, on Wednesday the 15th of this month.[1] It is said that there is some squabbling going on in the *ménage*, and that the reason is her jealousy of one of Madame's young ladies, named Fontanges, who has already, it seems, been enjoyed by the King, for, as you know, kings who have a desire seldom sigh for long. We must await the sequel; after the failure of the Ludre adventure, I would hesitate to predict success for this latest love-affair.

And, in his Histoire Amoureuse des Gaules, *Bussy remarks:*

Mme de Montespan, noticing that the *Grand Alcandre* [Louis XIV] was becoming increasingly estranged from her day by day, was so furious that she began denigrating Mlle de Fontanges publicly, saying that the *Grand Alcandre* showed a lack of discernment in becoming enamoured of a girl who had already been involved in several vulgar little love-affairs in the country, that she possessed neither wit nor schooling, and finally that she was really nothing more than a beautiful painting. And she repeated countless other libels of the same sort.

During April, Mme de Montespan received notice of her dismissal and at the same time was appointed superintendent of the Queen's Household, a post which had been refused her while she was still favourite. This time, it is Trichâteau who writes to Bussy, on April 14th:

On Wednesday, the Comtesse de Soissons received the order to resign from her post. The Comtesse was at Chaillot at the

---

[1] This hurried departure was no doubt connected with the arrest of La Voisin on March 12th.

time, staying in a small house she owned there. M. Colbert came and went several times. She had an interview with the King that evening, in the Queen's apartment and in her presence. The King spoke to her in extravagant terms about the pleasure she would occasion him by agreeing to relinquish her position, and she replied with complete submission. In the end, she went away 200,000 écus the richer, and Mme de Montespan became superintendent of the Queen's Household and, at the same time, ceased to be the King's mistress. It is rumoured that she wanted to give everything up and leave for Fontrevault, but that her friends persuaded her to remain at the Court. It is even said that she is seeking a reconciliation with her husband, and that Père de la Chaise is engaged in negotiations in this matter.

At the end of August, the Duchesse d'Osnabrück, aunt of the Princess Palatine, had arrived in Versailles to be present at the marriage of one of Monsieur's daughters with King Charles II of Spain. In the Chapel during the ceremony, she noticed that Mme de Montespan looked very much out of sorts. According to the Duchesse, she was sitting in the front row, but:

... with her dress in a state of great disorder, an embroidered coif on her head, showing the deepest gloom and irritation at the sight of the triumph of a woman younger than herself.

As for Mlle de Fontanges, she was radiant, observed the duchess, with her prayer book clutched in her hands:

The prayer book gave her an excuse to glance down towards the King whom she loved, no doubt, more than she loved the King of kings, which is understandable, for the former is a most lovable person.

While the Court derived some amusement from Mme de Montespan's discomfiture, the affaire des poisons was developing. A number of people who had had dealings with La Voisin and her friends were arrested, including Mme de Dreux, wife of a Maître des Requêtes, and Mme Le Féron, wife of a Président of the Parlement, both being accused of having wanted to poison their husbands. Then La Sage began naming other names, including those of the Duc de Luxembourg and the Marquis de Feuquières.

Louvois *reported to the King on October 8, 1679:*

I received yesterday M. de La Reynie, who informed me that the crimes of those detained at Vincennes appear more extraordinary each day. It seems that there are thirteen or fourteen witnesses of Mme La Féron's crime. He then gave me the original copy of the report of the interrogation of the man known as Le Sage, but was of the opinion that I should not send it to Your Majesty, since it is long and badly written, and Your Majesty would have had difficulty in deciphering the document. We agreed together that I should keep it for you until I may have the honour of reading it to Your Majesty at Saint-Germain.

All the evidence which Your Majesty has already seen against M. de Luxembourg and M. de Feuquières is nothing compared with the declaration contained in this report: M. de Luxembourg is accused of having sought to contrive the death of his wife, that of the Maréchal de Créqui, the marriage of his daughter to my son, his own reacquisition of the duchy of Montmorency, and that he should be enabled to perform heroic feats on the battlefield, to help Your Majesty forget his incompetence at Philippsburg. And M. de Feuquières is portrayed in this same declaration as the wickedest man in the world, who has willingly had communion with the Devil to induce the Voisin woman to poison the uncle or tutor of a girl he wished to marry.

In November, La Voisin implicated Jean Racine, poet, academician, and royal historiographer. He had once been the lover of the actress Du Parc. His son, Louis Racine, claimed that 'it was on his account that Molière's best actress left his company and joined a theatrical troupe in Burgundy'. And, according to a conversation with Boileau recorded by Mathieu Marais, 'M. Racine was in love with La Du Parc . . . He wrote Andromaque *for her. La Du Parc died shortly afterwards, in child-bed.'*

Suddenly the poisoner claimed to know that Racine had assassinated his mistress. The accusation is to be found in the official report of the interrogation of La Voisin on November 21, 1679; in answer to the question as to how well she knew La Du Parc, La Voisin replied:

I have known her for fourteen years, we were very good friends, and she confided in me completely during that period. I had meant to tell you earlier that La Du Parc must have been poisoned, and that suspicion fell on Jean Racine at the time, at least there were very strong rumours to that effect. I had some reason to believe them to be true because, although I was the good friend of La Du Parc, Racine had always prevented me from seeing her during the course of the illness from which she died, despite the fact that La Du Parc had kept on asking for me. Although I went to see her on several occasions, I was never allowed in, on Racine's orders; this I know through the step-mother of La Du Parc, known as Mlle de Gorle, and through La Du Parc's daughters, who are at the Hôtel de Soissons and have assured me that Racine was the cause of their misfortune.

De Gorle told me that Racine had married La Du Parc secretly, and was jealous of everyone, and particularly of me, whom he disliked extremely. She further told me that his violent jealousy had caused him to poison her, and that during her illness Racine never left her bedside, and at one point removed a valuable diamond ring from her finger. She also asserted that he had appropriated La Du Parc's jewellery and personal effects and had sold them for a considerable sum of money.

The evidence against Racine was extremely slim. Nevertheless, there exists in the archives of the Bastille a letter from Louvois to the judge of the Chambre Ardente, Bazin de Bezons, stating: 'The King's warrant necessary for the arrest of the Sieur Racine will be sent to you as soon as you request it.' Doubtless the judge (a colleague of Racine's in the Académie) never requested such a warrant. In any case, it seems that the great dramatist was never summoned for questioning. But other arrests were made during the beginning of 1680. On January 27th, Bussy-Rabutin wrote to La Rivière:

Here is extraordinary news, Monsieur: the Chambre des Poisons has issued warrants for the arrest of M. de Luxembourg, the Comtesse de Soissons, the Marquise d'Alluye and M. de Polignac.

Subpoenas have been handed personally to Mme de Bouillon, the Princesse de Tingry, the Maréchale de La Ferté and Mme de Roure. A warrant for the arrest of Cessac has just been issued.

M. de Luxembourg's crime is reputed to be that, while with the Army, he had poison administered to an Intendant des Contributions of Flanders, from whom he had extorted a sum of the King's money.

The Comtesse de Soissons is accused of having poisoned her husband; the Marquise d'Alluye, her brother-in-law Sourdis; the Princesse de Tingry, babies she had given birth to; Mme de Bouillon, a valet de chambre who had got to know of her love affairs. The King has sent back to the Duchesse de Foix a note which she had written to La Voisin, and which included the phrase: 'The more I rub, the less they project.' His Majesty demanded an explanation of this phrase, and she replied that she had asked La Voisin for a prescription to make her breasts grow larger.

Last Thursday, two priests were arrested, including one named Le Sage who claimed that a certain Mme de Brizy—who is already incarcerated at Vincennes—a young woman in love with Rubanstel, had come to him asking to be given secrets to have men fall in love with her. He had told her that an infallible method would be to have him say Mass while she stretched naked on the altar, the chalice on her stomach. She agreed to this ritual, but came back to him two weeks later to complain that Rubanstel seemed no more enamoured of her than before. He then assured her that it was necessary to add a new element to the ritual, and that if he lay with her after Late Mass, Rubanstel would be certain to acquire an insatiable passion for her; the lady performed all these ceremonies.

The Abbé de Choisy *has this to say about the Comtesse de Soissons:*

The King, out of consideration for the memory of the

Cardinal, sent M. de Bouillon to her to tell her that he offered her the choice of going the next day to the Bastille to undergo the rigours of prison and interrogation, or else leaving France immediately. The Duc de Villeroi and the Marquise d'Alluye were with her, and they discussed the Kings' ultimatum. They both urged her to go to the Bastille, in view of her constant protestations of innocence, but she did not dare take that risk. She declared to them: 'M. de Louvois is my mortal enemy, because I refused my daughter to his son. He has been powerful enough to have me accused, he has false witnesses at his command. Since things have gone so far that a warrant has been issued against a person of my quality, then I fear he will succeed in his criminal attempts and will have me die on the scaffold or, at least, keep me in prison for life. I would rather keep my freedom, and exonerate myself later on.' The Marquise d'Alluye, her faithful friend, followed her into exile.

La Voisin was condemned to death on January 19th, and the Duc de Luxembourg was imprisoned in the Bastille. Mme de Sévigné wrote, on the 29th, to the Comte de Guitaut:

Does it not seem to you from the distance at which you are able to survey these matters that we here are living in an atmosphere of poison, sacrilege and abortion? In truth, the whole of Europe is horrified by these accounts, and those who read them in a hundred years' time will be severe in their judgement of those who were witnesses of these accusations. You know how the unfortunate M. de Luxembourg surrendered himself voluntarily to the Bastille, acting as his own escort and himself showing the order of Bèzemaux. Coming from Saint-Germain, his carriage crossed that of Mme de Montespan *en route*; they both climbed down and spoke to each other in privacy, and he was seen to weep a great deal. He visited the Jesuits, asking for several of the fathers, then went to pray to God in the church, still in tears. It almost seemed that he was not sure which saint to evoke. He met M. de Vauvineux and told him that he was on his way to the Bastille, that he would leave it an innocent man, but after such indignities he would never return to society.

At first he was placed in a quite agreeable room, but two

hours later the order came to lock him up securely and so he is now in a bare cell high up in the building. He has been questioned for four hours by M. de Bezons and M. de La Reynie.

Mme de Soissons has conducted herself in an entirely different manner, making a great public show of her innocence. She disappeared at night, saying that she could not face the prospect of prison and the shame of being confronted with hags and villains. The Marquise d'Alluye went with her. They took the road for Namur, but there is no intention of following them. I consider her action to be perfectly natural and noble, and entirely approve of it. Yet it is said that the things of which she is accused consist of mere stupidities, things she herself has mentioned time and time again, as one does after visiting one of these so-called sorceresses. There is much that demands discussion in all these matters, and indeed people have no other theme for their correspondence, but I fear that they do not always write what they think. Events will show whether her crimes are as black as they are painted: up till now, they appear to be only grey, if that. You know the names of all those who have been summoned to appear. The Maréchal de Villeroi remarked: 'These ladies and gentlemen believe in the Devil but not in God.'

And here is the version of one of the accused, Antoine de Feuquières, Marquis de Pas, who wrote to his father, then Ambassador to Sweden, on January 29th of the same year:

The news which this post brings you will both surprise and horrify you, although M. de Tourmont will have already prepared you by the account he sent you by the previous post. However, I will repeat what you already know, that on Wednesday last an arrest warrant was issued by the Chambre des Poisons against M. de Luxembourg, and that he has gone voluntarily to the Bastille, accused of various crimes the details of which remain unknown, although I can assure you that they are very calumnious and that I am certain that events will justify him. And yet judge of the disgrace for a gentleman of his rank to find himself accused of a long list of black and infamous deeds. The whole story would take up a sheaf of paper, but to be brief, Monsieur, I will tell you simply that some male and female poisoners by trade have succeeded in prolonging their lives by making successive denunciations of men of quality, who have consequently to be arrested and interrogated, and thus the prisoners gain a respite. Apart from M. de Luxembourg, I am told that the latest denunciations have resulted in warrants being issued against the Comtesse de Soissons, the Marquise d'Alluye (both of whom have left the country rather than appear before the judges), M. de Cessac, Mme de Polignac, M. de Lusignan and M. de Vardes.

Subpoenas have been issued for the appearance of Mme de Bouillon, M. de Vendôme, Mme de Tingry and the Maréchale de La Ferté, a great number of other people, and myself, too, I hear. But although the others have already been notified, I have so far heard nothing. In any case, do not be alarmed. This whole business would be terribly unpleasant if I were alone, but the friends who surround me make the experience bearable and, besides, I have no idea as to the subject on which the Chamber desires to question me. So, to put it shortly, Monsieur, I wait perfectly calmly whatever directives they may choose to give me. I am convinced of M. de Luxembourg's innocence, but am outraged to think that a gentleman of his standing should be the victim of calumniators vile enough to accuse him of crimes as black as Hell—and as false. Finally, I beg you once again not to be in the least concerned about me, Monsieur.

In March, Feuquières *at least learned what were the charges against him. Writing again to his father, on March 16, 1680, he explains:*

As regards my own case, I will tell you immediately that I have never seen La Voisin, and that the accusations made against me are so ridiculous and baseless that they are hardly worth enumerating, and would take three days to set down in full, but I will try to give you the gist of them. There are two chief counts. The first is that I am supposed to have asked a certain Mme Vigoureux to marry me; this woman, who was one of the band of poisoners, died while undergoing torture a year ago. The only time I ever saw her was about two years ago, when she came to my house to tell me that her husband was a lady's tailor, that he had worked for my late mother, and that I would be doing her a great favour if I would take as a lackey a small boy whom she had with her, whom she claimed to be her son and my mother's godson. But, luckily for me, I thought him too small and refused to employ him. Apparently this woman also dabbled in fortune-telling. In any case, she must have told them some story which has obliged them to call me in for questioning. You can see that it does not amount to much.

The other charge has to do with a note written by the late La Vallière and myself and burnt in the presence of M. de Luxembourg. The fact is that a man known as Le Sage told us that he could bring us an answer to any note we wrote, without reading it, in three days; so, treating it as a huge joke, La Vallière filled a sheet of paper with nonsense and then we set fire to it. This villain now claims that the note contained matter of grave importance, and the tribunal has asked me what was written.

But all this unpleasantness is partially offset by the fact that the weather during my enforced stay here in Paris is absolutely beautiful. As for M. de Luxembourg, do not ask me what he is accused of, because no one knows positively; I am perfectly sure that he is no poisoner, at any rate. And pray do not worry about me.

In the end, Feuquières was not arrested, and the Duc de Luxembourg was soon released from the Bastille. La Voisin was burnt alive on February 22nd, and the scene was duly described by Mme de Sévigné:

I will only mention the La Voisin affair. She was not burnt on Wednesday, as I wrote you, but only yesterday. She knew her fate on the Monday, a most extraordinary circumstance! In the evening she said to her guards: 'What! no *medianoche?*'[1] She ate with them at midnight, out of whim for it was not a fast-day, drank a great deal of wine, and sang a number of drinking songs. On Tuesday she received the question ordinary and extraordinary, after having dined, and

[1] From the Spanish: *media noche* (middle of the night), a meal taken after midnight between a fast-day and a meat day.

slept for eight hours. She was confronted, while under torture, with Mesdames de Dreux and Le Féron [poisoners of their husbands] and several others. Her answers have not yet transpired, but everyone expects strange revelations. . . .

She appeared in the tumbril dressed in white, a kind of garb worn by those condemned to be burnt. She was very red in the face, and was seen to push away the confessor and the crucifix with great violence. M. de Chaulnes, M. de Sully, the Comtesse [de Fiesque], myself, and several others, saw her pass by the Hôtel de Sully [rue Saint-Antoine].

But the Affaire des Poisons *continued, and 'strange revelations' were indeed forthcoming.*

CHAPTER XI

FONTANGES,
'BELLE COMME UNE ANGE...'

'...et sotte comme un panier.'[1]
The ABBÉ DE CHOISY

PRINCIPAL PERSONALITIES MENTIONED IN CHAPTER XI

SIMON ARNAULT, MARQUIS DE POMPONNE, Minister of Foreign Affairs until 1679.

CHARLES COLBERT, MARQUIS DE CROISSY (brother of Jean Baptiste Colbert), successor to Pomponne.

MARIE ANNE CHRISTINE VICTOIRE OF BAVARIA, daughter of the Elector of Bavaria and fiancée of the Dauphin.

LOUIS, son of Louis XIV, Dauphin of France.

LOUIS SANGUIN, MARQUIS DE LIVRY, chief maître d'hôtel of the King.

MARIE ANNE DE BLOIS, daughter of Louis XIV and Mlle de La Vallière.

LOUIS ARMAND DE CONTI, eldest son of the Prince de Conti.

JEANNE DE SCORAILLE, Abbess of Maubuisson, sister of Mlle de Fontanges.

TRIMONT DE CABRIÈRES, Prior of Saint-Geniez-de-Malgoirez, 'a most charitable man possessing most singular remedies', according to Saint-Simon.

MARGUERITE MONVOISIN, daughter of La Voisin; ROMANI, valet; BERTRAND; VAUTIER; 'LE GRAND AUTEUR', Grand

---

[1] 'Beautiful as an angel, and stupid as a donkey.'

Master of the *cabbala*; LA FILASTRE; LA BRETESCHE (accomplices of La Voisin).

CLAUDE DE VIN DES OEILLETS, Mme de Montespan's maid.

The Affaire des Poisons was not the only matter to preoccupy the Court. During November it was stupefied to learn of the disgrace of Arnaud de Pomponne, Secretary of State for Foreign Affairs, and his sudden replacement by Charles Colbert de Croissy, brother of Jean Baptiste Colbert. Mme de Sévigné was quite overwhelmed by this news, as she makes clear to her daughter:

What I am going to tell you, my dear child, will both surprise and vex you: M. de Pomponne is in disgrace. He had orders, on Saturday evening, as he was returning from Pomponne, to resign his office. The King has directed that he shall receive 700,000 livres, and that he should continue to receive the pension of 20,000 livres a year he received as a Minister. His Majesty desired to show by this settlement that he was satisfied with his fidelity. It was M. Colbert who gave him this information, assuring him at the same time that he was extremely mortified to be obliged to . . ., etc. M. de Pomponne asked him whether he might not be allowed the honour of speaking to the King, and learning from his own mouth what fault he had committed that had brought this thunderbolt down upon him. He was told he could not, so he wrote to the King, expressing his extreme sorrow and his complete ignorance of what might have contributed to his disgrace; he mentioned his numerous family, and begged him to have compassion on his eight children. . . .

M. de Chaulnes, Caumartin and I had been, as I wrote you, at Pomponne on the Friday, where we found him and the ladies, who all received us with the greatest pleasure. We chatted all evening, and played chess. Ah! what a checkmate they were preparing for him at Saint-Germain! . . .

But you will understand more easily the ways of Providence when I tell you that it is the Président Colbert [de Croissy] who has replaced him. Since he is in Bavaria, his brother is officiating in his absence, and wrote to congratulate, and to surprise him, on the cover of the letter, as though by mistake: 'To M. Colbert, Minister and Secretary of State'. Reflect a little on the absolute power of this family.

At that moment, a marriage was being arranged between the Dauphin and Marie Christine of Bavaria, who, according to Mme de Caylus:

. . . was not just ugly, but so grotesque that Sanguin, the King's chief maître d'hôtel, who had been sent by the King to Bavaria during the negotiations for the marriage, could not resist saying to His Majesty, on his return: '*Sire, sauvez le premier coup d'oeil.*'[1] Yet Monseigneur loved her.

But, according to Primi Visconti, the future Dauphine had:

. . . a beautiful skin, perfect teeth and fine eyes, which compensates somewhat for her defects.

In addition, the King had decided upon a marriage between his daughter by La Vallière, Marie Anne de Blois, and Prince Louis Armand de Conti. A love-match, according to Mme de Sévigné in a letter of December 27, 1679:

The Court is overjoyed at the marriage of M. le Prince de Conti with Mademoiselle de Blois. They are real story-book lovers. The King was highly amused at the ardour of their passion: he spoke most affectionately to his daughter, assuring her that he loved her so much he would find it hard to be parted from her, and the sweet creature was so moved and so full of joy that she wept. So the King told her he saw that she was weeping from aversion to the husband he had chosen for her, at which she burst into tears a second time, her little heart unable to contain her joy. The King related this little scene, and everyone was charmed with it. As for the Prince de Conti, he too was in transports of delight, and hardly knew what he was doing or saying; on his way to visit Mademoiselle de Blois he bumped into people right and left. Madame Col-

[1] 'Sire, do not betray your first impression.'

bert[1] did not wish him to see her until the evening, but he burst open the doors, threw himself at her feet, and kissed her hand, whereat she embraced him without further ceremony, and burst into tears again. This dear little princess is so sweet and pretty that she seems good enough to eat. The Comte de Grammont was among those who paid his compliments to the Prince de Conti: 'Monsieur,' he said, 'I am delighted about your marriage; take my advice, stay on good terms with your father-in-law, do not argue with him or quibble with him about trifling matters, keep well with the family, and I can answer for it that you will have no reason to regret this alliance.'

In the same letter, Mme de Sévigné announces that:

The portrait of Madame la Dauphine has arrived. She appears to be far from beautiful: her intelligence, her teeth and her figure have been praised, but these virtues have given Troy [the King's official painter] precious little opportunity to display his talents.

A significant appointment now took place, with the naming of the widow Scarron to be Second Mistress of the Wardrobe to the future Dauphine. Her discreet ascendancy had been gradually establishing itself for four years now, but, in any event, she certainly deserved this new honour since, according to Mme de Caylus, the King and Mme de Montespan had often had occasion to make use of her services:

Mme de Maintenon used to be sent for whenever Mme de Montespan's labour pains commenced. She took the infant away, hiding it under her cloak, a mask over her own face, and hired a carriage to bring her to Paris. Think of her fear lest the child should start crying! Indeed, her fears must often have been renewed, since Mme de Montespan had seven children by the King.[2]

---

[1] Mme de Colbert had brought up Mlle de Blois.
[2] In 1669, a daughter, who died at the age of three; in 1670, Louis Auguste, Duc du Maine; in 1672, Louis César, Comte de Vexin; in 1673, Louise Fran-

Primi Visconti *relates:*

The entire Court is astonished that preference should have
been given to La Maintenon, a completely unknown figure,
widow of the poet Scarron, a person for whom the post of
governess of the King's natural children would seem to have
represented the height of her ambition. However, it was not
long before Mme de Rochefort became assiduous in her protestations of friendship towards her, for it was noticed that the
King spent the greater part of his time with Mme de Maintenon, and visited Mme de Montespan and Mlle de Fontanges
less and less frequently. No one knew what to make of this,
since she was quite old;[1] some regarded her as the King's
confidante, others as a go-between, still others as a gifted person whom the King was using to set down for him the Memoirs
of his reign. What is certain is that no one would have guessed,
from her clothes, her adornments or her general manner, the
kind of person with whom they were dealing. Many expressed
the opinion that some men are more attracted by old women
than by young women. In any case, Mme de Montespan and
the other enemies of the new favourite bent every effort to
uncover blemishes in her origin, upbringing and conduct, as
such people are used to do whenever a potential rival starts to
appear above the horizon. They whispered that while she was
young she had been seen, disguised as a page-boy, in the bed
of the Seigneur de Villarceaux; but one of my closest friends,
the Marquis de Marsilly, the Lieutenant General who defended
Barcelona for two months, and who had once been one of
Mme Scarron's suitors, has assured me that she was a woman
of virtue and had refused an offer from the Surintendant de
Lorme of 30,000 écus, although she was very poor. This I
believe, since Marsilly has no compunctions about speaking ill
of people when the occasion demands.

*As far as the virtue of Mme Scarron is concerned, we have
the testimony (if one can call it that) of Ninon de Lenclos, the*

çoise, known as Mlle de Nantes (married Louis de Bourbon-Condé); in
1674, Louise Marie, known as Mlle de Tours, who died at the age of seven;
in 1677, Françoise Marie, known as Mlle de Blois (married the Duc de
Chartres); in 1678, Louis Alexandre, Comte de Toulouse.
[1] She was forty-four years old at the time.

century's most notorious courtesan, in a letter to Saint-Evremond:

Scarron was my friend. His wife gave me immense pleasure by her conversation, but at the time I considered her awkward and unsuited to be a good lover. I knew nothing of the details, and never saw anything, but I often lent my yellow bedroom to her and Villarceaux.

Saint-Simon, *too, claimed that:*

Mme Scarron [after she became a widow] took a room for herself and her maid on one of the upper floors of a house, where she lived in very straitened circumstances. But her charms served gradually to improve her living conditions: Villars, the father of the Maréchal Beuvron (d'Harcourt's father), and Villarceaux were her three most regular supporters, and there were many others.

And Mme de Caylus noted discreetly:

Although I am persuaded of Mme de Maintenon's virtue, I would not go as far as M. de Lassay, who went on for so long one day defending her against all the rumours then circulating about her that he drew a most singular question from his wife, the natural daughter of M. le Prince. Bored with the lengthiness of the dispute, and surprised that her husband should be as convinced of the lady's virtue as he appeared to be, she said to him, with a splendid semblance of innocence: 'How does it come about, Monsieur, that you are so sure about these matters?'

In the space of a few years, the widow Scarron had gained the good graces of the King, and, according to Mme de Caylus, he was fated to witness the frequent incidents which flared up between her and the irascible Mme de Montespan:

I have heard it said about Mme de Maintenon that she was once engaged in a violent quarrel with Mme de Montespan when the King chanced to enter the room, saw that they were both in an excitable state, and asked what was the matter. Mme de Maintenon spoke up first, very calmly, and said to the King: 'If Your Majesty will be pleased to step into the next room, I shall have the honour of explaining the matter to him.' The King left the room, with Mme de Maintenon following him, so that Mme de Montespan was left alone. Her calmness on this occasion was astonishing, and would seem incredible if I did not know it to be true.

When Mme de Maintenon found herself alone with the King, her sang-froid left her and she painted a dramatic picture of Mme de Montespan's harshness and injustice, saying how greatly she feared the results of the other's anger. The examples she mentioned were not unknown to the King, but since he still loved Mme de Montespan, he attempted to make excuses for her, and to prove that she was not really so hard-hearted, said to Mme de Maintenon: 'Did you not often notice that her lovely eyes fill with tears whenever someone recounts to her some generous and touching action?'

The widow Scarron next did her best to dissuade Mlle de Fontanges from her passion for the King. In her Instructions à Saint-Cyr, *she herself relates how she was sent by Louis XIV to mollify his young mistress who was having a fit of the sulks about something, and how she spent two hours with her:*

I employed this time in trying to persuade her to leave the King and that such an action would be both beautiful and praiseworthy. I remember that she answered me heatedly: 'But, Madame, you speak to me of abandoning a passion as though it were as simple as stepping out of a chemise.'

The most succinct summing-up of the King's relationships with his favourites at that time was provided by La Beaumelle, *author of the* Mémoires pour servir à l'histoire de Mme de Maintenon:

The King gave himself to Mlle de Fontanges through human weakness; he returned to Mme de Montespan through habit; and allowed himself to be drawn, through personal preference, to Mme de Maintenon.

But during December, la belle Fontanges gave birth to a son, who died the following month. This death seems to have made little impression at the time, though Mme de Sévigné *mentions it in a letter to her daughter dated January 19th:*

La belle Fontanges did not appear [at the wedding of the Prince de Conti]. It is said that she is grieving over the death of a tiny person.

And many years later, the Princess Palatine *wrote:*

La Montespan was the wickedest woman in the world. I know of three people she had poisoned: La Fontanges, her little boy, and a young woman in her suite, without mentioning others whose names I do not know.

On April 6th, sensation! The indefatigable Mme de Sévigné *informs her daughter:*

I am going to tell you a piece of news which is no longer secret, but you will have the pleasure of being the first person to hear it: Mlle de Fontanges is a duchess, with a pension of 20,000 écus. She received the compliments of her friends to-day, reclining in bed; the King made her a public visit. To-morrow she takes her seat, then goes to spend Easter at an abbey which the King has presented to one of her sisters . . . Madame de Montespan is in a great rage; she wept bitterly yesterday. You can imagine what a cruel blow this is to her pride.

The new favourite returned to the Court on May 14th, and almost immediately fell ill. Again according to Mme de Sévigné:

You know how fortune has smiled on the Duchesse de Fontanges. But now it frowns upon her: she is so ill that she must remain at Maubuisson [abbey] in bed, having lost a great deal of blood and suffering from a high fever. Her body is beginning to swell, and even her beautiful face has become rather puffy. The Prieur de Cabrières does not leave her side:

if he effects this cure, his standing at the Court will rise considerably.

It began to be whispered that this illness was the result of poison. And the name of Mme de Montespan was mentioned: everyone knew that she used perfumes in prodigious quantities, and that even the King had become suspicious . . . Bussy-Rabutin, *writing to his friend Trichâteau on May 18th, tells him:*

I have just learned that on the day when the King left for Saint-Germain, as he was about to enter his carriage with the Queen, he exchanged some blunt words with Mme de Montespan on the subject of the scents of which she constantly reeks and which make His Majesty feel ill. The King spoke to her quite civilly to start with, but when she replied in a sour manner, His Majesty became angry. Personally, I do not think that she will remain at the Court much longer.

Meanwhile, the Affaire des Poisons *was continuing. For a year the Chambre de l'Arsenal had been pursuing its investigations, and La Voisin's accomplices had made some shocking revelations: a valet Romani, and his accomplice Bertrand both confessed that the poisoning gang was plotting to poison the King, by means of a petition which was to be presented to him at Saint-Germain, and to poison Mlle de Fontanges, by impregnating her clothes and gloves. Their friend, the woman Filastre confirmed these confessions.*

A priest had also been arrested, Guibourg, formerly sacristan of the church of Saint-Marcel, and now vicar-substitute of Vanves, who admitted to having celebrated Black Masses at La Voisin's request. And La Voisin's daughter Marguerite Monvoisin accused Mme de Montespan of having been her mother's client over a long period of time. At this juncture, the King intervened, and on August 2, 1680, wrote to La Reynie a letter which is still in the Archives of the Bastille:

Having seen the declaration which Marguerite Monvoisin, prisoner in my château of Vincennes, has made on the 12th of last month, I write you this letter to tell you that I desire you to use all means available to you to clarify the statements contained in this declaration and interrogation report, and I further desire that you will have carefully set down in separate books the verifications and confrontations and everything else which may be helpful in preparing any proceedings which might be instituted on the basis of this declaration and interrogation report. Meanwhile, you will refrain from handing over to my Royal Chamber in session at the Arsenal, until you receive orders from me, the interrogation reports on Romani and Bertrand. I am confident that you will fully comply with my wishes in all these matters, and I will say no more for the present.

The Voisin daughter *continued to talk, and her interrogatory of August 20th was damning for Mme de Montespan. In her statement she says:*

I saw Guibourg say two Masses in my mother's bedroom . . . The first took place, as far as I can remember, more than six years ago. I helped my mother to get the room ready for this Mass: a mattress was placed over a row of seats, and candlesticks with lighted candles in them were placed on stools on each side. After this, Guibourg would emerge from the small side room, wearing his chasuble, and then my mother would bring into the room the woman on whose belly Mass was to be celebrated. At that point, my mother made me leave the room.

When I was older, my mother came to trust me, and I was present at that kind of Mass and saw that the lady was stretched naked on the mattress, with her head thrown back at one end, supported by a pillow placed on a chair which had been turned on its side, and her legs hanging down at the other end, with a napkin spread over her belly and a crucifix placed in its centre, and the chalice was set on her groin.

Mme de Montespan had one of these kinds of Mass said for her by the Abbé Guibourg, at my mother's house. about three years ago; she came at ten in the evening and did not leave until midnight. I heard my mother tell the lady that she should let her know the dates on which they could say the other two Masses which had to be said if the affair was to succeed, but the lady told her she could not possibly find the time and that they would have to perform the remaining ceremonies designed to make the affair succeed without her presence. My mother promised to take Mme de Montespan's place for the remaining two Masses, and have the rituals performed on her own body. Some time after that, I was present at a Mass which Guibourg celebrated in the same manner, on my mother's stomach, and at the elevation of the host he repeated the name of Louis de Bourbon and that of the lady, which consisted of two or three names which did not include that of Montespan . . .

On several occasions I delivered to Mme de Montespan, on my mother's orders, powders which had previously been sprinkled into the chalice, and other powders of whose composition and usage I know nothing, because when I asked what I was to say when handing them over my mother told me to say nothing because all had already been said. Once I saw her concoct a preparation, and it consisted of powdered moles.

Finally, Marguerite Monvoisin declared that Mlle des Oeillets, a maid of Mme de Montespan's, had often come to collect powders of this sort for her mistress. She also mentioned a petition which was to be presented to the King at Saint-Germain:

. . . the sole purpose being to poison the King by means of this petition.

She added that:

Four or five weeks before my mother was arrested, she told me that she was going to send me to Clagny [Mme de Montespan's residence] with a note asking for 2,000 écus, because Romani said that without money it would be impossible to obtain the fabrics which were to be shown to Mlle de Fontanges and which he needed so that he could pass as a merchant. But Romani appeared to possess plenty of money, nevertheless.

At about the same time, according to Laurent de La Beaumelle in his Mémoires ..., Mme de Maintenon had written several letters to her friend, Anne de Frontenac, to tell her of a scene between the King and Mme de Montespan:

August 19th: M. de Louvois has arranged for Mme de Montespan a *tête à tête* with the King. The King had suspected this move on his part for some time, and had made every effort to avoid a suitable occasion presenting itself, but all to no avail, for in the end he fell into the trap carefully prepared for him and found himself confronted with the lady. At this moment they are in the throes of explanations, and love will hold sway today. The King is firm, but Mme de Montespan's tears are very affecting.

August 23rd: The explanations given have confirmed the King's resolution. I congratulated him on having vanquished so redoubtable an enemy. He concedes that M. de Louvois is a more dangerous man than the Prince of Orange, but declares he is necessary to him. Mme de Montespan wept at first, then upbraided him, then finally used an arrogant tone of voice. She attacked me furiously, as is her habit . . .

Are these letters hinting that the favourite had been called upon to explain her role in the Affaire des Poisons, or had Louvois simply been intriguing to effect a reconciliation between the King and herself? It must be said that La Beaumelle was considered a highly unreliable source by Voltaire and the other historians of that era.

Mlle de Fontanges' illness had become protracted. On September 1st, Mme de Sévigné wrote to her daughter:

It is said that the beauty now believes she has been poisoned, and that she will now have the right to demand Guards. She is still languishing, but so infatuated with a sense of grandeur that you must imagine her to be exactly the opposite of that little violet [La Vallière] who hid beneath the grass and blushed to be mistress, mother and duchess. There will never be the like again.

On September 30th, the poisoner La Filastre, who had also

accused *Mme de Montespan, was condemned to death and executed. On the same day, the King ordered the Chambre de l'Arsenal to suspend its sessions. In December, La Reynie summed up the situation in a memorandum sent to Louvois:*

There are 147 persons in the Bastille and the prison of Vincennes. There is not a single one among all this number who is not faced with grave charges of poisoning or traffic in poison. Yet, if the course of Justice should be halted now, most of these scoundrels are likely to escape scot-free . . . When the Voisin daughter was heard on the *sellette* she mentioned both Mme de Montespan and Mlle des Oeillets. Although some news of this has leaked out to the public, I am obliged to say that it is to the honour of the judges that they perceived, through the form of the interrogatories to which La Filastre was subjected while on the *sellette* by M. Boucherat, that the King must have issued some order that there should be no questioning concerning this woman's scheme to get into the presence of Mlle de Fontanges. The respect which the judges have for a royal order, the existence of which is only presumed, has ensured that no news of this has emerged, nor of the other crimes which the wretched creature has openly confessed, giving great offence in the process, declaring positively that the Mass which Guibourg had described to her had been recited by him in a cellar as part of his pact with Mme de Montespan . . .

But, adds La Reynie:

If the persons involved have any knowledge of what has been said against them, and if they are innocent, can one expect them to do nothing about it, or will they not rather go to some trouble to vindicate themselves against such serious accusations?

And if these same persons feel guilty, and if they knew that something to their disadvantage had been uncovered, they would surely be filled with disquiet and foreboding despite the freedom they are enjoying? Would it not follow that they would fear nothing more than a full exposure of these abominable crimes, and their state of fear and despair might provoke them into any desperate action, the more so because they had already proved themselves capable of entertaining strange and criminal thoughts? I even fear that the most dangerous time may be while they are actually being examined.

My duty, in so grave and important a matter, impels me, even on the supposition that the facts are dubious, to represent to the King, speaking as a judge and on the basis of the record, that in this matter the danger confronting us should not be examined more closely without taking certain precautions; this same duty obliges me to ask God that in continuing to protect His Majesty he will vouchsafe to him the knowledge of what should be done, in these circumstances, for the greater glory of God, for the preservation of His Majesty and for the ends of justice.

On January 29, 1681, Louvois asked La Reynie *to prepare bills of indictment; the latter duly sent these, accompanied by some* 'Observations to be placed on the file of the bills sent, at the King's command, to M. de Louvois, the whole enclosed in a locked case, with the sealed key thereto sent by separate messenger.' *These abridged notes confirm all the accusations made against Mme de Montespan:*

Le Sage, pressed on all these matters, declared that the aim was to procure the King's death through magic, that La Voisin had made him work towards these ends, that Vautier and his wife [two friends of La Voisin] had introduced to him the 'Grand Auteur' [title of the Grand Master of the Cabbala] for that, and that La Voisin, seeing that he, Le Sage, was achieving nothing with his apparatus, had put herself in the hands of the Grand Auteur; that the Auteur had blended poisonous powders at Vautier's home, and had given these to La Voisin, for Des Oeillets.

And the aim was to give these powders, as aphrodisiacs, to Mme de Montespan, and to have the King poisoned by this means and by the hand of Mme de Montespan, without her realizing what she was doing . . . It was established at the trial that, two or three years before Le Sage was arrested, he had said before witnesses that he feared this affair would be his undoing. He has testified that he had wanted to leave La Voisin because of her dealings with La Des Oeillets.

These same facts have been mentioned repeatedly since the beginning of our investigations. La Bosse was the first to appear before the tribunal, and was the first to mention these things, while being put to the question. But the King has so far withheld his permission for these kinds of accusation against persons of distinction to be recorded, and since nothing else that the woman had to say was of the slightest consequence, no mention was made in the report of La Bosse's questioning of the things she has said about Mme de Montespan.

As regards the second plot, that aiming to poison Mme de Fontanges by sprinkling her clothes and gloves with a deadly preparation, observe that the Voisin daughter states that at that time, that is to say at the time of the plot involving the petition, prior to March 1679, there was both a plot against the person of the King and another plot, to poison Mme de Fontanges, and this statement is confirmed by the other depositions.

Romani had sought to gain entry into Mme de Fontanges's house by posing as a pedlar, with a stock of fabrics and gloves, in which he was to be helped by La Bretesche, who is already accused, in quite different criminal proceedings, of being a notorious poisoner.

Meanwhile, Mlle de Fontanges had returned to the Court, but she was still listless, and in the spring of 1681 her condition became worse. She was taken to the Faubourg Saint-Jacques and lodged in a small pavilion belonging to the Convent of Port Royal, where she died on June 28th, with no one in attendance except the Duc de Noailles. Louis XIV wrote to him immediately:

Although I had long expected the news you have sent me, it has nevertheless shocked and grieved me. I see by your letter that you have given all the necessary orders to ensure that the instructions I gave you are carried out. You have only to continue what you have commenced. Stay as long as your presence may be required and then come and give me a full account of everything . . .

As regards the question of having the body opened up, I think it would be better if that could be avoided. Convey my compliments to the brothers and sisters and give them my assurances that, whenever the occasion may arise, they will always find me disposed to give them marks of my protection.

What were the instructions mentioned by the King? They were that the commissioner Delamare, under the direction of La Reynie, should find and secure Mlle de Fontanges's correspondence before the servants were able to get their hands on it. And on July 2nd, the Duc de Noailles *wrote to* Delamare:

If you have secured the letters of which I have spoken to you, as well as the portrait, you must either bring them to me yourself or send them to me by a reliable channel, the whole package well secured with your own seal.

According to Bussy-Rabutin *in his* Histoire Amoureuse des Gaules, *an autopsy did in fact take place, and appears to have justified the suspicions of poisoning:*

Having opened up the body, it was found that the heart and lungs were covered with black blotches, which, it is claimed, is a sure proof of poisoning. The King's grief was so great that it was apparent in his face, and it is certain that he would have revenged himself upon Mme de Montespan in spectacular fashion, had he not had powerful reasons to conceal his anger. For he was fully convinced that Mme de Fontanges had been sacrificed to the jealousy and despair of this ambitious woman who had cherished the illusion that she would always reign supreme.

A fragment of the report of the autopsy of Mlle de Fontanges is still preserved in the Archives of the Bastille:

The cause of death of this lady must be attributed solely to the total decay of the right lobes of the lung, which resulted from the hot, dry deterioration and intemperance of her liver which, having manufactured a great quantity of bilious and bitter blood, caused the preceding discharges.

Ezechiel Spanheim, *Envoy Extraordinary of the Elector Palatine at Versailles, attributed the young woman's death to:*

. . . an obstinate ailment remaining from the period of her confinement, and which widespread rumour, although perhaps baseless, attributed to a beverage which is supposed to have been given her on Mme de Montespan's orders.

But the Princess Palatine *was categorical:*

It is certain that La Fontanges died from poison. She herself accused La Montespan of her death. A lackey suborned by La Montespan contrived her death with poisoned milk, and did away with some of her followers: two have died, and it is said publicly that they were poisoned.

The Affaire des Poisons *received its epilogue in July 1682, when* La Reynie, *in a document preserved in the Archives of the Bastille, drew up his list: 210 sittings, 319 warrants for arrest issued and 318 persons actually arrested, eighty-eight condemnations . . . etc. The report concludes:*

It is appropriate that the Chamber should now be dissolved, but on no account must this be accomplished in a spirit of weariness or of criticism of the judges, to avoid any possibility that the considerable number of interested parties may seize the occasion to decry the working of justice.

And on December 15th of that year, the King signed an order for the deportation or imprisonment of all the accused still remaining in the Bastille or at Vincennes—seventy in all. Guibourg, Le Sage, Romani and eight others were incarcerated in the citadel of Besançon. On December 16th, minister Louvois wrote to M. Chauvelin, intendant of Franche Comté:

Above all, advise these gentlemen [the officers of the

garrison], if you please, to take measures to prevent anyone hearing the stupidities that they [the prisoners] may try to cry aloud, for previously they have often shouted remarks about Mme de Montespan which are wholly without foundation. Threaten them with such rigorous punishment, at the first sound they make, that not one will dare raise a murmur.

CHAPTER XII

'JEUX DE PRINCES . . .'[1]

All these young ladies and gentlemen dying of boredom, longing to enjoy themselves all the time but never finding anything to satisfy their insatiable desire for pleasure.

MME DE MAINTENON

PRINCIPAL PERSONALITIES MENTIONED IN CHAPTER XII

HENRI FRANÇOIS DE SENNETERRE DE LA FERTÉ, Peer of France.

BERAIN: presumably JACQUES LOUIS BERINGHEN, COMTE DE CHÂTEAUNEUF, who became Master of the King's Horse (already mentioned in Chapter IX).

JULES ARMAND COLBERT, MARQUIS D'ORMOY, known as the CHEVALIER COLBERT. The Minister's fourth son.

MARC RENÉ DE VOYER D'ARGENSON, who later became Lieutenant-General of Police.

JEAN BAPTISTE DE CASSAGNET, CHEVALIER DE TILLA-DET, cousin to Louvois, and colonel of dragoons.

BERTRAND DE LONGUEVAL, COMTE DE MANICAMP, nicknamed *Giton* by Bussy-Rabutin in his *Histoire Amoureuse des Gaules*.

LOUIS, COMTE DE VERMANDOIS, son of Louis XIV and Mlle de La Vallière; nearly fifteen years old.

M. LE GRAND (*Ecuyer*) LOUIS DE LORRAINE, COMTE

[1] *'Des jeux de princes qui ne plaisent qu'à ceux qui les font'* ('When royalty plays, only royalty is amused')—illustrative quotation for the word *jeu*, from the Dictionary of the Académie Française in process of being compiled during the reign of Louis XIV.

D'ARMAGNAC, elder brother of the Comte de Marsan and the Chevalier de Lorraine (already mentioned in Chapter IX).

FRANÇOIS DE LA ROCHE-SUR-YON, youngest son of the Prince de Conti, later to assume that name and title.

LOUIS JOSEPH, DUC DE VENDÔME (already mentioned in Chapter X).

On March 6, 1682, the Court installed itself at Versailles on a permanent basis. The programme of celebrations included the performance of comedies three times a week, a ball every Saturday, and on the other days music and dancing from six in the evening. A great deal of gaming at cards and dice went on, and the Dauphin, the Dauphine, Monsieur and Madame used to play together in one of the rooms. The Marquis de Sourches, *Provost of the King's Household and Grand Provost of France, wrote in his* Mémoires:

And in this same room were a number of tables covered with magnificent cloths, at which people were playing various games of their choice, and the players were waited on by a great number of servants who were meticulous in their service. In the fourth room was a billiard table, at which the King often played with the Court's most proficient players. In the fifth room, a magnificent collation awaited the company, who were free to eat and drink whenever the fancy took them. But what was most charming of all was the carefree atmosphere which prevailed, thanks to the indulgence of the King who, during such occasions, waived all ceremony towards him and came and went informally among the assembled players and spectators, escorted by no one except the captain of his Guards.

However, this 'carefree atmosphere' did not go far enough for the young princes and their courtiers. The Court, which had been so rudely shaken by the Affaires des Poisons, *indulged widely in another vice which was a source of concern to the King. It was not uncommon for incidents to be made public such as that described by* Bussy-Rabutin *in a letter to his relative La Rivière, dated January 27, 1680:*

Recently, the Duc de la Ferté, Berain, the Chevalier Colbert
and d'Argenson, all dead-drunk, sent out for ice-cream cones
and, finding that the vendor was a well-made young boy,
wanted nothing better than to use him as a whore. When he
struggled to defend himself, they struck him twice with the
flat of a sword. This incident came to the ears of the King,
who ordered M. de Louvois to apprise the Duc de La Ferté
of the abominable nature of his conduct . . . M. Colbert locked
his son up in his room and thrashed him unmercifully.

And even that amiable chronicler Primi Visconti *declared
that he had been forced to defend his virtue against the
advances of the Marquis de La Vallière, brother of the ex-
favourite:*

One day, while he was conducting me into his room, he
approached me and said: 'Monsieur, in Spain, the monks; in
France, the nobility; in Italy, everyone. . . !' I retreated hastily,
and replied jokingly that I was very far from such thoughts,
being twenty-five years old and having a beard on my chin.
He answered me that for Frenchmen of good taste neither age
nor growth of hair was a consideration. In short, I had quite a
task to extricate myself from this situation. The marquis died
soon afterwards of a disease of the anus, a disease which was
very widespread at that time.

Mme de Sévigné *was rather more discreet in her letter to her
daughter of October 16, 1676:*

M. de La Vallière has died, I know not how. But I always
feel sorry for men who have something wrong with their
behinds.

*These loose morals were condoned by some of the highest
in the land. François* Hebert, *curé of Versailles, mentions in
his* Mémoires *the 'shameful practices' indulged in by the courtiers and certain members of the royal family:*

I was most eager that the King should act firmly to put an
end to these detestable vices. With this in mind, I had a long

conversation with Mme de Maintenon, who was well aware of all that was going on in this sense. I urged her as strongly as was in my power that it was her duty to speak to the King and persuade him to use his full authority to put an end to such fearful corruption. She assured me that she had made such representations on several occasions.

'But, Madame,' I replied, 'was the King not entirely won over by your arguments? Did His Majesty not see clearly that such crimes are capable of bringing down on his kingdom all sorts of evils, as well as the wrath of God who never allows sin to go unpunished?'

'I have told him all this,' the lady answered me, 'and on one occasion when I was pressing him to take action, he replied: "Am I then to begin with my own brother?".'

Bussy-Rabutin, *in his* La France Galante, *depicted the Court's 'Italian morals':*

The complaisance with which all these ladies offered themselves had rendered their charms so unattractive to the more youthful courtiers that hardly any of these young men even glanced at them any longer. Debauch reigned more supremely here than anywhere else in the world, and although the King expressed on several occasions his absolute horror of these kinds of pleasure, it was the one matter in which he could never gain obedience. Wine-bibbing and the unmentionable vice were so fashionable that there remained very few who preferred to pass their time in a more agreeable manner. In any case, whatever inclination these few may have had to live in a manner acceptable to nature, there were so many more who lived disorderly lives that their evil example soon perverted the intentions of the more virtuous, so that they succumbed to the lure of viciousness.

Not only were most of the nobility of this persuasion, but some of the princes as well, a fact which angered the King exceedingly. But the princes concealed their activities as far as possible, so as not to displease him, and this obliged them to scurry through the night, hoping that the darkness would hide their misconduct. But the King (who was very well informed about all that went on) found out that one evening,

9. *Louis Joseph de Bourbon,*
Duc de Vendôme, after
de Largillière

The Marquis de
Puyguilhem, later
Duc de Lauzun

10.
Mlle de Fontages,
by Petitcot

Louis XIV, bust
by Bernini

after his *coucher*, they had gone to Paris and spent such a riotous and dissolute night that many of them were dead-drunk when they clambered into their carriages for the return journey. And since these scenes of debauchery had taken place in taverns (for they no longer bothered to hide their disorders), the King took the opportunity to give a great dressing-down to a young prince who had been a party to the escapade, and in whom the King took an interest. He told him that, if he was really unfortunate enough to be addicted to wine, he might at least get drunk in his own home rather than in an establishment of that nature, which was, in any case, a shameful place for a person of his high birth to be found in.

This youthful band overindulged so grossly in wine that each day brought some new tale of their excesses. But the most infamous debauch of all took place in a house of pleasure; the young men first dealt ignominiously, in the Italian manner, with the courtesans they had chosen as being most attractive, then they seized hold of one of them, tied her wrists and ankles to the bed-posts, thrust a firework into a part of her body which decency forbids me to mention, and put a match to it, pitilessly ignoring the unfortunate creature's cries for mercy. After committing this outrage, they carried their excesses to new levels of madness, running through the streets all night, breaking all the lanterns they came upon, until they reached the wooden bridge leading to the Île de Paris, where in a paroxysm of frenzy, or rather of impiety, they tore down the crucifix which was set up in the centre of the bridge; not content with that, they tried unsuccessfully to set fire to the bridge.

A kind of fraternity was set up by the young courtiers addicted to that vice so vigorously condemned by the King. Sandras de Courtilz, *in his* Intrigues amoureuses de la Cour de France, *relates:*

In order not to attract the King's wrath, they decided to pledge an oath of secrecy among themselves and to make all those who became members of the Fraternity swear that they would no longer have anything to do with women. They had suspected one of their number of having revealed their mysteries to a lady with whom he was on good terms, and believed that it was in this manner that the King had been able to learn of their activities; they therefore resolved to bar this member from their company, but when he applied for readmission and swore solemnly not to see this woman any more, they pardoned him, with the proviso that any repetition of his offence would result in immediate expulsion. This was the Fraternity's first rule, but several members pointed out that their Order was soon likely to become as extensive as that of St Francis and that it was necessary to draw up further rules of conduct. This resolution was approved by the rest, and a committee was chosen to work out the details.

Some squabbling took place among the candidates for office, it seems, according to the same source:

The Chevalier de Tilladet, speaking next, said that he would not at one time have found it strange to see Manicamp opposing him for office, since in those days it was rumoured that Manicamp was well endowed, but that today, when it was common knowledge that he was completely worn out, it would be outrageous for anyone to vote that he be elected to office.

Manicamp could not leave unanswered this personal attack delivered in the presence of so many people, for fear that the others would avoid him from then on, so he retorted that he was not yet so infirm that he had not been able to render certain services to Tilladet's sister, the Maréchale d'Estrées, that she had been so well satisfied that she desired to seek no further, and that although, as those who knew her would testify, she was not easily pleased, nevertheless she had never found fault with him.

No doubt Sandras de Courtilz was inclined to romanticize, but the Marquis de Sourches, *in his* Mémoires, *confirms that:*

The beginning of June [1682] was marked by the exile of a great number of distinguished figures, accused of 'ultramontane' debaucheries. The King did not expel them all from the Court at the same time: the first to be exiled were the

Prince de la Roche-sur-Yon, whom he sent to Chantilly, to his uncle M. le Prince; the Prince de Turenne; and the Marquis de Créquy (son of the Maréchal), who was ordered to go to Strasbourg and join the infantry regiment of which he was colonel.

A few days afterwards, the King exiled the Chevalier de Saint-Maure, one of the six gentlemen whom His Majesty had appointed to Monseigneur le Dauphin's suite, to accompany him everywhere;[1] the Chevalier de Mailly, who had been brought up from childhood in the company of Monseigneur; M. de Caillemotte, son of M. de Ruvigny, Deputy General of the Huguenots; M. de Mimeurre, who had been brought up as Monseigneur's personal page and was still in his service, with a pension of 1,000 écus; and the Chevalier de Tilladet, first cousin of M. de Louvois, and at one time a colonel of dragoons and maréchal de camp. The latter had remained for a few days, hoping for a reprieve, but in the end he had to leave like the others. Finally, the King expelled the Comte de Roucy and the Vidame de Laon, the children of the Comte de Roye, of the House of Rochefoucauld, a Huguenot, but one of the finest, most honest and most virtuous gentlemen in the kingdom. The Duc de La Rochefoucauld used all his influence with the King to plead with him to spare his kinsman, whom he loved dearly, so terrible a humiliation. But the King was inexorable. He did, however, grant M. le Grand's urgent plea that the Comte de Brionne, his eldest son, should not be exiled like the others, despite the fact that he was accused of the same misdeeds. But M. le Grand could not save his brother, the Comte de Marsan, who, although he was not expelled from the Court, was permanently banished from the King's thoughts and company. Many other courtiers also stood accused.

The Comte de Vermandois,[2] who was only fourteen or fifteen at the time, was heavily involved in these debaucheries; the King questioned him with all the authority of a father and a king, and the boy broke down and confessed everything, so

[1] These six gentlemen were Dangeau, Cheverny, Florensac, Grignan (brother of Mme de Sévigné's son-in-law), Thorigny and Saint-Maure. They each received an annual pension of 6,000 livres.

[2] The young prince was exiled to Normandy. He died the following year 'from a sudden fever' while with the Army in Flanders—where he had been sent when sixteen years old.

that the King found out through him the names of all those
who had taken part, and their disgrace followed. A great many
others were named as being guilty parties, but by June 10th
only those I have already named had been expelled.

*The exiles included, as we have seen, the young Prince de
La Roche-sur-Yon, nephew of the Prince de Condé and later,
after the death of his elder brother, Prince de Conti. The King
continued to show implacable hostility towards this remarkably handsome young man who was the darling of the Court,
and also towards his brother Armand, despite the fact that the
latter was married to the natural daughter of Louis XIV and
La Vallière. On this occasion, François Louis de La Roche-
sur-Yon was recalled to the Court, but placed under constant
surveillance.* Dangeau *noted later in his* Journal *(December
26, 1684):*

The Princes de Conti complained bitterly about the fact
that M. de La Feuillade had had them followed on Christmas
Eve when they had been the supper guests of M. de Langlée.
The King declared that this had been by his orders, and that
he had given this task to M. de La Feuillade to prevent any
incident occurring between the princes and the Comte de
Soissons.

*The King did not show the same severity towards the Duc
de Vendôme (great-grandson of Henri IV and Gabrielle
d'Estrées), a successful general who was in great favour at the
Court, a fact which aroused* Saint-Simon's *indignation:*

. . . This is all the more extraordinary to anyone who has
known the King, full of gallantry towards ladies for the
greater part of his life and, for the remainder of it, not only
pious himself but insistent that others maintain the same moral
standards; in any case, filled throughout his life with feelings of
horror towards all inhabitants of Sodom and even those who
might be suspected of a predilection for unnatural vice. M. de
Vendôme was vilely plunged in the mire of these perversions
all his life, behaving quite blatantly in public, as though he
were conducting trivial and normal love-affairs. Yet the King,

who was well aware of his habits, never gave any mark of disapproval and remained on excellent terms with him. This
scandal followed M. de Vendôme all his life, at Court, at Anet,
and in his army career. His servants and junior officers were
continually called upon to satisfy his unnatural lust, were
known to be his minions and as such were courted by M. de
Vendôme's intimate friends and by those trying to curry
favour with him, in the hope of gaining promotion.

*Other courtiers managed to avoid disgrace, and the Marquis
d'Effiat, for example, was seriously considered, a little later,
for the post of tutor to the Duc d'Orléans' son. The Princess
Palatine protested indignantly:*

To this, Monsieur replied to me: 'It is true, I admit, that the
Marquis d'Effiat has been a debauchee and has had a liking for
young boys, but he reformed his ways a long time ago.' To
this, I commented: 'It was only a few years ago that a handsome young German who was here excused himself to me for
not coming to see me as often as he would wish, explaining that
d'Effiat pestered him unbearably whenever he visited the Palais
Royal.'

*Fortunately, the heir to the throne was normal in his inclina-
tions: in July 1682, the great event at Versailles was the
announcement of the birth of the Duc de Bourgogne, son of
the Grand Dauphin. The Abbé de Choisy (who had been
present at the Grand Dauphin's birth) describes in his
Mémoires the atmosphere reigning at Versailles and in Paris
on this occasion:*

The King was the first to emerge from the anteroom and
announced to us: 'Madame la Dauphine has given birth to a
son.' I was present at both events and noticed a distinct difference between the first and second joyful occasions. The
news of the birth of Monseigneur le Dauphin was received
with great pleasure; bonfires were lit everywhere, and the
Spanish actors danced a ballet in the Cour des Fontaines, below
the Queen's balcony, with castanets, harps and guitars. But the
birth of Monsieur le Duc de Bourgogne brought wild en-

thusiasm. All those present permitted themselves the liberty of embracing the King. The crowd swept him along with them, from the Surintendance, where Madame la Dauphine had just been delivered, as far as his apartments. He allowed himself to be embraced by anyone who wished. The common people seemed to have lost leave of their senses. Bonfires were lit everywhere in celebration of the event. Some chairmen were so bold as to break up their mistress's gilded sedan-chair and burn it in the courtyard of the Galerie des Princes, adding to the blazing heap some pieces of panelling and flooring that were stacked there waiting to be installed in the gallery. Bontemps came running to the King in a rage to tell him of this vandalism, but the King simply laughed and said: 'Let them be, we can soon order new floorboards.' Joy was equally widespread in Paris; the celebrations went on for a long time, and the shops were closed for three days.

CHAPTER XIII

'MADAME DE MAINTENANT'

The King to Marly does retire—
Lover no more, a married sire.
At his age it's appropriate:
Retiring to the country life,
Old soldiers find it is their fate
To pick the village whore for wife.

Parisian popular song.

❧

PRINCIPAL PERSONALITIES MENTIONED IN CHAPTER XIII

FRANÇOIS DE HARLAY DE CHAMPVALLON, Archbishop of Paris.

FRANÇOIS D'AIX DE LA CHAISE, Jesuit, the King's confessor.

CLAUDE, CHEVALIER DE FORBIN, mariner, later ambassador to the King of Siam, then second-in-command to Jean Bart.

BONTEMPS, the King's head valet de chambre.

HENRY DE MORNAY, COMTE DE MONTCHEVREUIL, tutor of the Duc du Maine. His wife is one of Mme de Maintenon's closest friends.

FRANÇOIS DE SALIGNAC DE LA MOTHE FÉNELON, late preceptor of the Duc de Bourgogne (see Chapter XVI).

In the autumn of 1679, work was started at Marly on the building of a small château where the King could get away from the pomp and ritual of Versailles. Because, says Saint-Simon:

At last, the King grew tired of the grandeur and the pressing throng and made up his mind that he would like occasionally to enjoy the pleasures of privacy in some small place. He made expeditions round about Versailles, looking for a site suitable for his new plans, visiting various places, including the hills flanking Saint-Germain and the great plain stretching out below, where the Seine, as it winds out of Paris, waters so many great estates and rich pastures. He was urged to choose Luciennes, a spot where Cavoie later built a house with an enchanting view; but he replied that the very beauty of the sight would involve him in ruinous expenditure, and that since he had something very modest in mind he needed the kind of site which would not allow of development. Behind Luciennes he came across a deep, narrow valley with steep slopes, made inaccessible by the marshy nature of the terrain, lacking a view, hemmed in by hills on every side, extremely confined, in fact, and on the slope of one of the hills a wretched village called Marly. The chief merit of this enclosed space, in the King's eyes, was that it neither possessed a view nor offered an opportunity of creating one. An added advantage was the narrowness of the valley, which made large-scale building impossible.

It was a tremendous task to drain this bog, to divert all the channels which poured their streams of water into it, and to develop a base of solid soil. But finally the hermitage was built. Two or three times a year the King spent three nights there, from a Wednesday to a Saturday, with, at the very most, a dozen courtiers to perform the most essential offices.

Félibien *describes the château of Marly in his* Vie des Peintres:

This château is hidden in a park adjacent to the park of Versailles. The first sight to meet the eye is a circular court-yard whose buildings house the Bodyguard. At the far end are other courtyards set aside for stables and coach-houses. . . . From the round courtyard, the château is approached by an avenue 115 *toises* [about 745 feet] long, flanked by tree-lined terraces. At the end of this avenue is a forecourt containing two pavilions, one of which is the chapel . . ., and the other has the Salle des Gardes on the ground floor, and lodgings above for the use of several of the more important office-holders ...

The château itself consists of a great pavilion standing on its own and of similar design to twelve smaller ones which are set at some distance from each other, six on one side and six on the other.

The great pavilion is square, extending for twenty-one *toises* [about 135 feet] in each direction; the outside of the building is decorated with fresco paintings representing Corinthian pilasters, and trophies and devices placed between the window embrasures.

This is the place to which the King was to retire frequently in the future, accompanied only by a few privileged courtiers (two persons per pavilion), and with all rules of etiquette abolished for the duration of these visits.

Meanwhile, many other changes were making themselves felt at the Court. On September 18, 1680, Mme de Sévigné wrote to her daughter:

I do not know which forked tongue among the courtiers first pronounced the new name, but in any case they are calling Mme de Maintenon *Mme de Maintenant* under their breaths. . . . This *dame* de Maintenon or de Maintenant passes every evening between eight and ten o'clock with His Majesty. M. de Chamarande escorts her there and brings her back again quite openly.

During 1681, the new favourite gained further ground and even got into the Queen's good graces. Bossuet's protégé, Languet de Gergy, who later became almoner to the Duchesse de Bourgogne, explains how this situation developed:

The contrast between this modesty and prudence, so rare among those at the Court, and the insatiable greed of Mme de Montespan, persuaded the King gradually to draw away from the latter and to seek the company of Mme de Maintenon, but his feelings for Mme de Maintenon were those of esteem only, whereas his passion for Mme de Montespan continued unabated despite her terribly tired appearance. The reason for this attachment was perhaps the way in which the Queen behaved towards the King. The Queen was a saintly princess, but she was lacking in social graces, was often unobliging and possessed none of those arts and manners which win over a husband's heart. She had registered too openly her annoyance about the King's successive attachments to mistresses, and on innumerable occasions she failed to show him those delicate attentions which the King was used to receiving from a complaisant Court. Her devoutness led her to go to church at moments when the King would have wished her to accompany him on some outing, and she preferred to retire rather than please the King by taking part in the fêtes and other amusements with which he liked to divert his Court.

Nevertheless, the Queen showed consideration for Mme de Maintenon, and soon began to confide in her. She appreciated her liveliness of mind, her discretion, her modesty and her piety; and she profited from Mme de Maintenon's advice. Mme de Maintenon replied to these marks of affection by encouraging the King to be more tender and attentive in his manner towards the Queen, and her success in this constituted one of the first fruits of her coming into favour and the decline of Mme de Montespan. The Queen soon realized to whom she was indebted for the King's changed attitude; she was moved to tears by the marks of friendship which the King was showing her and was heard to say in tones of joy: 'God has created Mme de Maintenon to restore the King's heart to me!' She repeated her sense of gratitude shortly before her death, declaring to those in her confidence that she had never been so well treated by the King as since the time when Mme de Maintenon began to come to favour.

But the Princess Palatine *tells a very different story:*

La Montespan is responsible for the King's becoming infatuated with the old trollop.[1] To start with, so as to have her to look after her children, she hid from the King the fact that this idiot had led a thoroughly disorderly life. She persuaded everyone who had occasion to speak with the King to praise

[1] '*la vieille guenipe*': in the Princess's letters, Mme de Maintenon is invariably referred to in such unflattering terms.

this woman and give glowing reports of her virtue and piety. In this manner, the King was finally convinced that the bad or unfavourable things said about her were nothing but lies, and he remained firmly attached to this wholly erroneous opinion.

La Montespan was a capricious creature with no powers of self-control, always in search of amusement and bored when alone with the King; her proclaimed love for him was based entirely on self-interest and ambition, and she cared nothing about him as a person. She thought that by bringing La Maintenon along, she could provide a source of amusement for the King, so that he would not notice that she herself was having a jolly time among her own circle of friends ...

The old frump [La Maintenon] used her Duc du Maine to persuade his mother that since the King had taken other mistresses, including La Ludre and La Fontanges, she would have no more authority and would be an object of scorn for the whole Court. This annoyed her, and she showed her ill humour whenever the King came to visit her. La Maintenon, on the other hand, importuned the King endlessly, telling him that damnation awaited him if he did not behave better towards the Queen. The King repeated this to the Queen. She, being the most good-natured woman in the world, really imagined that she was greatly in debt to La Maintenon and arranged her advancement by having her appointed Mistress of the Wardrobe to the Dauphine of Bavaria, so that La Maintenon would no longer have any contact with La Montespan. La Montespan became so enraged by this that she told the King all the sordid details of the widow Scarron's life, but the King, knowing well that she was a vicious creature whose jealous rage spared no one, refused to believe anything she said.

However, Mme de Montespan does not seem to have entirely lost her influence with the King during this year 1681. She busied herself persuading Mlle de Montpensier to hand over some of her estates—the principality of Dombes and the county of Eu—to the Duc du Maine in exchange for a promise that her beloved Lauzun, who was still in prison, would be set free. The poor love-sick woman agreed to this proposition, and tells the sequel in her own words:

One day, when I was thinking of nothing in particular, Mme de Montespan sent a message to me while I was dining, asking if I would like to take a walk with her afterwards, since the weather was so fine. She requested me to pass by her apartment. When the King asked me what the message was about, I told him and he said: 'Well, go, since she wants to speak with you.' My heart began to beat faster, for I knew that it must be something to do with M. de Lauzun.

When I went in, Mme de Montespan said to me: 'You have certainly taken your time in coming; I was getting tired waiting for you. The King has told me that he will have M. de Lauzun released from Pignerol on condition that he goes to Bourbon.' I exclaimed: 'What? Is he not then to be allowed back here, after all my efforts?' To which she replied: 'I am not sure. He [the King] gives you the choice of place where he is to stay, but he intends that he shall remain as strictly confined as though he were still in prison.' When I started weeping, she said: 'How difficult you are to please. When you have got something you want still more.' We went for a walk in the Vale, which is a garden at the end of the park of Saint-Germain. When we arrived there, she said to me: 'The King has told me to tell you that he desires you should abandon any thought of marrying M. de Lauzun.' On hearing this I burst into tears again and protested that I had only made those property gifts on that condition, that all the arrangements hinged on that. Mme de Montespan retorted: 'I never promised you anything,' but she realized that she had dealt dishonestly with me, and so listened to me in silence when I spoke to her in strong terms about her behaviour. Selfish people look after their own interests and care nothing for the interests of others.

On July 30, 1683, Queen Marie Thérèse died, at Versailles, apparently from a neglected abscess. Louvois wrote to the Marquis de la Trousse, on that same day, in the following terms:

You will certainly be greatly surprised and saddened to learn that the King has today suffered a grievous loss. The Queen began to feel ill three days ago, apparently from the effects of a boil which had formed under her armpit and had become so painful as to give her a slight fever. Yesterday, at midday, before leaving Versailles to come here [to Meudon], I went into her anteroom and was told that the fever had increased somewhat, but that there was no cause for alarm since it resulted from the pain. This morning, at half-past eleven, M. de Gourville, coming from Paris, stopped in to tell me that he had just met M. de Briolle who was on his way to Paris to warn Monseigneur le Prince that the Queen's condition was worse, and that her life was in danger . . . Immediately after dinner, I had myself driven to Versailles as quickly as possible. When I arrived I learned that the Queen had taken communion at about ten in the morning, had been bled from one foot, against the advice of Fagon and the two surgeons, at about eleven o'clock, and had had an emetic administered shortly before midnight. I had not been in the anteroom for more than a quarter of an hour before a commotion could be heard coming from her bedroom. When I went in I found that the unfortunate princess had just passed away. The King is deeply affected. He left Versailles half an hour later, for Saint-Cloud, followed by Monseigneur.

According to the Princess Palatine:

Our Queen died from an abscess under one arm. Instead of drawing it out, Fagon, who, unfortunately for her, was her physician, had her bled; this made the abscess burst inwards. . . . After the bleeding, he gave her a powerful dose of emetic and, in the process, the Queen's spirit departed for the other world. It is not an exaggeration to say that all France's happiness has died with her. The King was very upset. That wicked old devil of a Fagon contrived her death on purpose, so as to promote the interests of the old trollop.

And, a few weeks later, Colbert died too. Spanheim *explains the circumstances:*

Minister Colbert was at Fontainebleau with the Court, when the news arrived that a new apartment being built at the château of Versailles had collapsed through the faulty work of those in charge of its construction. His Majesty felt bound to express his annoyance to him, since he was responsible for all such works in his capacity as Superintendent of Buildings. M. Colbert, unaccustomed to being scolded by his master, felt this reproach keenly; he went to Paris immediately and poured his wrath upon the building contractors who had botched their job. As a result, he fretted himself into a fever, fell ill and died soon afterwards.

Racine, *whose son published a small collection of memoirs and anecdotes under the title* Fragments Historiques, *had this to say:*

It is said that M. Colbert died an unhappy man. When the King wrote to him, a few days before his death, instructing him to eat and to take care of himself, he did not say a word after the letter was read out to him. Soon after this, a bowl of broth was brought to him but he refused to touch it. Madame Colbert said to him: 'Are you not going to answer the King?' He replied: 'It is a bit late for that! It is to the King of kings that I must think of answering now.' When she said something similar to him a little later, he retorted: 'Madame, when I was sitting in this room attending to the King's business, neither you nor any of the others would have dared disturb me, but now that I have to attend to the business of my soul's salvation you will not leave me in peace.'

Colbert was even accused of having harboured evil thoughts towards the King. A letter from Mme de Maintenon *to Mme de Saint-Géran, dated September 10th, remarks:*

The death of M. Colbert has grieved him [the King] and many people have taken pleasure in his grief. M. Colbert's pernicious schemes were so stupid that they are better not mentioned, and the King forgave him most willingly for having wanted to die without reading his letter, so that he might concentrate his thoughts better on God.

Mme de Maintenon was now favourite, though the word was no longer mentioned: the King had reformed his ways and was becoming concerned with spiritual questions. According to Languet de Gergy:

The slow and hesitant change in the King's attitude and behaviour became more clearly marked between 1683 and 1684. He grew less secretive about his newly-found virtuousness and no longer feared to appear in his true stature and to replace the amorous intrigues which had amused him hitherto with the sincere practice of religion.

Languet de Gergy *was convinced that Mme de Maintenon had indeed gone through a secret marriage ceremony with the King:*

I can bear witness that it was generally accepted that the King and Mme de Maintenon had gone through a genuine marriage ceremony blessed by the church, a marriage which the dignity of the throne did not permit to be declared openly but which conscience did not permit to conceal entirely, either.

It must be noted that the King acquired the habit increasingly of staying with her until ten o'clock each evening. Mme de Maintenon's infirmities and, later, her age necessitated her retiring at an early hour, sometimes even before ten o'clock, and Mme de Maintenon used to undress and get into bed in the alcove of the very room where the King was visiting her, a thing which decency would have forbidden to anyone but a wife. And when the King was ill in bed, she visited him with the same lack of formality, and rendered him all the services which a loving wife might be expected to render her husband.

One summer day, the King was ill in bed, and the weather was so hot that for his comfort he had discarded most of his clothing. Mme de Maintenon was sitting by the side of his bed when Monsieur, the King's brother, came into the room. The King, wishing to make it clear to him that there was no offence to decency in the scantiness of his attire, made the following significant remark: 'Brother, seeing my state of undress in the presence of Madame de Maintenon, you will know how much she means to me.'

And the Abbé de Choisy gives his own version of the background to the King's secret plan to marry his old friend:

One day he took M. de Louvois into his confidence, speaking to him as though the matter was not yet settled and he was in need of his advice. 'Ah! Sire,' exclaimed M. de Louvois, 'is it possible that Your Majesty has been speaking to me seriously? What: the greatest king in the world, covered in glory, marry the widow Scarron? Do you wish to dishonour yourself?'

He then threw himself down at the King's feet and declared between sobs: 'Forgive me, Sire, for taking such a liberty. Relieve me of my charges, put me in prison, but I will never condone such an indignity.' The King replied: 'Get up! Are you mad? Have you completely taken leave of your senses?' M. de Louvois got to his feet and left the room without knowing whether or not his protests had had any effect, but the following day he saw from Mme de Maintenon's embarrassed and formal air that the King had been weak enough to tell her the whole story. From that moment, he realized that she had become his mortal enemy.

. . . The secret marriage took place soon afterwards. M. de Harlay, Archbishop of Paris, and Père de la Chaise officiated, while Bontemps and the Chevalier de Forbin acted as witnesses. Three years later, a trifling incident provided me with some evidence of the truth of this. I had made a gift of a particular book to the King, and had asked Bontemps, who was a friend of mine, to present another copy with my compliments to Mme de Maintenon; she was ill at that time and seeing no one. He performed this service for me. A fortnight later, while recounting to me his conversation with the lady, he started to repeat something he had said to her, beginning with the phase: 'I am certain that Your M. . . .' Upon which he cut himself short, started, and changed the conversation, trying to distract my attention from his slip of the tongue. I pretended not to have heard the fateful words, and never brought the matter up again.

Most of Mme de Maintenon's chroniclers agree that the marriage must have taken place in October 1683. But Marie

Jeanne d'Aumale, *an ex-pupil of Saint-Cyr and now secretary to Mme de Maintenon, wrote:*

The marriage did take place, most probably during January 1686. The Archbishop of Paris, Harlay de Champvallon, officiated at the ceremony, assisted by Père de la Chaise. Bontemps, head valet de chambre, M. de Montchevreuil, M. de Fenelon and M. de Louvois were witnesses. That at least is what I have heard said by people who were in a position to know.

For Saint-Simon, *on the other hand, there was no doubt that the King married Mme de Maintenon in the months following the Queen's death:*

There is not the slightest shadow of doubt that a short time after the King returned to Fontainebleau, in the middle of the winter following the Queen's death (posterity will scarcely credit this, but it is perfectly true), Père la Chaise, the King's confessor, said Mass at midnight in one of the King's rooms at Versailles. Bontemps, governor of Versailles and head valet de chambre for that quarter of the year, who was the most trusted of the four, served that Mass at which the King and La Maintenon were married, in the presence of Harlay, Archbishop of Paris, acting as diocesan, and Louvois, both of whom extracted the King's solemn promise that he would never declare the marriage. The only other witness was Montchevreuil, cousin and friend of Villarceaux and bearing the same family name of Mornay, to whom in earlier days he had lent his country house each summer, while remaining there himself with his wife. There, Villarceaux entertained that queen' Mme de Maintenon, as he did in Paris, and paid all the expenses . . .

But by the end of 1684 Mme de Montespan was still playing the rôle of titular favourite. The Marquis de Dangeau *notes, in his diary entry for December 31st:*

Madame de Montespan presented the King, after supper, with a superbly bound book full of paintings in miniature representing all the towns of Holland captured by the King in 1672. This book had cost her 4,000 pistoles, she claimed. Racine and Despréaux had written the text, consisting of a series of descriptions and a historical eulogy of His Majesty. This New Year's present from Mme de Montespan to the King was exceedingly sumptuous, beautifully designed and most impressive to look at.

René Louis de Voyer d'Argenson, son of the Lieutenant of Police and himself, later, a counsellor of State and minister, made various accusations against Mme de Maintenon which have not been confirmed from other sources:

The King had certainly married her, and although it remained undeclared she still insisted on asserting all her rights. It is a law that no one else but the King may lie on the Queen's bed, even if it should be a question of saving the most precious life or of accommodating the greatest in the land after the King. As it happened, Mme la Duchesse de Bourgogne was taken very ill while in Mme de Maintenon's apartments, and there was no time to have her carried back to her own quarters. Mme de Maintenon arranged some cushions on a sofa so that Mme la Duchesse should not be placed on her bed, and in this way she prevented that happening . . .

It will be an interesting question for the chroniclers of our time to resolve one day, as to whether Louis XIV was Mme de Maintenon's lover as well as husband, or whether she was simply a good friend to him, trying to please him in everything. If the latter, it seems probable that, knowing the King's inordinate appetite for young women, she founded the community of Saint-Cyr in order to have available a plentiful supply of the prettiest among His Majesty's female subjects, able and willing to satisfy his needs. There is no doubt that the King often received in private some of the prettiest pupils from Saint-Cyr, and in this way he was able to take his pleasure discreetly, remaining unattached and avoiding both public and private pressure. Mme de XXX has assured me that this is what happened.

Mme de Maintenon's influence became increasingly power-

ful. Ten years later, the correspondence between two 'ladies of quality', published by Mme Dunoyer under the title Lettres historiques et galantes, *shows clearly that people remained puzzled by the high favour she continued to enjoy:*

It is astonishing that a woman possessing neither beauty nor youth can inspire such passion and confidence. But as the Prince of Orange once said: 'The King is exactly the opposite of all other monarchs, for he instals young ministers and an elderly mistress.' She never appears in public except when going on an outing with the King. Then she can be glimpsed at the back of the carriage, spectacles on her nose, working away at a piece of embroidery . . .

Yet I have had the honour of speaking with her occasionally, and have found her extremely gentle and forthright. Perhaps, under present circumstances, she is fearful of exciting envy, or perhaps she feels that at public appearances the order of precedence in seating arrangements might not work out to her advantage. Whatever the reason, she remains quietly in the background.

CHAPTER XIV

THE GRAND DESIGN

Nothing could have been more beneficial to the Kingdom than this highly desirable community of feeling, had it pleased God to give his blessing to him who had inspired such unanimity.

VAUBAN

※

PRINCIPAL PERSONALITIES MENTIONED IN CHAPTER XIV

FRANCESCO MARIA IMPERIALE LESCARO, Doge of Genoa.

LOUIS ARMAND DE CONTI, elder son of the Prince de Conti (already mentioned in Chapter XI).

FRANÇOIS LOUIS DE LA ROCHE-SUR-YON, younger brother of Louis Armand de Conti (already mentioned in Chapter XII).

FRANÇOIS DE LA ROCHE-GUYON and HENRI ROGER DE LIANCOURT, sons of the Duc de La Rochefoucauld.

LOUIS NICOLAS DE NEUFVILLE DE VILLEROI, son of the Maréchal de Villeroi.

JEAN BAPTISTE SEIGNELAY, elder son of Minister Colbert and Secretary of State for the Navy.

HENRI DE MASSUÉ, MARQUIS DE RUVIGNY, Deputy General of the Protestant Churches.

ANNE JULES, DUC ET MARÉCHAL DE NOAILLES, formerly Comte d'Ayen (already mentioned in Chapter IV).

PAUL PELLISSON, one time friend of Superintendent Fouquet. Had regained the King's favour by recanting his Protestant convictions, and now had charge of the Conversion Fund set up to reward Protestant converts.

LOUIS BOURDALOUE, preacher in ordinary to Louis XIV (already mentioned in Chapter VI).

VALENTIN (ESPRIT) FLÉCHIER, Bishop of Lavaur and lector to the Dauphin.

The COMTESSE DE ROYE, widow of FRANÇOIS DE LA ROCHEFOUCAULD, called De Roye, who died in 1680.

In the spring of 1685, Versailles awaited the arrival of the Doge of Genoa. The King had ordered the bombardment of the town to punish its ruler for having built and launched four galleys for the Spaniards, and now the Doge was compelled to come in person to beg for clemency. The Marquis de Sourche *was present at this spectacle:*

The entire Court was preoccupied with the subject of the Doge of Genoa's forthcoming audience with the King, knowing that his retinue was assembled and that he had already sent word to the King, asking on what day he would be pleased to receive him. The King had set May 15th as the date, but some complications had arisen, and it was feared that the audience would have to be postponed. The chief difficulty was that the King had named the Maréchal d'Humières to precede the Doge and escort him to the audience, but the marshal had been informed that the Doge was not prepared to shake his hand, and so was unwilling to precede him. It was then decided that the Doge should appear at the audience without any escort at all, to avoid providing him with a prince as was the normal practice with ambassadors extraordinary; but in every other respect he was to be treated with the respect due to an ambassador. There was another difficulty, too: the senators accompanying the Doge had asserted their right to remain covered in the presence of Monsieur, the King's brother, but this pretentious claim was treated with the contempt it deserved . . .

On May 15th the Doge of Genoa had his audience of the King. And despite all the precautions that had been taken to avoid any disorder at his reception, the crush of people was so terrible that complete disorder reigned from the outer courtyard of the Château to the great gallery where the King was to receive the Doge. The latter arrived at between ten and eleven o'clock in the morning, with a particularly magnificent retinue, and went to the room reserved for ambassadors, to change into his ceremonial robes . . .

When the Doge appeared, everybody pressed forward so hard to catch a glimpse of him that for some time he was quite unable to approach the King. When he finally managed to reach the foot of the dais, the King made a sign for him to approach and he began his prepared speech, bare-headed while the King remained covered. Then the King removed his hat and, after gesturing to the Doge to put on his hat, replaced his own. After doing this, the Doge resumed his speech, during the course of which he doffed his hat several times; on each such occasion the King touched his hat with his hand, without removing it. In the name of the Republic of Genoa, the Doge asked pardon for the acts they had committed which had caused offence. His speech was rather long but well constructed, and the King, who had had the text communicated to him beforehand, was entirely satisfied. In his reply, the King was haughty but frank, expressing his pleasure at seeing the Republic of Genoa so ready to forswear the courses of action which had offended him, and declaring that he would gladly offer it his friendship on condition that it behaved itself better in future.

Mlle de Scudéry *took it upon herself to eulogize in verse the King's extraordinary magnanimity:*

> On my path the other day
> I beheld the strangest sight.
> To explain myself I'll say
> 'Twas the Doge in all his might.
>
> I approached and said 'How dare
> You appear so bold in France?'
> 'By the grace,' did he declare,
> 'That your demi-god's hand grants!
>
> 'Noble hearts like his have got
> All the kindness to relent:

Our offence he soon forgot
When our knees bent to repent . . .'

. . . and so on.

Dangeau *records:*

After he [the Doge] had performed his penance, he was
received and treated like an ambassador. After dinner he paid
visits to Monseigneur, to Mme la Dauphine, to the princes and
princesses, all of whom received him reclining on their beds
so as not to be obliged to see him out. He was delighted by
the atmosphere in Mme la Princesse de Conti's apartment, and
stared at her for so long that one of his attendant senators said
to him: 'At least remember, Sire, that you are a Doge . . .'
He looked over all the apartments and, on leaving Monseigneur's study, referred to the bombardment of Genoa a year
previously by remarking: 'For a year we have been living
in hell, but today we have glimpsed paradise.'
Before leaving for Paris he said that his sorrow in having to
leave France was almost as great as the sorrow he had felt in
having to come there in the first place. It is said, too, that
when someone asked him what he had found most remarkable
in Paris, he replied: 'To find myself there.'

*During the month of July the King was oppressed by the
revelation of what seemed a great scandal: the two young
princes of the blood, nephews of the Great Condé, Louis
Armand de Conti and his brother François Louis de la Roche-
sur-Yon, had asked the King's permission to go and serve in
Poland under John III Sobieski who was waging war against
the infidels. Louis XIV had given his consent reluctantly, since
he had never liked the Contis, tainted as they were by their
father's involvement in the Fronde, and was equally distrustful
of their rebellious spirits. In fact, according to Dangeau, he
refused even to read their letters:*

Mme la Princesse de Conti entered the King's study to
bring him two letters, one from M. le Prince de Conti and the
other from M. de La Roche-sur-Yon. The King said to her:

'Madame, I could not refuse anything from your hand, but you shall see the use I make of what you are offering me.' At the same time he took the letters and threw them in the fire, despite all Monsieur's efforts to persuade him to read them.

The two young men finally joined the imperial army of Charles of Lorraine as volunteers, and performed prodigies of valour in the field. But they were in the service of the Emperor, whom the King quite justifiably considered to be his enemy. Mme de Sévigné *comments to her daughter:*

You seem to have a romantic regard for the Princes de Conti; for my part, I cannot help blaming them for leaving such a father-in-law, and not trusting him to show them enough of war. God knows, they only had to be a little patient and meanwhile enjoy the high station into which they were born; no one doubts their courage, so what need for them to set themselves up as adventurers and knights errant?

But the affair took a more serious turn when the young princes' courier was arrested on the King's orders. The facts are related by the Marquis de Sourches:

It became know at the Court that the King had ordered the arrest of young Mercy, M. le Prince de Conti's page, who had just visited the Court on his master's business and was now on his way back to Hungary to rejoin him. Mercy was seized near Strasbourg, while carrying a packet of letters. Since then, Mme la Princesse de Conti has had a long conversation with the King in his study, and left in tears . . . It soon became clear that the King had had ample reason to order Mercy's arrest and the seizure of the letters he was carrying, which were concealed about his person, some secured inside the crown of his hat and others sewn into the lining of his jacket. It was rumoured that most of these letters contained accounts of disgusting debaucheries and also outrageous remarks directed against the government and those in charge of it, and even against the person of the King and against Mme de Maintenon.

These letters had been written by some of the most highly-regarded young men at the Court . . . That same evening it was learned that the King had dismissed from the Court the Duc de La Roche-Guyon, the Marquis de Liancourt and the Marquis d'Alincourt because of the letters they had written to M. le Prince de Conti and M. de La Roche-sur-Yon. The first was banished to La Rochefoucauld, the second to the island of Oléron and the third to a small estate owned by the Maréchal de Villeroi in Berry, a property surrounded by woodland. They were all ordered not to stir from these places.

Mlle de Montpensier *adds:*

M. de Seignelay had organized a great fête at Sceaux, attended by the whole Court. While there, M. de Liancourt, the youngest son of M. de la Rochefoucauld, wrote a long letter to M. le Prince de Conti, in which he mocked everybody unmercifully, not sparing even the King and Mme de Maintenon. M. de la Roche-Guyon had added a signed footnote saying that his brother had left him nothing to say, and that he agreed with all he had written. The Marquis d'Alincourt also wrote a letter full of foul allusions.

The Marquis de Fare *is rather more precise as to the contents of these offending letters:*

They behaved with incredible irresponsibility in writing such letters; among other things they pictured the King as a simple country gentleman sunk into a stupor under the influence of his doddering old mistress, using such insulting terms that the King never forgave them. His anger was the greater because one of these gentlemen was the son of the Duc de Villeroi, in whom he reposed complete confidence, and the other two were the sons of the Duc de La Rochefoucauld, who could almost be described as being a favourite. He dismissed all three from the Court, and refused to see the Prince de la Roche-sur-Yon on his return, because it was to him that the letters had been addressed. As for his son-in-law the Prince de Conti, he preferred to believe that he was ignorant of the whole affair.

Louis XIV never really forgave the Contis for their conduct, but they were princes of the blood and so could not be

*treated as though they were ordinary courtiers. All that
happened to them was that they received an order from their
uncle, the Great Condé, to return to France, an order which
they obeyed with alacrity and a great display of penitence.
The Court had left Versailles on September 3rd for Chambord,
where the King inspected the progress of the works for bringing the waters of the Eure to Versailles, and then went on to
Chartres to spend the night. The two offenders joined him
there, and* Dangeau, *who was present, records the scene:*

They threw themselves at his feet, begging him to forgive
them for having displeased him, to which the King replied
that he was very glad that they had returned, since the princes
of the blood should always remain near their King and could
never be so well off elsewhere.

*But Louis XIV had graver preoccupations during this sum-
mer of 1685. He had conquered or subjugated the whole of
Europe. He was allied to the Kings of England, Denmark and
Sweden; the Emperor of Germany was fully occupied by his
campaign against the Turks, and Spain was remaining quiet.
The 'greatest king in the world' now anticipated a long period
of peace and, according to the Abbé de* Choisy, *set his mind
to other matters:*

The King, satisfied that the truce would last and confident
in his power to enforce it, began to think of directing his zeal
towards the banishment of heresy from his States. This had
always occupied his thoughts since he assumed power, and the
grand design had gradually formed itself in his mind. The
Chambers set up by the Edict of Nantes had all been suppressed. More than 400 temples had been destroyed; the
Huguenots were no longer allowed to hold posts in the police
forces or departments of finance; farming was barred to them;
no physicians or midwives might be members of their faith;
it was even becoming difficult for them to achieve advancement in a military career. These restrictions were both
reasonable and wise, but they did not seem vigorous enough
to a zealous and powerful king who imagined that he would
attain divine glory if he was prepared to sacrifice to politics

in this most important matter. In this he was encouraged by Louvois, a bold spirit who had long been accustomed to storming all barricades.

The King had, in fact, long desired to destroy the reformed Church, as François Hébert, curé of Versailles, confirms:

The Sieur de Ruvigny, a gentleman of distinction, a most zealous supporter of this accursed sect, born with the prejudices which a false religion usually inspires in those who embrace it, had been chosen by their consistories as their official representative at the Court. This office gave him fairly frequent opportunities to speak with the King in the interests of his co-religionists. One day, he was pointing out to the King that in many parts of France they were suffering persecution at the hands of Catholics and that the edicts of pacification were not being properly observed as they had been during the reign of Louis XIII, his father, and Henry IV, his grandfather. The King replied, as succinctly as was his wont: 'The King my grandfather loved you, the King my father feared you, but I neither fear nor love you.' This remark typifies the vigorous attitude which the King has adopted throughout his reign.

Massacres of Protestants had already taken place two years earlier in Languedoc, where the Duc de Noailles, Marshal of France had taken over the supreme command from the Duc du Maine who, although named governor of the province, was still only twelve years old. The Mémoires *edited by the Abbé Millot from the notes and documents of the Duc de Noailles and his son give us some idea of the way in which the attempts of the Huguenots to assemble in support of their rights were suppressed:*

Reaching Tournon on September 24th [1683], the Duke mounted a horse to reconnoitre the mountain passes. Having ascertained that armed bands of these insolent scoundrels were growing larger by the day, he and Saint-Ruth, the commander of the troops, decided to attack them the next day. After a few hours march he found five or six hundred men entrenched securely in a position above Pierre Gourde, and ordered his troops into action, following a prearranged plan. A small number of dragoons dismounted and drew them into minor skirmishes, while the infantry quickly deployed itself to encircle the rebel force. They defended themselves fiercely, and the only way to break them up was by hand to hand fighting. Whey they finally turned and fled they were able to make good their getaway through gaps in the woods which the infantry had been unable to block. But the dragoons pursued them and killed a great number. A dozen prisoners were hanged on the spot, with a thirteenth forced to act as hangman. It is terrible that Frenchmen should have to be so treated, but their fierce fanaticism had made them seditious and dangerous.

Most of the time, conversions were secured by gentle persuasion backed up by bribes, but even before the Revocation of the Edict of Nantes, dragoons were being used to obtain quick results. Nicolas Joseph Foucault, *intendant of the Pau region, noted in his day-to-day* Mémoires:

On April 18th, 1685, I asked M. de Louvois for blank warrants which would allow me to billet one or more companies in the towns where these religionists are strongly established, since I felt sure that the mere approach of the troops would produce a great number of conversions. I assured him that I would exercise strict control over the soldiers to see that they did no violence, and said I would accept responsibility for any complaints he might receive . . . M. de Louvois having sent me several blank warrants, six hundred people in five towns and villages were immediately converted on hearing the news that the companies were on the march.

Several influences seem to have been at work at Versailles urging the King to the final act of Revocation: Louvois, Mme de Maintenon, Père de la Chaise, the Archbishop of Paris were implicated. The Princess Palatine *states flatly:*

The old witch, in league with Père de la Chaise, was behind the whole business, persuading him [the King] that by taking this action he would efface before God and before the world the scandal of his double adultery.

On the other hand, Ezechiel Spanheim *partially exonerates Mme de Maintenon. He deplores:*

. . . the baneful influence she is reputed to have exercised in the unhappy and cruel persecution to which the people of the Religion in France were subjected; an influence all the more strange because she and her whole family were born into that Religion, her grandfather had lent it his zeal, his pen and his courage, and nearly all her relatives were still attached to the Religion and had not escaped suffering from the persecutions.

One can only guess that she has sacrificed everything to the King's inclinations and long-standing resolve in the matter, that she wanted to impress him with her loyalty, that she may even have deluded herself for a short time into thinking that this grand design might be achieved without the extraordinary and violent means which were eventually used, that when the violence occurred she had neither the power nor the will to oppose it, and finally, that bigotry came to the aid of her lack of resolution and, indeed, to her complete resignation to the King's wishes and commitments.

The Abbé Legendre, *protégé and secretary of the Archbishop of Paris, Harlay de Champvallon, had his own explanation of how matters went:*

Things gradually came to a point where only a mere shadow of the Edict of Nantes remained. The Archbishop, either from zeal for his religion or to cover up his differences with the Court of Rome, redoubled his efforts to have it revoked. When the princes are in disfavour with Rome, it is then that they display their greatest zeal for religion, for fear that the people, seeing them to be in dispute with the Pope, their master, may accuse them of lacking zeal entirely.

To prepare the way for the revocation of the Edicts of Nantes and Nîmes, M. de Paris had ordered in the 1682 Assembly of the Clergy that a pastoral letter of admonishment should be issued, exhorting the Huguenots to become converted; and in the 1685 Assembly he had ordered a further letter to be issued, intended this time to disabuse their minds with regard to the disgraceful calumnies with which the Catholic faith had been besmirched since the schism. I had a part in drafting this second text, and through my good offices the Theatine Father who had introduced me into the archbishopric (this Father had long specialized in disputation) was also associated in this work. He was well paid for his pains. The Archbishop, who had sole control over the payment of expenses, awarded him 300 pistoles. The Father made good use of the sum, buying books and using the rest to decorate his rooms and to instal a few of those small comforts which it is proper for a priest and a man of religion to possess.

But according to Ezechiel Spanheim, *the Archbishop of Paris was heartily disliked, and lampoons circulated in which:*

He was cruelly attacked for his immoral and dissolute way of living. The broadsheets mentioned in detail the scandalous commerce he is supposed to have had, while Archbishop of Rouen, with the abbesses of Pontoise and Andely, and claimed that since he had become Archbishop of Paris, he had had commerce with a certain présidente de Bretonvilliers and possessed several other mistresses who visited him at his fine mansion at Conflans, near Paris.

He was condemned equally strongly for the way in which he engineered the exile, imprisonment or even sentencing to death of Catholic scholars who were guilty of no other crime than that of having incurred the displeasure of the Jesuits . . . Amid all this scandal, the archbishop was all the more eager to ingratiate himself with the King by pursuing zealously the extirpation of the Reformed Religion in France, knowing that this project was foremost in His Majesty's thoughts . . . Consequently, he was quite unconcerned to justify the means that were used, or to defend himself against the reproaches of bad faith which were levelled against him on several occasions. He was most reluctant to share the glory of these supposed conversions and the success of the whole great enterprise with M. de Louvois. Apart from the fact that the archbishop had little liking for the minister in any case, being closer to the Colbert family, he resented the additional fact that M. de Louvois was the author of the scheme to apply pressure through the billeting of dragoons, fearing that the success of this scheme would enhance the minister's prestige at the expense of his own. Besides that, he was viewed with jealous dislike by the Archbishop of Rheims, the brother of the minister.

The Marquis de La Fare *puts forward yet another version:*

It is said that the Jesuit La Chaise, the King's confessor, was not personally in favour of the use of violence. It is said also that Le Tellier and Louvois did not desire the revocation of the Edict of Nantes for which the sanctimonious hypocrites were campaigning so enthusiastically. Yet when Le Tellier signed the declaration in his capacity as chancellor, he exclaimed in joy, in the words of Simeon: '*Nunc dimitte servum tuum, Domine.*'[1] And when Louvois realized that he would now have a free hand, he initiated harsh and cruel policies which led to shameful violations of religious and human dignity and produced 1,600,000 so-called converts in six months.

The Abbé de Choisy *flatly accuses Louvois:*

This minster was so thirsty for credit that he viewed with great irritation and impatience the frequent audiences that the King granted to the Archbishop of Paris, to Père de la Chaise, and even to Pellisson. The archbishop would speak of the books he was having written and printed for the edification of the Huguenots, the Father was always recommending the demolition of some temple, while Pellisson would itemize the sums of money distributed from the special fund to those who became converted. Louvois was most anxious to cut short these interviews which gave him increasing grounds for concern, and so he exerted all his influence in favour of the revocation of the Edict of Nantes.

[1] 'Lord, now let Thy servant depart in peace . . .', said by the 'just and devout' Simeon after seeing the Messiah in the Temple (*Luke* II, 25-35).

The King ordered that the question be deliberated in Council. Opinion was divided during this discussion. Some advocated moderation, claiming that consciences could never be governed by a raised cudgel. But others, carried away by a somewhat excessive zeal, proclaimed that there was no reason to fear a mere handful of people who would soon lose heart when they saw themselves despised and leaderless; that those persons of quality who were involved would soon abandon their cause; that whole towns had been converted at the first sight of the intendant of Poitou's troops; and that if the King spoke up directly and firmly they would all follow him like sheep.

The great day arrived. Dangeau *noted in his* Journal *on Friday, October 19th:*

Two days ago the King ordered all Huguenots established in Paris for less than a year to leave the city immediately, and it has just been learned that the chancellor set his seal this morning to the annulment of the Edict of Nantes. All the temples will be torn down, and the building of the temple in Charenton prohibited. The revocation of the Edict of Nantes is to be proclaimed everywhere on Sunday and Monday. The secretaries of State have dispatched couriers to every province so that the proclamation may be read out simultaneously throughout France. In addition to the annulment of the Edict of Nantes of 1598, the Edict of Nîmes of 1629 was also annulled, as well as all Edicts and Declarations in favour of the self-styled reformed religion.

The news was well received at the Court. According to the Marquis de Sourches:

The King at last proclaimed the celebrated declaration intended to achieve the destruction of the self-styled reformed religion. Just before this, Chancellor Le Tellier had fallen ill at his home in Chaville, from where he had himself carried to Paris. His advanced age gave rise to grave anxiety for his life, but he declared that he would die happy in the knowledge that he had sealed the declaration destined to abolish the self-

II.
*Mme de Maintenon with her niece, Françoise d'Aubigné,
by Elle*

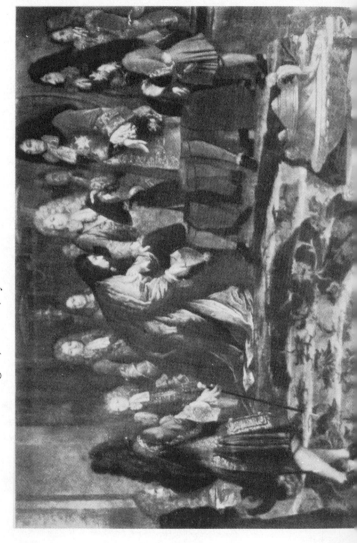

12. *Louis Receives the Doge of Venice*, by Le Brun

styled reformed church. Such noble sentiments made the public anticipate his demise with even greater regret.

The Abbé Le Dieu, Bossuet's secretary, writing of the ever-increasing conversions, boasts:

A great number of distinguished personalities continued to present themselves to M. de Meaux, to be converted through his ministrations . . . The most spectacular of all these conversions was that of Charles, Duke of Richmond, the illegitimate son of King Charles II of England and the Duchess of Portsmouth. It took place at Fontainebleau, on Sunday, October 21, 1685, just after the royal Mass had been celebrated. M. de Meaux officiated in full panoply, including crozier and mitre, and preached on the text of the day, *Compelle intrare* (*Matthew* XXII, 2 and *Luke* XIV, 25). Tears were in the eyes of all those present as they reflected on the mercy of God who chooses those He calls to Him. So the great movement of conversion of the Huguenots was set in motion. The King was enchanted to hear an explanation of the *compelle* and to learn of St Augustine's interpretation and the way in which he modelled his actions entirely on those of the Church in Africa. The sermon affected the whole Court most deeply, and Mme la Dauphine was so carried away with fervour that she talked about nothing else throughout dinner.

The dragonnades which ensued were generally approved or at least accepted as necessary. Hébert, the curé of Versailles, writes:

The King had missionaries sent throughout his territories to instruct the lost sheep. At the same time, he dispatched troops everywhere to maintain these people in their duty and to inspire in them the fear which would persuade them to return to the bosom of the mother Church. If, in the execution of the King's order, a few of the military officers may have committed acts of violence, it is certainly not the fault of the King but simply the result of the soldiery's tendency to act over-enthusiastically in carrying out assignments of this nature.

Mme de Sévigné *comments, in a letter of October 28th:*

Many people have become converted without knowing the reason, but Père Bourdaloue will soon teach them why. The dragoons have been excellent missionaries so far, and the preachers who are being sent out will complete the task.

Nicholas Joseph Foucault, *who had been appointed intendant of Poitiers, was eager to prove his zeal:*

On October 27th, I advised M. de Louvois that the Marquis de La Millière, a gentleman enjoying an annual income of 20,000 livres, was due to make his abjuration in the presence of other gentlemen at a special assembly in Haut Poitou, to provide a good example to them. This assembly did not produce many conversions, but it made a great impression on several gentlemen who were nevertheless ashamed to declare themselves in public. M. de Saint-Georges, the brother of M. de Vérac, was the first to declare openly, in this assembly, that he desired to embrace the Roman religion; I advised M. de Louvois that this gentleman deserved to be awarded a pension.

Gradually, the system was extended to most of the provinces, and the general feeling was that it was bound to have a salutary effect. 'Les Nouvelles à la main', *a collection of day-to-day confidential letters now in the Bibliothèque Nationale under the title* Lettres historiques est anecdotiques, *informs us that on November 7, 1685:*

It had been intended to send the 'missionaries in army boots' into Brittany, but the order was cancelled following a protest made by the Duc de Chaune, the governor of this province, who persuaded the authorities that there were very few followers of the Religion there, and that it was quite easy to make these few listen to reason. This duke tours his province with the Abbé Fléchier, and together they try to convert the dissidents through the powers of eloquence and logic. Several of the religionists who were caught trying to cross the frontier have been brought back here and will be sent to the galleys. Two young men of this number presented petitions claiming that they were only going abroad for purposes of travel. The answer they got was very simple. 'Mass or the galleys.'

Of course, the treatment differed according to whether commoners or gentlefolk were involved. On December 16th of that same year the Marquis de Seignelay wrote to La Reynie:

Mme la Comtesse de Roye has just been here to complain that her district commissioner has visited her home, demanding the names of her children and servants. And since people of this quality merit special consideration, the King desires you to order the commissioners to take no actions in the future which are not covered by specific orders, and to remind them that they are not to confuse persons of rank and quality with the ordinary citizens of Paris, who are to be dealt with in the manner already laid down.

The Maréchal de Tessé, in charge of the dragonnades in the Orange region, wrote to Louvois at the beginning of 1686:

Monseigneur, not only has the entire town of Orange become converted in a single day, but the États have passed a resolution approving this, and the members of the Parlement, who preferred to distinguish themselves by a show of obstinacy, passed an identical resolution twenty-four hours later. The whole business has been effected quietly, without violence or disorder. Only minister Chambrun, the patriarch of the province, still refuses to listen to reason. M. le Président of the Parlement, who so recently aspired to the glory of martyrdom, would now turn Mohammedan if I told him to do so, as would the rest of the Parlement . . .

Gradually, however, all the ministers of the reformed religion left the kingdom. This exodus of Protestants, together with their passive resistance, scandalized the honest Hébert:

The King was informed that the departure of these ministers of religion was causing great harm in his kingdom, because of the frequent so-called pastoral letters which they were addressing to their brethren to console them in their supposed

persecution and fortify them in their acquired beliefs. These
dangerous writings were being circulated everywhere and
making a most unfortunate impression upon the minds of
impressionable people of wavering faith . . .

These developments gave rise to considerable discussion
about the King's policy regarding these ministers. In the views
of some, it would have been preferable for the good of the
kingdom to have had them all arrested and kept locked up in
prisons or citadels for as long as might be necessary to convince them, through discussion of religious matters, that they
would not regain their freedom before giving convincing
proof of their true conversion; and, further, that if they gave
such assurances, they would not only enjoy once again the
freedom they had forfeited but would be awarded pensions
at least as great and probably considerably greater than those
they had enjoyed through their consistory funds. It was felt
that in this way most of the ministers would become genuinely
converted and would thus be in a position to exercise particular
influence over those who had originally been won over by
their heretical discourses, and that these people would then
abjure sincerely. I heard such ideas discussed every day, at the
Court and elsewhere. I particularly remember visiting M. de
Harlay, the Archbishop of Paris, one day and listening to him
express himself precisely along these lines.

The ex-courtier Daniel de Cosnac, *who had once been the
confidante of Henriette d'Angleterre, and was now Bishop of
Valence, has related what went on in his own diocese:*

Since several parishes of my diocese in the Vivarais region
were infected with heresy, it was necessary to visit the region
from time to time to help root out such opinion. M. d'Agues-
seau, the intendant, had already put on trial two ministers who
had been arrested with weapons in their hands after attacking
some soldiers of the King's troops. One of these ministers was
a leader of their party and had been found guilty of being in
Toulouse at the time when the decision was taken there to
plan a general uprising against the King. These two ministers
were in prison in the town of Tournon, in my diocese; I
learned that their trial had already taken place and that the

minister Homel, who was an important and greatly esteemed figure in their party, had been condemned to be broken, alive, on the wheel and his corpse then to be displayed at each of the four corners of the Vivarais, while his companion, also a minister, had been sentenced to be hanged.

I thought it my duty to go to Tournon to try to save both their souls and their lives, if that were possible, from their imminent peril. I left immediately and completed the journey with the greatest possible speed. As I reached the main square of the town I saw thirty paces away a gallows which had already been set up by the executioner. At that very moment, the second minister was being led by the executioner towards the gallows, wearing his criminal's shirt, a noose round his neck, and his arms bound behind his back. I shouted at the top of my voice: 'Halt!' Then I hurried forward, removed the condemned man from the custody of the executioner and had him taken under escort to a nearby house. Here I made it clear to him how greatly obliged he was to divine Providence for having sent me, and that I did not doubt I should be able to save his soul and deliver him without delay from the disgrace to which he was to be exposed, if he would only respond to God's merciful intervention, which he should consider as a kind of miracle. This man resisted my arguments for some time despite the mortal danger in which he stood, but eventually he promised to abjure his heresy. This he did, apparently in good faith, testifying that he accepted all the arguments I had put forward and regretted the trouble he had given me.

After accomplishing this conversion I questioned him about the minister Homel, in what state of mind I should find him, and whether he too might be persuaded to abjure. He dismissed my hopes in this matter entirely, assuring me that this man was prepared to undergo any kind of suffering and would be absolutely unwilling to pay heed to anything I might say to him regarding his conversion. He further informed me that this Homel had been condemned to be broken on the wheel, that he knew of the sentence, and that the only reason the execution had been delayed was because the local excutioner had never performed such an operation and so it had been necessary to send to Grenoble for an experienced man. I hoped that perhaps God had permitted this delay so that this minister too might be saved, and I hurried to the prison where he was being held. But, when I got there, one of the judges who had presided over the trial told me that in the orders which the intendant had received from the King to reprieve all heretics who abjured, three exceptions had been named, and that the minister Homel's name was the first on the list. Therefore, he said, even after I had converted him he would still be broken on the wheel.

But the agitation did not die down, and until the end of the century the Protestants continued 'conspiring against the State.' The Duc de Noailles, still in command in Languedoc, describes a typical incident, in a dispatch to Louvois dated November 15, 1688:

In the diocese of Castres, a young peasant woman had visions or pretended to have them. She proclaimed openly the frequent visits the angels paid to her, started to preach as though by divine inspiration, and soon collected a whole crowd of new converts who retracted their abjurations. A captain of dragoons was sent with his company of men to arrest this girl. When he entered the house where she was, pistol in his hand, a peasant seized him by the throat, then hurled him to the ground. He fired and killed the peasant. Another resisted arrest and levelled a musket at the lieutenant of the troop, but was killed by a dragoon before he had time to fire. The rest of the band escaped through the window. The girl was arrested and taken to prison . . .

We shall encounter these rebellious Protestants again fifteen years later, in the ranks of the Camisards, fighting under the direction of the 'Prophets of the desert.'

CHAPTER XV

HIS MAJESTY'S FISTULA

Already all things start to fade: gardens are less flowery, flowers less bright, colours less vivid, meadows less green, waters less limpid. The shadow of death hovers over all things.

(from a sermon by BOSSUET)

❦

PRINCIPAL PERSONALITIES MENTIONED IN CHAPTER XV

FRANÇOIS D'AUBUSSON, DUC DE LA FEUILLADE, colonel of the King's Guards and Marshal of France.

MARIE BONNEAU DE MIRAMION, founder of the Filles de Sainte-Geneviève.

MME DE BRINON, headmistress of the academy of Saint-Cyr.

JULES ARMAND COLBERT DE BLAINVILLE, Grand Master of Ceremonies.

NICOLAS DE SAINCTOT, Master of Ceremonies.

ANTOINE D'AQUIN and GUY CRESCENT FAGON, the King's chief physicians.

CHARLES FRANÇOIS TASSY, called FÉLIX, the King's chief surgeon.

FRANÇOIS LOUIS, PRINCE DE CONTI, who took the name of Conti on the death of his brother, in November 1685, of smallpox (already mentioned in Chapter XIV).

By 1686, Louis XIV had completely tamed his courtiers, transforming them into faithful followers of a quasi-religious cult. The Maréchal de La Feuillade surpassed all the others by having a statue of the King erected at his own expense. In March 1686, the Marquis de Sourches *noted:*

During the same period there occurred the celebrated dedication of the bronze statue of the King, made on the orders of the Maréchal de La Feuillade and installed by him in a small square he had had built in an area of the Hôtel de La Ferté-Sénecterre, on a plot of land he had bought from the creditors of the marshal of that name.

The Abbé de Choisy describes the scene thus:

Paris was the witness, before God and man, of the most extraordinary sight: a ceremony in which the Maréchal de La Feuillade consecrated the statue of the King he had had set up in a square called the Place des Victoires . . . La Feuillade circled the statue three times on horseback, at the head of the regiment of Guards of which he was the colonel, and performed the same sort of prostrations that pagans used to perform in olden days before the statues of their emperors . . .

Speaking of M. de La Feuillade, I have a rather curious story to tell about him. He was on very friendly terms with my mother and in talking to her he used always to call her *mon bon ami*. One day, at Saint-Germain, where my mother was accommodated at the Hôtel de Richelieu, La Feuillade entered her room. I was in the alcove by my mother's bed, engaged at her request in writing to the Queen of Poland. He told the lady's maid Marion to leave the room, closed the door and began to stride up and down in a most agitated manner. Then, after throwing his hat on to the ground, he burst out: 'No, I cannot go on any longer, I am at the end of my tether; three of my brothers have been killed in his service, he knows that I do not possess a single sou and yet he gives me nothing! Farewell, *mon bon ami*', he continued, still addressing my mother who was lying in bed, 'I am going to retire to my estates and get by as best I can.'

My mother replied: 'Are you mad? Do you not know by now that the King is the most artful man in his whole kingdom? He has no wish for his courtiers to give up in despair but he sometimes likes to make them wait a long time, and those whose patience holds out are lucky indeed, for they find themselves overwhelmed finally by his favours. Just wait a little longer.'

He accepted her advice, continued to appear at the Court as usual, and was indeed well rewarded in the end. His good fortune was similar to that of M. de La Rochefoucauld, another Griselda among the courtiers, who after spending fifteen years with scarcely the price of a pair of shoes, despite the fact that he was constantly in the King's presence and was practically his favourite, suddenly found his condition changed from the depths of penury to the heights of opulence.

Louis XIV was now forty-eight years old and in a deteriorating state of health. The Elector of Brandenburg's special envoy Ezechiel Spanheim *sent his master an account couched in rather mysterious terms:*

Apart from the attacks of vertigo to which he had occasionally been subject, it was only in the beginning of 1686 that the state of his health began to give cause for apprehension. At this time he first started suffering from an obstinate and trying indisposition. The nature of the ailment, which has been much discussed in public and may therefore be mentioned with propriety, appears to proceed from a malformation of the intestinal structures and is difficult to cure entirely, either because of the deep-rooted nature of the malady or because of the difficulty of applying appropriate remedies. It is for this reason that his illness was kept secret for some time, being known to no one except his personal physician, his chief valets de chambre, and those few people, such as the Marquis de Louvois and Mme de Maintenon, who were, for various reasons, honoured with his confidence.

At Whitsun, the King decided to take the waters at Barèges. He intended to take Mme de Maintenon with him, but not Mme de Montespan, a piece of news which enraged the latter when she heard it, according to Choisy:

Mme de Montespan had the bitter experience of hearing her dismissal proclaimed to her through the mouth of her detested rival. Mme de Maintenon announced to her in unambiguous terms, on behalf of the King, that he no longer wished to maintain a personal relationship with her and that he advised her to start thinking about the salvation of her soul, just as he himself desired to give serious thought to his own salvation. These were grave words and Mme de Maintenon was reluctant at first to be their messenger fearing that the King might not have the strength of will to maintain them. She expressed these doubts to the King on several occasions but he was so insistent that finally she did as he asked. Once her difficult mission had been accomplished, she had summoned up the courage to remind him occasionally of his words, for fear that his good nature would cause him to falter or even break down entirely in his resolution.

Mme de Montespan departed for Paris and installed herself in the house of the Filles de Saint-Joseph, where she proceeded to discharge herself of the black bile which was choking her. She sent for Mme de Miramion, famous for her devout nature, to see whether perhaps a conversation devoted entirely to God might help her to forget men. 'Ah! Madame,' Mme de Montespan exclaimed, embracing her, 'he treats me as though I were a low woman, and yet since the conception of the Comte de Toulouse I have not even touched him with the tip of my finger!' The devout old lady told me later that she would have been most glad to have been spared confidences of that nature.

But the King began to feel better and the trip to Barèges was cancelled. Mme de Montespan decided to make one more attempt to re-establish her position, and so she returned to Versailles. During the summer she was a member of the royal party which attended the opening ceremonies of the school of Saint-Cyr, a creation of her rival. Mme de Caylus, a former pupil, has described how the institution came to be founded:

She [Mme de Maintenon] knew an Ursuline nun at Mont-chevreuil whose convent had been disbanded for lack of funds. Although I suspect that this young woman did not have a true vocation and was probably not particularly distressed at the failure of her community, she appealed so successfully to Mme de Maintenon's sympathies that the latter bought a house for her out of her own personal funds. The number of pupils increased in proportion to the income from fees. Three other nuns joined Mme de Brinon (the young woman I have just mentioned) as teachers, and the community established itself first of all at Montmorency, then at Rueil. When the King abandoned Saint-Germain for Versailles and enlarged the limits of his park around Versailles, several houses became enclosed, including the property of Noisy-le-Sec. Mme de Maintenon asked the King to let her have this house so that she might instal Mme de Brinon and her community in it. It was at this point that she began to envisage the project of establishing Saint-Cyr: when she spoke to the King of her ambitions he offered no objections: on the contrary, he showed an enthusiasm worthy of his generosity of spirit. In less than a year a superb and extensive edifice was erected and ready to accommodate 250 young ladies, thirty-six ladies to teach them, and the domestic staff necessary to see to the needs of such a large community.

These young ladies were educated—in a rather rudimentary fashion—to become either nuns or women of the world. Sometimes Mme de Maintenon arranged marriages for them, and in the Lettres historiques et galantes, *Mme Dunoyer's correspondent explains how:*

Whenever a suitable match is proposed to her for one of these young ladies, she summons four of them into the parlour, one from each class. These classes are distinguishable only by the colours on their *fontanges*.[1] All four are made to parade in front of the gentleman, who remains invisible on the other side of a grille. When the young ladies have retired, Mme de Maintenon asks him which of them has pleased him the most, and he names the colour sported by his favourite. As soon as he has made his choice, the chosen beauty is brought back again, and after Mme de Maintenon has received an assurance from her that her prospective husband is not repugnant to her, a notary, Maître Carnot, who has been summoned before these proceedings start, draws up the articles of marriage. The girl's parents are neither informed nor required to contribute anything to the arrangement.

[1] A headdress named after Louis XIV's mistress: at Saint-Cyr, the four classes wore either a blue, green, yellow or red ribbon in their bonnets.

On September 1st, the Court was thrilled by an exotic cere-
mony. The King had sent an ambassador to the King of Siam,
wishing to establish trading-posts in that country to offset the
influence of the Dutch in Asia. The King of Siam reciprocated
by sending ambassadors to Versailles in the summer of 1686.
The visit, which proved a great attraction, was described by
Baron de Breteuil, the Grand Master of Ceremonies:

The ambassadors made their entry into Paris on August
12th. They were escorted to the Hôtel des Ambassadeurs
Extraordinaires.[1] The Maréchal-Duc de La Feuillade accompanied them to their apartments, and after a few minutes of
conversation he withdrew. The ambassadors reaccompanied
him to his carriage and watched him depart.

From that evening onwards, all their expenses were paid for
them, since it is an established principle that all ambassadors
sent by rulers whose realms lie outside Europe shall be treated
as guests, at the King's expense, during their stay in the
kingdom.

The first thing the First Ambassador did was to place the
letter to the King written by his own sovereign by the side of
the bed for lying in state, in a sort of casket which in their
language they call a *mordoe pratinan*. The ambassadors placed
fresh flowers on this letter from their king every day, and
each time they passed by this royal casket they made deep
reverences ...

The King suffered an attack of the quartan ague on the day
they arrived, so the audience he was to have granted them
on the 14th was postponed. Having recovered completely, the
King granted an audience to the ambassador on September 1st.
When the ambassadors arrived at Versailles at ten o'clock in
the morning they found the combined regiments of the French
and Swiss Guards drawn up on parade in the forecourt of the
Château, arms at the ready and drums rolling. They were
driven up to the entrance of the Salle des Ambassadeurs,
where they awaited the hour of their audience.

After performing ritual ablutions, they donned muslin
bonnets shaped like pyramids, the bases of which were circled

[1] Formerly the Hôtel du Maréchal d'Ancre, rue de Tournon.

by gold crowns two fingers high, the symbols of their dignity. From these crowns there dangled thin strips of gold-leaf encrusted with tiny rubies, to represent flowers: these adornments were so fragile that they trembled in the wind. The Third Ambassador's gold crown carried no such flowers. The eight mandarins wore similar muslin headdresses without crowns.

At the end of the Great Gallery, on the side where Mme la Dauphine's apartments were situated, a throne had been set up on a dais with six levels, the whole construction being covered with a gold-embroidered Persian carpet enriched with floral design in silver thread and silk. Great torchères and silver candelabras had been positioned at each level, while the foot of the throne was flanked on each side by great silver cassolettes containing silver vases. A space extending for several feet had been marked out round the dais, so that the mandarins in attendance upon the ambassadors would not be inconvenienced by the pressure of the courtiers during the audience . . .

The procession was led by six mandarins in long robes adorned with sashes, a dagger at their side, their silk bonnets pointed like pyramids, accompanied by a dozen drummers of the King's Chamber beating the march rhythm. Eight trumpeters of the King's Chamber preceded a pyramidal structure in gilded wood which they called the royal repository and which contained the letter from the King of Siam; it was carried by Swiss troops of the Regiment of Guards. Two Siamese walked on each side of this, each carrying a long wand in one hand and a parasol in the other, each parasol being of a different shape and design. The three ambassadors walked in front, side by side, with the Duc de La Feuillade on their right and the Sieur de Bonneuil, who had been appointed to introduce them, on the left. Two officers carried great round boxes with engraved surfaces and raised lids: these symbolize their titles and dignities and are presented to them by the King of Siam himself, so that they never appear in his presence without carrying these marks of distinction. The procession advanced in this order through the courtyard of the Château where the guards of the Provost Marshal's establishment were lining the route, and so to the doorway to the staircase leading to the Grand Appartement, outside which a contingent from the hundred-strong force of Suisses was standing guard, while the remaining members of the force lined the staircase, one on each step. Sieur de Blainville, Grand Master of Ceremonies, and Sieur Sainctot, Master of Ceremonies, at the head of the hundred Suisses, received the ambassadors . . .

On entering the Gallery, the entire ambassadorial delegation prostrated itself as soon as the secretary appointed by the King to conduct the ambassador had indicated the spot at which they were to position themselves in a row. They would have remained indefinitely with their faces against the floor had not the King given them permission to look at him; he told them that they had travelled too far to deny themselves the satisfaction of beholding him. The mandarins, seeing the King on his throne at some distance, saluted him without removing their bonnets, placing their hands together at the level of their mouths. At each obeisance they bowed three times in succession, then advanced a few paces and repeated the same procedure until they had reached the foot of the throne, where they went down on their knees. In this posture, they saluted the King by prostrating themselves three times, after which they remained seated on the floor for the rest of the audience . . .

The head of the Embassy, who was in the middle of the row of envoys, recited a ceremonial greeting to the King without removing his hands which were pressed together in front of his face. The two other ambassadors were seated in the same position and repeated his gestures.

When his speech was finished, the Abbé de Lionne, who had learned the Siamese language while serving with the missionary expedition to Siam, approached the King to translate the ambassador's remarks. The King replied in most courteous terms to the ambassador's compliments. Then the First Ambassador approached the throne, holding in his hand the letter from his own sovereign which had just been handed to him by one of the mandarins; he presented it to the King, who got up to receive it and placed it in the hands of M. de Croissy. The two other ambassadors, who had accompanied the First Ambassador to the throne, stood one step lower than him. The King spoke to them for some time, the Abbé de Lionne interpreting the remarks of both parties.

The Abbé de Choisy, who had been in Siam himself as a member of the suite of Louis XIV's envoy, the Chevalier de Chaumont, and had preceded the Siamese to Paris, was far from pleased with the attitude of minister Louvois:

The presents they had brought were on display in the room at the end of the gallery. M. de Louvois, who had little esteem for anything in which he had not taken a direct part, was extremely contemptuous about them. Passing me, he said: 'Monsieur l'Abbé, can all this stuff you have brought back really be worth as much as fifteen hundred pistoles?' 'I have no idea, Monsieur,' I replied, speaking as loud as I could so that I should be heard, 'but I do know very well that the gifts include more than 20,000 écus worth of gold, taking no account of the ornamentation of the objects, and not including the Japanese cabinets, the folding-screens, the pieces of porcelain . . .' He gave me a disdainful smile and walked on.

The state of the King's health continued to deteriorate. His Majesty was suffering from an anal fistula, and had decided to undergo an operation after his return from Fontainebleau to Versailles. D'Aquin, his physician, explains the operation:

The King had resolved some time ago to have himself operated upon for removal of the fistula, and on his return to Versailles he ordered that the operation should be carried out, but that nobody except those directly involved should have any knowledge of this momentous undertaking. At eight in the morning of November 18th, M. Félix, in the presence of M. le Marquis de Louvois, myself and M. Fagon, assisted by M. de Bessières, introduced a probe at the end of a specially designed bistoury into the whole length of the fistula as far as the bowel. Having reached the opening of the bowel with a finger of his right hand and then drawn his hand back and downwards, he was able to open the fistula quite easily; he then introduced the scissors into the wound in the fundament, cut the intestine just above the opening and cut all the tubes which attached the fistula to the intestine. The King bore all this with the greatest fortitude.

The Abbé de Choisy *adds:*

Mme de Maintenon was by the King's bedside. Mme de Montespan came to the door of the room and tried to enter, adopting that imperious air which came naturally to her after so long a period of domination. But the usher had his orders; she was not allowed in and had the additional vexation of seeing her place taken by a person worthier to occupy it.

A second operation was due to be performed in December. But meanwhile, from the same evening of the day on which the first operation took place, the King received visits and held councils in his room. According to Choisy :

One could see pain written on his face; his forehead was nearly always bathed in perspiration, from sheer faintness, and yet he continued to give orders and insisted that he be kept informed of events. He ate in bed, in public, and allowed himself to be seen twice a day even by the most minor courtiers. During the operation he gave no sign of impatience at all the scissor cuts being administered to him. All he said was: 'Is it done, Messieurs? Finish your work, and do not treat me like a king. I wish to recover as though I were a peasant . . .'

When the news leaked out, the whole of Paris was deeply affected and astonished . . . I heard with my own ears a weeping chair-carrier say: 'They cut him twenty times with a bistoury and the poor man did not say a word!' 'How they must have hurt him!' exclaimed another. The news spread through Paris in the space of a few minutes, and in the streets it was the only subject of conversation.

The reactions at the Court were rather different. La Fare *asserts that the King's illness was followed closely by all the Dauphin's friends:*

Since there was some reason to fear for his life, the cliques around Monseigneur renewed their intrigues; they became even more active when, after this operation, the King fell ill once again, from an anthrax resulting from tainted blood, which necessitated a second and more dangerous operation.

But the operation was successful. The King was cured.
Hébert, *the curé of Versailles, has related how for months beforehand the surgery which was to be performed on His Majesty was tried out experimentally. The Marquis de Louvois first tried having several patients suffering from fistulas treated with a balm, but this produced no results, and he had a better idea:*

He took wiser, juster and surer measures by having several of these sufferers installed in his mansion in Versailles, and having them treated there by the King's chief surgeon who was to carry out the operation on His Majesty. Some died under surgery, and he took the precaution to have these buried at daybreak, with no tolling of church bells, so that no one should know what was happening. But several patients were cured, including a priest named Sanga whose one thought, after his successful operation, was to profit from the situation, supposing that he was now in a good position to obtain the gift of a benefice from the King.

In fact, when the King was cured, this priest did present him with a petition in which he had the impudence to describe himself as a blood brother to His Majesty. The King eventually granted him a canonry in the metropolitan church of Sense. In his new post, the fellow continued to put on airs, and was even stupid enough to persuade the more simple-minded that he possessed influence at the Court. This earned him a sarcastic rebuke from M. Boileau, the dean of this church, one day, during a meeting of the chapter. The man had begun his usual foolish boasting about the royal protection he imagined he enjoyed, and the dean, whose wit was as biting as that of his brother Despréaux in his satires, held him up to ridicule by remarking: 'You do well, M. Sanga, to boast of the manner in which you entered our body, for after all you were made a canon for having displayed your arse.'

Meanwhile, Mme de Sévigné *had written to the Président de Moulceau, on December 13th, to tell him:*

. . . a melancholy and at the same time a pleasing piece of news: the death of M. le Prince [de Condé], which happened at Fontainebleau the day before yesterday, Wednesday 11th, at a quarter past seven in the evening; and the return to the Court of M. le Prince de Conti, through the kindness of the prince, who had asked this favour of the King shortly before drawing his last breath. The King immediately granted the request, and the prince had this consolation on his deathbed, but never was joy drowned in so many tears. The Prince de Conti is inconsolable at the loss he has sustained; it could not be greater, particularly as he passed the whole period of his disgrace at Chantilly, where he made admirable use of the prince's understanding and ability, drawing from its source all that was to be learned from so great a master, by whom he was dearly loved.

M. le Prince had flown, with a haste and speed which cost him his life, from Chantilly to Fontainebleau, when Mme de Bourbon fell ill there with the smallpox, in order to prevent M. le Duc, who had not had the complaint, from nursing her or remaining in contact with her . . . He was very ill, and eventually died of a great oppression which made him remark, as he was about to return to Paris, that he was setting out on a far longer journey . . . The letter he wrote to the King is the finest thing you can imagine, and His Majesty was forced several times by his tears to interrupt his reading of it.

This is what the Prince de Condé *wrote to the King from his deathbed:*

He [the Prince de Conti] has been under my guidance now for a year, and I am satisfied that I have moulded his character in a way which will meet with Your Majesty's entire approval. This prince possesses very real virtues, and it is only my knowledge of his entire submission to Your Majesty and of his very sincere desire to be guided in his conduct solely by Your Majesty's desires that allows me to address Your Majesty now and to beg Your Majesty, as I now do most humbly, to be pleased to grant him once more what he esteems more than anything else in the world, namely the honour of His good graces. For more than a year now he has been languishing in a state of such misery that he might as well have been in purgatory. I beseech Your Majesty to release him from his misery and to grant him a general pardon. Perhaps my expectations are too high, but what may one not hope from the greatest King on earth, of whom I die, as I have lived, His most humble, most obedient and most faithful servant and subject.

The King could not resist this appeal. Conti was readmitted to the Court of Versailles, and immediately attached himself to the circle around the Dauphin who was increasingly becoming the focal point of the hopes of the younger courtiers.

CHAPTER XVI

THE DEATH OF LOUVOIS.
POISON AGAIN?

Here lies he whom no foe could resist,
Who knew the secrets of each man's mind,
Louvois, by people unloved and unmissed,
But mourned by the whole of mankind.
(Lampoon of 1691)

✦

PRINCIPAL PERSONALITIES MENTIONED IN CHAPTER XVI

SÉBASTIEN LE PRESTRE, MARQUIS DE VAUBAN, later
created a Marshal of France. 'No one,' wrote Fontenelle,
'ever invoked the principle of truthfulness so frequently. He
had an almost imprudent passion for truth.'

JAMES II, KING OF ENGLAND, dethroned and expelled by
his son-in-law William of Orange.

JEAN BART, Flemish corsair and commodore in the service
of Louis XIV.

The PRINCESSE DE MONTAUBAN: CHARLOTTE DE BEAU-
TRU, MARQUISE DE RANNES.

The PRINCESSE D'HARCOURT: MARIE FRANÇOISE DE
BRANCAS D'OISE.

MARIE MADELEINE GABRIELLE DE ROCHECHOUART,
Abbess of Frontrevault and sister of Mme de Montespan.

JEAN BAPTISTE SEIGNELAY, Secretary of State for the Navy
(already mentioned in Chapter XIV).

LOUIS PHELIPPEAUX, COMTE DE PONTCHARTRAIN,
Secretary of State for the Navy in succession to Seignelay on
the latter's death in 1691.

LOUIS FRANÇOIS LE TELLIER, MARQUIS DE BARBEZIEUX, son of Louvois, who succeeded his father as Secretary of State for War.

Louis XIV had recovered his health, his enemies had been defeated, the Protestants had been brought to heel or expelled from the country, and the future looked bright during the course of 1687. But the Prince of Orange had, the previous year, signed a treaty of alliance at Augsburg with the Emperor of Germany, joined subsequently by Spain and Savoy. And the War of the League of Augsburg started in 1688. The Dauphin, now twenty-six years old, was placed at the head of an army which invaded the German States and lay siege to Philippsburg. Mme de Sévigné's grandson was at the front, which led to an anxious exchange of letters between her and her daughter. Vauban's presence at the Dauphin's side re-assured them somewhat. On October 22nd, Mme de Sévigné writes:

We know that M. le Dauphin often visits the trenches, and it is reported that the other day he was covered with earth from the impact of a cannonball . . . The Chevalier [Mme de Sévigné's son] has reassured me with his conviction that the siege will soon be over, and that Vauban is so much the master of the situation that he has every reason to be more than usually sparing of the lives of his men; and you know what admirable care he always takes to conserve the forces under his command. Monseigneur is adored by all: he is generous; he gives to all the wounded; he has sent 300 louis to the Marquis de Nesle; he provides arms and equipment for those who lack it; he awards bounties to the soldiers; he writes glowing reports to the King about all his officers and begs him to reward them suitably. He himself says that he gives gener-ously because he sees how great is the misery and suffering. The King has his letters read out aloud.

A letter from Vauban to Louvois, dated October 23rd, appears to confirm this high praise of the Dauphin:

Monseigneur can hardly be restrained from visiting the

trenches every day, but the cannon has been so dangerous that I have found myself obliged to invent all sorts of excuses to dissuade him. I hardly dare tell you that, on the second occasion he was at the front during a major attack, a cannon-ball whistled by so close to him that M. de Beauvilliers, the Marquis d'Uxelles and I, who were walking ahead of him, all felt queasy for the next quarter of an hour, and that only happens when one has felt the breath of the cannonball against one's cheek.

And on All Saint's Day, Mme de Sévigné proclaimed some joyful news to Mme de Grignan (the post arrived much more quickly in Paris than in Provence where Grignan was the King's lieutenant general):

Philippsburg is taken, and your son is well! I shall do no more than turn this phrase in every possible way, for I refuse to change my text. Learn then again from this note, that *your son is well, and that Philippsburg is taken!* A courier has just arrived at M. de Villacerf's, who says that Monseigneur's courier reached Fontainebleau while Père Gaillard was preaching. The sermon was immediately interrupted and thanks returned to God for this happiest of events and most brilliant of victories.

The Palatinate was rapidly conquered by the French. But during the first days of 1689, the thoughts of the Court were elsewhere: it was attending the performances of Jean Racine's tragedy Esther, *acted by the young ladies of Saint-Cyr. One of the actresses, Mme de Caylus, a protégée of Mme de Maintenon, has described how she came to join the cast:*

There had never been any question of asking me to play a rôle. But I was present on the occasions when M. Racine read out to Mme de Maintenon the scenes of the play, one by one as he finished writing them; I was able to memorize some of the verses and when I recited these to M. Racine one day he was so pleased that he begged Mme de Maintenon to instruct me to take on one of the parts. This she did, but I did not care to portray any of the characters so far written into the play, which obliged him to create specially for me the prologue spoken by Piety. But I heard the play so often that I ended up knowing all the parts by heart, and I played them all at one time or another, whenever one of the other actresses was indisposed. Performances of *Esther* continued to be given throughout the winter, and although it had originally been intended only to show it privately within the walls of Saint-Cyr it was, in fact, seen several times by the King and the whole Court, and received on each occasion with great applause.

These theatrical performances did not meet with the approval of the curé of Versailles, Hébert, who expressed his misgivings:

I do not know who can have inspired in this illustrious lady the desire to have the young ladies who were being educated there [at Saint-Cyr] to perform plays, but I feel sure she would not have undertaken this without having spoken beforehand to the Bishop of Chartres and to MM. Tiberge and Brisacier, the directors of the Seminary of Foreign Missions, who all enjoyed her full confidence at that time. Although she also reposed confidence in me, she did not do me the honour of speaking to me on the subject; perhaps she foresaw that I would have dissuaded her from the project, as indeed I did my best to do later on.

M. Racine, delighted to find so favourable an opportunity to make his mark at the Court and also to make his fortune there, did not hesitate for a moment to resume his profession of poet; he saw very well that his art would be incomparably more advantageous to him here than it had been in Paris, where he had worked for a long time without becoming very rich. He composed the tragedy of *Esther* to get into Mme de Maintenon's good graces, and its public performances resulted from the generally favourable opinion of it. The play achieved a great reputation, and there was great talk at the Court about this new manner of creating innocent dramas able to deserve universal approval. This general approbation may make it seem strange that contrary opinions and feelings should have existed. Nevertheless, I was profoundly grieved to see matters

going so far, and I awaited a suitable occasion to be able to
state my views about the propriety of theatrical performances
being permitted in a community established to provide young
ladies with a Christian education. The opportunity soon arose.

Hébert was able to vent his opinion at the conclusion of an
assembly of the Ladies of Charity, attended by Mme de Main-
tenon. When he was invited to attend a performance of Esther,
he declared that since he condemned such public entertain-
ments in his sermons he would be judged severely by the public
if he frequented them himself. He added:

Can you really consider it decent for persons of our
character to attend the performance of a tragedy by exceedingly attractive young girls whom one is thus obliged to look
at for hours on end? Is that not to expose oneself to tempta-
tions, and may one in all conscience allow oneself to do this?
In this connection, I must tell you frankly that some courtiers
have admitted to me that the sight of these young ladies made
a very strong impression on their hearts. Indeed, knowing that
these were virtuous ladies, they were far more affected than
they would have been by the sight of professional actresses;
and even such actresses provide constant temptation towards
dishonour for the courtiers, despite the fact they are well
aware that these women often lead immoral lives.

Esther *was even performed before James II, King of Eng-*
land, and his Queen, driven out of their kingdom by William
of Orange and now installed at Saint-Germain since the begin-
ning of this year 1689. They appeared frequently at the Court
of Versailles, and Louis XIV, who had not entirely renounced
the amorous disposition of former years, became attracted by
the charms of the queen without a kingdom. According to
Mme de La Fayette:

His manner towards her was so agreeable and so affectionate
that it was generally agreed that he must be in love with her. I
think it very probable. Even those who were not close to the
centre of events all agreed that Mme de Maintenon, although
she was supposed to be just a friend, viewed the King's attitude
towards the Queen of England with rage and disquiet. She had

good reason to react in this way, for any mistress will very soon win a contest against a woman who is only a 'friend'.

During the course of this year, tales began to spread about the exploits of a certain Jean Bart, a native of Dunkirk, an intrepid corsair who had been successfully harassing English and Dutch shipping. But in May, while convoying a French merchant fleet, he ran afoul of two English men-of-war and was taken prisoner together with his second-in-command, the Chevalier Claude de Forbin. The two men succeeded in escaping at Plymouth and getting back safely to France. But while Jean Bart, ashamed of his unfortunate adventure, returned to Dunkirk, Forbin, on the contrary, went straight to Versailles, glorified his part in their escape from the enemy, and was rewarded with a command.

Sébastien Le Prestre, Marquis de Vauban, who had a high regard for the achievements of Jean Bart, was indignant at this and wrote to Seignelay (son of Colbert and Minister for the Navy):

Bart is here, awaiting your orders for his next assignment. The whole town of Dunkirk has given him a hero's welcome and I too have been glad to see him back, though I scolded him thoroughly for not having gone straight to you as did M. de Forbin. The latter behaved like a typical Frenchman (pray God he is not a Provençal!), while the first acted like a sensible Fleming and went home. Believe it or not, the excuse he gave me was that, since he spoke indifferent French, and since he had just suffered defeat, he had not dared to appear before the King, but that when he had taken his revenge he would go there if he was desired to do so. That, Monseigneur, is more or less how I would wish all warfaring men to be, and I wish to God that every man in your navy was of so bluff and honest a nature. As for me, I like a man who owes all to his merit and nothing to favour. The value of those who owe their advancement to another's favours is usually further vitiated by their need to provide themselves with protectors who are to broadcast their virtues and actions in such terms as will scarcely permit the rules of modesty to be observed; such officers are rarely the best ones, but often the most successful, to the great prejudice of their master, whose service inevitably suffers. Do not fall into the error of those who allow such undesirable developments to occur, and remember that the greatest service you can offer the King is to create good officers for him. It is entirely a matter for you whether or not Bart shall soon be counted among our very best fighters. Grant him your protection in compensation for his poor standing at the Court, and remember, too, if you please, what kind of men were old Tromp, Ruyter and Du Quesne: their antecedents were no less humble. It is quite possible that he will achieve as much fame and honour as they did, but for that he needs help and support.

The war still raged. Louvois had persuaded Louis XIV that in order to safeguard Alsace it was necessary to embark on a policy of ruthless destruction in the Palatinate: Heidelberg and Mannheim had already been ravaged during the first months of the year. The Princess Palatine *was grief-stricken. On March 20th, she wrote:*

What distresses me the most is that the King gave his assent to the policy of devastation after I had implored him to spare Heidelberg and Mannheim. And yet some people take it ill that I am so overcome with sorrow!

The atrocities continued during the spring: Worms, Spire, Oppenheim and Bingen were razed, and their populations massacred or driven out. The cries of hatred against France which were being sent up throughout Europe began to be heard even in Versailles: Mme de Maintenon became alarmed by this chorus of protest, and so did the King. Languet de Gergy *notes in his* Mémoires *that:*

M. de Louvois did not like Mme de Maintenon and she was well aware of the fact. He had always behaved towards her in the most unfriendly manner possible and had intrigued with Mme de Montespan to destroy her credit with the King, with whom, there is reason to believe, she exercised a certain influence.

The same chronicler comments further on Louvois that:

This minister had heaped indignity upon the greatest princes of Europe and no one doubts that he acted deliberately in order to increase the heat of the war and so produce a situation in which his abilities and his command of the situation would render him indispensable. Mme de Maintenon, despite her moderation and patience and her aversion for all affairs of State, could not ignore the cries of the peoples and the indignation of all the nations. She felt she was bound to point out to the King the way in which his chief minister had harmed his cause under the guise of serving him. It is not surprising that she showed the true strength of her character in involving herself in a matter which was of vital importance to the State, to the King's glory and to the people's happiness. This was *Esther* denouncing to *Asahuerus* the pernicious designs of his minister *Aman*.

What is really surprising is that Louis XIV should have been prepared to endure his minister's insolence so patiently, for so long ...

I remember a story that went the rounds in the days when I was at the Court: it seems that once things went so far that the King lost his temper and threatened Louvois with his cane —or, some said, with some fire-tongs—and that Mme de Maintenon, who was present, had to throw herself between them and persuade the King not to take an action which Louvois might well have merited but which would have been unworthy of Louis XIV.

But Saint-Simon *describes this dramatic scene in far greater detail:*

He [Louvois] wanted to destroy Trier by fire, claiming such action necessary to deprive the enemy of a fortified position which would otherwise have to be occupied, together with the surrounding country, by troops who could be better employed elsewhere. He had already brought down on his head so many reproaches for so many other acts of pillage that he did not dare assume responsibility for so odious a destruction. So he decided to speak to the King about his plan, but His Majesty rejected it and repeated his refusal twice. Making one last effort to gain his way, Louvois remarked to the King while securing his dispatch case that he had taken it upon his conscience to govern the King's conscience in this matter, since the latter was the sole reason for the preservation of Trier against the many decisive reasons to destroy the town; for this reason, he had sent the order for the burning of Trier. At these words the King was beside himself with rage, seized the tongs from the fireplace and ran at his minister, who ducked quickly. At the same moment Mme de Maintenon threw herself between them and tried to disarm the King of the fire-tongs. The King raged at Louvois and concluded by advising him to dispatch a counter-order without delay and to take care to choose a good courier, since if he did not arrive in time Louvois would answer for it with his head.

The shocked minister left the room, alarm written on his face, and confessed to his closest friends that he knew himself to be a lost man. It was not that he feared the counter-order would arrive too late: he had had no intention of sending the order to burn Trier until he saw how successful his ruse turned out to be. The order was ready and was to be issued on his return, had the King confined himself to expressing regret. But so terrible a fit of rage in a master who was already estranged from him, and who never gave way even to slight fits of temper, and the fact that this scene had taken place in the presence of his enemy, left Louvois in a state of great anxiety.

The whole of Europe was now united against France and its régime. Lampoons had started to circulate throughout the kingdom: one of those most widely distributed was entitled 'The Groans of an Enslaved France' and was attributed by some to the Protestant Jurieu, and by others to Michel Le Vassor, a pamphleteer who published his lampoons from Amsterdam:

In spite of the saying that one is not rendered less miserable by having several companions in misery, it remains true that the heart is more deeply wounded when it suffers alone, surrounded by happiness. For the comparison one makes between one's own unhappiness and the happiness of others makes one feel one's state more acutely. Of all the blessings of mankind, liberty is surely that whose loss must affect us most deeply. It is difficult to be a slave when surrounded by thousands of free people without becoming bitterly conscious of one's state of servitude.

This is why France must awake and become aware of the weight of the fearful tyranny under which she groans, and must consider the happy freedom enjoyed by all her neighbouring States under their legitimate princes and in the possession of their ancient laws.

Only France, the loveliest country in Europe, the noblest segment of the world, sees itself subjected to a cruel and tyrannical domination and to a limitless authority. Free peoples who have inherited from their ancient freedom the names of Franks or Frenchmen, are today the most downtrodden of peoples, without excepting those who groaned under the tyranny of the Turk. Today, all freedom is lost, even the freedom of speech and protest . . .

Vauban, *indignant at the appearance of these lampoons, proposed to the King a plan of propaganda to answer his enemies' calumnies:*

It is well known that all the States bordering or near France are her avowed enemies, and most of the rest of Christendom is either her secret or indirect enemy. We also know that the lampoons published against her are circulated throughout the nations of Europe; far from diminishing the aversion they feel naturally for us, these pamphlets exacerbate such feelings, all the more so because they see nothing coming from our side refuting the attacks against us, and so are convinced that we are in the wrong and that we make no reply because we have no answer . . .

France boasts today more excellent pens than ever before, and all that needs to be done is to select a certain number of the liveliest writers and set them to work. The King may easily accomplish this at no cost to himself, simply rewarding the most successful with the grant of benifices yielding two, three, four or even six thousand livres in annual income. These writers may be divided into separate groups, of counter-satirists and counter-newsmongers. Others, again, will dissect the lampoons and separate the true from the false, replying in an appropriate manner, asserting the truth modestly and exposing falsehood. In this way we shall soon be able to turn these publications and their authors to ridicule, nobly and honestly, and avoiding insult and invective.

But Louis XIV did not seem unduly worried by what his adversaries were saying. He was spending more and more time at Marly, where the Court was able to relax from the etiquette imposed at Versailles. Charles Honoré d'Albert, Duc de Luynes, relates:

During the extremely lively suppers which took place there, it was even known to happen that the King, who had an excellent aim, would amuse himself by throwing bread pellets at the ladies and allowing them all to hurl pellets at him. M. de Lassay, who was too young at the time to have been a table guest at these meals, told me one day how astonished he had been to see the King throw not only bread pellets but apples and oranges. On one such occasion, apparently, Mlle de Viantais, maid-of-honour of Mme la Princesse de Conti, was slightly hurt by the impact of some piece of fruit thrown by the King, and retorted by hurling at his head a whole dish of dressed salad.

And Mme Dunoyer's correspondent assured her that the courtiers sometimes bought their invitations to Marly:

The Princesse de Montauban, annoyed at never having figured on the famous list, sought out the Princesse d'Harcourt, who was on it, and offered her 1,000 écus to yield her place to her. The Princesse d'Harcourt accepted the proposition, but she still needed the King's agreement for the exchange to be made. So she went in search of the King.

'It seems to me, Sir,' she commenced boldly, 'that the Princesse de Montauban has never been to Marly.' 'I know it,' said the King. 'Yet I believe that she would be most gratified to go there.' 'I do not doubt it, Madame.' 'But, Sire, will Your Majesty not deign to name her?' 'It is not necessary, Madame.' 'But the point is,' continued the princess, 'it would be worth

1,000 écus to me, Sire, and Your Majesty knows that I am short of money.'

On April 20, 1690, occurred the death of the Dauphine, Marie Christine of Bavaria. She had exercised little influence over her husband, and her death affected the Court very little. Primi Visconti claimed that she was an intelligent woman, but that soon after her marriage·

She began to talk of nothing but dress and fashion. She had been warned that such subjects were the only ones permissible, and that the interest the King had shown in her had diminished because she had begun to inform herself in affairs of State.

The Princess Palatine *exclaims indignantly:*

The Dauphine is unhappy, and although she does her best to please the King, the old hag sees to it that she is made thoroughly miserable every day. They force her to spend her life being bored and becoming pregnant. Her M. le Dauphin cares about nothing in the world. He finds his pleasures where he can and is horribly debauched.

Mme de Caylus describes how Marie Christine died:

She spent her life shut up in a small room behind her apartment, an ill-ventilated place with no view. This, added to her naturally melancholic disposition, brought on dizzy spells. These vapours were taken to be symptoms of a serious illness and she was subjected to violent remedies. In the end it was these remedies rather than her ailments which caused her death, after she had given us three princes. She died convinced that her last child-bed had been the death of her and she said, while giving her blessing to M. le Duc de Berry: 'Ah! my son, how dearly your days have cost your mother!'[1]

The Dauphin, after having commanded the army in Germany without great distinction (Louis XIV had advised him not to give battle, since 'for his particular glory, it would be appropriate to fight, but not to endanger himself for the sake

[1] But, in Mme de Sévigné's version, she said, while blessing her children: 'And you too, my little Berry, although you are the cause of my death.'

of the State'), withdrew increasingly to his residence at Anet,
where he was surrounded by a miniature court of gentlemen of
his own age. The King was preparing his forthcoming spring
campaign. At the same time he had confided the education of
his youngest legitimized daughter, Mlle de Blois, not to any
friend of her mother, Mme de Montespan, but to a protégée
of Mme de Maintenon, the Marquise de Montchevreuil. This
time, Mme de Montespan, weary of undergoing humiliations,
quit Versailles for good. The Princess Palatine *explains exactly*
how this came about:

The Duc du Maine persuaded his mother to withdraw from
the Court for a little time, since that would give the King the
incentive to recall her. She loved her son and thought he
reciprocated her sentiments. So she went to Paris, writing to
the King that she would never return. The Duc du Maine
immediately had all his mother's baggage sent to Paris, without
telling her beforehand. As for her furniture, he had it thrown
out of the windows. In short, he made it impossible for her
return to Versailles.

And Mme de Dunoyer's correspondent *partially cor-*
roborates this version of the favourite's withdrawal from the
Court:

It was the Duc du Maine, her son, who was heartless enough
to inform her that it was necessary for her to leave the Court,
since the King needed her apartment. On the following day,
her son was installed in it. You can well understand how dis-
traught his mother was. She asked to speak to the King for the
last time and, realizing that she had no reason any longer for
mincing words, she spoke to him angrily, reproaching him for
his ingratitude after all she had done for him. The King endured her anger calmly, because she was a woman and because
he realized this was the last time he would have to listen to her
complaints. She divided the rest of her days between the house
of her sister, the Abbess of Fontrevault, and the community of
Saint-Joseph in the Faubourg Saint-Germain which she had
founded herself.

Echoes of the war reached Versailles every day. The in-

trepid Jean Bart was back in action: in July 1691 he succeeded in running the English blockade, and during the summer his men pounced pitilessly upon shipping in the North Sea and even undertook a skirmishing attack on Newcastle. The Chevalier de Forbin, who had become his second-in-command once again, relates his version of the events:

The orders that Bart had received from the Court instructed him to burn all the vessels he captured, but the intendant of Dunkirk, with his own interests in mind, had amended these orders, explaining to him that although the Court's instructions regarding the burning of prize vessels should be obeyed in general, exception should be made in the case of captures above a certain value and that such vessels should be kept intact. To ensure the carrying out of this new policy, the intendant appointed a commissioner with orders to return to him prize vessels of a certain value and put them under his command. Since the four vessels we had just seized were worth more than three millions, after taking off their crews we had a frigate from our squadron escort them to Bergen in Norway, in the Kingdom of Denmark, a country with which we were at peace . . .

A few days out of Bergen we found ourselves off the coast of Scotland. I proposed to Bart that we should make a landing and burn a few villages and a fine castle which had come into view. Such a sortie seemed to me to present the two advantages of creating a stir in the country and of enhancing the reputation of our squadron. Bart approved my plan and left me in sole charge of the enterprise.

After landing, I had twenty-five men entrench themselves in a position where they could guard the sloops and dinghies and keep open a line of retreat in case I was repulsed by the enemy. I then advanced upon the enemy territory at the head of my band, and began my attack. We burned and sacked the villages and the castle, although I had some regret at the pillage of the castle since I could see by the ornaments looted from its chapel that the owner was a Roman Catholic . . .

One morning a Dutch ship hoved into view and I broke away and pursued it. My ship suddenly ran into bad weather which drew me so far away from the squadron that it became

impossible for me to rejoin it. I set course for our destination
[Bergen] and burned four English vessels on the way, arriving, with our supplies almost exhausted, to find that the
squadron had got there a few days ahead of me. When I dis-
embarked I was confronted by a scene of complete confusion.
M. Bart was carousing in a tavern which had become his more
or less permanent home, and was completely oblivious of his
responsibilities; and the governor, who took him to be an
ordinary privateer, held him in such small regard that he had
taken away from him the ships we had captured at the start of
our campaign and had handed them over to the Danes, without
the slightest show of opposition from Bart . . .

Forbin *continues his partisan account of events to claim
that it was he who restored the situation and managed to get
the prize ships back from the Danes after a series of brawls
and disputes. They returned to France to find that the King
had ordered them to report to him to give an account of their
conduct:*

The apparent ill-will shown towards us by the Court
resulted from the intendant Patoulet's treacherous behaviour
towards us. We found out that the commissioner, who had
been attached to our party solely so that the intendant might
have a chance to appropriate part of our booty, had written
to the intendant complaining that Bart—who acted on my
advice in all matters—had put him in irons for fear he should
witness our thievery. On hearing this story, the intendant had
complained to the minister, exaggerating the commissioner's
tale in the process. We decided between us that we should
behave as though nothing was wrong. I was to travel post to
the Court, and Bart would follow me at a more leisurely pace;
we agreed that when he arrived in Paris he would see no one
before consulting with me. So I left for the Court the day
after I landed at Dunkirk and reported immediately to M. de
Pontchartrain. I made out such a good case for the actions we
had pursued that the minister was won over from his initial
prejudice and declared himself entirely satisfied with our conduct. I then went to pay my respects to the King, and he
received me affably.

Bart arrived a few days later. He was received far better than he deserved, since he had played almost no part at all in the operations we had carried out. Nevertheless, he was rewarded with a bonus of 1,000 écus for the campaign, simply because he was officially the commander, whereas I, who had taken all the decisions and done all the work, got nothing. This was a very great mortification to me.

Bart's fame made everybody in the Court want to meet him. I introduced him everywhere, which led to a few wits saying jokingly: 'Let us go and see Forbin leading his Bear!' I must admit that there was some truth in their jibe: Bart was dull and stupid and could not even read or write, except that he had learned how to sign his name; he spoke haltingly and seldom; he was always raring for a fight but he was quite incapable of planning any kind of long-term project.

During this summer, on July 16, 1691, the Marquis de Louvois died 'rather abruptly', in the words of the Abbé de Choisy:

His family was convinced that he had been poisoned, but I think this idea is nonsense. His behaviour was very different to that of the King, who began several years ago to think about his salvation. It is certainly true that he was most dissatisfied with his ministry, and that his patience had become exhausted on innumerable occasions.

In a letter to the Maréchal de Tessé, dated July 28th, the Marquis de Barbezieux, Louvois' son, describes his father's death:

He died on Monday, very suddenly. A quarter of an hour earlier he had complained of a burning sensation in his stomach. He was bled from the left arm and, feeling himself relieved by this bleeding, asked to be bled from the other arm as well, but his physician would not allow this because of his extreme weakness. He asked where I was and sent for me. I was ill in bed, but got up to go to him. Meanwhile, M. Fagon, for whom he had a high regard, had entered his room. He began to describe to M. Fagon what was hurting him, but a moment

later said that he was suffocating. He asked for me again
urgently, saying that he was dying. After these last words his
head slumped against his shoulder and he expired. I arrived just
as his head fell back. I could scarcely believe the sad truth
which was written in the grief-stricken faces of those present,
and rushed up to him, but it was all over and he remained
insensible to my caresses. His body was opened up on the
following day, and though they found no indications positive
enough to make it certain that he had been poisoned, it still
seems most probable that that was in fact the manner in which
he died. So I lost all that was dearest to me in the world.

Dionis, *Louvois' surgeon also gave an account of this
death:*

On July 16, 1691, the Marquis de Louvois, after having
dined at home in good company, went to the Council. While
reading out a letter to the King, he had to break off because
he felt so ill. He tried to start reading again, but found it impossible, so he left the King's study and made his way to the
Surintendance, where he lodged, assisted by one of the gentlemen of his suite.

Passing by the gallery which leads from the King's apartments to his own rooms, he told one of his people to fetch me
as quickly as possible. I got to his bedroom just as they were
undressing him and he said to me: 'Bleed me quickly, I am
suffocating!' I asked him if the pain was greater on one side of
his chest or the other, to which he replied: 'This is where the
pain is,' placing his hand over the region of his heart. I bled him
in the presence of M. Séron, his physician, but a moment later
he urged me to bleed him again because he felt no relief.
M. d'Aquin and M. Fagon arrived and examined him, noticing
his enfeebled state and the great pain he was clearly suffering.
He suddenly felt a movement in his stomach as though it were
about to burst. He called for the *chaise percée* and, after sitting on it for a moment, exclaimed: 'I am fainting.' He threw
himself backwards, supported by M. Séron on one side and one
of his valets on the other. His death-rattle lasted several minutes
before he expired.

On the following day, M. Fagon visited me to tell me that

the family had expressed the hope that I would undertake the opening up of the body. I did so, in the presence of MM. d'Aquin, Fagon, Duchesne and Séron . . . I am definitely of the opinion that death was caused by the interception of the circulation of the blood; the lungs were filled with blood because it had been retained there, while there was none at all in the heart because the blood was blocked from it. The heart had to stop because it was receiving no supplies of blood to keep its movements going, and the stoppage caused this sudden death.

Dionis, as can be seen, does not commit himself, but the detective Saint-Simon is better informed:

On July 16th I was at Versailles. After dining with the King that day, I came across him [Louvois] at the far end of a very small room which lies between the great Salle des Gardes and the great salon which gives on to the small Cour des Princes. He was speaking with M. de Marsan. He told me he was going to work with the King in Mme de Maintenon's apartments, and that afterwards the King intended to walk in the gardens of the château. This the King used to do regularly, and all the people at the Court were free to follow him and speak with him on such occasions.

At four o'clock in the afternoon of that same day, I visited Mme de Châteauneuf in her apartment, and learned from her that he had become ill while at Mme de Maintenon's, that the King had insisted that he retire, and that he had gone back to his own apartment on foot. There his condition had suddenly grown worse, the physician had hastily administered an enema which he had not been able to retain, and that he died immediately after this, while asking for his son Barbezieux, who arrived too late even though he had come running from his room as soon as he was summoned.

The suddenness of Louvois' illness and death gave rise to a great deal of talk, and to even more talk after the opening of the body revealed that he had been poisoned.

He was a great drinker of water and a jug of water, from which he used to drink directly, was always to be found on the chimney-piece in his study. It is known that he had taken a drink from this jug before leaving for his appointment with

the King. It is also known that between the time he left the
King's dinner-table with a number of other guests and the time
he entered his study to collect some papers he required for his
afternoon's session with the King, one of the household's blue
footmen had entered his study and remained there alone for a
few moments. He was arrested and imprisoned,[1] but when he
had been in custody only four days, and the judicial enquiry
was already under way, he was released on the King's orders,
the documents in the case thrown in the fire, and an absolute
ban placed on any further investigation of events. It even
became dangerous to speak about it and the Louvois family
suppressed all the rumours with a determination which left no
doubt that very strict orders had been given.

The Princess Palatine, *too, had her suspicions:*

I do not know if it is true that Mme de Maintenon had
Louvois poisoned, but it is certain that he died poisoned, as did
his own physician who was instrumental in his murder. The
doctor confessed on his deathbed: 'I die poisoned, and I
deserve my fate for having poisoned my master, M. de Louvois,
in the hope of becoming the King's physician, as Mme de
Maintenon had promised me.' But here at the Court attempts
have been made to shrug off this statement by Doctor Séron as
sheer invention.[2]

If she did in fact have Louvois poisoned it was because he
had decided to oppose her actively and open the King's mind
to her intrigues. To achieve his aims more easily he had
advised the King not to allow this woman to accompany him
to the armies. The King had been weak enough to tell her this.

[1] On July 27th, Barbezieux wrote to La Reynie: 'I think you will by now
have received the King's order authorizing the transfer to Vincennes of the
Savoyard in our household who was arrested. I think I should advise you
that I have received information that an attempt may be made to murder
this man to prevent him talking.'
[2] Saint-Simon also reports the story told him by a gentleman in the Louvois
household, according to which this physician Séron, four or five months
after the minister's death, had barricaded himself in his room and let himself die, saying that he deserved his fate for doing what he had done to his
master and that he was a miserable creature beyond help; he died in this
state of despair, after ten or eleven hours, without making any further
statement or naming any names.

And the death of Louvois followed. He was a wicked fellow, believing in neither God nor devil, but it must be admitted that he served his King faithfully.

Guilty or not, Louis XIV apparently showed a certain satisfaction at the death of Louvois. At any rate, the Abbé de Choisy, *after recalling the grave differences which affected the relationship between the King and his minister, states:*

The death of Louvois altered everything, and the King made no attempt to hide his joy at the news. One evening, when he was taking supper at Marly with the ladies, the Comte de Marsan, who was behind Madame, was speaking of the King's heroic deeds at the siege of Mons. 'It is true,' remarked the King, 'that that was a lucky year for me. I was rid of three men I could not endure any longer: M. de Louvois, Seignelay and La Feuillade.' Madame, who is quick in repartee, said to him: 'Ha, Monsieur, why did you not simply have them disposed of?' At which the King lowered his eyes and stared at his plate.

CHAPTER XVII

CONTI,
DARLING OF THE COURT

No prince was ever more greatly loved, and no prince ever
had more royal propensities.

MME DUNOYER

✦

PRINCIPAL PERSONALITIES MENTIONED IN CHAPTER XVII

FRANÇOIS LOUIS, PRINCE DE CONTI (already mentioned in
Chapter XV).

HENRI JULES, DUC D'ENGHIEN, son of the Great Condé,
known as Monsieur le Prince.

LOUIS DE BOURBON, son of the Duc d'Enghien, known as
Monsieur le Duc.

LOUIS FRANÇOIS, DUC DE BOUFFLERS, Marshal of France.

JEAN ARMAND, DUC DE JOYEUSE, Marshal of France.

CHARLES EUGÈNE, PRINCE D'ELBEUF, Marshal of France.

MARIE ANNE, widow of the first Prince de Conti (Louis
Armand), daughter of Louis XIV and La Vallière.

MARIE EMILIE JOLY DE CHOIN, lady-in-waiting to the Princess de Conti, and the Dauphin's mistress.

ANNET DE CLERMONT-CHASTE, called Clermont-Chatte,
a Guard's officer.

LOUISE FRANÇOISE, daughter of Louis XIV and Mme de
Montespan, married to the Duc de Bourbon and known as
Mme la Duchesse.

ABBÉ MELCHIOR DE POLIGNAC, French Ambassador to Poland.

During the spring of 1692, the King prepared a fresh campaign in Flanders. The Great Condé's son, M. le Prince, was placed in command of the army and had under his orders his own son (M. le Duc), the Duc du Maine, the King's natural son, and Prince François Louis de Conti who, as we have seen, remained in disgrace at the Court until the appeal to the King by his uncle, the Great Condé. Louis XIV detested this handsome young man, but the Court, despite its habit of submitting to the royal will, made him their 'darling'. According to Saint-Simon:

The King hated him and showed his dislike so openly and so constantly that everyone was aware of it. He was not just out of favour; every courtier knew quite well that to be seen in his company would risk the royal displeasure . . .

But despite such powerful arguments and the Court's usually servile attitude, M. le Prince de Conti only had to put in an appearance (which he did frequently) to be surrounded immediately by the greatest and distinguished courtiers, young and old. They clustered around him so assiduously that at Versailles his room was filled every morning with the most important and brilliant figures at the Court; while at Marly—where the King was in a position to keep a much closer watch on things than at Versailles—the Prince de Conti was always surrounded the moment he appeared in the salon. Indeed, those who frequented his company comprised the most illustrious, distinguished and important of all the courtiers, who were happy to sit at his feet, and often forgot the moments when they should have been paying their respects to the King or attending meals . . . In short, he was an Orpheus able to charm the trees and the rocks around him with his lyre and to triumph over the King's powerful hatred even in the centre of his Court, without ever seeming to make the least effort in that direction. Equally, the sheer force of his graciousness and discretion placed all the ladies completely under his spell.

Conti was to cover himself with glory at Steinkirk. An

account of this battle has been left by another soldier who took part in it, James Fitzjames, Duke of Berwick, natural son of James II of England, who was serving under the command of the Maréchal de Luxembourg:

After several camps and marches made by both opposing armies, we finally camped on August 1st at Steinkirk, near Enghien, and the enemy at Tubize, near Hall.

When the Prince of Orange discovered that a secretary of the Elector of Bavaria was passing information to the Maréchal de Luxembourg he decided to profit from this by trying to surprise our army. He forced this man to provide the false information that his army would be spending the following day foraging, so that when M. de Luxembourg was warned at daybreak that the enemy had been sighted, he paid no attention at first. However, after receiving repeated reports about a build-up of enemy strength, he rode out of the camp and saw the columns of infantry; whereupon, he first ordered that the troops who had been camped on the side of the Enghien stream from which the enemy were approaching should cross back to this side, but soon after that he decided to allow no troop movements and to keep the army in its present positions, although the stream cut our army in two . . .

Meanwhile, the enemy arrived in column and started forming into line, but because of the broken nature of the country their battle formations were not completed until about one o'clock in the forenoon. Then they launched a furious attack upon our right flank and, despite the resistance put up by our troops, succeeded in forcing our retreat from the ground we were holding and captured our cannon . . .

At this, M. de Luxembourg, seeing the necessity of a vigorous counter-attack to re-establish the position, called up the brigade of Guards, which charged, sword in hand, and mowed down all opposition. Several other brigades flanking us also charged, so together we managed to push the enemy back a good quarter of a league, to beyond the woods, with a great loss of men on their side. Our *troupe dorée*, consisting of Monseigneur le Duc d'Orléans together with Messieurs the Duc de Bourbon, the Prince de Conti, the Duc de Vendôme, his brother the Grand Prieur and a number of others, was in the thick of the battle during the entire engagement, and under heavy fire ... During the two hours the engagement lasted, both sides lost a total of seven thousand men, and M. de Luxembourg swore he had never taken part in a more hotly-contested action.

The Marquis de Sources *records an account of the same engagement from the mouth of an infantry brigadier, Albergotti, who had arrived at Versailles the following day to bring the news, and adds:*

The Duc d'Enghien and the Prince de Conti performed prodigies of valour. The prince had two horses shot from under him and another wounded.

And Jean de Fontaine *wrote to Sillery, Conti's Master of the Horse:*

Your prince's name is on everybody's lips here. It is acknowledged by all that we owe to him our success at the battle of Steinkirk.

Conti had so far given proof of nothing but courage, yet he had somehow acquired the reputation of being a great military leader, so the Court was astonished that the King steadfastly refused to appoint him to a command. It became even more indignant the following year when Louis XIV, by refusing an opportunity to attack the enemy, disillusioned his generals, his army, his courtiers and his people. Saint-Simon, who was going through his first campaign, has given an account of the Gembloux affair:

The King left on May 18th with the ladies, spent a week or more with them at Quesnoy, then sent them on to Namur and himself went, on June 2nd, to put himself at the head of M. de Boufflers' army. On the 7th of that month, he and the marshal drew up their army in battle order at Gembloux, in such a fashion that there was no gap between his left flank and M. de Luxembourg's right flank, and it was possible to come and go between the two armies in perfect safety. The Prince of Orange had disposed his forces in the area of Pure Abbey, and found that his supply-lines were cut off and that he could not even retreat without risking being outflanked by the King's two armies. He entrenched his army at Pure as speedily as possible, regretting heartily that he had allowed himself to be manoeuvred into a defensive position at such an early stage of the engagement. It has since been learned that he wrote several times to his close friend, the Prince de Vaudémont, saying that he was lost and that only a miracle could save him and his men. His army was inferior in numbers to the smaller of the two armies commanded by the King; in addition, the King's armies were plentifully provided with siege equipment, military provisions and artillery, and were, as one may imagine, in a most favourable position.

Here was an absolutely perfect situation which gave us at least four months to plan and carry out a major campaign assured of victory. But on June 8th the King informed M. de Luxembourg that he was returning to Versailles, and that he intended to send Monseigneur to Germany, together with the Maréchal de Boufflers and a large contingent of troops ... Luxembourg was so dismayed to see so glorious and so easy a campaign escape from his grasp that he went down on his knees to the King in supplication, but all to no avail. Mme de Maintenon had tried unsuccessfully to persuade the King not to make the journey, for she did not like to let him out of her sight. So splendid an opening to the campaign would have kept the King away from her for a considerable time, and she would not be able to share in his achievements. In the end, the tears she shed at their parting and the letters she then wrote to him weighed more heavily with the King than the most pressing reasons of State, war and glory.

On the evening of that doleful day, M. de Luxembourg went back to his quarters stunned with grief, and broke the news to the Maréchal de Villeroi, to Monsieur le Duc, to Monsieur le Prince de Conti and to his own son: they could hardly believe their ears and groaned with despair. But by the following day, June 9th, there could no longer be room for any doubt. It so happened that on that morning I went alone to report for general orders to M. de Luxembourg's headquarters, as I frequently did, to find out what was happening and what was planned for the following day. I was most surprised to find the place deserted and to learn that everybody was at the King's headquarters. I was sitting on my horse pondering this strange situation and wondering whether to return or to ride on to the King's camp, when I saw M. le Prince de Conti arrive from our own camp, alone like myself, followed by a page and a groom with a pack-horse. He cantered up to me, asked me what I was doing there and laughed at my surprise. He told me he was about to take leave of the King and advised me I would do well to go with him and do likewise. I asked him what he meant by 'taking leave', and before replying he had his page and groom drop back and suggested that I also should tell my page and groom and a lackey who was accompanying me to follow us at a small distance. He then told me the whole story of the King's order for a retreat, laughing all the time and, despite my youth, embroidering the account with various scandalous details, for he had confidence in my discretion. I listened with utter astonishment and my confusion allowed me only to ask a few questions . . .

This retreat created a sensation not only among the troops but among the common people also. The general officers discussed the matter heatedly between themselves, while the reserve officers spoke out openly, unable to contain their feelings. The enemy gave full vent to their surprise and joy, but nothing that they said could have matched the ridicule and contempt expressed by those in our armies, by the townspeople, and even in the Court where the courtiers who were usually so pleased to find themselves back at Versailles, on this occasion made it a point of honour to show their shame . . . Amid all these rumours, the King arrived at Versailles on June 25th, accompanied by the ladies.[1]

The Marquis de La Fare, *on the staff of Monsieur, who had remained in France with a force of seven or eight thousand men to defend the coast against a possible English landing, confirms that the King's brother was stupefied on learning that the King had refused battle:*

The whole thing seemed so incredible to him that he admitted later that he had suspected the Emperor and his allies

---

[1] The Princess Palatine noted in her diary, on June 28th: 'Mme de Chartres, Mme la Duchesse, and the wife of the Prince de Condé have all become pregnant, so the King cannot say that his expedition was unfruitful.'

of having negotiated with the King behind his back. No one
ever found out who had given the King the advice to retreat,
but it was suspected that Mme de Maintenon was responsible,
her reason being that he had a slight attack of fever. It was
certainly a typical piece of female advice, and it was immediately disowned by M. de Luxembourg and all the other
ministers. This retreat did the King no honour, and he has
never since found himself at the head of his army.

*The Maréchal de Luxembourg succeeded in rescuing the
army's honour a month later, at the battle of Nerwinden, and
became the idol of the Parisians, as did the Prince de Conti
who had once again given proof of his valour. The Prince
gave his own account of that battle, in a letter to the Prince de
Condé dated August 3rd. This report was subsequently published by the* Mercure Galant *(the 15 sol paper founded by
Donneau de Visé and Thomas Corneille) in a special issue
devoted to the victory of Nerwinden:*

The attack on the village of Nerwinden was quite successful
at first, despite the enemy's resistance. Our men pushed them
back to the foot of their entrenchments, but were unable to
hold the position for long because of the intense cannon and
musket fire from the enemy, whose superior strength soon
forced us to abandon the ground we had won. M. de Luxembourg was well aware that victory depended on the success
of this attack, and ordered the Guiche brigade commanded by
Albergotti to advance; the Duc d'Enghien and the Comte de
Marsin, who had placed themselves at its head, won back from
the enemy all the ground our own troops had lost, but suffered
the same fate later and were repulsed . . .

When M. de Luxembourg saw that the attack by the Guiche
brigade had succeeded no better than the first he ordered the
brigade of guards to advance on the right of the village of
Nerwinden; after a most obstinate engagement, the Guards
made themselves masters of the outskirts of the village as far as
the enemy trench-works. The Surbeck and Zurlauben
brigades went in on the left flank of the Guards and occupied
that part of the village, while the Piedmont brigade and the
Royal brigade seized the rest of it. This time we were able to

hold our positions despite the frequent attacks the enemy made in their attempts to dislodge us.

We captured seventy-six pieces of cannon and eight mortars, several pontoons and most of their artillery equipment, sixty standards and drum-aprons and twenty-two flags. We took 1,500 prisoners, including 150 officers . . .

It would take too long to give adequate praise to all those who were involved, but I cannot refrain from saying that the part played by the Maréchal de Luxembourg in the undertaking and execution of this action was supreme. The Maréchal de Villeroi and the Maréchal de Joyeuse also distinguished themselves exceedingly in this encounter. The Maréchal de Villeroi cannot be too highly praised for his speedy occupation of the enemy trenches at the head of the Household brigade; his successful action was an important factor in our victory. M. le Duc de Chartres conducted himself in his usual manner, which is to say with great valour. M. le Duc d'Enghien led the charge repeatedly, sometimes at the head of the cavalry and sometimes at the head of the infantry. In short, all our general officers, brigadiers and colonels had no other thought but to give fully of their services, and in this they succeeded admirably.

Mme de Sévigné's *comment on the battle, in a letter to the Comtesse de Guitaut, is as follows:*

Good Lord, Madame, how many deaths and casualties have resulted from this battle, and how many visits of consolation we shall now have to make! Yet this engagement which first seemed to be an advantage that had cost us too dear has now turned into a great victory: we have so many cannons, so many kettledrums, so many flags and standards, so many prisoners, that it can safely be said that no pitched battle fought during the last fifty years has resulted in so signal a victory . . .

On the same day that a Te Deum was sung in Notre Dame for the Nerwinden victory, the King fell ill. This marked the end of his martial career. At the beginning of 1694, he developed gout and had to be pushed around the palace in an armchair fitted with felt-lined wheels. The courtiers became increasingly bored, but the younger ones tried hard to amuse

*themselves in other ways, and on March 1st, a group organized
the first coach race in French history. The Marquis de*
Sourches *has recorded the scene:*

On the first day of March, the Prince d'Elbeuf organized a
famous race and one which had been long awaited. He had
wagered 1,000 pistoles that six coach-horses he had in his
stables would draw a coach from Paris to Versailles and back
to Paris in less than two hours. It was the Marquis de
Chêmerault who had wagered against him, and both were
backed to win by rival groups. All the parties concerned
agreed to appoint M. le Prince de Conti judge of the event and
to accept his rulings. The prince made every effort beforehand
to ensure that the route was kept clear. Then he started off
from the Parte de la Conférence.[1]
On arrival at Versailles, the Prince d'Elbeuf was several
minutes ahead, and was so sure of winning that he himself
entered the box and drove the team back to Paris, getting back
a quarter of an hour ahead of the two hour limit. An extraordinary number of people came out into the streets to witness
this spectacle, both in Paris and in Versailles, lining the route
from eight in the morning onwards, although the race was not
due to start until ten o'clock.

*During this year, the King's health continued to deteriorate.
According to the* Princess Palatine *in a letter dated May 9,
1694:*

The King is letting himself go. He is visibly sinking, and
appears fat and old. His Majesty appears to have shrunk. His
face has changed so that he is hardly recognizable; it becomes
more lined from day to day.

*The Dauphin, presiding over his small court at Meudon, was
becoming increasingly the centre of attention. He was surrounded by a clique of rowdy courtiers who indulged in
pleasure and intrigue with equal vigour. Among his followers
were François Louis de Conti, the widow of his brother Louis
Armand, the Maréchal de Luxembourg, the Duc de Vendôme,*

[1] The city wall formed the far boundary of the Tuileries gardens, and the
Porte de la Conférence in the middle of that section of the wall gave access to
the Cours la Reine and the countryside.

and—among the least important of the gentlemen in residence
—a certain Clermont-Chatte, a Guards officer who was
energetic enough to seduce simultaneously Conti's widow, the
Princess, and the Dauphin's mistress Mlle Choin.

This Emilie Joly de Choin was the daughter of a governor
of Bourg-en-Bresse, of the lesser nobility, but she had become
a maid-of-honour of the Princesse de Conti and had exercised
some attraction upon the heir to the throne. The Princess
Palatine *describes her with her usual benevolence:*

It has been suggested that he [the Dauphin] married her
secretly, but I am convinced that this is not so. She looked just
like a pug-dog: she was low-built, with short legs, a round
face, a snub nose, and a large mouth filled with rotting teeth
the stink from which could be smelled at the other end of the
room. Her bosom was horribly overdeveloped, but Monseigneur was enchanted by this phenomenon and used to play
on them like drums. However, this fat, stocky little creature
was witty enough. I understand that the Dauphin accustomed
himself to the smell of tobacco smoke so that he should no
longer smell the vile odour of La Choin's rotting teeth.

Saint-Simon *confirms that the Dauphin was never particu-*
larly discerning as regards his pleasures:

He relieved his appetites in a transitory and secretive manner, being incapable of a more romantic approach, and was
served in these matters by Du Mont and Francine, Lully's sons-
in-law, who had been co-directors of the Opéra for a long
time.

In this connection, I cannot refrain from giving a typical
example of his fastidiousness. He had conceived some desire
for an exceedingly pretty young woman from this troupe, and
on an agreed date she was brought to Versailles with an unattractive older woman as chaperone, and shown into the anteroom of Monseigneur's apartments. Advised that the women
were there, Monseigneur opened the door and grabbed hold of
the woman standing nearest to it, who, being the ugly one,
resisted vigorously, realizing the mistake he had made. He, on
the other hand, simply thought she was being coy, pulled her
in and locked the door.

The other woman was highly amused by this error, and anticipated with pleasure her companion's discomfiture when she was ejected from the room and she herself was called in. Just then, Du Mont entered the anteroom, was astonished to see her alone, and asked her what she was doing there and what had become of her friend. She then told him the whole story, and Du Mont rushed up to the door, crying: 'That's not the one you want, you've taken the wrong one!' No answer. Du Mont shouted and banged again, but still no reply. Finally, Monseigneur opened the door and pushed the woman out. Du Mont presented the other, saying: 'Wait, here she is.' 'No, the business is done,' replied Monseigneur, 'she will have to await another occasion.' And he closed his door again.

. . . It is incredible how stingy he was with his beloved Choin. He never gave her more than 400 golden louis a quarter, making 1,600 louis a year, and even then made a point of paying her personally, ensuring that not one pistole extra slipped through his fingers by mistake. He gave her one or two presents each year, but even those were carefully chosen so as not to be too expensive.

One must do this young woman justice so far as to admit that she was completely unselfish, either because she knew she had no choice with this particular prince or else because it was an ingrained characteristic, which seems more probable. No one can say for sure whether or not she was married to him, but those most closely acquainted with their personal affairs were always adamant that no marriage ever took place. She was never anything more than a fat, swarthy bedfellow who, despite all her wit and playfulness, looked like a servant and had long since become fat, old and stinking.

Emilie Choin found herself appointed lady-in-waiting to the Princesse de Conti, the widow of the first Prince de Conti, although Mme de Caylus agrees with the other witnesses that she was:

. . . remarkably ugly and possessed the kind of mind which shone in anteroom chatter, with her eternal recitation of everything she had just seen. It was these stories which ingratiated her with her mistress.

Yet this same Mlle Choin stole the heart of M. de Clermont-Chatte, at that time a Guards officer, away from the most beautiful princess in the world. Indeed, it is considered certain that they intended to marry, and no doubt they counted on gaining the consent of the Princess de Conti first of all and then obtaining, through her and Monseigneur, the blessing of the Court, which would have been absolutely necessary for them. But the imprudence of a courier during a campaign wrecked their plans and revealed in the cruellest manner to the Princesse de Conti that she had been doubly betrayed, by her lover and by her favourite. M. de Luxembourg's courier gave M. de Barbezieux all the letters he had in his care, and the latter promised to have them returned, but instead he took the packet to the King. One may easily imagine the effect produced by the discovery of this correspondence: Mme la Princesse de Conti was heartbroken, Mlle Choin was expelled from the Court, and M. de Clermont was exiled and his status as an exempt officer withdrawn.

M. de Coulanges *commented to Mme de Sévigné on August 27, 1694:*

Mlle Choin's disgrace is much discussed at Versailles . . . For if Monseigneur ever loved anyone, it was that young woman. Was she expelled without his knowledge? The Princesse de Conti had some very private conversations with the King, much to everyone's surprise. And the result of their deliberations is that Mlle Choin finds herself in Paris, in Mme de Lillebonne's house, and it is said that a small apartment is being prepared for her at the Hospitalières.

But by now another intrigue was the talk of the Court: Conti had fallen in love with the Princesse de Condé, the wife of the Great Condé's grandson, called Mme la Duchesse. Mme de Caylus, *who observed this love affair at first hand, remarked that this natural daughter of Louis XIV and Mme de Montespan was ravishingly beautiful:*

Her face was shaped by the tenderest passions and her spirit was fashioned to play with love at its leisure without ever becoming its slave . . . Until M. le Prince de Conti fell in love with Mme la Duchesse he had never seemed capable of showing serious intentions towards a lady; he had had several affairs involving flirtation more than love, but it was only when he met Mme la Duchesse that he became violently enamoured for the first time. Perhaps this passion was created not only by their mutual sympathy but also by the very schemes of those hostile to their interests.

M. le Prince de Conti first became aware of the charms of Mme la Duchesse as a result of being constantly advised to pay no attention to her. He loved her passionately and, for her part, if she ever loved anyone he was that person ... And they had a go-between against whom the duke's rage and jealousy were powerless: the Dauphin himself. He was, I believe the only confidant they ever had. They conducted their affair so wisely and discreetly that no one was ever able to accuse them of misconduct. Indeed, Mme la Princesse [the duchess's mother-in-law] was reduced to agreeing with her daughter-in-law that her sole reason for suspecting that a love-affair was in progress was that M. le Prince de Conti and herself seemed made for each other.

A little later on, the charming Conti thought he was about to become a king. The Poles were in the habit of choosing their sovereigns by election, and had decided to offer him the throne. Louis XIV gave his consent and opened his treasury for the purpose. The French ambassador to Poland, the Abbé de Polignac, considered his election a certainty. And the Marquis de Sources *commented:*

Care was taken that the three millions the King had sent would be suitably distributed, it was known that the courier carrying the other 600,000 livres had been very well received, and it seemed that the Senate and the nobility were very well disposed towards the Prince de Conti, and that if he failed to gain his cause it could only be as a result of the eccentricity and capriciousness of a few drunkards.

Conti himself was not overenthusiastic about the idea of abandoning the French Court for Polish society, but the King had made his decision for him. On July 11th it was learned that the election had taken place. Dangeau *notes:*

The news immediately spread everywhere. The Prince de Conti was overwhelmed with compliments and went to Saint-Germain to inform the King and Queen of England. The King also sent the Duc de la Trémoïlle to advise Their Majesties of the news, and sent another messenger to Monsieur at Saint-Cloud.

The Duchesse de Bourbon-Condé, still madly in love with Conti, was far from happy at these developments, and Saint-Simon describes the rather different feelings of her husband:

M. le Duc floundered between two states of mind: jealous rage at so superior an ability and one rewarded by so flattering a choice, and on the other hand the satisfaction of seeing himself at last immune from the daily realization of the extent of this superior ability, including that in a certain sphere about which a husband of his humour was particularly sensitive.

Mme de Maintenon herself was delighted by this promotion of a prince of the blood, and recorded her personal interest in the journey undertaken by Conti to reach his future kingdom:

We received the news yesterday that the Prince de Conti has passed through Denmark without encountering any difficulties. He is in good health and is due in Danzig on either the 19th or the 20th of this month [July]. There he will place himself at the head of his supporters to contend with the Duke of Saxony for the crown. We must all pray for our prince of the blood, for it is in the interests of both Religion and State that he should reign rather than the other claimant.

The fact was that in the Kingdom of Poland on this occasion to be elected was not enough: the winner was faced with the prospect of fighting it out with the rival candidate who refused to accept defeat. The Duke of Saxony was in militant mood, whereas Conti lacked enthusiasm for the contest, and his support gradually dwindled. On November 14th, according to the Marquis de Sourches, news reached Versailles that he was on his way back:

The King announced at his *coucher* that the Prince de Conti was returning home. He praised highly the prudence of this prince, his honourable conduct and the insight he had shown, even before leaving France, in uncovering the details of the intrigues being conducted in Poland. He pointed out too, that the Prince had been reluctant to go there in the first place. He also emphasized that there was no question of his having been short of money since he [the King] had assured him that he had such confidence in him he would send him as much money as he needed, provided that he wrote personally to him stating his needs. It was clear, added the King, that he had been deceived in that country by everybody, beginning with his own ambassador. By that remark the King was certainly not impugning the loyalty of the Abbé de Polignac, who was indisputably loyal, but suggesting rather that he had perhaps placed too much confidence in the promises of the Poles.

A scapegoat was required and so the Abbé Melchior de Polignac found himself in disgrace. But there were doubts among the courtiers as to whether the King had really been entirely sincere in his avowed support of the Prince de Conti's claim. Mme Dunoyer's correspondent confided to her, when the Polish election was first announced, that:

The fact of being a prince of the blood is not an unmixed blessing under this reign. Indeed I doubt whether the King will take any pleasure in seeing him mount a throne from which he will be in a position to retaliate for the ill treatment he has suffered at the King's hands.

And after the débacle, the same correspondent hinted darkly:

The Prince de Conti is just back from Poland, abandoning whatever prospects he may have had there. The Elector of Saxony gained the upper hand over him, and the King has dismissed the Abbé de Polignac who is accused of being insufficiently zealous on this occasion. But perhaps he did his duty only too well? Nobody knows what secret orders he may have received from the Court, and it may well be that his disgrace is a mere feint.[1]

[1] But it lasted until 1702.

CHAPTER XVIII

MADAME GUYON'S QUIETISM AND THE DISGRACE OF FENELON

With this impostor guiding one's leisures
Through the flowery paths of sweet quietism,
One must soon be absorbed by real *Molinism*,
And so be enabled, through Lucifer's measures,
To sample in heaven all hellish pleasures.

BOILEAU

PRINCIPAL PERSONALITIES MENTIONED IN CHAPTER XVIII

MADAME GUYON, née JEANNE BOUVIER DE LA MOTTE, who introduced the doctrine of Quietism into the Court.

PAUL DE SAINT-AIGNAN, DUC DE BEAUVILLIERS, tutor to the Duc de Bourgogne.

CHARLES HONORÉ D'ALBERT, DUC DE CHEVREUSE, married to Anne Marie Colbert, daughter of the minister.

LOUIS ANTOINE DE NOAILLES, Cardinal, Bishop of Châlons and later Archbishop of Paris.

LOUIS AUGUSTE DE BOURBON, DUC DU MAINE, natural son of Louis XIV and Mme de Montespan (already mentioned in Chapter V).

JEAN RACINE, poet and royal historiographer (already mentioned in Chapter X).

The heated controversy over the doctrine of Quietism, which had been brewing for five years, finally boiled over in 1694. Quietism had been thought up by a Spanish Jesuit named Molinos who taught that when the soul attained pure contemplation it achieved a state of absolute quietude in which it had no thought of salvation and no fear of death. A young widow, Mme Guyon, introduced this doctrine into France. The curé of Versailles, François Hébert, *describes her in these terms:*

This lady came from Montargis, a pretty town in the Gâtinais. She had married M. Guyon, a counsellor at the Parlement of Paris and, like herself, a person of considerable means, but her marriage did not last long for her husband died and left her free again. She had a most intelligent and lively spirit, possessed a most attractive presence, and was strongly drawn towards virtue, piety and the performance of good works, especially those directed towards the poor. From her early youth onwards, and during the period of her marriage, she had always applied herself to devotions. When she became a widow she gave herself up entirely to pious activities and was famed for them not only in Montargis but throughout the entire region.

While I was staying at the Sens seminary, where I was teaching theology, I had occasion to visit this town, and became acquainted with this lady's brother: he was the local Procureur du Roi and lived in a most exemplary manner. It was clear from the testimony of all the good folks of Montargis that Mme Guyon's virtue and person were held in high respect; everybody praised her to the skies.

Mme Guyon had published a treatise, Le Moyen court et facile pour faire oraison, *and so gained the confidence of Fénelon, tutor to the King's grandsons since 1689. Mme du* Pérou, *in charge of the novices at Saint-Cyr, relates in her* Mémoires:

Mme de Maintenon entertained Mme Guyon on several occasions and even had her dine with her at her own table. She considered that Mme Guyon displayed more of her arms and chest than was proper for one who made so great a profession of piety, but she was impressed, nevertheless, by her method of saying prayers.

Mme Guyon soon began to exercise a considerable influence at the Court, and especially at Saint-Cyr. Again in Mme du Pérou's *account:*

The entire establishment became indubitably Quietist. The sole subject of conversation was pure love, surrender, holy indifference and simplicity, all of which were to provide the basis for a comfortable attitude in which one would be troubled by no problems, not even that of salvation. They derived from this attitude a supposed resignation to the will of God, stretched so far as to accept openly the possibility of damnation as much as the hope of salvation. This constituted the famous act of surrender which they taught, after which they took no thought whatsoever to prepare their souls for eternity . . .

Apart from Mme de Maintenon, Mme Guyon's most ardent supporters were the Duc and Duchesse de Chevreuse, and the Duc de Beauvilliers. But some highly-placed dignitaries of the Church were far from pleased at these goings on. Hébert *continues:*

It now became clear to everyone what was going on at the Court. Mme Guyon was seen to appear frequently, and it was noticed that she made a point of arriving at times when the King was at Marly, so that she would have a better opportunity of seeing those persons I have mentioned [Mme de Maintenon and the Chevreuses]. In addition, it was known that she exercised influence over other great ladies of the Court who, after being instructed in the principles of her new spirituality, suddenly appeared wafted on to a plane of sublime contemplation. It is known, too, that she went so far as to give them spiritual direction, so that they had far greater confidence in this lady than they did in their own confessors and directors, which was a complete reversal of the order established by God in his Church.

All this, together with the goings-on at Saint-Cyr, about

which the Bishop of Chartres had been informed, impelled him to order a close examination of this lady's feelings, principles, conduct, conversation and writings. The Abbé de Fénelon, who believed her innocent and righteous, undertook her defence. Mme de Maintenon was advised by the Bishop of Chartres of the impending investigation, and realized immediately the importance of the affair, but hoped that it would remain secret so that the King should have no occasion for alarm about the Saint-Cyr establishment.

The Abbé de Fénelon, who had been showered with favours by the King, was guilty of something else besides defending Mme Guyon: at some indeterminate date between 1691 and 1695—probably 1694—he had written a letter to the King in terms which contrasted violently with the laudatory messages to which Louis XIV was accustomed:[1]

For thiry years or more, Your principal ministers have disturbed and even overturned all the ancient maxims of State in order to elevate Your authority to a new peak, an authority which had become their concern because it was in their hands. No one spoke any longer of State or law; they spoke only of the King and his good pleasure. Your revenues and Your expenses have been blown up to huge proportions. You have been elevated to the level of the heavens themselves for having, it is said, effaced the greatness of all Your predecessors put together, which is to say for having impoverished the whole of France so that You might introduce a monstrous and incurable luxury into the Court. They have desired to set You up upon the ruins of all the principles of State, as though You could be great by ruining all Your subjects upon whom Your very greatness is founded.

Your peoples, whom You should love as Your children and who have up till now been so devoted to You, are dying of hunger. Agriculture is almost abandoned; the towns and the

[1] The context of the letter shows that Louvois was dead, but that the Archbishop of Paris, Harlay de Champvallon (who died in August 1965) was still alive; Mme de Maintenon refers, in letters dated December 2 and 27, 1695, to an 'excessively harsh letter' addressed to the King, but it cannot be this one.

countryside are become depopulated; all the crafts and trades are languishing and no longer provide jobs for their workmen; commerce has been entirely crushed. What results is that You have destroyed half of the real strength inherent in Your State in order to make and maintain vain conquests abroad. Instead of extracting money from Your impoverished subjects You should have succoured them and fed them. The whole of France is one vast poorhouse without hope or sustenance. The magistrates have become degraded and exhausted. The nobility, whose estates are all in pawn, survive only by means of letters of State [letters from the King suspending civil actions for a period of six months]. You are importuned by the massive demands and murmurings of your peoples. It is You, Sire, who have drawn all this trouble down upon Yourself, for having ruined the entire kingdom You now find that everything is in Your hands and that everybody depends for his existence entirely on Your charity.

Here, then, is a great and flourishing kingdom ruled by a king who is portrayed daily as the joy of his people and would, indeed, be that if he had not been poisoned by counsels of flattery. Your peoples—one must be frank—who loved You so much and had such confidence in You, have begun to lose their feelings of friendship, confidence and even respect. Your victories and conquests no longer inspire joy in the hearts of the masses, who have become filled with bitterness and despair. Sedition is flaring up on all sides. They believe that You no longer have any pity for their miseries, that You love only Your authority and Your glory. They claim that if the King was in his heart a father towards his people he would surely find it more glorious to give them bread and provide them with relief after so many misfortunes, than to contend for a few territories on our frontiers, the possession of which is the sole reason for the present war. What can You reply to that, Sire? Popular agitation, so long unknown, is now widespread. Even Paris, so near to Your presence, is not immune. The magistrates are obliged to tolerate the insolence of rebellious spirits and even to bribe them secretly in order to appease them, so that those who should be punished are in fact being rewarded. You are reduced to the shameful and deplorable extremity of either leaving sedition unpunished and so allowing it to thrive on its impunity, or of ordering the savage massacre of peoples whom You have reduced to despair by Your war taxes which have taken out of their mouths the bread they have striven to win with the sweat of their brow.

But while they are without bread, You Yourself are without money and refuse to recognize the extremity to which You are reduced. Because You have always been happy, You are incapable of imagining that You could ever cease to be so. You fear to open Your eyes. You fear to have anyone open them for You. You fear the prospect of having to diminish a fragment of Your glory. This glory which hardens Your heart is dearer to You than justice, than Your own peace of mind, than the welfare of Your peoples who perish every day from diseases caused by famine, and, worse still, is dearer to You than Your eternal salvation which is incompatible with this idol of glory . . .

One had hoped, Sire, that Your Council would have drawn You away from so misguided a path, but Your Council has shown itself neither forceful nor vigorous in its pursuit of the common good. At least Mme de Maintenon and the Duc de Beauvilliers, who enjoy Your confidence, should have put it to good use and disabused You, but their weakness and timidity dishonour them and are the subject of public scandal. France is in desperate straits: why, then, do they hesitate to speak out frankly? You may ask, Sire, what it is that they should say to You? I answer: they should try to persuade You that You must humble Yourself; that You must sue for peace and so expiate, by this humiliation, all the glory which You have made Your evil; that You must reject the unjust councils of political toadies; and, finally, that, to save the State, You must return to Your enemies as soon as possible the conquered territories which You cannot, in any case, retain without injustice. You should be only too happy, surrounded as You are by misery, to see God sweep away those ambitions which have blinded You, and to have Him compel You to make those restitutions which are essential for Your salvation, and which You would never have resolved to make in a peaceful and triumphant State. The person who addresses these truths to You, Sire, far from opposing Your interests, would give his life to see You appear as God would wish You to be, and prays constantly for You.

It seems possible that Fénelon's appointment to the arch-bishopric of Cambrai in January, 1695, and his consequent separation from the Court, may have been the result of this letter. The curé of Versailles, Hébert, considered it an advancement rather than a rebuff, but Saint-Simon was of a different opinion and described the effect of the news on Fénelon's friends:

Cambrai was a thunderbolt for the whole little clique. They saw that the Archbishop of Paris was now in a position to ruin all their schemes. They had all wanted Paris for their leader, and not Cambrai, which they despised as a country diocese; also, the necessity of his occasional residence there would deprive them of their pastor. Paris, on the other hand, would have placed him at the head of the clergy and would have given him a position of immediate and lasting influence. It would have allowed him the authority to give his full backing to Mme Guyon and her doctrine which was at that time still a secret between them. So what the rest of the world took to be a brilliant stroke of fortune was a source of deep gloom for them.

The King had other things on his mind than Fénelon's criticisms and the state of his kingdom. In the Netherlands, the Duc du Maine, his favourite natural son, had shirked battle near Namur and had allowed the enemy to escape. Attempts were made to hide this news from the King, but he soon learned the truth. Saint-Simon describes how:

Lavienne, a very fashionable Parisian bath attendant, had won the King's confidence during the period of the royal amours: he had administered drugs to the King which had, on several occasions, allowed His Majesty to achieve greater satisfaction than would otherwise have been possible, and this facility had eventually resulted in his being appointed one of the four chief valets de chambre. He was a most honest man, though coarse and outspoken. But this frankness in an obviously trustworthy man led the King to ask him for the kind of information he could never hope to obtain from other sources, though he only raised matters which were within

Lavienne's competence to discuss. During a visit to Marly the King questioned Lavienne about the progress of the war, and the latter, being taken by surprise, could not avoid showing his embarrassment. This reaction redoubled the King's curiosity and he then ordered Lavienne to tell him all he knew. Not daring to resist the royal command, Lavienne gave the King that distasteful information which rankled with him for the rest of his life and put him in a state of despair when he heard it. His whole purpose in putting M. de Vendôme at the head of an army was to facilitate the introduction into it of M. du Maine, for he was chiefly concerned to abridge the powers of the princes of the blood by setting them in competition with each other. The Comte de Toulouse was already an admiral and so his future was secure. It was M. du Maine, then, who occupied all his thoughts, and he was heartbroken to see all his hopes now dashed to the ground. He was most conscious of the fact that his darling son was the laughing-stock of the army, and the gazettes revealed to him that his son was equally the butt of foreign lampoons, so he was most extraordinarily vexed.

On this one occasion, the King, who was normally so even-tempered and so much master of his emotions even in the most difficult circumstances, lost his self-control. Leaving the dinner-table at Marly, accompanied by all the ladies and in the presence of all his courtiers, he noticed that a valet who had been serving the dessert had put a biscuit in his pocket. He utterly forgot his dignity, and raising his cane, which had just been presented to him together with his hat, rushed upon this valet who was absolutely dumbfounded, as was another valet who was standing between them and was thrust rudely out of the way. The King belaboured the man with his cane, cursing him soundly, until the cane, which was not very robust, broke over his back. Then, wildly brandishing the stump of the cane in his hand and continuing to curse the wretched man, who had by this time escaped from the scene, he crossed this small salon and an anteroom and entered Mme de Maintenon's apartment where he remained for an hour, as was his habit at Marly after dinner. Leaving there to return to his own apartments, he saw Père de la Chaise among the courtiers and called out to him at the top of his voice: 'Mon père, I have just beaten a rogue and broken my cane over his back, but I do not think that I have offended God in doing so.'

The facts eventually came out, and it was learned that Lavienne, pressed by the King, had been indirectly responsible for this disgraceful exhibition of behaviour.

In January, 1687, Fénelon provoked a future crisis by publishing his Explication des maximes des saints sur la vie intérieure, *an apology of pure love and a justification of Quietism. He wrote to the Duc de Chevreuse, asking him to show this work, which was already partly printed, to the curé of Versailles, Hébert, who comments:*

The Duc de Chevreuse promptly brought me this letter, together with his prelate's thesis. He had me read the part of the letter referring to myself. I took this work from him and, holding it in my hands, spoke courteously yet firmly to this lord in these words:

'I am most unhappy, Monsieur, that the Archbishop of Cambrai has finally resolved to write about mystical life. Had he been at the Court I would have begged him not to allow this work to be printed. Only a few months ago, when he did me the honour of asking me whether I though it advisable to write on these kind of abstract questions I replied that one should not do so unless one exercised the greatest possible prudence.'

Nevertheless, Hébert applied himself to the task of reading and criticizing the book, but a few days later:

I was obliged to visit the King's grand apartments at the Château. The Cardinal de Noailles (who had become Archbishop of Paris) was just emerging from an audience. As soon as he caught sight of me he came up to me to say that he had just learned that the gentlemen charged with the printing of M. de Cambrai's book were pressing forward with its publication and were unwilling to agree to what had been decided, which was that M. de Cambrai's book should not be put on sale until one month after the Bishop of Meaux's book had appeared. The cardinal urged me to read and examine this book of M. de Cambrai's as speedily as possible. The reason why these gentlemen were in such a hurry to complete the printing of the book was that they feared that if M. de Meaux found out that it was printed or in process of being printed he would have the whole edition suppressed.

In fact, Bossuet was beside himself with rage when the book was published:

The Bishop of Meaux accused the Archbishop of Cambrai of heresy . . . He rushed to the King and demanded his pardon for not having warned His Majesty earlier of this prelate's erroneous doctrinal views. This was sufficient to turn the King against the archbishop. His Majesty was most concerned that all these things had happened without his having been informed about them, and he reproached several people, including Mme de Maintenon and Cardinal de Noailles.

The Marquis de Sources noted on February 22nd:

Everybody took sides, some supporting the archbishop, others censuring him openly, while others were more moderate in their opinions and considered that, during a time when the Church was being attacked by heresy, he would perhaps have been better advised not to write on so delicate a subject.

Then, during March, Boussuet in his turn published his Instruction sur les états d'oraison, *and the courtiers started marking the score.* Dangeau:

M. de Meaux recently gave the King a copy of his book. Since the Archbishop of Cambrai and the Bishop of Meaux do not see eye to eye, their books, which are very different, are causing a great stir, and the King seems well pleased with M. de Meaux.

According to Mme Dunoyer's correspondent, there may have been an additional reason for the attack which was now being launched on Fénelon:

13. *François Fénelon,* by Vivien

Jacques Bossuet, by Rigaud

14. *Louis, Duc de Bourgogne,*
after Troye

*Marie Adélaïde
of Savoy, Duchesse
de Bourgogne,*
by Gobert

I know how highly you regard M. de Cambrai and so I will tell you his story, but to do so I shall have to let you into a secret which is known by only a very few people. You may know that no one here doubts that the King married Mme de Maintenon long ago; this seems clear from many signs, including her blunt behaviour towards Monseigneur and towards Mme la Princesse de Conti. It is said that for some time now her desire to be openly acknowledged as Queen has become so strong that she has nagged the King unmercifully on the subject. He resisted at first, but eventually, in a moment of tenderness, he promised her he would consult his confessor about the matter. Mme de Maintenon felt sure, now, that her ambitions would be satisfied, thinking that Père La Chaise would be eager to curry favour with her. But he was far too shrewd to commit himself, knowing too well that to declare himself in favour of one party would bring down on him the wrath of the other party; so he was clever enough to extract himself from his predicament like the good Jesuit he was, by persuading the King that he did not believe himself to be a good enough casuist to decide such an important question, and asking his permission to consult an enlightened person whose discretion he guaranteed. The King was most reluctant to have his secret made known, but when Père La Chaise named M. de Fénelon, the King willingly gave his consent and told the Father to go and find him.

When the archbishop learned why he was wanted, he was extremely put out and said to the Jesuit: 'What I have done to you, mon Père, to deserve this? This will ruin me.' After a moment he added: 'Ah well, it cannot be helped. Let us go and find the King.' They found him waiting for them in his study. The archbishop immediately knelt at the King's feet and begged him to forgive him in advance for anything he might say to cause offence. This the King promised and then explained the matter on which he required advice. M. de Fénelon, with his usual forthrightness, emphasized in reply what damage to his cause would result from a declaration of the marriage, and what harmful effects might ensue. The King was persuaded by the soundness of these arguments and resolved to go no further in the matter.

Mme de Maintenon continued to press the King after this

event, but the King was adamant in his refusal. She demanded to know if it was Père La Chaise who had dissuaded him. The King refused for some time to tell her who it had been, but eventually, in a most blameworthy moment of weakness, he explained the course of events to her. Mme de Maintenon concealed her anger from the King and plotted to revenge herself. The first victim of her rage was the archbishop, although the Jesuit's turn was to come later, despite the fact that his sole sin was one of omission. Her faction pondered for a long time on how best to attack M. de Cambrai successfully, since nothing he had done so far gave room for hostile action. Finally, the Bishop of Meaux, who was annoyed because the King had confided the education of Monseigneur le Duc de Bourgogne to the Abbé de Fénelon rather than to himself, hit upon a plan. The archbishop had written a book treating the theme of pure love, and M. de Meaux thought he might cunningly achieve M. de Cambrai's downfall by wilfully misinterpreting certain passages which, in fact, expressed thoughts no more extravagant than those of St Theresa and many others revered by the Church. Mme de Maintenon had invoked his aid in achieving her revenge and he had been only too happy to oblige her, so he now gave her this advice. It is feared that she will make use of it ruthlessly.

Fénelon, however, was not the only one to express alarm at the state of the kingdom; several other serious-minded people in Court circles were becoming disquieted. Jean Racine, still sure of Mme de Maintenon's protection, summoned up the courage to present a list of criticisms and propose some solutions. They were not well received, as Louis Racine explains in his memoirs of his father's life:

Mme de Maintenon had the highest regard for him, and although she could not see him very often she always enjoyed listening to him talk on various subjects, for he had the knowledge and wit to discuss any matter at all. One day she mentioned to him the misery which afflicted the common people; he replied that that was a usual result of long wars, but that it could be alleviated by those in positions of power if they were acquainted with the facts by individuals concerned with the

problem. He began to expatiate on this theme, with the enthusiasm and eloquence which came naturally to him when
his interest was aroused by the subject under discussion;
Madame de Maintenon was so impressed by his observations
that she persuaded him he should reflect further upon his
opinions and then write them down for her. Unfortunately for
him, he agreed to do this, not in the least in a sycophantic
spirit but because he really hoped that his views might be of
some use to the public. So he sent Mme. de Maintenon a
cogently argued and excellently well written memorandum.
She was engaged in reading this when the King entered her
room, took it from her and, after reading a few lines, asked her
heatedly who was the author. She replied that she was bound
to secrecy but the King was so imperative in his insistence on
being told that she had no alternative but to obey, and the
author was named.

The King praised M. Racine's zeal but expressed disapproval
that a man of letters should concern himself with things which
were none of his business. He even added, rather petulantly:
'Because he is an accomplished versifier does he think he knows
everything? And because he is a poet has he now ambitions to
be a minister?' If the King had realized the effect his words
would cause he would never have uttered them. He was
always kind towards those around him and never deliberately
offended anybody, but in this instance he cannot have guessed
that these words would deeply wound M. Racine's very sensitive heart. When Mme de Maintenon sent a message to the
author of the memorandum, informing him of what had happened and telling him at the same time not to visit her again
until further notice, he was completely overwhelmed. He
began to brood on melancholy ideas, and soon afterwards was
attacked by a violent fever which the physicians were finally
able to cure by administering quinine . . .

During this period, the posts of secretary to the King
became subject to a tax, and since M. Racine had had great
difficulty in raising sufficient funds to pay the cost of his own
post, he was now hard put to find an additional sum to pay
this tax as well. He hoped that the King might grant him
exemption . . . He wrote out a petition but did not dare present
it himself, so he prevailed upon some influential friends to

present it for him, and this they did willingly. 'This cannot be,' the King replied, then added: 'But if an occasion should arise, later, to compensate him, I shall be very glad to do so.' These last words should have consoled M. Racine, but he only paid attention to the first words of refusal, and became convinced that the King had set his mind against him for reasons which he could only guess . . .

Still according to Louis Racine's *account, Mme de Maintenon became worried by her favourite poet's state of despondency, although she was unwilling to intercede for him with the King:*

Seeing him one day in the garden of Versailles, she turned aside into a nearby *allée* so that he could join her there. As soon as he had approached her she said to him: 'What is it you fear? I am the cause of your unhappiness, and I owe it to my own interests as well as to my honour to repair the damage I have done. Your fortune is one with my own. Let this cloud pass by, I shall bring back the fine weather.' 'No, no, Madame,' he replied, 'you can never bring it back for me.' 'And why,' she asked, 'should you have such a thought? Do you doubt my heart or my influence?' He answered: 'I know, Madame, how great your influence is, and I know how kind you are towards me, but I have an aunt who loves me in a very different manner; this saintly lady prays every day to God to subject me to disgraces, humiliations and subjects for penitence, and she has greater influence than you.' While he was still speaking they heard the sound of a carriage. 'It is the King out for a drive!' exclaimed Mme de Maintenon in alarm, 'hide quickly!', and he fled into the shrubbery.

Saint-Simon, however, explained Racine's fall from favour very differently; according to his account, the poet had offended both the King and his protectress by an unfortunate phrase:

He was sometimes exceedingly absent-minded. One evening, when he was in the company of the King and Mme de Maintenon in her apartment, the conversation turned to the state of the theatre in Paris ... The King inquired about the plays and actors of the moment, and asked Racine why, according to what he had been told, the drama had sunk to a very low level of quality compared to that of previous years. Racine gave him several reasons, concluding with what he considered the most important one, namely that for lack of authors and good new plays the actors were falling back upon old works, including plays by Scarron which were worthless and repugnant to everybody.

At these words the unfortunate widow [of Scarron] blushed, not at this attack upon the reputation of the poor cripple, but to hear his name pronounced at all, especially in the presence of his successor. The King was embarrassed. The silence which suddenly descended awakened the wretched Racine to a realization of his offence and to the depths of the pit into which his fatal distraction had just plunged him. He remained the most disconcerted of the three, and stood there not daring to raise his eyes or open his mouth, while the other two were so stunned by surprise that the silence lasted for several long moments. Finally, the King dismissed Racine from the room, saying that he had work to do. The latter left in a state of shock and made his way as best he could to the room of his friend Cavoye, to whom he recounted his dreadful blunder. Its enormity was such that there were no steps he could take to make amends. After that incident, neither the King nor Mme de Maintenon ever spoke to Racine again or even recognized his presence. His chagrin was so great that he fell into a decline and died after a period of two years which he put to good use in seeking the salvation of his soul ...

Meanwhile, the affair of Quietism was still smouldering. In June 1698, the King finally took drastic action, and on the 2nd of that month Dangeau noted in his Journal:

This morning, before the Council, the King was closeted for a considerable time with M. de Beauvilliers, and this evening it was learned that His Majesty has expelled from his Court Messieurs the Abbés de Langeron and de Beaumont, and Messieurs Dupuy and de l'Echelle. The Abbé de Langeron was lector and the Abbé de Beaumont assistant preceptor to the

Duc de Bourgogne, while Messieurs Dupuy and de l'Echelle were gentlemen of his suite. All these gentlemen are accused of having become strongly attached to the new opinions. The Abbé de Beaumont is the nephew of the Archbishop of Cambrai. At the same time, the King has cashiered Fénelon, an exempt officer of his Guards, who is the brother of M. de Cambrai.

In a further entry, dated June 7th, Dangeau *notes:*

I have just learned that Mme Guyon was confined in the Bastille a few days ago. It is believed she will remain there for the rest of her life; she has been left two women to attend upon her.

As for the Princess Palatine, *she declared that Mme Guyon, Fénelon and their friends were preparing great changes at the Court in the event that the King should die. She even accused Mme de Maintenon of having been their accomplice:*

Entire lists have been found of posts that were to be awarded: they wanted to change the composition of the whole Court and distribute the highest posts among the members of their faction. Religion played the least part of all in this affair. But Mme de Maintenon saw that M. de Meaux had discovered this underhand manoeuvre, realized that there might be repercussions, and feared that the King might discover her double-dealing, so she promptly changed sides and abandoned Mme Guyon and all her spirituality. Then everything was unmasked. I can assure you that this whole quarrel between bishops has absolutely nothing to do with questions of faith: the whole thing is simply a clash between rival ambitions.

With the publication of his Relations sur le Quiétisme, *Bossuet succeeded in crushing his adversaries. And the following year Fénelon was condemned by Rome.* Dangeau *announced, on March 22, 1699:*

The courier from Rome has brought the condemnation of M. de Cambrai's book, which contains twenty-three propositions qualified with the words: dangerous, rash or erroneous. The Pope decrees the excommunication of all those who read it or keep a copy. The King announced this news to M. de La Rochefoucauld, who spoke well of M. de Cambrai, assuring the King that he should submit unhesitatingly.

Indeed, as Dangeau *added, on April 12th:*

The Archbishop of Cambrai has issued a pastoral letter in which he forbids all in his diocese to read his book. Everybody here is well satisfied with his pastoral letter.

Eleven years after his condemnation, Fénelon *wrote to Père Le Tellier:*

He who was in error prevailed; he who was free from error was crushed. May God be praised.

CHAPTER XIX

MESSIEURS! BEHOLD THE KING OF SPAIN

My brother, it is not chance which has made you great and
powerful by birth. God, since the start of the centuries, pre-
destined you to this temporal glory.

BISHOP MASSILLON: *Lenten Sermon*

❦

PRINCIPAL PERSONALITIES MENTIONED IN
CHAPTER XIX

LOUIS DE FRANCE, DUC DE BOURGOGNE, eldest son of the
Dauphin.

MARIE ADÉLAÏDE, daughter of the Duke of Savoy, married
at the age of twelve to the Duc de Bourgogne.

MME DE LUDE: MARGUERITE LOUISE DE BÉTHUNE-
SULLY, widow of Henri de Daillon, Duc de Lude, previously lady-in-waiting to the Queen and now governess of
the Duchesse de Bourgogne.

CHARLES, DUC DE BERRY, third son of the Dauphin.

PHILIPPE, DUC D'ANJOU, second son of the Dauphin, who
now becomes King Philip V of Spain.

JEAN BAPTISTE COLBERT, MARQUIS DE TORCY, Foreign
Minister, son of Jean Baptiste Colbert's brother, Colbert de
Croissy.

*The Peace of Ryswick was signed in October 1697. This
time, Louis XIV appears to have followed the advice of Fénelon: he gave up all his conquered territories in Spain, Flanders
and Germany. Surprise was general, and Mme Dunoyer's
correspondent wrote to her:*

At last, Madame, we have peace. Since it is claimed that this peace is not to France's advantage, it has not been marked by much joy. It has furnished material for a quantity of satires against the plenipotentiaries and even against the Court, and this has grieved the King, who had expected to witness great celebrations, and has expressed his astonishment at the general lack of enthusiasm. As a result, the following anonymous verses have been written:

> The King, it's said, is very sad
> To find, in giving peace to France,
> That Paris folk are not so glad
> And show entire indifference.
> To prove to us we've not been had,
> Peace-signing's not the only way!
> Did he treat his subjects like his foes
> And give them back all that he owes,
> He'd see a fine firework display!

The King of England, who is called King William to distinguish him from the other king at Saint-Germain, has sent his favourite, Lord Portland, here as ambassador extraordinary, and Monsieur d'Odyck has arrived here as envoy of the States-General. These gentlemen have been received with great pomp; indeed, Paris is a splendid sight these days, filled as it is with a prodigious number of foreigners who all boast magnificent retinues and spend a great deal of money.

The Court was preparing to celebrate the marriage of the Duc de Bourgogne, the Dauphin's eldest son, to Marie Adélaïde, daughter of the Duke of Savoy, who, one year earlier, had signed a separate peace treaty with France. The young princess, who was then eleven years old, had arrived at Versailles at that time. According to the Marquis de Sourches:

She was very small, but she had a pretty figure and even her slightest movement was vivacious. Her hair was very long, a beautiful light brown which looked as if it was growing darker. Her complexion was fresh and clear. Her eyes were very large, almost too open, her nose straight and rather short,

her forehead too wide and rather bulging, her mouth rather
wide and full-lipped, attractive enough except when she
laughed, for her teeth, though white, were large and unsym-
metrical. Her bosom seemed well developed for her age. She
had a serious and gentle air and already knew how to instil a
majestic presence into her natural vivacity. She spoke little but
answered questions intelligently and spontaneously. But she
was still a child, played with her dolls and joined in games of
blind man's buff.

Madame de Maintenon, *too, was charmed by the young
princess's character. She wrote to the Duchess of Savoy (the
daughter of Monsieur and his first wife, Henriette d'Angleterre) to tell her her impressions of her daughter:*

This letter is hardly appropriate to the respect I owe Your
Royal Highness, but I think you will pardon my informality as
resulting from the fact that we are all in transports of joy at
the treasure we have received. The Duchesse de Lude has tears
in her eyes when she describes the princess's behaviour, which,
she assures us, is as accomplished as seems evident to all who
watch her. As for her natural wit, she only has to speak to show
it, and her manner of listening and all the motions of her face
make it abundantly clear that nothing escapes her. Your Royal
Highness can scarcely imagine how great is the King's satisfaction; indeed, he did me the honour yesterday of telling me
that he would have to be on guard against himself because
otherwise people would have found his pleasure excessive. The
princess thought Monsieur rather fat; but she found Monseigneur slim and considered that the King had the finest
figure in the world. Her politeness is such that she is incapable
of saying anything disagreeable. Yesterday, when I tried to
stop her caressing me because, as I said to her, I was too old, she
replied: 'Ah, you are not very old!' Then she pressed herself
eagerly against my lap and said: 'Mama has told me to express
to you the great affection she has for you, and to ask you for
your own affection towards me; do teach me, I beg you, what
I must do to please you.' Those are just words, Madame, but
the air of gaiety, gentleness and charm which accompanied
them cannot be described in a letter.

The marriage ceremony took place on December 7, 1697, at Versailles, and the Mercure Galant *gave this account of it:*

Never before has a king kept his word with such exactitude. By the treaty concluded with the Duke of Savoy, His Majesty agreed that M. le Duc de Bourgogne should marry the Princess of Savoy as soon as she was twelve years old. She celebrated her twelfth birthday on the 6th of this month and the marriage took place on the following day.

On that day, which was a Saturday, all the princes, princesses and principal ladies of the Court went to the Princess of Savoy's room between eleven o'clock and midday. Monseigneur le Duc de Bourgogne, accompanied by M. de Beauvilliers, was conducted there at half-past eleven by the Marquis de Blainville, Grand Master of Ceremonies, and by M. Des Granges, Master of Ceremonies; and Monseigneur took a seat not far from the princess, who was still completing her toilet. When the King, on emerging from his Council, sent word to her she left her room to join His Majesty, who was waiting for her in the gallery. Monseigneur le Duc de Bourgogne gave her his right hand. The Marquis de Dangeau, his gentleman-in-waiting, walked behind Monseigneur holding up his robe, while the Comte de Tessé, his first equerry, went in front of him to assist him from time to time because of the weight of his garments, but he accomplished this duty walking backwards so as not to appear to precede Monseigneur . . .

But the young bride was only twelve, and the bridegroom fifteen. That evening:

The King of England came to present the shirt to Monseigneur le Duc de Bourgogne and the Queen presented the nightgown to Madame la Duchesse de Bourgogne who, in her turn, presented her garters and bouquet to Mademoiselle [d'Orléans]. As soon as Madame la Duchesse de Bourgogne was in bed, the King summoned Monseigneur le Duc de Bourgogne, who entered the room, holding his bonnet in his hand, his hair knotted at the back by a flame-coloured ribbon, and got into the bed on the right-hand side. The curtains at the foot were closed, but those at the sides remained half open.

The King called for the Ambassador of Savoy to enter the
room, and told him he could report that he had seen the married couple in bed together. Then the King and Their
Britannic Majesties retired, but Monseigneur [the King's
brother] remained in the room. Shortly afterwards, Monseigneur le Duc de Bourgogne got up, went into the large study,
where he dressed again, and went back to his own apartments
to sleep.

Saint-Simon *adds:*

The little Duc de Berry, so naughty and bold, thought very
ill of his brother's meekness in this respect, and maintained
stoutly that had it been him he would have stayed in the bed.

But according to Mme Dunoyer's correspondent, *the Duc
de Bourgogne was not resigned to waiting:*

Not long ago, M. de Bourgogne, with the aid of a chambermaid, found the means to hide himself in his wife's room and
to slip into her bed when Mme de Lude, who slept in the same
room, was sound asleep. But that lady awoke at a most incon-
venient moment and ordered the prince to retire to his room.
The following morning she went straight to the King to complain of his conduct and the King said very curtly to the Duc
de Bourgogne: 'I have learned, Monsieur, that certain things
have occurred which might be injurious to your health, and
I pray you to see this does not happen again.' The prince
replied hastily: 'Sire, I am very well,' and the matter was not
mentioned again.

*The same correspondent went on to announce what she
termed a most extraordinary piece of news:*

... which is that the Emperor of Morocco has sent to ask
for the hand of Mme la Princesse de Conti who, as you see, has
extended her conquests further than Hercules, since the kingdom of Morocco lies beyond this hero's pillars. It is said that
this swarthy emperor was so impressed by the description
given to him of our beautiful princess that he decided to come

to France himself, incognito, and that he was one of those *margageas* whom we saw in the suite of the Moroccan ambassador. However that may be, he seems very much smitten with love and offers very favourable terms which the King, however, has no desire to accept. Mme la Princesse de Conti has even less desire to go to Africa ... This adventure has given a good laugh to the Court and the whole town. But since the King wishes to treat the Moroccan prince tactfully he made his refusal in most courteous terms, limiting his reasons to the question of the difference in religions.

In the autumn of 1699, a new ceremony diverted the Court. On October 22nd, the Duc and Duchesse de Bourgogne were at last authorized to conduct themselves as man and wife. The Baron de Breteuil, Master of Ceremonies, who had come to escort the prince, relates:

His hair had been set in a mass of curls and the magnificence of his dishabille was most proper for a wedding-day. He left his room with a firm step and a joyful air, and since I had the honour of bearing the candlestick I conducted him to the door of the field of battle. This all took place so quickly that the King, who had told them he would come along, through the back rooms of their apartment, to see them together in their bed, arrived too late and did not enter their room at all.

According to Mme Dunoyer's correspondent:

Since the duchess's [the Princesse de Condé's] songs give you pleasure, here is one she has just composed to celebrate the freedom just granted to the Duc and Duchesse de Bourgogne to enjoy their conjugal rights:

> Frenchmen, you all shall rejoice,
> And sing aloud with one voice:
> May God to this good task enjoin
> M. le Duc de Bourgogne.
>
> Thank God he is youthful and bold,
> And Madame his wife is not old,
> And with pleasure herself will join
> With M. le Duc de Bourgogne.

> Grandpapa's joy will be great,
> And the happy event celebrate,
> When he sees the fruit of the loins
> Of M. le Duc de Bourgogne.

Nobody sings anything else at present. M. d'Argenson, our lieutenant of police, tried to stop it but failed in his efforts.

And Dangeau *noted in his diary on November 11th:*

Monseigneur le Duc de Bourgogne has begun sleeping every night in the bed of Madame la Duchesse, for he no longer wishes to sleep by himself.

The Court was in festive mood that winter, thanks to the young bride, who adored fêtes. The Marquis de Coulanges wrote to Mme de Grignan on February 2, 1700:

You can scarcely imagine, Madame, the furious quest for pleasure on which the Court has embarked. The King desires Mme la Duchesse de Bourgogne to do exactly as she pleases from morn to night, and he is sufficiently rewarded if she is happy. Life is a constant succession of expeditions to Marly and Meudon, comings and goings to Paris for operas, balls and masquerades, and the gentlemen are practically at daggers drawn to attract the princess's favourable attention. The ladies who take part in these festivities have to look to their appearance, and they spend four times as much on their finery as they used to. For masquerades they wear gowns made from fabrics costing at least 150 francs an ell, and when a lady is unfortunate enough to be obliged to appear twice in the same costume she becomes the object of jests to the effect that it is obvious she has only come to Paris to buy second-hand clothes.

In November 1700 there was great agitation at the Court. The King of Spain, Charles II, had just died childless: in his will he designated as his successor Louis XIV's grandson, the Duc d'Anjou.
The sovereigns of Europe had become concerned by the problems of this succession. The Marquis de Feuquières explains in his Mémoires:

The failing health of the King of Spain, Charles II, who had no children, gave rise to anxiety among the powers which had no interest in the succession. King William and the Dutch had the idea of proposing to the King and the Emperor a partition treaty covering the future succession to the Spanish throne, its purpose being that the House of France and the House of German Austria should benefit equally from an aggrandizement of their territories which would serve also to retain the balance of power between these two Houses, thus preserving the tranquillity of the other European powers.

The King agreed to this proposal for a partition treaty, but the Emperor, who felt sure of winning the succession to the entire Spanish monarchy, refused to enter into any negotiations . . . The King was called on by the English and the Dutch to accept the partition, which he did, but the Emperor refused a similar summons. During these negotiations the King of Spain died, having made a will in which he made amends to the House of France, which had been unjustly disinherited by the wills of Philip III and Philip IV, by nominating M. le Duc d'Anjou as the universal heir to the whole Spanish monarchy. The King had no reason to refuse to accept the will in favour of the prince, his grandson, since the Emperor's refusal to accept the partition treaty restored to His Majesty every legal right to press the legitimate claims of his House in the Spanish succession.

It was this acceptance of Charles II's will, without the agreement and permission of the English and the Dutch, that determined them to support the Emperor . . .

At Versailles, according to Pierre Narbonne, *commissaire of police of that town (and appointed its governor the following year), the following disrespectful jingle was being sung by the people:*

> Here Charles the Second, King of Spain,
> Lies sleeping. He led no campaign,
> He conquered nothing, left no heirs:
> What did he do for thirty years,
> This mighty prince, while he did reign?
> His fragile health caused him such pain

That though we search with all our skill
We find he only made his will!

According to Mme Dunoyer's correspondent:

Our monarch understands his interests too well to be con-
tented with a portion when he can have the whole. However
the matter was deliberated by the Council, which decided in
accordance with the King's desires; only M. de Torcy held the
opposite opinion and was in favour of partition. But just as a
swallow does not make a summer, so M. de Torcy's opinion
carried no weight at all.

Nicolas de Sainctot, *who had succeeded his uncle and his
father in the post of Master of Ceremonies at the royal palace,
has left an account of the manner in which the King announced the great news to the courtiers:*

On November 16th, the Spanish ambassador, the Marquis
of Castel dos Rios, presented to the King, after his *lever* at a
secret audience, letters signed by the persons composing the
Regency of Spain. These letters expressed the eagerness with
which Spain awaited the arrival of M. le Duc d'Anjou, whom
the will of the late King Charles II declared to be his heir
presumptive and the successor to all his kingdoms.

Before the audience, the King had told M. le Duc d'Anjou
to wait in a small adjacent room. After reading the letters, the
King summoned him, placed him at his right-hand side, and
said to the ambassador: 'Here is the King for whom Spain
calls.' Then the ambassador went down on one knee, bowed
to His Catholic Majesty, offered him his compliments while
still in this posture, and then kissed his hand, which is the way
the Spaniards salute their sovereign. When the ambassador had
made his compliments, the Marquis de Torcy opened the door
to me and I re-escorted the ambassador from the room. The
King told me to let everybody come in. The two folding doors
were pushed to each side, and the King announced in a loud
voice: 'Recognize the Duc d'Anjou as King of Spain.' At once,
all the courtiers present hastened to express their joy to the
new King.

And the Marquis de Breteuil *adds:*

That evening, the King of Spain supped with the King who made him sit above him at the table. After washing their hands they were proffered one dish containing a double towel, which they both took at the same time . . . and when the King of Spain retired to go to bed, the King accompanied him as far as the door of his bedroom, that is to say nearly as far as the entrance-way of the anteroom nearest the bedroom. The whole Court was much astonished by the novelty of this cere-mony and by the sight of it. And the King, when taking his leave, said to him: 'I hope Your Majesty sleeps well tonight.' His Majesty could not refrain from smiling as he acted out this little comedy.

Louis XIV's grandson prepared to leave for Spain. The afternoon of December 3rd was devoted to leave-taking, ac-cording to Breteuil, *and the new King and Queen of Spain made their entrance into the salon followed by the entire royal household in tears:*

At this sight, all those lining the way began to weep as well. The King, who was more moved and more tearful than anyone else, embraced His Catholic Majesty at the door of that apart-ment which gives on to the peristyle, but then his emotions were so strong that he desired to embrace his dear child once more, so His Majesty took three steps into the gallery and gave him one last very tender and very close embrace. His Majesty immediately returned to the apartment, and the King of Spain went out to his carriage, followed by the whole Court.

But according to Mme *Dunoyer's correspondent, the fare-wells took place at Sceaux, where the Duc du Maine—uncle 'of the left hand' of the new King of Spain—had given a mag-nificent reception in his honour:*

I shall say only that the whole Court and town was at Sceaux, that I was there with the rest, that the King had a private conversation there with the King of Spain and that after giving him his instructions he embraced him tenderly and left him in the arms of Monseigneur le Dauphin. Monseigneur le Dauphin wept as he parted from his dear son and after saying good-bye to him started following him from a distance, holding a handkerchief to his eyes, but the King grasped him by the arm, saying: 'Where are you going, my son?' and drawing him back into the apartment. I had gone downstairs to see the young king enter his carriage and I noticed, when he did me the honour of greeting me, that his eyes were very red. I am not surprised: he knows what he is leaving behind and does not know what lies ahead of him. Everybody was weeping that day, except the princes his brothers, who were delighted by the prospect of the journey involved in accompanying him as far as the Spanish frontier. M. le Duc de Berry, with his usual vivacity, said to the Duc de Bourgogne: 'Do you know, brother, why the King is having us accompany the King of Spain?' 'Why,' replied the prince, 'to procure for us the pleasure of remaining together as long as possible, and so that we may have a chance of seeing something of France at the same time.' 'No,' retorted the Duc de Berry, 'you are far off the mark; it is to show the Spaniards that they have been given the one of us three who was the most worthy.'

It was clear that the great powers were not prepared to accept the fact of a grandson of Louis XIV occupying the throne of Spain. The same correspondent expressed the fears of the Court:

Everybody here expects a terrible war to break out next spring, and preparations are already being made for this eventuality. So now the kingdom is going to be ruined once again, before it has had time even to make good the ravages of the last war. Frankly, I think that we are going to pay dearly for this crown of Spain which the King has bought for his grandson at our expense. It will cost us a fortune to prevent it being seized away from him. Frankly, we are great fools to ruin ourselves for the aggrandizement of others, and for people at that who, far from doing us honour and being grateful to us, regard us as a worthless servant of the Gospel who does not perform his allotted tasks—but I say no more for fear that I have already said too much.

CHAPTER XX

PREDICANTS AND CAMISARDS

'Alas! no sooner is one leader slain, than others spring up.'
MARÉCHAL DE BROGLIO

PRINCIPAL PERSONALITIES MENTIONED IN CHAPTER XX

FRANÇOIS DE NEUFVILLE, MARÉCHAL DE VILLEROI, a favourite of Louis XIV since the beginning of his reign (already mentioned in Chapter III).

GÉDÉON LAPORTE, JEAN CAVALIER, 'ROLAND', leaders of the Camisards.

MARÉCHAL VICTOR MAURICE DE BROGLIO, MARÉCHAL NICOLAS AUGUSTE DE LA BAUME DE MONTREVEL, MARÉCHAL LOUIS CLAUDE DE VILLARS, charged with re-establishing order in Languedoc.

On June 9, 1701, the Court went into mourning. Monsieur, the King's brother was dead. Mme Dunoyer's correspondent *informed her that:*

This good prince died suddenly, during a game of lansquenet, of a heating of the blood which caused a kind of apoplexy. A fortune-teller had predicted to him long ago that gaming would sooner or later play him a nasty trick but he could not resolve to give up playing. The King appears most affected by his death. Madame has gone into retreat, and M. le Duc d Orléans is consoling himself with Mlle de Séri, Madam's maid-of-honour, who is at present his declared mistress.

In the opinion of Saint-Simon it was not the lansquenet which had heated Monsieur's blood but an acrimonious dispute with his brother: the King was irate with Monsieur's son, the Duc de Chartres, whom he accused of infidelity to the wife he himself had given him (his own daughter, Mlle de Bois) and of causing a scandal throughout the Court by his debaucheries.

On June 8th, at Marly, where the Court was spending a few days, sounds of quarrelling were heard coming from the King's room and an usher had hurried to warn His Majesty that every single word could be clearly heard in the adjoining salon where the courtiers were waiting:

The usher's warning made them lower their voices but failed to stop the recriminations, in fact Monsieur finally flew into an absolute rage and reminded the King that when he had arranged the marriage of M. le Duc de Chartres he had promised him the earth, but that so far all he had been able to extract from him was a governorship. Monsieur went on to say that he had wished passionately for his son to be honourably employed to divert him from these petty love-affairs and that his son too had also desired it keenly, as the King well knew, since he had again and again asked it as a favour, but since the King had refused him persistently he had no intention of preventing the young man from finding consolation in his pleasures. He added that at the time of the marriage he had been warned that he would reap nothing but shame and dishonour and gain no advantage whatsoever, and he now saw how true that warning was. The King, growing more and more furious in his turn, retorted that the war would soon make him economize in various directions, and that since Monsieur had shown himself so disobliging his pensions should go first, before the King made any personal economies.

At that point dinner was announced to the King and they left the room together to take their places at table. Monsieur was quite scarlet, his eyes sparkling with anger; indeed his inflamed appearance led some of the ladies who were at table and some of the courtiers standing behind to whisper to each other that Monsieur looked in great need of bleeding. The same had been said about him a short while before at Saint-Cloud; he admitted himself that he was in urgent need of it, and despite the ill-feeling between them, the King had more than once urged Monsieur to be bled.

Dinner passed off as usual, Monsieur eating prodigiously as he always did at his two meals, not to mention the many cups of chocolate he drank every morning and the amount he gobbled throughout the day in the way of fruit, pastries, preserves and all kinds of titbits with which his pockets bulged and which covered the tables in his private rooms.

That same evening, after supper, the Duc de Chartres sent a message to the King to advise him that Monsieur had just been stricken by an attack of apoplexy:

At this news, the King, who usually sped to Monsieur's side for the most trivial occasion, went instead to Mme de Maintenon's apartments and had her woken up. After spending a short time with her, he returned to his own apartments at about midnight, ordered his carriages to be got ready, and despatched the Marquis de Gevres to Saint-Cloud with instructions to return and wake him should Monsieur grow any worse. Then he went to bed. It is my belief that, as a result of the quarrel they had just had, the King suspected some kind of plot to relieve the tension between them, and that he had gone to consult with Mme de Maintenon because he preferred to fail signally in the proprieties rather than be duped. Mme de Maintenon disliked and feared Monsieur. He seldom paid his respects to her, and despite his meekness and his more than deferential attitude, he had occasionally let slip remarks, when talking to the King, which betrayed his contempt for her and his respect for public opinion. She was therefore in no hurry to urge the King to visit him, and still less to encourage him to travel through the night, lose his sleep, and witness a mournful scene which would probably so touch his heart that he might relent. And she hoped, too, that it would all be over quickly so that the King should be spared prolonged pain.

But in the middle of the night the King was informed that his brother was at the point of death, and he set out for Saint-Cloud:

The King arrived at Saint-Cloud shortly before three in the morning to find that Monsieur had not regained consciousness for a single moment since he was first taken ill. There had been a glimmer of awareness when Père du Trévoux had been about to say Mass at daybreak, but it had not lasted. Even the most solemn and awful scenes often produce ridiculous incidents. Père du Trévoux, at that moment, had bent down and shouted into Monsieur's ear: 'Monsieur, don't you recognize your own confessor? It's me, dear old Père du Trévoux, speaking to you?' which made those who were least moved laugh out loud in a rather indecent manner. The King himself appeared very moved. He was naturally prone to weep and on this occasion, too, he burst into tears. Indeed, he had never had cause to do other than love Monsieur dearly, and although they had been on bad terms for two months this sad occasion must have reminded him of their past affection for each other. Perhaps he blamed himself for hastening Monsieur's death by the previous morning's quarrel. And, too, he may have felt some concern because Monsieur was two years younger than him and had all his life been as healthy as himself, if not more so. The King heard Mass at Saint-Cloud and then, at eight o'clock, when there was no longer any hope for Monsieur's life, he allowed himself to be persuaded by Mme de Maintenon and Mme la Duchesse de Bourgogne not to wait any longer but to return with them in his coach. When he was about to leave he said a few kind words to M. de Chartres, both of them weeping bitterly; whereupon the young prince took advantage of the situation to clasp the King's knees, sobbing: 'Ah, Sire, what will become of me? I have lost Monsieur, and I know that you do not love me.' The King, who was surprised and deeply touched, embraced him and spoke to him most affectionately . . .

On arriving at Marly the King went straight to Mme de Maintenon's apartments, accompanied by Mme la Duchesse de Bourgogne. Three hours later, Fagon appeared. Since the King had ordered him not to leave Monsieur's side until he was dead, or until he had recovered, which could only happen by a miracle, he said to him as soon as he saw him: 'Well, Monsieur Fagon, is my brother dead?' 'Yes, Sire,' he replied, 'no treatment could save him.' The King wept bitterly.

But his grief did not last long:

After such a shocking event, so many tears and such demonstrations of love, everybody took it for granted that the remaining three days of that Marly excursion would be exceedingly dull. However, when on the morning after Monsieur's
death the ladies in attendance went at midday to Mme de
Maintenon's apartments, they found the King already there
with Mme la Duchesse de Bourgogne, and heard them, from
the adjoining room where they were waiting, singing a selection of opera prologues. Shortly afterwards the King noticed
that Mme la Duchesse de Bourgogne was sitting in a corner
of the room looking miserable. He asked Mme de Maintenon in
surprise what could have upset her, and then tried to cheer her
up by playing with her, after which he sent for several ladies
to entertain them both. That was not the only strange scene.
When they came out from dinner at the usual time, that is to
say, shortly after two o'clock, just twenty-six hours after
Monsieur's death, M. le Duc de Bourgogne invited the Duc de
Montfort to play a hand of brelan. 'Brelan!' exclaimed Montfort in utter astonishment, 'you must have forgotten, Monsieur
is not yet cold.' 'Indeed,' replied the prince, 'I know it very
well, but the King will not allow anyone at Marly to be bored;
he has ordered me to start everyone playing and, in case no
one dares to be the first, I am to set the example myself.' They
then sat down to a hand of brelan and before very long the
drawing-room was full of gaming-tables.

Such, then, was the sorrow of the King, and that of Mme de
Maintenon. She felt the loss of Monsieur as a positive de-
liverance. She found it hard to dissimulate her joy, and she
would have found it a great deal harder to simulate an appearance of grief. She saw that the King was already entirely consoled, and nothing suited her purposes better than to try to
divert him.

*France was launched into a fresh war, during the spring of
this year 1701, this time against the Empire and England. The
dethroned king of England, James II, had died the previous
September, still in exile at Saint-Germain. Louis XIV recognized James's son as the legitimate sovereign of Great Britain,*

whereas the British parliament had declared him guilty of high treason and set a price on his head.

The Emperor Leopold attacked in Italy and the year 1702 began badly for France: in February, the Maréchal de Villeroi let himself be surprised in Cremona. The French troops retook the town, but their commander remained in enemy hands. The Marquis de Dangeau was present when the King related the marshal's misfortunes to the assembled courtiers:

He spoke for some time about the Maréchal de Villeroi, using the most affectionate and obliging terms. He expressed his surprise and indignation at the behaviour of those who mocked the marshal's ill fortune, and added that he suspected that the hatred being shown towards the marshal resulted partly from the friendship with which he honoured him. He even made use of the word favourite, a word which had never before passed his lips in referring to any person. He continued speaking for a long time, in the tones of a man who is determined to defend the interests of the unfortunate. This will be a great consolation to the marshal's family, and shows the great goodness of the King, who never abandons those who serve him and are loyal to him.

This did not prevent Paris and the Court from humming a jingle about the incident:

> Frenchmen, thank Bellona,
> Your fortune is double:
> You have kept Cremona
> And lost your general!

At this same moment, the Protestants of the Cevennes were in a ferment: they had either refused to be converted or else had abjured. Following the call of their 'prophets' and predicants, they were holding assemblies in the mountains. In 1698, a secret memorandum prepared by Lamoignon de Basville, intendant of Languedoc, at the request of the Duc de Bourgogne, had already drawn attention to the dangerous situation:

The predicants are beginning to organize small-scale assemblies at night in inaccessible places. They do not preach rebellion at first. But if one tolerates these assemblies then they are soon attended by increasing numbers of people and the predicants, seeing that they are not being proceeded against, begin to introduce fanaticism, calling on the people to take up arms and inciting them to all kinds of violent excesses.

There is only one way of putting a stop to this menace and that is to forbid any assembly of any nature whatsoever and to punish all those taking part in any assembly which is uncovered ... The second most important objective is to take all possible measures to capture the predicants and, when they have been taken, to give them no quarter and to apply the full rigour of the law by sentencing them to death.

The simmering revolt finally boiled over into action in July 1702, in the small town of Pont-de-Montvert on the Tarn, with the murder of the Abbé du Chayla, inspector of missions for the Bishop of Mende. The rebels soon assumed the name of Camisards, because, stated one of them, Abraham Mazel, in his Mémoires:

We often found that our garments hindered our movements, so whenever action threatened we stripped to our shirts or camisoles so that we might be more nimble.

Charles Joseph de La Baume, *counsellor at the Nîmes Présidial and consul of the town, was an on-the-spot observer of the rebellion. He wrote a book about it and gave this account of its outbreak:*

July 22, 1702, was the date on which they resolved to mass together and start armed rebellion. Their first project was the assassination of the Abbé du Chayla, who had been at Pont-de-Montvert for a month, acting as a missionary, accompanied by two clerics and two Capuchins. He also had with him four soldiers to guard the prisoners, a manservant, a cook, the schoolmaster of Pont-de-Montvert, M. Blanc, a judge at Florac, who was there to draw up the proceedings against the prisoners, and lastly two pensioners he had brought with him from Saint-Germain-de-Calberte.

At about ten in the evening, a band of these ruffians, about two hundred strong, entered Pont-de-Montvert. Only about a quarter of them carried arms, and they were led by a certain Laporte . . . They massed outside the house of the Abbé du Chayla, who thought at first that they had come for the sole purpose of releasing six young men who had been found armed at various assemblies and had been arrested through his perseverance . . . When the street doors were opened from the inside for the six prisoners to be handed over to their friends, the whole mob burst in. Its first victim was M. Raouls, a cleric and school governor, whom they wounded fatally. Then they ran towards the staircase, emitting blood-curdling yells. The Abbé du Chayla, seeing that all was lost, resigned himself to death. He gave absolution to his servants and exhorted them briefly to die like good Catholics. The servants stationed themselves at the head of the stairs and fired two shots which killed one of the scoundrels and severely wounded another.

The two pensioners fled at the first sound, jumping from a window into the garden and thence into the river, which they succeeded in swimming across safely despite a fusillade of musket shots directed at them. One of them hid in the branches of a great tree and witnessed everything that happened; it was he who gave me the account later on.

Laporte, who had not expected to encounter such resistance and did not wish to lose any more men, cried out: 'Children of God, cease the attack. It will delay us for too long. Let us burn the house and all those in it!' So they piled up in the centre of the hall all the pieces of wooden furniture they could find and threw straw on the pyre to make it burn more quickly. In a few moments the house was ablaze.

The Abbé du Chayla, whose arm was badly burned, succeeded with the help of his servants in reaching the garden by means of a rope fashioned from bedsheets knotted together and lowered from a window. But he fell and broke a thigh. With the aid of the manservant who had followed him down he managed to drag himself into a thicket which covered part of the garden, but was soon revealed by the glare of the flames. They rushed up to him, crying: 'Let us strangle this persecutor of the children of God!' They said to him: 'Today you shall expiate the crimes of violence you have committed for so long

against our relatives and our friends.' The prophet called them
to silence and said in a solemn voice: 'God does not desire the
death of the sinner, but that he should live and repent. Let us
spare him his life if he will agree to join us as a minister of the
Eternal.'

'I would rather die a thousand times,' the Abbé cried out.

'Then you shall die,' replied the false prophet, 'and your sins
be upon your head.'

They dragged him to the bridge, where they stabbed him to
death, but with many glancing blows struck at intervals, so
that his suffering should be more prolonged.

*This first leader of the Camisards, Gédéon Laporte, was
killed in a pitched battle that same year, but his nephew, Pierre
Laporte, known as Roland, together with a twenty-two-year-
old shepherd, Jean Cavalier, took over from him. One of the
Camisards, Jacques Bonbonnoux, explains in his Mémoires how
the rebels lived and fought. A Protestant himself, he had been
weak enough to marry according to the Catholic rite. When
his wife died after a year of marriage he was filled with remorse
for having betrayed his faith and decided to 'enter the wilderness' and join Cavalier's men:*

So I left my home, one evening after supper, at the beginning of the year 1703. I was accompanied by a few young men,
including one, Pierre Claris, who had already been with the
Camisards. We travelled about two leagues that night, making
for a certain house near the village of Montaud, above Durfort,
where an honest and obliging man, Olivier by name, was to
lodge us and feed us during the day we were to stay there. The
following night we headed for another little hamlet, Paussan,
near Miolet in the Cevennes. I remember that before we
reached this hamlet we went down on our knees several times
to thank God for having saved us from being ambushed by our
enemies . . .

From this second haven we retraced our steps and headed in
the direction of Monoblet and lodged in a house at Verdeilhe.
While there we could hear, with heavy hearts, the sound of
gunfire being directed against our persecuted brethren at Pompignan. On the evening of that fatal day, while on our way to

a fresh refuge, we crossed paths with a few survivors of that engagement who had saved themselves by flight. We were all together in a village called Les Montèzes, and here Daniel Guy, the most distinguished member of this scattered band, after dressing a wound he had received in the fighting, recited with such zeal the prayer to be found at the end of the 'Christian observances for a flock' that I almost swooned with ecstasy. After this prayer the chiefs of this small band decided— although I knew nothing of it at the time—that, to show our enemies that not all the Camisards had been killed at the battle of Pompignan, we should burn the church of Durfort. And this resolution was executed that same night ...

Gradually the lives of these outlaws became more organized:

We were continually on the move and rarely stayed more than two days in the same spot. The Protestants living in the districts where we camped brought us food supplies, each bringing a different commodity, one bread, another wine, and a third meat. Our troop was divided into brigades, with about forty men to each brigade and two brigadiers to command each one.

Here is Bonbonnoux's *account of his first engagement:*

One day we received a warning from some source or other that a large detachment of military was about to pass along the main road above Vézenoble. We decided we should engage them in battle, and this was the first time I found myself involved in fighting. Before launching our attack on the troops the sieur Daire, a young predicant aged about twenty, exhorted us with prayers of zeal in face of combat and death. Then we burst on to the enemy, while a certain Adam intoned Psalm LI (he was sixty years of age, a shoemaker by trade, and came from Saint-Maurice, near Saint-Hippolyte in the Caton district). They took to their heels without so much as firing a shot, and we pursued them. As we advanced, one of my comrades, named Douzon de Quissac, who was ahead of me, picked up a rifle from the ground and handed it to me. I had never yet carried one. A little further on I found one myself and took that; it is the rifle I have always used, and though I have had the choice of finer ones since, I have remained faithful to that one.

Denunciations, repressions, reprisals against the rebels was the order of the day. The rebellion developed into partisan warfare, as can be seen from a letter written by the Camisards of the Cevennes to their brethren of Bagnols and dated Avignon, March 12, 1703, 'From the Camp of the Eternal, towards the end of the new moon':

Our very dear brothers in Christ,

We have learned with very great sorrow of the terrible executions of four of our brethren in your town of Bagnols, as a result of the treachery of the miserable Dornac. Our band hitherto held your town in high regard, because you, our dear brothers, had never sent us messages of complaint about conditions there, but now that we know of the indignities meted out to our brethren, we notify you that we shall sweep all your lands with fire and blood. If the Eternal who controls this great universe will give us grace to enter your town, as we hope to do, by an easy means of ingress, then we swear to you that people will talk of what we shall have done there as long as the world lasts. And Dornac and his family may consider themselves warned that his treachery towards our poor brethren is engraved in our hearts in letters of blood.

Be patient until the 15th of next month and you will see things happen then which will astonish you. Our band grows larger every day. Julian[1] has been somewhat troublesome but, thanks be to the Eternal, for every one he kills a hundred join us. That, my dear brethren, is the gist of the present communication. We advise you to keep your doors closed from the 26th to the 28th, and to mark the lintels with a white spot. He who will deliver this letter into your hands is a Prophet.

The Maréchal de Broglio, who had been unable to suppress the rebellion, was recalled and replaced as commander by the

---

[1] A Protestant converted to Catholicism, now a maréchal de camp in the French army and nicknamed Julian the Apostate by the rebels.

Maréchal de Montrevel. The Marquis de Dangeau, *in an entry in his diary dated March 11, 1703, notes:*

News has just been received from Languedoc. The marines who are stationed in that part of the country have attacked and beaten four or five hundred of these fanatics, killing sixty of them. They have had the insolence to have medallions struck which bear a design of two crossed darts surrounded by three letters, C R S. These have been interpreted in two ways, as COMES ROLANDUS SEREVERONORUM[1] or else as CALVINISTE ROMANOS SACRIFICATE.[2] The fanatics are commanded by one known as Roland, to whom they give the title of Comte de Cévennes.

On April 6th:

The news from Languedoc is such that all here are well pleased with the Maréchal de Montrevel. We shall soon have fifteen or sixteen battalions in that country. After which, it is hoped that we shall be in a position to exterminate these fanatics ...

But on August 23rd:

The latest news from Languedoc is not good. The fanatics there are still creating great havoc and are crueller than ever.

However, the principal leader of the Camisards, Cavalier, was ready to negotiate, according to La Baume :

There appeared a letter from the Wilderness, September 14, 1703, signed by Cavalier and addressed to the King. It is extremely long, and crammed with ill-digested passages from the Scriptures designed to prove that they were forced to take up arms in order to win freedom of conscience. He refers at length to the cruel treatment they claim to have received at the hands of the bishops and priests, which forced them to take up arms, and promises that they will lay down their arms if His

---

[1] Comte Roland des Cévennes.
[2] Calvinists, exterminate all Roman Catholics.

Majesty agrees to grant them freedom of conscience and to release their prisoners. He assures the King that then no subjects would be more faithful to him than they, and that they would lay down their last drop of blood in his service. But since their first duty of obedience was to God rather than to the King, they would defend themselves to the bitter end if their just demands were not granted. He signs himself 'Cavalier, commander of the troops sent by God'.

The petition was rejected and the skirmishes continued. Fléchier, *Bishop of Nîmes, wrote on October 23rd:*

Our affairs are still in the same state. The situation deteriorates day by day and our province is ruined and without resources. The rebels are the masters of the countryside. Our forces ravage their mountain fastnesses and they ravage our plains. Hardly any churches are left standing in our diocese, while our lands can be neither sown nor cultivated and so bring us in no revenue. The local defence forces of Catholics which were formed in the villages have nearly all been wiped out. Neither God nor the King have any faithful servants any longer in this province.

When Camisards were captured, the tribunals showed pitiless severity. Père Louvreleuil, *curé of Saint-Germain-de-Calberte and author of a book,* Le Fanatisme renouvelé, *reports:*

The Presidial of Nîmes, at the beginning of March [1704], ordered two executions, following, as usual, the laws and forms of Justice. It condemned to death Louis Jonquet, aged twenty-eight, a native of Lice near Castelnau in the diocese of Uzès, who is celebrated among the rebels and a brigadier in Cavalier's band. He is convicted of having committed acts of extreme cruelty. It pronounced sentence of death at the same time against La Grande Marie, aged thirty, who, under the false name of the Prophetess of Lussan, had caused the death of a great number of innocent people through her fraudulent revelations. In addition, she had appointed herself a collector of funds for Cavalier's troops, with whom she spent nearly all her time, and had succeeded in obtaining large sums of money and huge supplies of provisions.

The King decided to replace Montrevel with Villars.
Dangeau *recorded, on March 27th of the same year, that:*

The King has told the Maréchal de Villars that he is to have audience of him tomorrow and receive his orders. It is believed that His Majesty wishes to send him into Languedoc to assume the Maréchal de Montrevel's command.

Villars decided to negotiate with the Camisard leaders.
Louvreleuil *tells how he went about it:*

M. d'Aygalliers, a gentleman of Uzès, recently converted, who had accompanied the Maréchal de Villars from Paris, had proposed several schemes for winning back the rebellious fanatics by peaceful means. In the hopes that at least one of these ideas might prove successful, he obtained the marshal's permission to ride with thirty other well-disposed recent converts to find and meet Cavalier, to try to persuade him to lay down his arms. It seemed to him that Cavalier might not prove entirely intractable, and therefore the Maréchal de Villars hoped to win over this particular leader. Towards this end, the marshal made a point of making a display of generosity towards those soldiers of the rebel band who had surrendered to him. He also made use of another intermediary in the shape of the Sieur La Combe, a bourgeois of Vézenoble, who had been Cavalier's teacher. The marshal spoke to him more or less in these words: 'I know you are an honest man and a good servant of the King, that you used to know Cavalier and that he has shown on several occasions that he holds you in esteem, that you have spoken to him on several occasions and have done your best to persuade him to abandon his venture. It is imperative that you should render service to the State by acting as our agent: go to him, find out what are his claims and his demands, and report back to us.'

Cavalier was by no means impervious to these overtures. He justified his co-operative attitude in his Memoirs of the Wars of the Cévennes, *published in English in Dublin in 1726:*

15.
Louis XIV and
his heirs: his son
the Grand Dauphin,
his grandson the
Duc de Bourgogne,
his great-grandson
the Duc de Bret-
agne, with the
latter's governess
the Duchesse de
Ventadour,
by de Largil-
lière

16. *Court Ball in* 1682

I had lost all at once a great quantity of arms, all my ammunition, all my money, but above all a body of soldiers toughened by fire and immune to fatigue, men with whom I could have performed any deed ... My last loss [that of his store of guns and ammunition] was the most fatal: previously I had always had some resources to fall back on, but now I had none. The whole province was devastated, the friendship of our friends had cooled, their purses were empty, a hundred towns and villages had been pillaged and burned, the prisons were all full of Protestants, the countryside was deserted. Add to this that help from England, promised for so long, never arrived.

Negotiations got under way and eventually produced results, as Dangeau *noted in his diary entry for May 17th:*

While the King was walking in his garden, near the Pavillon des Globes, one of M. de Chamillart's equerries approached him, followed by a man in riding-boots who was obviously a courier. This courier was the Marquis de Saint-Pierre, the Maréchal de Villar's aide de camp, bringing news of the gradual elimination of the fanatics. These are the details of his dispatch: the Brigadier de Menou having beaten the fanatics in a small skirmish in which thirty or forty of them were killed, Cavalier, their chief, sent a message to M. de La Lande asking for a parley on parole, giving his own assurances of safe-conduct. M. de La Lande went to the designated meeting place, which he found to be in a state of defence. When he had passed through the barriers he found the fanatics, both cavalry and infantry, drawn up in line, and the infantry presented arms to him as he passed through their ranks. The result of the parley was that Cavalier asked for the King's pardon, and demanded an amnesty for himself, for one of his chiefs named Roland, for an officer named Catinat, and for the four hundred men they had with them ... Cavalier was given a commission with the rank of lieutenant-colonel and a pension of 1,200 livres. Roland has not yet accepted this agreement.

Roland did not accept the agreement at all. And Cavalier was only able to win over part of his troops. According to Bonbonnoux:

His proposal surprised us and disgusted us in equal measure. Forgetting that he had been our commander and that we had obeyed him almost as implicitly as we would have obeyed God Himself, we turned our backs and marched away with Ravanel at our head, took the road leading to the Cévennes and went to rejoin Roland, shouting slogans such as: 'All power to the sword of the Eternal!' and 'The Edict of Nantes or death!'

Roland's small army was now augmented by many of Cavalier's soldiers. It was then decided, writes La Baume, to capture Roland by a ruse:

A man of Uzès named Malorte who owned property at Castelnau was promised a hundred louis d'or if he would pass on any information he could obtain about the plans of the rebels. He succeeded in joining Roland's band and remaining with it without arousing anybody's suspicion. He occasionally brought them gifts of pigeons and chickens, and acted with such skill and discretion that he was able to accompany them on their most secret expeditions ...

This Malorte was instrumental in Roland's eventual capture:

Roland, and his companion in debauchery, Maillet, a native of Courbès near Anduze, were enamoured of two sisters, the daughters of M. de Cornelli, a gentleman of Lassalle. These two young ladies, under pretext of going to take the waters at Yeuset, went to Castelnau, which is close nearby, at the beginning of August. Roland and Maillet, who were very much in love with them, used to go and visit them occasionally at night, but they made their stays so brief that Malorte never had enough time to make arrangements to have them surprised. On August 13th, Roland pitched camp half a league away from Lassalle, and he and Maillet rode to Castelnau, arriving there at nightfall. They went straight to the house where the sisters were staying ...

Malorte was with them and left the house under the pretext of feeling ill. He galloped at full speed to Uzès, two leagues away, and M. Coste de l'Abadie, commander of the second battalion of Charolais, was despatched immediately with all the officers and dragoons to be found in Uzès . . .

Roland, Maillet and a few men who had followed them to Castelnau succeeded in getting away. But they were found hiding in a nearby valley by the King's troops:

Roland fired one shot, then, seeing that they were surrounded and that escape was impossible, gave himself up to a captain of the Charolais regiment. At that very moment a dragoon killed him with a single shot from his carbine. The others were taken prisoner and escorted to Nîmes, together with Roland's corpse. That same night M. de Basville, sitting with the Président de Nîmes, condemned Grimaud, Couterau, Guérin, Raspal and Maillet to be broken alive on the wheel. Maillet was a tanner, aged twenty-six. His appearance was impressive and his manner full of confidence; he betrayed neither fear nor weakness during his execution. Roland's corpse was dragged on a hurdle, after which it was burned and the ashes thrown to the wind.

Indeed, La Baume, *writing about the last of the executions, which took place in 1705, confirmed that:*

All these scoundrels died with astonishing courage and calmness.

Before being sentenced, they appeared quite unconcerned by the tortures with which they were menaced, and they endured those tortures with a steadfastness which would have deserved admiration had not the cause for which they suffered horrified the whole nation . . . May God grant that a Christian country shall never again be the theatre of so terrible a tragedy.

THE MADCAP DUCHESSE DE BOURGOGNE

I am in despair, my dear aunt, at always committing such follies.

Letter from the DUCHESSE DE BOURGOGNE
to Mme de Maintenon

❦

PRINCIPAL PERSONALITIES MENTIONED IN CHAPTER XXI

MME DE LA VRILLIÈRE: FRANÇOISE DE MAILLY, wife of the Marquis de Châteauneuf de la Vrillière.

FRANÇOIS COLBERT, COMTE DE MAULÉVRIER, son of one of Colbert's brothers, Edouard, Comte de Maulévrier, and married to a daughter of the Maréchal de Tessé. He died by his own hand, in 1706, at the age of thirty-one.

LOUIS ARMAND DE BRICHANTEAU, COMTE DE NANGIS, later a Marshal of France under Louis XV.

MARGUERITE LOUISE DE BÉTHUNE-SULLY, DUCHESSE DE LUDE, Lady-in-waiting to the Duchesse de Bourgogne (already mentioned in Chapter XIX).

LOUIS FRANÇOIS, DUC DE BOUFFLERS, Marshal of France (already mentioned in Chapter XVII).

FRANÇOIS VII, DUC DE LA ROCHEFOUCAULD, Grand Veneur of France (already mentioned in Chapter XII).

LOUIS JOSEPH, DUC DE VENDÔME, Marshal of France (already mentioned in Chapters X and XII).

The little Marie Adélaïde of Savoy, whose marriage to the

Duc de Bourgogne we have already recorded, soon achieved a position of supremacy in the Court. The King adored her, and she got on well with Mme de Maintenon—which is more than could be said for her husband, according to Benjamino Priolo, the Venetian ambassador, who has left us a series of more or less malicious portraits of the royal family in his Relation de la Cour de France:

The little Duchesse de Bourgogne is shrewd and spiteful. She absolutely loathes the Duchesse de Lude, her lady-in-waiting, and mimics and teases her continuously. But she is quite servile in her attachment to Mme de Maintenon, whom she calls her 'dear mama'. The Duc and Duchesse de Bourgogne appear completely indifferent to each other.

When, soon after his marriage, this prince was in Mme de Maintenon's room one day, his cold and abstracted air induced her to reproach him gently, saying that he seemed not to know her. 'Indeed I do, Madame,' he answered sharply and haughtily, 'I know you very well and I know, furthermore, that I am the Duc de Bourgogne and that I am in your room.' This harsh reply reduced her to embarrassed silence. The Duc de Beauvilliers went up to her and said in a low voice: 'Time will teach us, Madame, with what kind of a man we have to deal.'

It can be anticipated that, if the King dies, many things in the Court will be changed and Mme de Maintenon will emerge with little satisfaction from the process. It is not that she harms anyone or abuses her power, it is simply that she is an odious person and has the whole of the royal family under her thumb. Furthermore, she is considered to have been instrumental, through ambition, in the acceptance by the King of the conditions of the Peace of Ryswick, which are so contrary to France's interests.

The Princess Palatine, *however, thought, on the contrary, that the Duc de Bourgogne was an excellent husband but that he was less amused than was the Court by the Duchess's practical jokes, which were not always in the best of taste:*

M. le Duc de Bourgogne is so faithful that he cannot even look at another woman. One evening his wife thought it would be amusing to play a joke on him, so she prevailed on Mme de La Vrillière to get into his bed, and then made a great show herself of being tired. The prince, happy that for once his wife wanted to go to bed early, and before him at that, hastened to undress so that he too might go to bed. He entered their bedroom and called out: 'Where are you?' 'Here I am,' replied a muffled voice from beneath the bed-covers. The prince quickly took off his dressing-gown and slipped into bed next to the sleeping form. Just then he saw the duchess approach, fully dressed. 'What is this, monsieur?' she exclaimed indignantly, 'you play the devoted husband, and then I find you between the sheets with one of the prettiest women in the country?' 'What do you mean?' stammered the prince. 'Why, look, monsieur, who is lying next to you!'

... She [La Vrillière] had no time to arrange her clothing or put on her slippers, because the duke looked as if he had every intention of beating her with one of his own slippers. She fled barefoot, and he was unable to catch her, but he shouted all manner of invective after her. 'Shameless hussy' was one of the more printable expressions he used. Those who came in to see what was going on tried to calm him down, but they were all almost speechless with laughter.

Later, the Princess Palatine *had this to say about the Duchesse de Bourgogne, who had now become the Dauphine:*

At Marly she used to roam around at night with all the young people, sometimes staying in the gardens until three or four in the morning. The King never knew of these nocturnal escapades. La Maintenon had forbidden the Duchesse de Lude ever to reproach the Duchesse de Bourgogne, for fear that she might become sulky and so no longer be in the mood to amuse the King. Indeed, La Maintenon had made it clear that she would never forgive anyone who dared report the Dauphine's misdemeanours to the King. This is why no one had the courage to speak to the King about her and why he remained entirely ignorant of what was going on, although the whole Court and the foreign community knew every detail.

One of the Dauphine's favourite games was to have herself dragged over the ground on her back by lackeys pulling her by the feet. The servants used to say to each other: 'How about going over to the Duchesse de Bourgogne's place for a bit of fun?' (for she was not yet Dauphine at that time).

It is difficult to believe that the King was entirely ignorant of the goings-on, especially since, according to Saint-Simon, *everyone at the Court was under constant surveillance by the King's Swiss guards:*

Treated less as soldiers than as domestic servants and clad in the livery of the King, their task was to lurk around the staircases morning, noon and night, and when the weather was fine, around the courtyards and gardens too. They had to patrol, hide themselves, lie in ambush, notice people, follow them, watch them enter and leave the places they were visiting, know who was there, listen to everything they could hear, remember how long people stayed in other people's rooms, and finally give an account of their observations to Bontemps, the King's valet de chambre, and to Bloin, governor of Versailles. This system of spying, which was also indulged in by other minor officials and a few male servants, was assiduously practised at Versailles, Marly, Trianon and wherever else the Court happened to be.

It is also Saint-Simon *who tells an anecdote revealing a most curious habit of the Duchesse de Bourgogne's:*

One evening there was to be a play at Versailles and the princess was showing off her mastery of various languages when Mme de Maintenon's old nurse, Nanon, came into the room. Immediately, arrayed as she was in full Court dress and bedecked with jewels, she went and stood with her back to the fireplace and leaned forward against a little screen placed between two tables. Nanon, who seemed to have one hand in her pocket, slipped behind her and went down on her knees, whereupon the King, who was nearest to them, asked what they were doing. The princess burst out laughing and said that she was only doing what she usually did before a play, but the King persisted. Then she said: 'Must I really tell you, since you have not seen for yourself? The truth is that I am having an enema.' 'What?' said the King, roaring with laughter, 'are you seriously telling me that you are actually having an enema at this moment?' 'Indeed I am,' she replied. 'But how?' he asked the King, and they all four went into fits of laughter. And, indeed, Nanon had brought the syringe already prepared, hidden under her petticoats, had lifted up the princess's skirts, who held them up as though warming herself, and then had inserted the nozzle. In this way nothing could be noticed. The King and Mme de Maintenon paid no particular attention, thinking that Nanon was simply rearranging some part of the princess's dress. So they were taken completely by surprise and found the whole thing extremely amusing. What is extraordinary is that she used to attend the play holding the *lavement*, and in no hurry to be quit of it. Sometimes she held it throughout the entire time of the King's supper and the conversation afterwards in the study. She said that she found it refreshing and that it prevented her from getting a headache in the stuffy theatre.

But the Duchesse de Bourgogne indulged in less innocent pleasures, and it was whispered that she was unfaithful to her husband, though Mme Caylus was of the opinion that these were merely rumours.

Madame la Dauphine was young and she was a woman and so flirtatious by nature, which is in itself sufficient explanation of the fact that her day-to-day conduct inevitably revealed many small faults which she would have preferred to keep hidden. That does not constitute being unfaithful. All I will say in her defence is that many of these small faults resulted from her being too easily led on by others; indeed, the greatest fault I knew in her was that of being too easy-going, and of allowing the young people who surrounded her to exercise too much influence over her. It was this amiability which precipitated her into a few awkward situations that may have harmed her reputation to some extent.

There has been talk of two men with whom she is supposed to have been involved. The first was M. de Maulévrier, who was completely mad. He went to Spain as a child and later fell in love with the Queen of Spain, the sister of the Duchesse de

Bourgogne. I use the word 'mad' deliberately, since he eventually committed suicide by throwing himself out of a window. Mme de Maulévrier, the daughter of the Maréchal de Tessé, who was very friendly with Mme la Dauphine before her husband's death, broke with her afterwards, supposedly because the Dauphine refused to give back the letters he had written to her, but most probably, in fact because she had spread this baseless rumour of his infatuation.

Mme la Dauphine's second conquest is supposed to have been the Comte de Nangis, and his was a different case altogether to that of Maulévrier, in fact I agree with public gossip that there was something between them. The only thing I doubt is whether this affair went as far as people claimed. My own view is that their liaison was limited to mutual regard and an exchange of letters. I think this for two reasons: first, because Nangis was too much in love with another woman, who was watching him closely and who assured me that at the times when rumour had it he was with the Dauphine he was in fact with her.

This woman was Mme de La Vrillière. And the Princess Palatine *was less credulous than Mme de Caylus:*

Mme la Dauphine was on friendly terms with all the young men, but the one man she really loved was Nangis. She suggested to him he should pretend to be in love with Mme de La Vrillière, who did not have such a good figure nor such winning ways as Mme la Dauphine, but whose face was far prettier and who was an incurable flirt. It seems probable that this game resulted in something more serious. The poor Dauphin was like all husbands of ladies of easy virtue: they are always the last to notice what is going on. The Duc de Bourgogne never dreamed that his wife's thoughts were on Nangis, although this was perfectly obvious to everybody else. He genuinely liked Nangis and thought that his wife talked to Nangis simply to please him, being persuaded that his best friend was carrying on an affair with Mme de La Vrillière.

The little Duc de Bretagne, son of the Duchesse de Bourgogne, died when ten months old, but he was replaced the same year by another son who also bore the title of Duc de Bretagne. And in 1706, the Duchesse de Bourgogne was pregnant once again. Saint-Simon *relates her subsequent ordeal:*

The Duchesse de Bourgogne was pregnant and felt extremely unwell. Contrary to his usual custom, the King wished to go to Fontainebleau at the beginning of the summer and had announced this intention. In the meantime he still wanted to make his usual excursions to Marly. His grand-daughter amused him so much that he found her company indispensable, but travelling was bad for her condition. Fagon put in a discreet word, but this merely annoyed the King, who was not used to being crossed and had been spoiled by his mistresses, who had always accompanied him on journeys when pregnant or just risen from child-bed, wearing full court-dress. The objections made to him about the Marly visits irritated him but failed to change his mind. The most that he would concede was to postpone twice the voyage set for Low Monday, but he insisted on going no later than the Wednesday of the following week, despite all that could be said or done to stop him, or to gain permission for the princess to remain at Versailles.

On the following Saturday, at Marly, the King went strolling in the gardens after Mass, and was diverting himself with the carp in the ornamental basin between the château and the vista when he saw the Duchesse de Lude approach us on foot, alone, although there were no ladies with the King, for they seldom accompanied him on his morning walks. He realized that she must have something important to say to him, so he went to meet her, and as they approached each other we stopped and left him to join her alone.

Their private conversation did not last long. The duchess retraced her steps and the King walked back to us and continued towards the carp basin without uttering a word. Everyone knew quite well what was afoot but no one was anxious to speak first. Eventually, when the King had reached the basin, he turned to the chief persons present and, without addressing anyone in particular, said crossly: 'The Duchesse de Bourgogne has had a miscarriage' and not a word more. Whereupon, M. de La Rochefoucauld exclaimed his shock, M. de Bouillon, the Duc de Tresmes and the Maréchal de

Boufflers echoed his words in an undertone, and then M. de La Rochefoucauld remarked loudly that it was a great misfortune, since she had already had previous miscarriages and might no longer be able to have children.

The King, who had remained silent so far, suddenly interrupted furiously. 'What does it matter to me,' he said, 'if that is so? She already has a son, has she not? And if he were to die, is not the Duc de Berry old enough to marry and have children? What do I care which of them succeeds me; are they not all grandchildren of mine?' Then, in a sudden fit of impatience: 'Thank God she has miscarried, since it had to happen. Perhaps, now, I shall no longer be thwarted in my excursions and everything else I want to do, by the eternal objections and arguments of doctors and midwives. Now I can come and go as I please and they will leave me in peace.'

A silence during which you could have heard a pin drop succeeded this extraordinary outburst. All eyes were lowered, and those present scarcely dared breathe. Stupefaction reigned. Even the men working on the buildings close by remained motionless. The silence lasted an appreciable time, but finally the King broke the silence himself by leaning over the rim of the basin and speaking of a carp. No one answered him. At this, he addressed his remarks about the carp to the building workers, who were hardly used to being included in the King's conversation, though on this occasion he spoke only of carp to them. The atmosphere remained strained and the King went away soon afterwards. As soon as he was out of sight and we dared look at one another, our eyes met and spoke volumes. For that one moment, all those who were there felt a sense of mutual trust. They expressed their astonishment, then their grief, and finally shrugged their shoulders . . . I was all eyes and ears as I studied these people, and I complimented myself on having long ago come to the conclusion that the King only loved and considered himself, and was his own prime object. His strange and unnatural speech had repercussions far beyond Marly.

The Duchesse de Bourgogne occasionally dabbled in politics. Mme de Caylus claimed that it was she who successfully persuaded the Maréchal de La Feuillade to spare Turin, during the course of the Italian campaign of 1706:

Exercising all her charms by the use of flattery, she said to him half proudly and half pleadingly: 'Do not drive my father to extremities.' These few words, spoken most touchingly, had exactly the effect that was intended. M. de La Feuillade went off to the war, laid siege to Turin, launched a romantic attack on the citadel and not only did not capture it but was forced, on the contrary, to lift the siege. He had taken the precaution, before leaving, of speaking to his father-in-law, M. Chamillart, pointing out to him how upset the Duchesse de Bourgogne would be if he took Turin.

But the duchess's great enemy was the Maréchal de Vendôme, since she had firmly taken sides with her husband in the vendetta between him and the marshal. In July 1708, the French, under the command of the King's grandson, had suffered a fresh defeat at Oudenarde. Rumours circulated that this reverse was due to the duke's hesitations and his disputes with Vendôme. The latter's friends launched a campaign against the duke, says Saint-Simon:

The cabal unleashed its campaign gradually but with ever-increasing fury. Its emissaries distributed doctored versions of the despatches from the front among the newsmongering rabble, in the coffee-houses, in public places, in gaming rooms and houses of assignation. Even Les Halles was filled with them, and with satirical songs, doggerel verses and every kind of atrocious libel on the heir to the throne.[1] These same lam-

---

[1] such as:

> Who would have thought he'd be able to jeer
> At the sight of our Burgundy back on the spot,
> After running so fast from the cannon and shot
> And shitting his pants in fear?

and:

> The grandfather's a braggart brave,
> His son a silly poop,
> The grandson is an arrant knave:
> Oh what a family group!

poons made out Vendôme to be the hero of the day. They swept Paris and the whole kingdom with a speed and licence which authority made no attempt to check, while at the Court and in the world at large the libertines and fashionable people applauded. Courtiers with a nose for politics, seeing which way the wind was blowing, joined the campaign and persuaded the majority of the others so effectively that within a week it became shameful to speak well of the son of the house in the paternal home itself.

The reverses continued. The enemy laid siege to Lille, which surrendered on October 26th. This time, public opinion blamed Vendôme as well, but was still no less severe towards the Duc de Bourgogne, who now left the army and returned to Versailles. This is how, according to Saint-Simon, *he was received by the King:*

The King was working in Mme de Maintenon's apartments, together with M. de Pontchartrain. Mme de Maintenon was sitting, musing, in her red damask-lined alcove. The King, in his armchair, was a prey to emotions which made shadows pass over his face, though he remained, as always, the complete master of his feelings. The minister was sitting, grave and silent, on a folding-stool, while the Duchesse de Bourgogne, her face flushed, her manner agitated and her body trembling, darted across the room from one door to another. Suddenly the doors opened and the prince entered. He stepped forward and stood in front of the King who, overwhelmed by paternal love, took two steps forward, opening his arms as he did so, and clasped his grandson to his chest. Then he pointed towards the duchess, who was in a complete daze, and said smilingly: 'Do you say nothing to her?' The Duc de Bourgogne turned towards his wife and looked at her tenderly but without daring to go over to her. Then he made his bow to Mme de Maintenon, and spoke with her and the King for five minutes or so. Finally the King put an end to the scene by saying that it was not fair to delay any longer the pleasure that the duke would have in being with the duchess, and sent them away, saying that they would have ample opportunity to meet again later on.

The young princess's attitude towards the Duc de Vendôme was one of scorn and loathing. When he came to her room to take his leave, accompanied by the Duc du Maine, who had a private feud of his own with the Bourgogne family, she gave them one single glance:

... and after this first glance, which propriety dictated, she stared over their heads and remained silent, although she was at her toilet and a moment before had been behaving in her usual manner, looking around and chatting with people and paying precious little attention to her mirror and her make-up. The chilly atmosphere which now descended on the room embarrassed M. du Maine and M. de Vendôme all the more because the others completely ignored their presence. They remained frozen there for several minutes, surrounded by the blank silence of everyone in the room, and with all eyes fixed on them. When they were unable to endure this any longer, they beat a stealthy retreat.

In the end it was the duchess who triumphed over Vendôme and engineered his downfall after the disastrous Flanders campaign:

This giant column crashed to the ground, blown over by a single breath of a good and courageous princess who received the approbation she so well deserved. All those who cared for her were delighted to witness her triumph, while those who were hostile to her—and to her husband—shivered with fear. Gloom and panic suddenly descended on that cabal, which had been so formidable, so well-entrenched, so influential, so firmly united in its aim of destroying the Duc and Duchesse de Bourgogne and to enjoy power, after the King's death, under Monseigneur's rule instead, at the risk of devouring each other subsequently in the struggle to hold the reins of the kingdom. It was a sad downfall for these male and female chieftains who had been so enterprising and audacious, whose past successes had promised such a rich future, whose imperious utterances had cowed so many people. It was a pleasure to see them come sneaking up now, and sidle artfully and basely around those of the opposite party whom they deemed to be important and whom they had previously driven to loathe and despise them through their arrogant behaviour. It was especially satisfying to see the embarrassment, fear and timidity with which they began to grovel before the young princess, to watch them edge shiftily around Monseigneur le Duc de Bourgogne and all those in his vicinity, and to observe their desperate attempts to ingratiate themselves with him and his friends.

CHAPTER XXII

DIFFICULT DAYS

The people are no longer living like human beings. It is no longer possible to count on their patience. The worn-out machine will surely break down at the first shock.

FÉNELON

PRINCIPAL PERSONALITIES MENTIONED IN CHAPTER XXII

SÉBASTIEN LE PRESTRE, MARQUIS DE VAUBAN, Marshal of France (already mentioned in Chapter XVI).

COUNT BERGHEYCK, a Flemish nobleman appointed governor of the Netherlands by the young King of Spain, Philip V (previously the Duc d'Anjou).

MICHEL CHAMILLART, Secretary of State for War since 1701.

NICOLAS DESMARETS, Comptroller General of Finance since 1708.

SAMUEL BERNARD, financier and Protestant, whose fortune was estimated at more than 30 million livres, but who went bankrupt a year after the events described in this chapter.

LOUIS FRANÇOIS, DUC DE BOUFFLERS, Marshal of France (already mentioned in Chapters XVII and XXI).

ANTOINE CHARLES, DUC DE GRAMMONT, Marshal of France.

ELIZABETH HAMILTON, COMTESSE DE GRAMMONT, wife of the Duc de Grammont. Saint-Simon referred to her as 'that nasty woman'.

MARC RENÉ DE VOYER D'ARGENSON, Lieutenant of Police of Paris in succession to La Reynie on the latter's death in June 1709.

PÈRE MICHEL LE TELLIER, the King's confessor in succession to Père La Chaise on the latter's death in January 1709. (Not to be confused, of course, with Michel Le Tellier, Secretary of State until 1666 and father of the Marquis de Louvois.)

Since the summer of 1706, the French armies had been reeling under a series of defeats. Conditions of appalling poverty prevailed throughout the kingdom, and revolt seemed imminent. Sébastien Le Prestre, Marquis de Vauban, a marshal of France since 1703, 'the most honest and most virtuous man of his century,' believed that the injustices to which the common people were subjected had become intolerable, and considered fiscal reform to be the prime necessity. So in 1706 he proceeded to publish a work he had written almost eight years previously, his Projet d'une dîme royale *or—to give it its English title in a translation published in London two years later—*Project for a Royal Tithe or General Tax which, by suppressing all the Ancient Funds and Later Projects for Raising the Public Revenues, and for ever abolishing all Exemptions, unequal Assessments, and all rigorous and oppressive Distraining on the People, will furnish the Government a Fixed and Certain Revenue, sufficient for all its Exigencies and Occasions, without oppressing the Subjects.

His proposal was simple: it was to tax everybody according to their income, including the King, the Dauphin and the princes of the blood!
Here is how he justified his project:

The wandering life I have led for more than forty years has given me opportunities of seeing and observing, often and in different manners, the greater part of the provinces of this kingdom, sometimes accompanied only by my own domestic servants, sometimes with some engineers. I have often given full scope to my reflections, and remarked what I found was good and what I found was bad in the various parts of the country, and so was led to examine their situation, and the state and condition of the people, whose poverty had often moved me to compassion and to set me on an inquiry into the causes of it . . . The high-roads in the country and the streets of our cities and towns are already crowded with beggars driven from their homes by hunger and cold.

During the several years that I have made it my business to enquire into that matter, I have chiefly observed that, lately, nearly a tenth part of the people is actually reduced to beggary and does, in fact, beg for a living; that, of the other nine parts, not five of them are in a condition to give alms to that tenth, by reason of the miserable condition they are reduced to, and the small pittance left to them. Of the four other parts of the people, three are in hard circumstances by reason of their great debts and the inextricable law-suits in which they are entangled; as for the other tenth part, in which I include the gentlemen of the sword, those of the robe, both clergy and laity, the nobility of all sorts, all those who bear civil or military offices, the rich merchants and burgesses who own estates and the others who are comfortably placed, one cannot reckon in all above a hundred thousand families, and of these I make bold to claim that not even ten thousand live in easy circumstances . . .

I am further obliged, in honour and conscience, to represent to His Majesty that I have at all times, and upon all occasions, observed that here in France too little regard has been paid to the meaner sort of people, and that they have been always despised, so that they have become the most impoverished and miserable part of the kingdom. Nevertheless, they are the most important of all, both because of their numbers and because of the real and effectual services they perform for the public. For it is they who bear the charges, who have always suffered and who still suffer more than any other group, and it is upon them that the great decrease of men in the kingdom falls . . . It is the lowest sort of people that by their labour and business, and by what they pay to the King, enrich both him and all his kingdom . . .

The King's revenues ought to be distinguished from those of his subjects, though they all come from the same fountain. For it is well known that it is the people who cultivate, gather and

keep together the King's revenues: his officers' business being
no other than to impose and collect them . . . The people are
the true revenues of Kings, it being from these that princes
draw all their revenues, and it is them they dispose of and
employ in all their affairs.

There is all the reason in the world, then, that this revenue
should be well managed, that all possible care be taken to improve and increase it by all lawful and just means, that it be
maintained and supported, and that nothing be permitted
which may contribue in any way to its destruction. This will
be achieved effectively when the impositions are proportioned
to everyone's ability; when the public revenues are properly
managed, when the people shall cease to be exposed to the
extortions of tax-farmers and shall be harassed no longer by
arbitrary taxes, tolls and customs; when the villainies committed in the *gabelle* and a thousand other burdensome duties
and consequent vexations, exercised at pleasure upon the
people, are abolished, so that these great numbers of people
will no longer be forced into poor-houses, or to beg in the
streets, or to leave the kingdom.

The vast swarms of tax-farmers and under-farmers, with
their creatures of all sorts, those horse-leeches of the State,
whose number is more than sufficient to man all the galleys,
carry their heads high in the streets of Paris, where they appear adorned with the spoils of their fellow-subjects, with as
much assurance and pride as though they had just saved the
country. It is from the oppression of these harpies that this
fund, by which I mean the people, ought to be preserved, a
people who love and obey their King more entirely than any
other people in the universe. And to conclude, what makes it
the more the King's interest to use them well is that, as he is
their King, his happiness and prosperity are so indispensably
and inseparably linked to their welfare that nothing but death
can separate them.

This is what I thought necessary to say at the end of these
memoirs, so that nothing should be omitted which might serve
to clarify the scheme I have put forward.

Following Fénelon's example, Vauban had his book printed
secretly, at Rouen. In November 1706 he went to fetch it from

*the printers and started distributing it, a few copies at a time,
in Paris. Immediately the storm broke about the head of the
marshal, who had already asked the King for an audience. According to* Saint-Simon, *the unfortunate would-be reformer
was accused of all the crimes under the sun:*

Having been deluged with all these hostile reports, it was not
surprising that the King gave the Maréchal de Vauban a very
cool reception when he presented him with his book, which
was dedicated to him, and disapproved thoroughly of its contents. As can well be imagined, none of the ministers to whom
he gave copies received him any more warmly. From that
moment, his services, his incomparable military genius, his
virtues, the King's affection for him, which was such that His
Majesty was thinking of crowning him with laurels by raising
him to the peerage—all this went by the board now. The King
suddenly saw in him nothing more than a man hungry for the
people's love, a criminal subverting his ministers' authority and
consequently his own. He told the marshal all this, without
mincing words . . .

On February 14, 1707, the Projet d'une dîme royale *was
banned. On March 14th, an order issued by the Privy Council
charged the Lieutenant of Police of Paris to discover its author
—whose identity was, in fact, common knowledge—and bring
him to book. Vauban, who had meanwhile been stricken with
bronchitis, found himself confronted with both a search-
warrant and a lettre de cachet. His state of health deteriorated.
On March 29th, the Marquis de* Dangeau *noted in his diary:*

Yesterday evening, while the King was at supper, M. Fagon
approached him to tell him that the Maréchal de Vauban was
very ill and had asked for M. Boudin, Monseigneur's chief
physician. The King ordered that Boudin should leave immediately to attend the marshal. He then spoke of M. de
Vauban in terms of great esteem and affection, praised him on
several scores, and remarked: 'I am losing a man who is very
dear both to my person and to the State.'

On March 30th, Vauban died: Saint-Simon *comments:*

The unfortunate marshal, revered in the hearts of all Frenchmen, could not survive the treatment meted out to him by his master, for whom he had done so much. He died a few months later, having cut himself off from all his friends, consumed with a grief which nothing could assuage and to which the King was so insensible that he seemed not even to notice that he had lost a most useful and a most illustrious servant. He was admired and respected throughout Europe, even by his enemies, and his passing was mourned by all in France except the bankers and money-lenders and their tools.

In fact, Vauban's analysis of the state of the kingdom had been perfectly accurate. The King's need for money was becoming increasingly urgent. His ministers were in despair and thought up various strange schemes for raising funds. One such scheme has been recorded by Pierre Narbonne, *Versailles' commissaire of police at that time:*

During the year 1708, a charlatan arrived in Versailles asking for Boudin, the King's chief physician. He gave him to understand that he possessed the secret of the philosopher's stone and that he was able to make gold and silver. Boudin believed him and spoke about it to the King, after which he installed this charlatan in a little house he owned in Montreuil. Furnaces were built for him, and he was provided with crucibles and with everything else necessary for his operations. He was guarded by a sergeant and two guardsmen, for the two months that he stayed there, and during this time Chamillart, then Comptroller of Finance, the other ministers, and even the princes and seigneurs of the Court went to watch him in his laboratory and listened open-mouthed to his disquisitions. Despite all this, he got no results. Boudin faced the shame of having recommended him, and the Court faced the shame of having been too credulous and of having permitted a charlatan to operate at the very gates of Versailles and in full view of the public. To preserve the honour of the King and his ministers, the man should at least have been made to carry out his experiments in the château of Noisy, where nobody would have had any inkling of the whole sorry business. The need for secrecy was all the greater because, in view of the dire state of the country's economy and the miserable condition of the armies, our enemies might have thought the kingdom to be in desperate straits if they came to know that we were trying to obtain money by such extraordinary and uncertain methods.

The charlatan was locked up for having abused the confidence of the Court in this way.

The simplest means of obtaining money was borrowing from financiers, and Louis XIV set about seducing the richest of them all. Saint-Simon *describes the successful gambit:*

The King came out at about five in the afternoon and proceeded on foot past all the pavilions on the Marly side.[1] Bergheyck emerged from Chamillart's pavilion to join the King's party. The King stopped at the next pavilion, which was the one in which Desmarets was lodging. Thereupon Desmarets came out, accompanied by the famous banker Samuel Bernard, whom he had invited to dine with him and discuss matters of finance. Bernard was the richest man in Europe and the owner of the most reliable banking business. He knew his own power and required to be treated with appropriate respect. Since the comptrollers general usually had far greater need of him than he of them, they were always most deferential in their manner towards him.

The King told Desmarets that he was very glad to see that he had M. Bernard with him, then he suddenly turned to the latter, saying: 'It is a shame that you of all people have never seen Marly. Come with me now, and I will show it you and then hand you back to Desmarets.' Bernard accordingly followed him, and during the entire walk the King talked mostly to Bergheyck and him, addressing only an occasional remark to the others. The King took them everywhere and showed them everything, with the charm which he knew so well how to assume when he had some purpose in mind. I was not the

---

[1] Marly comprised twelve pavilions for ministers or courtiers, set in two parallel rows of six a side, leading up to the wings of the central building which contained the royal apartments.

only one to marvel that the King, who was usually so miserly with words, should so prostitute himself, in a manner of speaking, to a man of Bernard's quality. It was not long, however, before I learned the reason, and then I marvelled even more at the straits to which the greatest kings sometimes find themselves reduced.

Desmarets no longer knew which way to turn. Money was needed for everything, and all funds were exhausted. He had been to Paris cap in hand, but so often and so flagrantly had all sorts of contracts been dishonoured and firm promises broken that he had met with nothing but apologies and closed doors. Bernard, like the rest, would lend nothing, since he was already owed large amounts. In vain Desmarets had stressed to him the many and pressing needs of the State and had reminded him of the enormous profits he had made in the past from the King's business. Bernard remained unshakeable. So there were the King and his minister sorely puzzled what to do. Desmarets told the King that, all things being considered, Bernard was the only man who could extricate him from his predicament because it was certain that he had enormous sums at his command in various financial centres. The problem was to make him change his mind and to overcome the stubbornness verging on insolence which characterized him. Desmarets added that Bernard was excessively vain and might be more willing to open up his purse if the King should deign to flatter him. In view of the critical state of his affairs the King agreed, and so, to give an air of respectability to this dubious enterprise and to avoid the risk of a refusal, Desmarets proposed the expedient which I have already described.

Bernard fell for the bait: he returned to Desmarets from his walk with the King so dazzled by the experience that, of his own accord, he told him he would rather risk ruin than leave in difficulties a prince who had just shown him such great honour, and he proceeded to praise him to the skies. Desmarets took immediate advantage of the situation and succeeded in extracting from him far more than he had originally intended to ask for.

Sadness had descended upon the Court. On February 22, 1709, the Prince de Conti died after an illness of several months. Ironically, the King had finally been persuaded to appoint him to a command—in Flanders—a few days before he fell ill. His death was universally mourned, according to Saint-Simon:

Everybody at the Court and in town asked continuously about the prince's condition, and exchanged the information they were able to glean. Passers-by stopped each other in the street. Groups gathered at the town gates and around the shops and questioned every new arrival.

And the Marquis de Sourche *commented:*

It would be difficult to describe the extent of public concern for this prince's recovery. Throughout his illness, his hôtel was always full of people of all conditions. Towards the end of his life, the princess his wife sent to Sainte-Geneviève to have Masses said for him, but the sacristan replied that it was pointless to give him money for this purpose, since it would take his community more than two weeks to say all the Masses for the prince which had been requested by so many individuals already.

This winter of 1709 was terrible. According to the Princess Palatine, *in a letter written from Versailles on March 2nd:*

I have never in my life seen such miserable times. The people are dying of the cold like flies. The windmill sails are frozen in their sockets, no corn can be ground, and thus many people are dying of starvation. Yesterday I was told a pathetic story about a woman in Paris who had stolen a loaf from a baker's shop. The baker wanted to have her arrested, so she said, weeping: 'If you knew my misery you would not be so cruel as to take this bread from me. My three little children are naked and starving.' The commissaire before whom this woman was taken told her to lead him to her home. When they arrived there they found three tiny children wrapped in rags and huddled in a corner, shivering with cold as though with a fever. He asked the eldest one: 'Where is your father?' 'Behind the door,' the child replied. The commissaire opened the door to see what the father could be doing there and retreated in horror: the wretched man, in a fit of despair, had hanged himself. Similar incidents occur every day.

And Mme de Maintenon's secretary, Mlle d'Aumale, commented in her Mémoires:

This year 1709 will not soon be forgotten in France. Never had the kingdom found itself in such a sad and unpleasant position . . . The common people were suffering greatly and beginning to lose patience. They accused Mme de Maintenon of being partly responsible for their miseries, despite her tremendous efforts on behalf of the poor.

It was claimed that, because she counted the loss of the King the greatest misfortune which could occur, not only for the State but more particularly for herself, she feared that any mention to His Majesty of the misfortunes which were following each other in quick succession might endanger his health, so she conspired with his ministers to conceal most of the bad news from him . . .

But no one, even if he had wanted to, could have concealed from the King either the capture of his towns or his losses in battle. He knew quite well what was going on. He worked with his ministers every day and settled everything himself . . . Several people made a point of telling him how matters really stood. The answer made to the King by M. de Harlay, Premier Président of the Parlement of Paris, is sufficient proof. The King had asked him during conversation if there was anything new in Paris, to which the illustrious magistrate replied, with greater brevity than tact: 'Sire, the poor are dying, but the rich are taking their place and becoming poor.'

Mme de Maintenon was busily engaged in succouring the needy, according to the same source:

The sums she dispensed every year in alms were considerable. I have made up her accounts on more than one occasion. She donated between fifty-four and sixty thousand livres a year from her income alone, without counting all the extra donations she managed to obtain from the King, the princes and all the seigneurs of the Court by dint of persuasion. In view of the added misery caused by the dreadful winter, she more than doubled her charities this year: she fed a great number of families, and maintained several convents for young girls who, without her aid, would either have died of hunger or would have been forced to beg their bread in the streets. On several occasions, when she had run out of money, she sold pieces of her furniture so that she could help some poor family whose needs had just been drawn to her attention.

The summer brought widespread famine with it. The Princess Palatine, *writing on August 24th, relates:*

Last Wednesday I was in Paris. Everything there is in a state of alarm because of the shortage of bread. As I was on my way to the Palais Royal someone yelled to me: 'A revolt has started. More than forty people have been killed already!' An hour later, the Maréchal de Boufflers and the Duc de Grammont had completely calmed the populace. We went to the Opéra without incident.

Saint-Simon *describes this minor disturbance more precisely:*

To keep the rabble occupied, some idlers and beggars had been given the job of levelling a large mound of earth which was obstructing the boulevard between the Porte Saint-Denis and the Porte Saint-Martin. For this work, the labourers' sole pay was a daily ration of mouldy bread, and a small ration at that.

On the morning of Tuesday, August 20th, it turned out that the supplies of bread were insufficient and many had to go without. One woman protested more loudly than the rest and so aroused the passions of those around her. The archers who had been detailed to distribute the bread threatened the woman, which only made her shout all the louder. Then the archers were misguided enough to seize her and put her in a nearby pillory. At that, the mob of labourers all rushed up, toppled the pillory and ran through the streets looting the bakeries and pastry-shops. The shutters of the shops began to go up fast, while the turmoil increased and spread to the adjoining streets, with the mob doing no physical harm to anyone but shouting: 'Bread, bread!' and seizing it right and left.

The Maréchal de Boufflers arrived on the scene, in the Rue Saint-Denis, to try to appease the fury of the mob:

He advanced on foot, accompanied by the Duc de Grammont, among this huge and raging mass of people. The marshal asked them what was the matter and why they were creating this uproar. He promised them bread and, speaking to them in calm but firm tones, pointed out to them that this was not the way to go about asking for it. His words did not fall on deaf ears, for after he had spoken repeated cries went up of 'Long live the Maréchal de Boufflers!'

... As soon as he had arrived in Versailles, the marshal went straight to Mme de Maintenon's apartments, where he found her with the King, both of them being in a state of great distress. He explained what had brought him there and was thanked profusely. The King offered him the military governorship of Paris, troops, police, burgesses to form night patrols, and pressed him to accept, but the marshal had too generous a soul to relish this kind of honour and preferred to see order restored by normal means.

Armed robbery, fraud and blackmail became increasingly widespread. The Marquis d'Argenson, Lieutenant of Police, who had succeeded La Reynie, wrote to the Marquis de Pontchartrain on January 24, 1710:

A most dangerous mendicant has been arrested this evening, and it is of the greatest importance that an example should be made of him. His name is Nicolas Chauveau and he is a native of Tours, though he claims to be a gentleman cadet of Normandy. He has been demanding alms while wearing a sword, and has been forced to admit that he was the author of the letter written to the dame Thévenin in which he advised her that if she valued her life she had better send her porter to him with thirty pistoles. His letter went on to threaten her that if she failed to do as he ordered, there was a band of desperate officers waiting for her in the street to take measures against her person. The rough draft of this letter was found in his pocket, and when the commissaire interrogated him about the letter he confessed to being its author . . .

I have no doubt that the Lieutenant Criminel will make every effort to discover all the facts which may have some bearing on these seditious letters which multiply with impunity and will soon become commonplace unless we profit by the arrest of this rogue, whose conviction seems certain.

As though the defeats abroad and the misery at home were not enough, the kingdom was now forced to witness the re-kindling of the old Jansenist controversy. The quarrel had been going on for about fifty years, interspersed by a few intervals of calm; it had originated in the publication by Cornelius Jansenius, Bishop of Ypres, of a large book on St Augustine which had made the claim that man, in order to achieve salvation, must have received the grace of God through predestination. The Petites Ecoles of Port-Royal-des-Champs had been propagating this doctrine despite the fact that it had been condemned by the Pope. The great Pascal had come to the defence of Port-Royal. Racine had originally attacked the establishment violently; but later came to support it and expressed the wish to be buried in its grounds. Dozens of learned treatises had been devoted to the praise or condemnation of the Jansenists.

By 1709, twenty or so nuns of the abbey of Port-Royal were still ignoring the Papal bulls and observing a 'respectful silence' about them which Pope Clement XI could no longer tolerate. Louis XIV, who was horrified by the very notion of independence, in matters of religion as much as in matters of politics, had always shown himself an enemy of the Jansenists. The Princess Palatine had her own—typically ingenious—explanation for the King's hostility:

The King had had such a fear of Hell instilled into him that he fondly believed all those who had not been instructed by the Jesuits to be damned in advance, and he was scared of being damned himself if he associated with such people. Anyone who wanted to contrive the ruin of an enemy had only to whisper in

the King's ear: 'He is a Huguenot' or 'He is a Jansenist' to be
sure that the victim's fate was sealed. My son [the Duc de
Chartres] wished to take into his service a gentleman whose
mother was an avowed Jansenist. The Jesuits, to create trouble
between my son and the King, told His Majesty that the prince
wished to take a Jansenist into his service. The King sent for
my son to admonish him, saying: 'How now, nephew, what
can you be thinking of, proposing to take a Jansenist into your
service?' My son replied, laughing: 'I can assure Your
Majesty that he is most certainly not a Jansenist; indeed I fear
it is improbable that he even believes in God.' 'Oh!' said the
King, in relief, 'if that is all, and you promise me solemnly that
he is not a Jansenist, you may certainly have him.'

*It was considered a black mark for any courtier to go into
retreat at Port-Royal. Hébert, curé of Versailles, had this to
say about it:*

His Majesty had for some years been in the habit of spending
a few days, from time to time, in the château of Marly, and on
these occasions nobody might stay there unless they were
nominated for the expedition or their presence was absolutely
indispensable. The King had given Mme de Maintenon the task
of nominating a certain number of ladies for these expeditions.
There was tremendous competition among the ladies at the
Court to secure a place on this list, since inclusion was a sure
mark of influence or favour. A few fortunate ladies were
always included in the Marly invitation lists, among them the
Comtesse de Grammont who was in great favour with the
King because of her pleasant manner and witty conversation.
But when the King learned that she had just spent a week at
Port-Royal, he decided to mark his displeasure with her in
the most mortifying way possible: he forbade Mme de Main-
tenon to include her on the list of ladies for Marly.

*And when the countess made her humble apologies to the
King, he replied:*

'How now, Madame, you who know better than anyone my
views on Port-Royal, who cannot doubt the degree of my

hatred for this Jansenist monastery, you, whom I have always held in the highest esteem, nevertheless visit the place, stay there, go into retreat there? Well, I will try to forget what you have done, but pray be more careful in the future.'

Hébert *relates this further anecdote:*

I once knew an unbeneficed priest in a Paris parish who might well have been called the scourge of the Jansenists. His main occupation consisted in denouncing all sorts and manner of people to the King's confessor as Jansenists. Since he possessed neither merit nor talent and precious little ability, he had adopted the profession of informer in order to gain a benefice of some kind. During the fourteen years I knew him, he never failed to appear at Versailles on the days when the King was due to take communion. On those occasions, he would position himself in the queue of aspirants, which used to stretch like a thick hedge from his Majesty's prie-dieu to the balusters of the altar or the presbytery. I often had occasion to admonish this cleric for the ignoble trade he pursued, and to reproach him for abandoning his parish on the very days when he should have been most assiduous in his duties. He once answered me, with most coarse directness, that all that he did in this connection was with the advice of his directors . . . In the end, he managed to obtain a minor canonry worth 200 livres a year, and I am of the opinion that Père La Chaise gave him that solely in order to be rid of his importunities and to get him out of Paris.

In 1709, matters came to a head. Pope Clement XI issued his bull Vineam Domini, *which condemned, yet again, the doctrine of Jansenius and reproved all those who were observing the 'respectful silence'. The nuns of Port-Royal were ordered to sign this bull and declare their agreement with its terms; they did this, but added a restrictive clause. Louis XIV then intervened, as* Saint-Simon *relates:*

The Council handed down a decree by virtue of which the abbey of Port-Royal-des-Champs found itself secretly invested, during the night of October 28th-29th, by detachments from the regiments of the French and Swiss guards. Then in mid-morning of the 29th d'Argenson arrived at the abbey with squads of constables of the watch and archers. He had the doors opened, ordered the entire community to assemble in the chapter-house, showed them a lettre de cachet and then gave them just fifteen minutes to pack their belongings and be out of the place. He had brought with him a number of coaches, with a matron in charge of each one. Into these coaches he directed the nuns according to their assigned destination, which was in each case some convent ten, forty or even as far as a hundred leagues away. When he gave the signal for the coaches to pull away, each left escorted by a few mounted archers, as though whores were being removed from a brothel . . .

After they had all gone, d'Argenson inspected the storehouse from attic to cellar, seized the entire stock, and had it taken away, with the exception of items which appeared to belong to Port-Royal in Paris and the little he felt obliged to set aside for the abducted nuns. Then he went to Versailles to give the King and Père Le Tellier an account of his successful expedition.

But Père Le Tellier was not the man to stop at half measures, and from then until the beginning of the following year a steady stream of orders in council and lettres de cachet were produced to serve his purposes. Families who had relatives buried at Port-Royal-des-Champs were ordered to have them exhumed and reburied elsewhere. All the unclaimed remains were dumped ignominiously into the cemetery of a neighbouring parish. Then the house, the chapel and all the out-buildings were razed to the ground, a treatment hitherto reserved for the houses of regicides. In the end, not one stone stood upon another. The rubble was all sold, and the ground ploughed and sowed: in truth, the only indignity they spared the place was sprinkling salt in the furrows. The resulting scandal spread even as far as Rome. I confine myself to this plain account of a disgraceful quasi-military expedition.

CHAPTER XXIII

TRAGEDIES AND TRIUMPHS

As the son bewailing his father
Falls, struck down by the same hand,
So brother is followed by brother,
And the wife dies before her husband.
Now the saddest blow descends,
From the sword which cruel Death extends,
On our country's two only sons:
The first has breathed his last breath,
While the second is close to death.

LAGRANGE-CHANCEL: *Philippiques*

PRINCIPAL PERSONALITIES MENTIONED IN
CHAPTER XXIII

CHARLES, DUC DE BERRY, the Dauphin's youngest son (already mentioned in Chapter XIX).

MARIE LOUISE ELISABETH (Mlle de Valois), daughter of the Duc d'Orléans, betrothed to the Duc de Berry.

MME DE FONTAINE-MARTEL, lady-in-waiting to the Duchesse d'Orléans.

JEAN LOUIS DE PARDAILLAN, DUC D'ANTIN, legitimate son of Mme de Montespan.

LOUIS, DUC DE BOURBON, grandson of the Great Condé (already mentioned in Chapter XVII).

FRANÇOIS DE LA ROCHEFOUCAULD, COMTE DE ROUSSY, one of the Dauphin's cronies.

HONORÉ, COMTE DE SAINT-MAURE, one-time page to the Dauphin.

PÈRE LE TELLIER, the King's confessor (already mentioned in Chapter XXII).

GEORGES MARÉCHAL, the King's chief surgeon.

CHIRAC, one of the King's physicians.

LOUIS, DUC DE BRETAGNE, elder son of the Duc de Bourgogne (later the Dauphin), who died at the age of five, one
month after his father.

LOUIS, DUC D'ANJOU, younger brother of the Duc de
Bretagne, who became Dauphin on his brother's death and
later succeeded to the throne.

LOUIS CLAUDE, DUC DE VILLARS, Marshal of France
(already mentioned in Chapter XX).

PIERRE DE MONTESQUIOU, COMTE D'ARTAGNAN, Marshal
of France.

*On February 15, 1710, the Duchesse de Bourgogne gave
birth to another son, destined to become Louis XV. The*
Princess Palatine *wrote to her aunt:*

I have just come from the Duchesse de Bourgogne who,
at half-past eight, was delivered of the prince who is to be
named Duc d'Anjou. She had a swift delivery, having only
been in labour for an hour, but she suffered terribly, because
the child appeared bottom first and had to be drawn out by
the legs!

The Marquis de Sourches *noted that:*

The King dispatched Des Granges, Master of Ceremonies,
to Paris, to arrange for a salute of cannon and to ensure that a
Te Deum was sung in all the churches. The King had a Te
Deum sung that same day at Mass.

*And the life of the Court continued to unfold according to
its normal ritual. A great marriage was in prospect: the Duc
d'Orléans, nephew of Louis XIV, was very eager for his
daughter, Mlle de Valois, to marry the King's youngest grandson, the Duc de Berry.* Saint-Simon *composed for the anxious
father the letter which he was to address to the King on this
subject. Suddenly, however, enemies of the proposed union*

*started spreading the vilest slanders concerning the nature of
the duke's affection for his daughter. Mme de Fontaine-Martel,
lady-in-waiting to the duchess, put* Saint-Simon *on his guard,
as he recounts:*

Taking advantage of an occasion when M. le Duc d'Orléans
was on an outing with Mademoiselle, she told me confidentially
that he would do well to hurry the marriage along if he had
any means to do so, because the most horrible lies were being
put about by those who wished to prevent it. Without divulg-
ing too many details, she gave me to understand that the
calumnies involved horrible suggestions about the father's love
for his daughter. It was enough to make my hair stand on end.
I felt more keenly than ever before, in that one moment, what
devils we had to deal with, and how vital it was for us to bring
matters to a speedy conclusion. For this reason, after returning
from a long walk with M. le Duc d'Orléans that evening, I
took him aside just as he was about to return to the château. I
told him that just one more effort would bring him success
but that all would be lost for him if the marriage did not take
place. I warned him further that in counting on the marriage
he should also count on the certainty that if he did not clinch
matters by obtaining a marriage announcement before the end
of this particular stay at Marly then the marriage would never
take place.

*After some hesitation, the King agreed to the marriage,
which was celebrated on July 6th, 'without any pomp',
and marked only by a great banquet that evening, according
to* Sourches:

At ten o'clock the King left Mme de Maintenon's apartments and entered those of the Duchesse de Bourgogne, where
all the princes and princesses of the royal household were
gathered . . . From there, he crossed the gallery and entered the
salon, where his supper was served to him at the end of a long
table at which he took his place, followed by all the princes
and princesses, who seated themselves on either side of the
table in decreasing order of rank. The supper was magnificent
and lasted until almost midnight.

During the month of April 1711, the Dauphin fell ill. This docile and carefree prince did not enjoy great prestige at the Court. In the opinion of the Princess Palatine:

The Dauphin did not lack wit and had an excellent sense of humour which recognized his own frailties as well as those of other people. When he felt in the mood he could talk most entertainingly, but his laziness was so ingrained in him that his sense of purpose was paralysed. He would have preferred a life of indolence to all the empires and kingdoms of the world. He never in his life opposed any of the King's wishes and his submission to La Maintenon was as complete as anyone could have desired. Those who said that he would have withdrawn from the Court if the King had made a public announcement of his marriage to the old trollop did not know him well enough.

Pierre Narbonne, *commissaire of police of Versailles, thought, on the contrary, that the Dauphin got on very badly with Mme de Maintenon:*

Just to please Louis XIV, Monseigneur used occasionally to call on Mme de Maintenon, this lady who had succeeded in capturing the King's heart. During one of these visits it so happened that the Dauphin, on entering, placed his hat and gloves on Mme de Maintenon's bed before going to sit down. Mme de Maintenon got up immediately and handed them back to Monseigneur, saying that only the King had the right to place his hat and gloves on her bed. Monseigneur sprang to his feet and walked out (weeping, according to some reports), went back to his apartment and then left soon afterwards for Meudon.

As soon as the King had learned of his son's departure he dispatched a group of seigneurs to Meudon, including M. le Duc de Bourbon, the Comte de Saint-Maure, the Marquis d'Antin and the Comte de Roussy. The Comte de Roussy, who was always witnessing the sight of Monseigneur bowed beneath the weight of grief caused him by Mme de Maintenon, proposed to him a plot whereby Mme. de Maintenon should be kidnapped on the road to Saint-Cyr the next time she went to visit that establishment, and then smuggled into England. But Monseigneur would hear none of it. When the Marquis d'Antin got back to Versailles he hastened to tell the King everything that had taken place at Meudon, which earned him later on the post of Superintendent of the Royal Buildings. The Comte de Roussy, on the other hand, was obliged to resign his army commission. The King produced reconciliations on two separate occasions between the Dauphin and Mme de Maintenon, and the prince continued to pay her occasional courtesy calls.

It is said that in 1710, during a journey to Fontainebleau, the King, who had married Mme de Maintenon secretly, proposed to Monseigneur that he should recognize her as queen, but that Monseigneur was adamant in his refusal. He left the Court on that occasion, too, and returned to Meudon.

This news spread throughout Paris, and a few practical jokers posted bills in several streets, bearing the message: 'Miracle! Miracle! Child of forty-nine learns to speak!'

On April 11, 1711, the Duc de Saint-Simon received a letter from his wife informing him that the Dauphin was ill and thought to be suffering from smallpox. The duke returned to the Court on the 13th. The Dauphin was at Meudon and was said to be recovering, but the following day:

All was quiet at Versailles and we had no inkling of the turn of events at Meudon. We had finished our supper, the guests had retired some time after that, and I was chatting with Mme de Saint-Simon as she undressed to go to bed, when suddenly one of our former valets, whom she had given to Mme la Duchesse as groom of the chamber and who served her at table, entered in a great state of alarm. He told us that bad news must have come from Meudon, because Monseigneur le Duc de Bourgogne had just whispered something to M. le Duc de Berry, whose eyes had immediately filled with tears. He had left the table at once, and when a second message arrived very soon afterwards, the entire company had risen precipitately and gone into the drawing-room. So sudden a change astonished me, and I hurried off to Mme la Duchesse de Berry's apartment, but found no one there. They had all gone to

Mme la Duchesse be Bourgogne and I followed as quickly as I could.

When I arrived I found all Versailles assembled there, or so it seemed. The ladies were in dishabille, most of them ready for bed, the doors were all wide open and confusion reigned everywhere. I soon learned that Monseigneur had received Extreme Unction, that he was unconscious, and that his life was now despaired of. I also heard that the King had sent word to Mme la Duchesse de Bourgogne that he would be leaving for Marly later that night and that she was to wait for him in the avenue, between the two stables, where he would pick her up as he passed by.

Distracted as I was by the force of my emotions and by the many thoughts that were crowding my mind, I did my best to direct all my attention to the scene around me. The two princes and the two princesses were in the small anteroom behind the bedside alcove. The toilet accessories had been laid out as usual in Mme la Duchesse de Bourgogne's bedroom, ready for her going to bed, and the room was in a complete turmoil, filled to overflowing with courtiers. She herself came and went between the two rooms, waiting until it was time for her to go to meet the King. She bore herself as graciously as usual, but there was a troubled, compassionate air about her which everybody seemed to mistake for grief. She spoke a few words to people as she passed by, or answered their enquiries briefly. The expressions on the faces of the onlookers were truly revealing; one only needed one's eyes, and no knowledge of the Court whatsoever, to distinguish the selfish desire painted on the faces of some from the blank look of those who had nothing to gain. Some were self-possessed, others seemed plunged in grief, while others looked deeply serious from their efforts to conceal their relief and joy.

Mme de Maintenon *gave every appearance of showing grief at the death of the Dauphin, an event which she described to her friend the Princesse des Ursins in a letter dated April 16, 1711:*

At eleven o'clock, a messenger was sent to the King to inform him that Monseigneur was gravely ill. The King went down and found him in convulsions and quite unconscious. The curé of Meudon had arrived before Père Le Tellier, although the King had taken the precaution of instructing the latter to remain at Meudon, and was shouting at the unconscious prince: 'Monseigneur, do you repent your offences against God?' Maréchal, who was supporting the prince, assured the curé that he had replied 'yes'. The curé went on: 'If you were in a state to confess, would you do so?' The prince answered 'Yes.' Père Le Tellier told us later that the prince had clasped his hand, upon which he gave him absolution.

What a sight confronted my eyes, Madame, when I entered Monseigneur's large drawing-room! The King was sitting on a sofa, dry-eyed but shaking like a leaf. Mme la Duchesse [de Bourbon] was in despair; Mme la Princesse de Conti was prostrate with grief; the courtiers did not say a word to each other, and the silence was broken only by the occasional sobs and cries that arose in the room each time it seemed that Monseigneur was about to expire.

The King had gone into the bedroom three or four times before I arrived, to see if the moment had come to send Père Le Tellier in to him and to have Extreme Unction administered. I had sent word to the Duchesse de Bourgogne to meet the King on the road, since she had expressed a desire to accompany him to Marly. I must say, in passing, that she has behaved splendidly, and done much to comfort the King, M. le Duc de Bourgogne and M. le Duc de Berry.

In a letter written during October 1711, the Princess Palatine mentioned—she was the only one to do so at the time—the mysterious masked prisoner in the Bastille whose identity has intrigued historians and novelists ever since:

A man remained for many years in the Bastille, and died there, wearing a mask. He was guarded by two musketeers who had orders to kill him if he removed the mask. He ate and slept in this mask. There must have been some compelling reason for his face to remain hidden, because in every other respect he was very well treated, was comfortably accommodated and given everything he asked for. He even used to take communion still wearing his mask. He was very devout, and read continuously. No one ever succeeded in finding out who he was.

On the 22nd of that month, the Princess Palatine *recorded an additional piece of 'information' she had gleaned:*

I have just found out who was the masked man in the Bastille. The mask he wore was not inflicted on him as a barbarous punishment. He was an English lord who had been involved in the Duke of Berwick's intrigues against King William, and he wore this mask until the day of his death so that that king should never learn what had become of him.

The Duke of Berwick, natural son of James II of England, had indeed waged war against the 'usurper' William of Orange, but it is impossible to establish the identity of the 'English lord' to whom the Princess Palatine was alluding. One legend attributed the rôle of the masked prisoner to the Duke of Monmouth, but he had conspired against James II, not William, and in any case he had been beheaded on July 25, 1685. But, in any event, the prisoner is mentioned in several documents in the archives of the Bastille, and Voltaire *has this to say about him in his* Le Siècle de Louis XIV :

An old physician in the Bastille who often attended this remarkable man in his illnesses declared that he never saw his face, although he had often examined his tongue and the rest of his body. He was a wonderfully well-made man, said this physician, who added that his skin was rather swarthy. He charmed by the mere tone of his voice, never complaining of his lot nor giving a hint as to his identity . . .

M. de Chamillart was the last minister to be in possession of this strange secret. His son-in-law, the second Maréchal de La Feuillade, told me that when his father-in-law lay dying, he implored him on his knees to tell him the name of this man who had been known simply as 'the man in the iron mask'. Chamillart replied that it was a State secret, and that he had sworn never to reveal it. Lastly, there are still many of my contemporaries who can confirm the truth of the account I have given. I know of no more extraordinary and at the same time better authenticated story than this one.

Later, in his Questions sur l'Encyclopédie, Voltaire *returned
to the problem of the masked man:*

It is clear that if he was not permitted to exercise himself in
the courtyard of the Bastille, and if he was allowed to speak to
his physician only with his face concealed by a mask, it was for
fear that his features might reveal some dangerously striking
resemblance to someone. He was allowed to show his tongue
but not his face. As for his age, he himself told the apothecary
of the Bastille, a few days before he died, that he thought he
was sixty years old; at least, this is what was told me more
than once by the apothecary's son-in-law, M. Marsolan, surgeon to the Maréchal de Richelieu and later to the Regent, the
Duc d'Orléans.

*Finally, in the same book, an 'editorial note' puts forward
the idea that 'the Man in the Iron Mask was no doubt an elder
brother of Louis XIV'. The legend was born, and continued
to blossom during the following century.*

*At the beginning of February 1712, the Dauphine, Marie
Adélaïde, died of purpural measles, a disease which had claimed
many victims in Paris that year.*

For once, the Princess Palatine *does not suggest poison; this
time she places the responsibility for the Dauphine's death on
the shoulders of her physicians—and Mme de Maintenon:*

Doctor Chirac went on assuring everybody right up to the
end that she [the Dauphine] would recover. In fact, had she
not been allowed to get up while she had the measles, and had
they not bled her from the foot, she would indeed still be
alive. Immediately after she was bled, her face, which had been
fiery red, became deathly pale and she complained of feeling
very ill.

When they made her get out of bed, I protested that they
should at least wait for her sweating fit to pass before they bled
her, but Chirac and Fagon insisted and jeered at me. The old
trollop came up to me and said: 'Do you think you know
better than all these doctors here?' I replied: 'No, Madame,
but one does not have to be very clever to know that it is best
to follow nature, and since her present tendency is to sweat it

would be far better to let her go on sweating rather than force a sick and perspiring woman to get out of bed to be bled.' She shrugged her shoulders and smiled sardonically, and I turned away without saying a word.

The Princess Palatine's suspicion of, and consuming hatred for, the King's consort may be explained, perhaps, by the comment of her aunt, the Princesse de Tarente, that she was 'violently attracted' by Louis XIV and 'did not know her own feelings'. But Saint-Simon hinted at a more sinister cause of death than measles compounded by the ill-will of Mme de Maintenon:

On Friday, February 5th, before midday, the Duc de Noailles presented the Dauphine with a beautiful snuff-box filled with fine Spanish snuff, which she tried and found excellent. She then took the box with her into her private boudoir, placed it on a table and left it there. That same evening she was attacked by an ague, retired to bed, and felt too ill to get up again, even to go to the King's study after supper. Although her fever continued throughout the night, she still got up at her usual time the following morning and spent the day pursuing her normal activities. That evening, however, the fever returned. She had an uncomfortable night, but felt a little better on the Sunday. Then, at about six in the evening, she was seized with a sudden pain below the temples, small in area but so excruciating that she sent a message to the King, who had come to visit her, begging him not to enter the room. This maddening pain lasted without respite until Monday, 8th, and was not relieved by smoking or chewing tobacco, or by large doses of opium and two bleedings from the arm. When the pain grew less, the fever increased. She said that she had suffered more even than in childbirth.

The violence of her illness led to rumours among her circle about the snuff-box which the Duc de Noailles had given her. When going to bed on the day she was given the snuff-box and first became ill, she had spoken of it to her ladies, praising both the box and the snuff, and had then asked Mme de Lévi to fetch it from her boudoir, where she would find it on the table. But Mme de Lévi hunted high and low without being able to find it and, to cut a long story short, it was never seen again from the moment that the Dauphine first placed it on the table. The disappearance seemed strange enough in itself, but the long and fruitless search, followed by such strange and sudden fatalities, could not fail to arouse the darkest suspicions. These suspicions did not go so far as to point to the one who had given the box, or if they did they were couched in such careful generalizations that the name of the person in question was never mentioned . . .

By Thursday 11th, the princess was so ill that the sacraments were administered to her. She was bled from the foot. The next day she became unconscious and died during the night. Saint-Simon *mourned:*

With her death, all joy, pleasure, gaiety and charm were eclipsed, and darkness covered the face of the Court, for she was its light and its life. She was everywhere at once, she filled its every corner, her presence permeated its inner life. If the Court continued to exist after her death, it was only to languish and pine for her.

Almost immediately, the Dauphin fell ill too. He had left for Marly on the morning of February 13th:

Since the time was approaching for the King's *réveil*, his three pages entered the Dauphin's room to announce it and I made so bold as to enter with them. He showed me that he had noticed me by glancing at me gently and affectionately, which moved me deeply. But I was horrified at his appearance. His eyes were glazed and staring, almost wild; his face had changed and was covered with large blotches which were livid rather than inflamed. The other people in the room also noticed this discoloration of his skin. He was standing up, and when, a few moments later, they came to announce that the King was awake, the tears which he had held back started to spring to his eyes . . . Seeing that he was just standing there, saying nothing, I ventured to take his arm, pointing out to him that he would have to see the King sooner or later, for he was waiting for him and certainly anxious to see and embrace him, so that it would be best not to delay any longer. Then, gently urging him on, I took the liberty of giving him a little push. He gave me a look which pierced my heart and then he left the room. I followed him a little of the way, then withdrew to try to regain my composure. I never saw him again.

The Dauphin died on February 18th. And the Princess Palatine *made much of the fact that he survived his wife by only a few days:*

The good prince showed how great was his love for his wife, in that he certainly died of grief at her loss, indeed he had always predicted that he would not survive her. A learned astrologer of Turin had once cast Mme la Duchesse's horoscope, in which was set down everything that was to happen to her during her life, including the prediction that she would die at the age of twenty-seven. She often spoke of it. One day she said to her husband: 'The time is approaching when I am fated to die. Your rank and your sense of duty will not allow you to remain without a wife. Whom, pray, will you marry?' He replied: 'I hope that God will never punish me so harshly as to see you die, but if this calamity ever befell me I would never remarry, for in a week I would have followed you to your tomb.' And this, in fact, is exactly what happened.

But a fresh blow was about to descend on the royal family. In the words of the Marquis de Sourches:

On March 7th it became known that both M. le Dauphin [the late Dauphin's elder son, the Duc de Bretagne] and M. le Duc d'Anjou [his younger son, later King Louis XV] were showing symptoms of having measles. From this moment onwards, the whole Court feared the worst, and even Fagon and the other physicians admitted that it was the same malady that had carried off M. le Dauphin and Mme la Dauphine . . .

On the 8th it was learned that both the young princes were extremely ill, and that the physicians had wanted to bleed M. le Dauphin, but had been prevented from doing so by a great sweat which had overcome him. Later, however, they did bleed him and also gave him an emetic. The Duc d'Anjou, too, was covered in spots and in great danger of his life . . .

On the morning of the 9th we learned that M. le Dauphin had died between midnight and one in the morning.

Three deaths in a single month! The courtiers were terrified and rumours began to spread. After the Duc de Berry, the Duc d'Orléans was the closest relative of the infant Duc d'Anjou who, at the age of two, had become Dauphin in his turn. If that child died it seemed probable that the succession would pass to the Duc d'Orléans. And now idle rumour began to whisper that Louis XIV's nephew, who was an enthusiastic student of chemistry, was engaged in suspicious experiments in his laboratory, assisted by a certain Humbert. On February 14th, the Princess Palatine *wrote to her aunt:*

People with wicked minds have been spreading the rumour throughout Paris that my son has poisoned the Dauphin and Dauphine ... At first I thought it must be just a bad joke. I could not believe that anyone was capable of suggesting such a thing seriously, yet that is how it has been told to the King. However, the King spoke to my son afterwards, in a most kindly manner, and assured him that he believed none of all this. But he advised my son to send his chemist, the poor learned Homberg [Humbert] to the Bastille to clear his master of this accusation. I am absolutely furious.

And on March 10th she added:

No doubt you will share my fears at the news that the little Dauphin is dead. Although my son never went near the child, the word has already gone around that he poisoned the little Dauphin.

Saint-Simon *takes up the story:*

On February 17th, when M. le Duc d'Orléans and Madame went to sprinkle holy water over the remains of the Dauphine, the mob lining their route yelled all sorts of stupidities at them, which he and Madame heard quite plainly without daring to show that they had done so, although their pain, embarrassment and indignation can be imagined. There was even reason to fear worse from a turbulent and credulous populace when, on February 21st, he went alone to sprinkle holy water on the Dauphin. On this occasion, too, he had to brave the vilest insults on the way . . . When his procession passed by the Palais Royal, the fury of the jeers, hoots and insults became so violent that for a few moments the situation seemed likely to get out of hand.

One may well imagine the good use M. du Maine made of this public frenzy . . . The death of the little Dauphin and the report of the opening up of his body by the surgeons added fresh fuel to the rage and licence of the mob, and provided M. du Maine, his inner circle of friends and Mme de Maintenon with a new means of turning this rage to good account. As for the King, he was utterly downcast, filled with fear and suspicion and resentment.

Finally, the unfortunate Humbert appeared at the Bastille to give himself up, but meanwhile the King's chief surgeon, Maréchal, had spoken to his master with 'the freedom which his virtue permitted him', and the King was persuaded to change his mind. Humbert was not imprisoned, but the Duc d'Orléans derived little benefit from this concession:

He was not only abandoned by all his friends and acquaintances. When he entered the King's apartments or the salon the courtiers drew back as he passed, and if he approached a group each member of it would make a half-turn to the left or to the right, in the most obvious fashion, and thus they would regroup themselves on either side of him. And if he succeeded in approaching someone unawares, that person would quit his company in the most indecent haste . . .

The kingdom seemed to be fighting for its life during this summer of 1712. France was in a desperate situation: arrayed against her were England, Prussia, Holland, Austria, Portugal and Savoy. Louis XIV had decided to sue for peace, and had sent his Foreign Minister, the Marquis de Torcy, to The Hague, but the demands of the Allies were so humiliating (they included the restitution of all territories conquered within the previous fifty years, and a declaration of war against the

King of Spain, the King's own grandson) that these pre-
liminary negotiations were broken off.

The Duc de Vendôme had succeeded in maintaining Philip
V on the throne of Spain through a series of victories in the
field against the English, Portuguese and Austrians, but France
had been invaded from the north, and the town of Landrecies
was under siege. Voltaire *commented:*

At this very time [June 1712] the Duc de Vendôme died
in Spain. The spirit of despondency which pervaded the
whole of France, and which I myself can remember, led
people to fear again that Spain, though temporarily sustained
by Vendôme, would once more fall now that her saviour was
gone. Landrecies could not hold out for long. The question of
the King withdrawing to Chambord on the Loire was raised at
Versailles.

The only French army left to bar the way to the enemy
was that under the command of the Maréchal de Villars. On
April 16th, Villars had had an audience with the King at
Marly, and subsequently described their conversation in his
memoirs:

On that day, the firmness of a monarch gave way to the
sensibility of a man. The King shed a few tears and then spoke
to me in a voice which shook with emotion and affected me
deeply. He said: 'You can see the state I am in, M. le Maréchal. Few people have suffered as I have suffered: in the space
of a few weeks I have lost my grandson, my granddaughter,
and their son. I had great hopes in them all and loved them all
dearly. God is punishing me, and I deserve his judgement, but
I hope I shall suffer less in the world to come. Now, let us
think no more about my personal misfortunes and consider,
rather, what we can do to cure the misfortunes of the kingdom.
You can be in no doubt about the confidence I repose in you,
since I have entrusted you with the resources of the State and
placed its safety in your hands. I know your zeal and the valour
of my troops. But even so, fortune may be fickle with you. If
the army which you command met with a reverse, what would
be your feeling about the part which I personally should play?'
Faced with such a grave and momentous question, I

remained silent for a few moments. Seeing this, the King started
to speak again, saying: 'I am not surprised that you should
hesitate before answering, but while waiting to hear your views
I will acquaint you with my own.' 'Your Majesty,' I replied,
'would relieve me greatly by doing so. The matter requires
deliberation, and it is natural that one should wish to think
about it for a while.' 'Well, then,' said the King, 'here are my
thoughts. Afterwards you may give me your own views.

'I know the reasonings of my courtiers. Nearly all of them
desire me to withdraw to Blois and not to wait for the enemy
to approach the gates of Paris, which they might well do if my
army were to be defeated. For my part, I know that armies
as powerful as mine can never be so utterly defeated as to
prevent numerous contingents from retreating across the
Somme. I know this river; it is very difficult to cross, but there
are points where it can be made fordable. My idea was to go to
Peronne or Saint-Quentin, rally all my remaining forces, and
make one last effort with you, in which we would either perish
together or save the State, for I shall never willingly permit the
enemy to approach my capital. That is how I reason. Now give
me your advice.'

'Your Majesty,' I replied, 'has relieved me immeasurably,
since it is painful for a faithful servant of the State to advise
the greatest King on earth to expose his person in the field.
However, I confess, Sire, that knowing Your Majesty's ardour
for glory, and having been privileged to have his heroic resolutions confided to me in the past, during less critical times, I
would have been bold enough to advise him that paths of glory
are also often paths of wisdom, and I can envisage no nobler
course to follow—for a King who is a great man as much as a
great King—than that which Your Majesty proposes.

*On July 24th, the Maréchal de Villars attacked Denain,
broke through the enemy's entrenchments, and took prisoner
General the Earl of Albemarle (Joost van Keppel). But
Saint-Simon gives all the credit for this victory to d'Artagnan,
the Maréchal de Montesquiou. According to him, the marshal,
sure of the King's support, began by harrying the enemy's
supply-wagons, then proceeded to advance on the enemy at the
head of a column, without waiting for any orders from Villars:*

Villars was advancing very slowly with the main body of the army. He was already vexed to see a part of the army ahead with Montesquiou, without orders from him, and he was even more vexed when he heard the sound of gunfire. He sent him repeated orders instructing him to halt his advance, to refrain from attack, to wait for him, and all the time continuing his own leisurely progress, for the fact is that he had no stomach for battle. Montesquiou sent him his aides de camp with the message that the wine was drawn and had to be drunk, and then launched such a vigorous attack on the enemy that he broke through their entrenchments, entered Denain, captured all their artillery and magazines, and inflicted heavy losses on their troops, many of whom were drowned while attempting to escape across the river. He then disposed his victorious forces in defensive positions, in case Prince Eugene should decide on a counter-attack. The prince had reached the opposite bank of the river with his army, had been an eye-witness of the successful assault on the town, and had now been joined by the defeated remnant which had succeeded in fleeing across the river. But he decided that he was not in a position to attempt to retake Denain and so he withdrew.

. . . Montesquiou had the sense to be modest, to allow Villars to play the hero and make a fool of himself, to respect the open protection offered Villars by Mme de Maintenon, and to content himself with the credit which he deserved and received. Fontainebleau was the scene of wild rejoicings and demonstrations of enthusiasm for the King, who was so flattered that for the first time in his life he thanked the courtiers. Prince Eugene, lacking provisions and equipment of all kinds, soon lifted the siege of Landrecies, and his troops started deserting at an alarming rate . . .

DEATH OF THE GOD

The Earl of Stair, the English ambassador, wagered, after the fashion of his country, that the King would not outlive the month of September.

VOLTAIRE

❧

PRINCIPAL PERSONALITIES MENTIONED IN CHAPTER XXIV

The DUC DE LAUZUN: ANTONIN NOMPAR DE GAUMONT, MARQUIS DE PUYGUILHEM, readmitted to the royal favour after a long exile, now brother-in-law of the Duc de Saint-Simon (already mentioned in Chapter V).

The PRÉSIDENT DE MAISONS, brother-in-law of the Maréchal de Villars, friend of Philippe d'Orléans and 'idol of the Parlement'.

ANNE JULES, DUC DE NOAILLES, Marshal of France, who conducted the campaign in Catalonia and was created a Grandee of Spain. His daughter married Saint-Simon's son. (Already mentioned in Chapters IV and XIV.)

MME DE VENTADOUR: CHARLOTTE ELÉONORE DE LA MOTHE-HOUDANCOURT, DUCHESSE DE VENTADOUR, formerly lady-in-waiting to Madame, now governess of the future Louis XV.

GUY CRESCENT FAGON, the King's chief physician: the Princess Palatine referred to him as 'that wicked old devil' (already mentioned in Chapters XV and XXIII).

LE BRUN, a quack doctor.

LOUIS AUGUSTE DE BOURBON, DUC DU MAINE, elder of

the two natural sons of Louis XIV by Mme de Montespan (the other was the Comte de Toulouse) and favourite of Mme de Maintenon (already mentioned in Chapters V and XVIII).

PHILIPPE, DUC D'ORLÉANS, Louis XIV's only legitimate nephew, future Regent of the kingdom during Louis XV's minority. He and the Duc du Maine loathed each other with equal intensity.

By the treaty of Utrecht in 1713, France secured peace terms from all her adversaries except the Emperor, but a brilliant campaign by Villars in Germany forced the former to negotiate the Treaty of Radstadt the following year. Louis XIV lost none of his conquered territories, but ceded Acadia (Nova Scotia) and Newfoundland to England and recognized the English sovereigns of the House of Hanover.

The Court, after so many misfortunes and apprehensions, began to breathe more easily. The King's health was excellent. Mme de Maintenon wrote, in August 1713, to the Princesse des Ursins:

There is a chamberlain of the Pope here who says that if he sent word to Rome that the King of France, at the age of seventy-four, was going out during the dog-days at two every afternoon, driving in the forest, over rough ground, surrounded by horses and dogs, they would think him mad, so he says laughingly that he will refrain from mentioning the fact in his letters.

But by the following spring Versailles was in mourning yet again. This time death came, on May 4, 1714, to the Duc de Berry, the King's youngest grandson. He had fallen from his horse and had concealed the incident for fear of worrying his father. According to the Princess Palatine:

The Duc de Berry killed himself by his horrible intemperance in eating and drinking. Furthermore, in falling from his horse while hunting he had ruptured a vein, which had resulted in a great loss of blood, but he had threatened to dismiss instantly any of his attendants who mentioned the accident or told anyone that he was losing blood. After his death, containers full of blood were found under his bed and under various pieces of furniture.

When he finally admitted this injury it was too late to treat it, and since no one had known about his accident the physicians had thought that his illness resulted entirely from his excesses at table. They made him take repeated doses of emetic, which served further to hasten his death. He himself said to his confessor, Père de La Rue: 'Ah! mon Père, I am the only cause of my own death!' He had repented, but too late.

Louis XIV's sole remaining heir was now a four-year-old child. The King's bastards now began agitating and intriguing to secure positions of power in relation to the little Dauphin.

In July 1714, these legitimized princes, whose rank had hitherto been intermediate between the Princes of the Blood and the Dukes and Peers, were declared princes of the blood. Saint-Simon *learned the news in the following manner:*

. . . Returning home from Marly, towards the end of the morning of Sunday, July 29th, I found one of Maisons' lackeys at my house with a message from his master imploring me to put all other business aside and come immediately to Paris, where he would be waiting for me alone. The note added that when I heard what he had to say I would realize that the matter in question brooked no delay, could not safely be set down in writing, and was of the utmost importance. The lackey had arrived some time ago and my people had been searching high and low for me. Mme de Saint-Simon was at Versailles, with Mme la Duchesse de Berry, who used to take supper with the King every evening without staying overnight at Marly, and I had an engagement to dine with M. and Mme de Lauzun. To have failed to appear would have aroused M. de Lauzun's curiosity and suspicion, so I ordered my coachman to drive me over to the Lauzuns and wait for me outside. As soon as dinner was over I vanished discreetly, and no one saw me get into my post-chaise and drive off. I made all possible speed to reach my own house in Paris, and then went directly to Maisons' house, still in great haste, as can be imagined.

I found him alone with the Duc de Noailles. My first glance told me that something was seriously wrong, for both men looked utterly downcast. After a short but succinct preliminary explanation, they told me, in lugubrious tones, that the King had declared his two bastards and their male descendents *ad infinitum* to be true princes of the blood, entitled to assume the quality and all the titles and honours of their new rank, and qualified to succeed to the throne in default of any other living prince of the blood. I was completely taken aback by this news, for not a word of this secret had leaked out. My arms dropped to my sides, I bowed my head, and I stood there, absorbed in deep and silent reflections; but my thoughts were soon interrupted by a most extraordinary din. I looked up to see these two men striding up and down the room, stamping their feet, kicking and striking the furniture, and vying with each other in making the house re-echo with their shouts and curses. I could hardly believe my eyes: it seemed scarcely credible that two such men, one so wise and temperate, and not in the least affected by the new decree, and the other so quizzical and self-possessed, could be responsible for such an outburst.

I asked them if they had both gone completely mad and whether, instead of creating this noisy and angry scene, it would not be more useful for us to put our heads together and see if there was anything to be done about the matter. They cried out that they were behaving as they did precisely because there *was* nothing to be done about something which had been not only decided upon but executed, issued as a declaration and sent to the Parlement. Furthermore, they said, M. le Duc d'Orléans was on such bad terms with the King that he would not dare lift a finger, the princes of the blood who were of age were as scared as the children they still were at heart, the dukes were entirely incapable of intervening, and the Parlement was reduced to a state of silence and slavery. Whereupon the two renewed their antics, each yelling and cursing louder than the other and sparing neither persons nor institutions in their abuse.

... Seeing that our deliberations were getting nowhere, I

took my leave and hastened back to Marly so that my absence should not be remarked upon. I arrived there just in time to take my place at the King's supper table, and went straight to the salon, where I found him looking extremely doleful. The others present were exchanging glances but scarcely daring to approach each other, contenting themselves with a surreptitious gesture or a few whispered words. When the King took his seat at table, he seemed to me to have a haughtier air than usual, and he stared hard at the people on either side of him. The news had broken only an hour previously, and all those present were still chilled with dismay and on their guard. When a situation cannot be retrieved, one must make up one's mind what one's future course of action is to be, and one can do this more easily and more honestly when the matter does not involve immediate repercussions. Since the intermediary rank granted to the bastards had never received the slightest compliment or acknowledgment from me, I did not have to consider too hard. I had already made up my mind what to do.

This time, however, Saint-Simon *did go to pay his respects to the Duc du Maine and the Comte de Toulouse. He comments:*

The Court was seething with suppressed resentment. Paris and the provinces had already exploded with wrath. The individual members of the Parlement could scarcely contain themselves, so indignant were they. Mme de Maintenon, preening herself at the success of her campaign, was receiving the adoration of her cronies . . . M. du Maine made no attempt to conceal his glee at the sad, doleful, stricken expressions on the faces of all those members of a subservient Court who had come to pay their reluctant but unavoidable compliments. Mme du Maine, at Sceaux, was equally triumphant, and showed herself completely indifferent to the general feelings of bitterness by organizing countless fêtes and entertainments. She accepted at their face value the driest and most formal compliments, and seemed not to notice the absence of the great number of people who were unable to stomach the prospect of appearing personally as adorers at her shrine. The deified bastards appeared only briefly at Marly.

But the Duc du Maine was not satisfied with his elevation to the rank of prince of the blood: his next objective was to persuade the King to draw up a will in his favour. In league with Mme de Maintenon, the duke launched a 'campaign of boredom', in which they both sulked and brooded and provoked an atmosphere of gloom and strain throughout the Court until they finally got their way with the King. And on August 27th, the representatives of the Parlement, Mesmes,[1] the Premier Président, and Joly de Fleury, the Procureur Général, were summoned to Versailles. Still following Saint-Simon's *account of events:*

When they were alone, the King unlocked a drawer and took out a large packet sealed with seven seals (I do not know if M. du Maine, in so sanctifying this packet, wished to imitate the mysterious Book with the Seven Seals mentioned in the Apocalypse). He handed it to them, saying: 'Messieurs, this is my will. No one but myself knows its contents. I consign it to your care for safe keeping by the Parlement, to whom I can show no greater proof of my trust and esteem than to make it the depository of this document. The fate of the wills of the kings who preceded me, including that of the King my father, makes me well aware of what may become of it. But they insisted. They have pestered me, they have allowed me no peace, whatever I said. Now I have purchased my rest. Here, take it, for what it is worth. At least I shall have some peace now and hear no more about it.' Then, giving them a curt nod, he turned and went into an adjoining room, leaving them standing there rigid with terror. They looked at each other, stupefied by what they had just heard and horrified by the look in the King's eyes and the expression on his face. When they had come to their senses they withdrew and returned to Paris.

What did this will contain? In place of a single regent during the minority of the heir to the throne, Louis XIV appointed a Regency Council, of which the Duc d'Orléans

---

[1] Jean Antoine de Mesmes, Comte d'Avaux. He was a close friend of the Duc du Maine, and the following year presided most reluctantly over the defeat in the Parlement of the duke's bid for power.

*would only be president. Its thirteen other members would
include the two bastards, the Duc du Maine and the Comte de
Toulouse. This new disposition reflected the King's continuing
mistrust of his nephew and the degree to which he was subservient to the wishes of Mme de Maintenon and the Duc du
Maine:*

Their impeccable devotion to him and their continual discretion gave the King great confidence in them. They had
perfected the art of presenting M. du Maine to him as someone
who, though intelligent and practical-minded, was wholly
without views or ambitions and was, indeed, incapable of
asserting his interests. He was pictured as being concerned
solely with his children, a good, quiet family man, touched by
greatness only as a reflection of the greatness of the King, and
his attachment to the person of the King led to his undying
love for that greatness. There was no more to it than that,
supposedly . . .

All this gave great pleasure to the King and put him perfectly at ease with his son, who was in any case his favourite
child. M. du Maine was always very close to him and assiduous
in his attentions, and amused him exceedingly with his anecdotes and jokes. I must admit that I have never known a more
accomplished story-teller, or a more charming and relaxed
companion when it suited his purpose to be so, although he was
equally adept at making malicious comments and at mocking
the infirmities of others. Whatever he did was done with great
care and deliberation, taking into account the time and occasion and the mood the King happened to be in, which he
could divine at a glance. If things went well, he had the art of
producing a most congenial and happy atmosphere, seemingly
effortlessly, by drawing on his great resources of guile, natural
charm and graciousness. If one takes all these factors into
consideration in assessing his character, one may well be
plunged into terror at the thought of this rattlesnake which
nestled in the King's bosom.

*However, the King did not conceal the regrets he felt in
the matter of his will.* Saint-Simon *records:*

On the following day, Monday, 28th, the Queen of England

[Mary of Modena, widow of James II] arrived from Chaillot, where she spent most of her time, on a visit to Mme de Maintenon. The King found her there and as soon as he set eyes on her he exclaimed in an exasperated tone of voice: 'Madame, I have made a will, they have nagged me into doing so.' Then, looking hard at Mme de Maintenon, he continued: 'I have bought some rest. I know how futile it all is. We do what we choose while we are alive, but when we are dead we have less power than the lowliest individual. You only have to think of what happened to the will made by the King my father, and that immediately after his death, and to the wills of so many other kings. I know this all too well; nevertheless, they insisted, and granted me no peace or forebearance or rest until it was done . . .'

These words, so expressive of outraged feelings and a long and bitter struggle before yielding, of chagrin and weary resignation, so plain and unambiguous in their delivery, require clear proof of their authenticity . . . What the King said to the premier président and the procureur général, I had from the former who had good reason never to forget it . . . As for the King's remarks to the Queen of England, which were far stronger and more direct, partly because he was more familiar with her and partly, perhaps, because Mme de Maintenon was also there and was the main target for the reproaches wrung from him as a result of the bullying he had undergone, I had them word for word two days later, from M. de Lauzun. The Queen of England had repeated the King's remarks to M. de Lauzun in her first astonishment.

During the spring of 1715, the King's health gave rise to some disquiet. He was suffering frequent bouts of illness, but still continued in his usual routine of going on outings, hunting, and reviewing his troops. Jean Buvat, employed as a cataloguer in the royal library, noted in his diary on June 18th:

His Majesty remarked during supper: 'If I go on eating with as good an appetite as I do at present, I shall be the ruin of a whole host of Englishmen who have wagered huge sums that I will die before the first day of September.'

At the beginning of August, the King received the ambassador of the King of Persia. The Marquis de Dangeau has given this description of the reception:

The King arose at his usual hour. He put on a costume made from a black and gold material encrusted with diamonds to the tune of more than 12,500,000 livres, and the costume was so heavy that the King changed out of it immediately after dinner.

The Persian ambassador arrived at eleven o'clock. Just beforehand, the King had appeared on the balcony of his room and the crowd, which filled the courtyard to bursting point, cheered him to the echo with enthusiastic cries of 'Long live the King!'

The ceremony took place in the long gallery, following the usual ritual:

The King mounted the throne. On his right stood the Duchesse de Ventadour, holding Monseigneur le Dauphin by his leading-strings: the little prince was wearing a dress and bonnet covered in precious stones. Monseigneur le Duc d'Orléans was standing on his left, and all the princes of the blood to the right and left of him according to rank. Circular platforms had been set up at each side of the throne to accommodate Mme la Duchesse de Berry, Madame [the Duchesse d'Orléans], and all the princesses of the blood, with their ladies-in-waiting . . .

After the audience, the ambassador visited Monseigneur le Dauphin in the apartments of the late Madame la Dauphine. He found the prince so enchanting that he said he would have liked to kiss him. He called him the Necessary Prince, which is the name they give in Persia to the heir to the throne . . .

But the gifts brought by the ambassador failed to impress the courtiers:

The presents were worthy neither of the King of France who received them nor of the King of Persia who sent them, consisting, in all, of four hundred very commonplace pearls, two hundred exceedingly poor turquoises, and two gold boxes full of balm of Muni, which is said to be marvellous for healing wounds: it is exceedingly rare, and seeps slowly from a rock enclosed within another, so that it takes a considerable time to collect enough to fill a single phial.

A few days later, the King was obliged to stay in bed. On August 13, 1715, Mme de Maintenon wrote to the Archbishop of Rouen:

Since we returned to Marly, the King has been complaining of a pain in his left leg which makes itself felt when he moves it and while walking. It appears to be a kind of cramp or gout. He had been appearing dejected and weary, but now his pulse is normal again and his appetite has returned. But he has decided to stay in bed today to see if the heat reduces the pain he is suffering. He has passed the last few days in my room, following his usual occupations, and looks very well.

Saint-Simon *notes that from now on the King stayed in bed most of the time and seemed to be weakening:*

On Wednesday, August 21st, four physicians examined the King and were careful to say nothing afterwards except to praise Fagon who has been treating the King with a liquid diet of senna water. His Majesty postponed until the following Friday his engagement to review the gendarmerie from his window, held the Council of State after his dinner, then worked with the Chancellor.[1] Afterwards he went to the *grande musique* at Mme de Maintenon's apartment, accompanied by the ladies of the royal family. He took his supper in his armchair, wearing a dressing-gown. It had been apparent for some days now that he was having difficulty in eating meat and even bread. But throughout his life he had always eaten very little bread, and since he lost his teeth only crumby bread, at that . . .

By the following day, the King's condition had become worse. He was examined by four others doctors who merely

[1] Daniel François Voysin, who had become Chancellor of France and Keeper of the Seals the previous year.

repeated the extravagant praise directed by the first four to Fagon's wide learning and extraordinary skill. That evening, Fagon made the King take some quinine in water, and at night he gave him some ass's milk.

By August 24 there was no longer any room for doubt as to the gravity of the King's condition:

He [the King] supped, standing up, in his dressing-gown in the presence of the Court for the last time. I noticed that he could swallow nothing but liquids, and that it irritated him to be looked at. He was unable to finish and requested the courtiers to pass, that is to say, to leave the room. He then asked to be put back in bed. His leg was examined and was seen to have black spots on it. He sent for Père Le Tellier and confessed. By now confusion reigned among the doctors. They had tried milk, and quinine with water; now both were discontinued without their having the slightest idea what to do next. They admitted that they thought he had had a slow fever since Whitsun, but excused themselves for having done nothing about it on the grounds that he disliked remedies, and that they did not think his condition was very serious . . .

In the October issue of the Mercure Galant, *Le Febvre de* Fontenay *recounted the King's last days:*

We shall relate for our readers the greatest, most moving, most heroic spectacle which mankind can ever hope to witness. On Saturday, August 24th, the eleventh day of the King's illness, His Majesty supped in public in his bedroom, as he had done ever since Tuesday, 13th of the same month. After supper, His Majesty felt extremely weak and sent for his confessor, and he confessed at eleven that evening. Having managed to get a little sleep the following morning, His Majesty found the strength and courage to give the courtiers entry at his dinner-time.

The next day, the 25th, was the feast of the King's patron, St Louis, and a national holiday. The King insisted that the drums and fifes should play beneath his windows as soon as he woke up. He ordered them to be brought up close under his balcony so that he could hear them better, since his bed was some distance from the window. Twenty-four violins and oboes played in the anteroom as usual during his dinner, and he desired the doors to be left open so that he could hear them.

The King was in the habit of going every evening to Mme de Maintenon's apartment for the *petite musique*. But for the last few days he had been listening to it in his own room. On that particular evening the musicians were standing waiting to be admitted, but he had fallen asleep and woke up later with a very feeble pulse and an appearance of lassitude which frightened the doctors. The King was confused in spirit when he awoke, but after a short period of time his mind cleared and, fearing a relapse into a similar condition, decided that he should receive the Holy Sacrament without delaying any longer. From this moment he acted as though he had only a few hours to live, and started giving the orders to those round him which a man who is about to die must give, but his bearing showed a firmness, presence of mind and greatness of soul which can surely never have been equalled.

The Cardinal de Rohan, Grand Almoner of France, preceded by two of the King's almoners and the curé of the parish of Versailles, brought the Host and the Holy Oils shortly before eight o'clock, entering by way of the concealed staircase which gives access to His Majesty's study. This pious and sad function was arranged and executed in such grief and haste that it was accompanied by no embellishments. There were only seven or eight torches, carried by the blue footmen of the Château, two of the chief physician's lackeys, and one in Mme de Maintenon's service. The Cardinal de Rohan carried the Host and the curè carried the Holy Oils, while Monseigneur le Duc d'Orléans, who had had some advance notice, accompanied the Host. Meanwhile, messengers were being sent around to warn all the princesses and their ladies-in-waiting, and the grand officers of the Household, and as they arrived they all entered the King's apartment through the back offices. No one else was allowed to enter.

The prayers for the Host and the ceremonies of Extreme Unction lasted more than half an hour. The princes and officers of the Household who were closest to the King's bedroom entered it during this time, but the princesses all remained in the council chamber. The princes and officers of the Household left the room in procession, following the Holy Sacrament.

As soon as the Host was gone, Mme de Maintenon, who had remained in the King's room for the entire period since he dined, left the apartment, accompanied by the Duc de Noailles. At the same time, the King ordered that a small table should be placed on his bed. Then he wrote four or five lines with his own hand on the fourth page of a codicil which he had been drawing up and of which the first three pages were already completed. The only other person in his bedroom at the time was the Chancellor. The door that gave on to the council chamber remained open, and the courtiers inside the council chamber were pressed closely around the door.

While the King was writing, Mme de Maintenon entered his room and took up a position in the alcove furthest from the council chamber door, so that she could not be seen. As soon as the King had finished writing, he asked for a drink. The courtiers who had been standing nearest the door advanced a few steps into the room, and could now be seen by the King, whose bed-curtains were open on the side of the fireplace and the side facing the door leading into the council chamber.

The King caught sight of the Maréchal de Villeroi and called him in a sturdy voice which certainly did not seem to come from a dying man. The marshal returned to the council chamber shortly afterwards, bathed in tears.

After speaking with the Maréchal de Villeroi, the King called M. Desmarets and spoke with him briefly. He then sipped a cup of broth. After this, M. le Duc d'Orléans, who had been summoned by His Majesty earlier, entered, and the King spoke with him for an appreciable time. The Duc du Maine, who had also been called for by His Majesty, entered the room immediately the Duc d'Orleans' interview was over. The prince came out again in a few moments, sobbing and weeping bitterly.

As soon as His Majesty had finished talking to the princes, the surgeons and apothecaries came in to treat the gangrenous leg as well as they could, and while they were changing the bandages the Chancellor left the room and went to speak to M. le Duc d'Orléans, who was seated in the Council chamber, in the window embrasure nearest the door into the bedroom ... The Chancellor drew from an unsealed envelope the sheet of paper on which the King had just written and handed it to M. le Duc d'Orléans, who placed the paper on a table and read it without sitting down ...

When M. le Duc d'Orléans had finished reading what was written on the sheet of paper, the Chancellor replaced it in its envelope and after showing M. le Duc d'Orléans what was written on the envelope, put it back, still unsealed, in his pocket.

This piece of paper was the codicil by which Louis XIV appointed the Duc du Maine tutor and guardian of the future King.

But according to Saint-Simon, *when the King had sent for the Duc d'Orléans and spoken with him privately, he had expressed his esteem, confidence and affection:*

And, what was most terrible, with Jesus Christ still upon his lips, having just received the Host, the King assured him that he would find nothing in the will which would displease him, then recommended to his care the State, and the person of the future King. Not half an hour had elapsed between his taking communion and receiving Extreme Unction and this conversation. He could not have forgotten the extraordinary provisions which they had extracted from him with such great difficulty. Moreover, during that short interval he had added further words to the codicil he had so recently drawn up, words which placed a knife at the throat of M. le Duc d'Orléans and its handle in the grasp of the Duc du Maine ...

On Wednesday, August 28th, he made an affectionate remark to Mme de Maintenon which she did not relish at all and did not answer. He told her that he derived some consolation in leaving her from the thought that at her age the parting would not be for long. At seven in the morning he sent for Père Le Tellier, and as they were speaking of God he saw reflected in the mirror above the chimney-piece two of his pages who were seated at the foot of the bed, weeping. He said to them: 'Why do you weep? Did you think that I was immortal? I have never thought so and, considering my age, you should have been prepared to lose me.'

The Anthoine *family, father and sons, who were respec-*
tively Gun-bearer and Grooms of the Chamber to the King,
recorded everything that happened during the last days of
Louis XIV, including the following story:

A doctor who had travelled from Marseilles sought an interview with M. le Duc d'Orléans, saying that he had a medicine
which purified the blood and cured all kinds of gangrene.
Hearing this claim, the Duc d'Orléans, seeing that the King's
life was despaired of, and that he had been practically abandoned by his own physicians, brought the Marseillais to the
Court and introduced him to His Majesty's physicians. This
man talked with them in the presence of several princes of the
blood, explained the nature of his remedy and assured them
that he had cured several people of the malady from which the
King was suffering.

Saint-Simon *confirms this account:*

An uncouth sort of yokel had learned of the King's illness
while on the way from Marseilles to Paris, and appeared that
same day at Versailles with a remedy which he claimed to be a
certain cure for gangrene. By this time, the King was so ill and
the doctors so desperate that they readily agreed, in the
presence of Mme de Maintenon and the Duc du Maine. Fagon
did try to intervene, but this yokel, Le Brun by name, turned
on him so fiercely that Fagon, who was in the habit of bullying
others, was quite taken aback and remained silent. They gave
the King ten drops of the medicine in a glass of Alicante wine
at eleven in the morning. For a little while he felt better, but
then his pulse weakened and nearly failed altogether, so they
offered him another dose at about four in the afternoon, telling
him it would revive him. As he took the glass he said: 'For life
or death, as God wills.'

The King's condition continued to deteriorate through
August 29th and 30th. By the 31st, says Saint-Simon:

There were only a few short moments of consciousness. The
gangrene had spread over the knee and the whole of the thigh.

They gave him a medicine of the late Abbé Aignan, which had been suggested by the Duchesse du Maine; it was an excellent remedy against the smallpox, but by this time the doctors were agreeing to anything because they no longer had any hope. By eleven at night the King was so ill that the prayers for the dying were recited. The ceremony restored him to consciousness, and he said the responses so loudly that he could be heard clearly above all the assembled priests and the other persons who had entered the room. When the prayers were over, he recognized Cardinal de Rohan and said to him: 'This is the last favour that the Church can do for me.' The Cardinal was the last person to whom he ever spoke. He repeated several times: '*Nunc et in hora mortis.*' Then he said: 'Help, O God, help me quickly!' Those were his last words. He was unconscious through the night, and his long-protracted agony ended at a quarter past eight in the morning of Sunday, September 1, 1715, just three days before his seventy-seventh birthday, in the seventy-second year of his reign.

The Anthoines *relate the sequel:*

As soon as the King had breathed his last, M. Maréchal, assisted by the Grooms of the Chamber, removed the body from the bed and dressed it in fresh linen. Then they replaced it in the bed, propped up against the pillows so that the dead King might be clearly visible to everyone for the rest of that day. Since he had died with his eyes and mouth open, Tartellière and La Gamie fils, the Grooms of the Chamber, rendered their last services to their master by drawing the eyelids down and closing the lips. His face was yellowish and pinched, but otherwise little changed, and his eyes seemed as penetrating and as fine as they had been during his life.

When the body had been arranged in the bed, all the doors of the apartments were thrown wide open and immediately all the princes and seigneurs of the Court and the great and minor officials who were there crowded in to pay their last honours to the remains of their dead King.

M. le Duc d'Orléans arrived, paid his last honours to the remains of the dead King, then went into the apartment and announced in a loud voice that King Louis XIV was dead.

Then the new King was immediately proclaimed: Louis XV, son of Louis, Dauphin of France and of Marie Adélaïde of Savoy, and great-grandson of the King, aged five years, six months and sixteen days . . .

On the following day, September 2nd, the body of the late King was carried by the officers of the Chamber and of the Wardrobe, to whom this honour belonged, into the anteroom and placed upon a table to be opened up, in the presence of M. le Duc d'Elbeuf and M. de Montesquiou, both nominated by M. le Duc d'Orléans, of the Duc de Tresmes, first gentleman of the Chamber, and of Maillebois, one of the Masters of the Wardrobe. All the doctors were there, led by M. Fagon, the chief physician, who described the proceedings to the assembled company while M. Maréchal, the chief surgeon, opened up the body. It was found to be in the condition described in the official report.

This official report stated:

We found the exterior of the left side of the body affected by gangrene from the foot to the head, the epidermis swollen on both sides, but less on the right than on the left, the stomach extremely distended, very bloated, the intestines much deteriorated and inflamed, especially on the left side . . .

After the opening, the body was embalmed and placed by the Duc de Tresmes in a lead coffin . . . The coffin was closed and then carried by the officers of the Chamber and the Wardrobe into the Great Apartment where the King used to hold the grand audiences. The coffin was magnificently adorned with the finest of the Crown jewels. It was set down on a bed for lying in state and covered by a pall of very rich cloth of gold. On each side of the catafalque an altar had been set up, and at these a great number of priests and more than a hundred nuns from all the different orders took turns to celebrate Mass during the mornings, and to chant psalms throughout the remaining hours, night and day, without interruption, until September 9th when the body was carried to Saint-Denis. During the whole period of the lying in state the body was watched over by the reverend fathers of the Feuillant order of strict Bernardines, who have the prerogative of watching over the bodies of deceased Kings until the day of their obsequies.

But the Duc d'Orléans had already convoked the Parlement on September 2nd, with the aim of breaking the King's will which imposed a regency council on him, and the codicil which appointed the Duc du Maine tutor of the young Louis XV. The Regency was bestowed on the Duc d'Orléans by acclamation, and he then proceeded to launch his attack on the codicil. Saint-Simon, who took a leading part in these political manoeuvres on behalf of his dear friend Philippe d'Orléans, and emerged triumphant, describes the crucial scene:

After a few moments of silence, M. le Duc d'Orléans began to speak again. He expressed his astonishment that the provisions of the will should have seemed inadequate to those who had contrived them, and that, not content with making themselves masters of the kingdom, they had themselves found the clauses so outrageous that they found it necessary to consolidate their power by gaining control of the person of the young King himself, the Court and Paris. He added that while the will wounded his honour to an extent which the assembly seemed to feel as deeply as he did, the codicil injured it still more, since it left him secure in neither life nor liberty, and placed the person of the King in the absolute power of a man who had not scrupled to take advantage of the weakness of a dying King to wring from him privileges which he cannot have intended to grant. He ended by declaring that it would be impossible to exercise the regency under such conditions, and so he did not doubt that the assembly, in its wisdom, would annul a codicil which was indefensible since its rules and conditions would spell disaster for France . . .

The Parlement then voted the total annulment of the codicil:

They took the vote without even waiting for the Premier Président to finish speaking. It was given unanimously.

The royal bastards had been effectively put in their place. Saint-Simon was exultant.

Pierre Narbonne, commissaire of police and governor of Versailles recorded in his diary that while this session of the Parlement was in progress:

The Royal Bodyguard had been booted and saddled since August 30th, ready to escort the new King to Vincennes[1] immediately after the death of Louis XIV, but the Duc d'Orléans had altered the arrangements and remained at Versailles until September 9th.

On that day, the obsequies took place. They were brief and simple, according to Saint-Simon:

To avoid the expense and complication of long drawn out ceremonies, it was decided to follow the practice in the case of the funeral of Louis XIII. That monarch had himself ordered that his own funeral rites should be celebrated as simply as possible.

And on the Pont Neuf in Paris the people sang:

> Shriven at last and shrouded, he
> Was taken to rest at Saint-Denis,
> In simple pauper's poverty.
> His son got nothing from his will
> To pay the undertaker's bill.

And according to Narbonne:

Many people rejoiced at the death of this prince, and in all the popular quarters of Paris violins could be heard playing.

Voltaire *commented:*

I saw several small booths erected by the roadway of Saint-Denis, in which people were drinking, singing and laughing. The feelings of the citizens of Paris had been adopted by the general populace. The Jesuit Le Tellier was the principal cause of this widespread joy. I heard several members of the crowd suggest that the houses of all the Jesuits should be set on fire with the torches which had lit the funeral ceremony.

[1] Louis XIV had ordered that his successor should be taken to Vincennes while the Château of Versailles was aired and cleaned.

Versailles was now destined to sink into a two year slumber. And in Paris, only tattered fragments still remained on the walls of the posters put up on September 1st:

Pray to God for the soul of the most exalted, most powerful, most excellent Prince Louis the Great, by the grace of God King of France and Navarre, most Christian, most majestic, most victorious, incomparable in clemency, in justice and in piety.

TABLE OF SOURCES

The reports, comments and opinion which constitute the body of this volume are drawn from the following works and documents:

Anonymous: Letters concerning the trial of the Chevalier de Rohan, included in a manuscript in the collection of the Bibliothèque Sainte-Genevieve, Paris, and reproduced in Fourier: *Variétés historiques*, Paris, 1855.

Anonymous: *Lettre des Camisards aux habitants de Bagnols*, French National Archives, quoted in Almeras: *La révolte des Camisards*, Paris, 1959.

Anonymous: *Lettres historiques et anécdotiques*, a collection of chronicles published during the reign of Louis XIV, Bibliothèque Nationale, Paris, French ms. no. 10,265.

Anonymous: *Relation des Plaisirs de l'île enchantée*, Paris, 1665.

ANTHOINE, Jacques, and his sons: *Journal historique ou récit fidèle de ce qui s'est passé de plus considérable pendant la maladie et la mort de Louis XIV, roi de France et de Navarre*, Paris, 1891.

ARGENSON, Marc René de Voyer d', Lieutenant of Police of Paris: *Rapports inédits*, Paris, 1891.

ARGENSON, René Louis de Voyer d', Foreign Minister during the reign of Louis XV: *Journal et mémoires inédits*, Paris, 1859.

ARTAGNAN, Charles de Baatz, seigneur d'. see SANDRAS DE COURTILZ.

AUMALE, Marie Jeanne de Moureuil d', secretary of Mme de Maintenon: *Mémoires*, Paris, n. d.

Bastille, Archives of the: published Paris, 1873.

BASVILLE, Lamoignon de la, intendant of Languedoc: *Mémoires pour servir à l'histoire du Languedoc*, Amsterdam, 1734.

BAYLE, Pierre, professor of philosophy at the Protestant Academy of Sedan and author of the 'Dictionnaire historique et critique': *Lettres*, Amsterdam, 1729.

BEAUVAU, Gabriel Henri, Marquis de: *Mémoires pour servir à l'histoire de Charles IV duc de Lorraine et de Bar*, Cologne, 1691.

BERWICK, James Fitzjames, Duke of, natural son of James II of England and Arabella Churchill, a commander in the French army: *Memoirs . . .*, London, 1779.

BOILEAU-DESPRÉAUX, Nicolas: *Oeuvres complètes*, Paris, 1873.

BONBONNOUX, Jacques, Camisard leader and 'prophet': *Mémoires*, Anduze, 1838.

BOSSUET, Jacques Bénigne: *Sermons*, Paris, 1862.

BRETEUIL, Louis Nicolas de Tonnelier, Baron de, Master of Ceremonies at the Court of Louis XIV: *Fragments*, Paris, 1855.

BRIENNE, Louis Henri de Loménie, Comte de, Secretary of State for Foreign Affairs in succession to his father: *Mémoires*, Paris, 1828.

BUSSY-RABUTIN, Roger de Rabutin, Comte de Bussy, cousin of Mme de Sévigné: *Histoire amoureuse des Gaules*, followed by *La France galante*, Paris, 1868.
Correspondance avec sa famille et ses amis, Paris, 1857.

BUVAT, Jean, a librarian in the royal library at Versailles: *Journal de la Régence*, Paris, 1865.

CAVALIER, Jean, Camisard leader: *Memoirs of the Wars of the Cevennes*, Dublin, 1726.

CAYLUS, Marguerite Marie Le Valois de Villette de Murçay, cousin of Mme de Maintenon: *Souvenirs* (edited by her son), Paris, 1881.

CHOISY, François Timoléon, Abbé de, courtier and diplomat: *Mémoires*, Paris, 1888.

COLBERT, Jean Baptiste: *Lettres, instructions et mémoires*, Paris, 1861-2.

Comptes des Bâtiments du Roi, the accounts of the royal building works under the reign of Louis XIV, edited by Jules Guiffrey, Paris, 1881.

CONDÉ, Louis II de Bourbon, Prince de: *Lettres inédites à Marie-Louise de Gonzague, reine de Pologne*, Paris, 1920.

CONTI, François Louis, Prince de: *Lettre au Prince de Condé* (concerning the capture of Nerwinden), published in the *Mercure Galant*, August, 1693.

COSNAC, Daniel de, Archbishop of Aix and Chief Almoner to the Duc d'Orléans: *Mémoires*, Paris, 1852.

COULANGES, Philippe Emanuel, Marquis de: *Mémoires*, Paris, 1820.
Lettres (à Mme de Grignan) in SÉVIGNÉ (q.v.).

COURTILZ, Sandras de: see SANDRAS DE COURTILZ.

DANGEAU, Philippe de Courcillon, Marquis de: *Journal de la Cour de Louis XIV*, Paris, 1854-60.

DIONIS, Pierre, Chief Surgeon to the Dauphine, to the Duchesse de Bourgogne and to Louvois: *Dissertation sur la mort subite*, Paris, 1710.

DUCLOS, Charles Pinot: *Mémoires secrets sur les regnes de Louis XIV et de Louis XV*, Paris, 1846.

DUNOYER, Mme, Anne Marguerite Petit, known as: *Lettres historiques et galantes de deux dames de condition, dont l'une était à Paris et l'autre en province*, Cologne, 1723.

DU PÉROU, Mme: *Mémoires sur Mme de Maintenon*, Paris, 1846.

DUPLESSIS-BELLIÈRE, Susanne, Marquise de: *Lettre au Surintendent Fouquet*, in the manuscript collection of the Bibliothèque de l'Arsenal, Paris.

FELIBIEN, Jean François, sier des Avaux et de Javercy, Louis XIV's official historiographer: *Relation de la Fête de Versailles du 18 juillet 1668*, Paris, 1668.
Description de Versailles, Paris, 1703.
Entretien sur la vie et les ouvrages des plus excellents peintres, London, 1705.

FÉNELON, François de la Mothe: *Lettre à Louis XIV*, Paris, 1825.

FLÉCHIER, Valentin 'Esprit', Bishop of Nîmes: *Lettres choisies*, Paris, 1715.

FEUQUIÈRES, Antoine du Pas, Marquis de: *Mémoires*, London, 1736.
Lettres inédites, Paris, 1845.

FORBIN, Claude, Comte de, naval commander, buccaneer and associate of Jean Bart: *Mémoires*, Paris, 1839.

FOUCAULT, Nicolas Joseph, intendant of Pau, Poitiers and Caen: *Mémoires*, Paris, 1862

GAIGNIÈRES: *Chansonnier*, Bibliothèque Nationale, Paris, French ms. no. 12,693.

Gazette de France, edited by Théophraste Renaudot.

GOURVILLE, Jean Hérault de, secretary to the Prince de Condé: *Mémoires*, Paris, 1838.

GRANDET, François, counsellor in the Présidial of Angers: *Mémoires*, Angers, 1901.

Journal de la santé du Roi, edited by Louis XIV's chief physicians, Antoine Vallot, Antoine D'Aquin and Guy Crescent Fagon, Paris, 1862.

LA BAUME, Charles Joseph de, counsellor in the Présidial of Nîmes: *Relation historique de la révolte des fanatiques ou des Camisards*, Nîmes, 1874.

LA BAUMELLE, Laurent Angliviel de: *Mémoires pour servir à l'histoire de Mme de Maintenon*, Amsterdam, 1755.

LA BRUYÈRE, Jean de: *Les caractères de Théophraste*, Paris, 1908.

LA FARE, Charles August, Marquis de: *Mémoires et réflexions sur les principaux événements du règne de Louis XIV*, Paris, 1838.

LA FAYETTE, Marie Madeleine Pioche de la Vergne, Comtesse

de: *Mémoires de la Cour de France pendant les années 1688 et 1689—Histoire de Mme Henriette d'Angleterre*, Paris, 1839.

LA FONTAINE, Jean de: *Fables*, Paris, 1828.

LA GRANGE, Charles Varlet de, actor and friend of Molière: *Registres* published by the Société de l'Histoire du Théâtre, Paris, 1942.

LAGRANGE-CHANCEL, François Joseph Chancel, known as: *Les Philippiques*, Paris, 1858.

LANGUET DE GERGY, Jean Joseph, Archbishop of Sens and Almoner of the Duchesse de Bourgogne: *Mémoires inédits sur Mme de Maintenon*, Paris, 1863.

LA REYNIE, Nicolas Gabriel de, Lieutenant of Police of Paris: *Lettres et notes*, Bibliothèque Nationale, Paris, French mss. no. 7,629 and 7,608.

LE DIEU, Abbé François, secretary of Bossuet: *Mémoires et Journal sur la vie et les ouvrages de Bossuet*, Paris, 1856.

LE GENDRE, Abbé Louis, secretary of the Archbishop of Paris, Cardinal de Noailles: *Mémoires*, Paris, 1865.

LENCLOS, Ninon de: *Lettre à Saint-Evremond*, included in Feuillet de Conches: *Les Causeries d'un curieux*, Paris, 1862.

LE VASSOR, Michel: *Les Soupirs de la France esclave*, Amsterdam, 1689.

LIONNE, Hugues de, Foreign Minister: *Lettres à Colbert de Croissy* (French ambassador to England), Valence, 1877.

LOCATELLI, Sebastiano, priest of Bologna: *Voyage de France, 1664-5*, Paris, 1905.

LOUIS XIV: *Mémoires et lettres*, Paris, 1927.

LOUVOIS, François Michel Le Tellier, Marquis de, War Minister: *Lettres*, Paris, 1827.

LOUVRELEUIL, Jean Baptiste, curé of Saint-Germain de Calberte: *Histoire du Fanatisme renouvelé*, Avignon, 1704.

LUYNES, Charles Philippe d'Albert, Duc de: *Mémoires*, Paris, 1862.

MAINTENON, Françoise d'Aubigné, Marquise de: *Conseils et instructions aux demoiselles de Saint-Cyr*, Limoges, 1875. *Correspondance*, Paris, 1865.

MARIGNY, Jacques Carpentier de: *Relation des divertissements que le Roi a donnés aux Reines dans le parc de Versailles*, Paris, 1664.

MASSILLON, Jean Baptiste, Bishop: *Sermons*, Paris 1791.

MAZEL, Abraham and MARION, Elie: *Mémoires*, Paris, 1931.

Mercure Galant, Le, newspaper founded in 1672 by Donneau de Visé and Thomas Corneille.

MONTAGU, Lord Edward, English ambassador to France: *Letters to Lord Arlington*, published as a supplement to LA FAYETTE: *Histoire de Madame Henriette d'Angleterre* (q.v.).

MONTPENSIER, Anne Marie Louise d'Orléans, Duchesse de: *Mémoires*, Paris, 1839.

MOTTEVILLE, Françoise Bertaud, Dame Langlois de, personal maid to Anne of Austria: *Mémoires*, Paris, 1886.

NARBONNE, Pierre, commissaire of police of Versailles: *Journal des régnes de Louis XIV et Louis XV*, Versailles, 1866.

NAZELLES, Cauzé de, former officer of the French army: *Mémoires du temps de Louis XIV*, Paris, 1899.

NOAILLES, Anne Jules, Duc de: *Mémoires politiques et militaires*, edited by Adrien Maurice, Duc de Noailles, Paris, 1839.

ORLÉANS, Charlotte Elizabeth of Bavaria, Duchesse d': see PALATINE, The Princess.

ORMESSON, Olivier Le Fèvre d': *Journal*, Paris, 1860-2.

PALATINE, The Princess, Charlotte Elizabeth of Bavaria, second wife of the Duc d'Orléans, known as: *Correspondance*, Paris, 1904.

PELLISSON, Paul, official historiographer to Louis XIV: *Correspondance inédite*, Paris, 1859.

PERRAULT, Charles, Controller of the Royal Buildings: *Mémoires de ma vie*, Paris, 1909.

PIROT, Abbé Edme: *La Marquise de Brinvilliers; récit de ses derniers moments*, Paris, 1883.

PRIMI VISCONTI, Giovanni Battista, Count di San Majole: *Mémoires sur la Cour de Louis XIV*, Paris, 1909.

PRIOLO, Benjamino, Venetian ambassador to France: *Relation de la Cour de France*, Amsterdam, 1731.

RACINE, Jean: *Fragments historiques de l'année 1682*, included by his son Louis RACINE in his *Mémoires de la vie de Jean Racine*, Paris, 1844.

ROHAN, *Procés du chevalier de*, Bibliothèque Nationale, Paris, French mss. nos. 7,629 and 16,565.

ROU, Jean: *Mémoires inédits et opuscules*, Paris, 1857.

SAINCTOT, Nicolas de, Master of Ceremonies at the Court of Versailles: *Cérémonial de France à la Cour de Louis XIV*, Paris, 1936.

SAINT-MAURICE, Thomas François Chabod, Marquis de, the Duke of Savoy's representative at the French Court: *Lettres sur la Cour de Louis XIV*, Paris, 1911-12.

SAINT-SIMON, Louis de Rouvroy, Duc de: *Mémoires*, the

selection edited by Chéruel and Régnier and prefaced by Saint-Beuve, 22 vols., Paris, 1904.

SANDRAS DE COURTILZ, Gatien de: *Le Prince infortuné*, Amsterdam, 1713.
Intrigues amoureuses de la Cour de France, Cologne, 1685.
Mémoires de Charles de Baatz, Seigneur d'Artagnan, Capitaine-Lieutenant des Mousquetaires du Roi, Cologne, 1700.

SCUDÉRY, Madeleine de: *La Promenade à Versailles*, Paris, 1669.

SEIGNELAY, Jean Baptiste Colbert, Marquis de: *Lettres*, Paris, 1867.

SÉVIGNÉ, Marie de Rabutin-Chantal, Marquise de: *Lettres*, Nodier edition, Paris, 1836; Monmerqué edition, Paris, 1862.

SOURCHES, Louis François de Bouchet, Marquis de, Grand Provost of France: *Mémoires sur le règne de Louis XIV*, Paris, 1882-92.

SPANHEIM, Ezechiel, the Elector of Brandenburg's special envoy to the Court of France: *Relation de la Cour de France*, Paris, 1900.

TESSÉ, René de Froullay, Maréchal de: *Lettres*, Paris, 1806.

VARLET DE LA GRANGE, Charles: see LA GRANGE.

VAUBAN, Sébastien Le Prestre, Marquis de: *Les Oisivités de M. de Vauban et sa correspondance*, Paris, 1910.
Projet d'une dîme royale, Paris, 1933.

VILLARS, Louis Claude, Duc et Maréchal de: *Mémoires*, Paris, 1904.

VISCONTI, Giovanni Battista Primi: see PRIMI VISCONTI.

VOLTAIRE, Jean François Marie Arouet de: *Le Siècle de Louis XIV*, Flandrin edition, Paris-Lille, 1925.

INDEX